Windows onto Jewish Legal Culture

Fourteen Exploratory Essays

The Institute of Jewish Law
Boston University School of Law
765 Commonwealth Avenue
Boston MA 02215

Publication No. 36

Windows onto Jewish Legal Culture
Fourteen Exploratory Essays

Hanina Ben-Menahem
Arye Edrei
Neil S. Hecht
Editors

VOLUME TWO

Routledge
Taylor & Francis Group
LONDON AND NEW YORK

First published in paperback 2024

First published 2011
by Routledge
4 Park Square, Milton Park, Abingdon, Oxon OX14 4RN

and by Routledge
605 Third Avenue, New York, NY 10158

Routledge is an imprint of the Taylor & Francis Group, an informa business

Publisher's Note
The publisher has gone to great lengths to ensure the quality of this reprint but points out that some imperfections in the original copies may be apparent.

British Library Cataloguing in Publication Data
A catalogue record for this book is available from the British Library

Library of Congress Cataloging in Publication Data
A catalog record for this book has been requested

ISBN: 978-0-415-78251-7 (hbk) (vol.02)
ISBN: 978-1-03-292105-1 (pbk)
ISBN: 978-1-00-312602-7 (ebk)
ISBN: 978-0-415-50049-4 (hbk) (set)

DOI: 10.4324/9781003126027

Typeset in Palatino
by RefineCatch Limited, Bungay, Suffolk

For Elly Leary, Richard Pearlstone,
and the Pearlstone Foundation,
whose support made possible
the publication of these volumes

Table of Contents

VOLUME TWO

Note to the reader

The chapters of *Windows onto Jewish Legal Culture: Fourteen Exploratory Essays* are replete with references to halakhic authorities and their writings. Many of these authorities are customarily referred to by acronyms of their names (e.g., Rashi, the Hida) or of the titles of their best-known works (e.g., the Shela, the Shakh); or by the titles of these works themselves (the Tur, the Arukh Hashulhan). To assist the reader in identifying these individuals, a list of the rabbinical authorities cited or referred to is provided at the end of each volume, along with a brief bio-bibliographic description. The authorities and scholars are listed alphabetically by their first name in English; in some cases they are also listed by their acronym (Rashi, the Rabad) or other commonly-used appellation (Maimonides, Gerondi). When a book title is used to refer to an individual, it is not italicized.

In references to the Talmud, m, b, j, or t prefixed to the tractate name indicates whether the Mishnah, the Babylonian Talmud, Jerusalem Talmud, or Tosefta is being referred to.

Law and ethics

8 Equity

1 Introduction

The notion of equity was first articulated by Aristotle, who observed that laws are formulated in a general manner and intended to cover hypothetical cases. An actual case to which we apply the law may well differ somewhat from the hypothetical case contemplated by the lawgiver, and may not be covered by the law. Hence the judge must invoke equity to save the law from insensitivity, unfairness, or inappropriateness, by moderating and adjusting it to fit the circumstances of the case being adjudicated. The principles of equity are general guidelines that by their very nature defy precise formulation, since their meaning and application vary with the cases to which they are applied, which cannot be predicted in advance.

> All law is universal, but about some things it is not possible to make a universal statement which shall be correct. In those cases, then, in which it is necessary to speak universally, but not possible to do so correctly, the law takes the usual case, though it is not ignorant of the possibility of error. And it is none the less correct; for the error is not in the law nor in the legislator but in the nature of the thing.... When the law speaks universally, then, and a case arises on it which is not covered by the universal statement, then it is right, where the legislator fails us and has erred by over-simplicity, to correct the omission—to say what the legislator himself would have said had he been present, and would have put into his law if he had known. Hence the equitable is just, and better than one kind of justice—not better than absolute justice, but better than the error that arises from the absoluteness of the statement. And this is the nature of the equitable, a correction of law where it is defective owing to its universality. In fact this is the reason why all things are not determined by law, namely, that about some things it is impossible to lay down a law, so that a decree is needed.
>
> *Nicomachean Ethics*, Book V, ch. 10, translated by W.D. Ross

Aristotle's concept of equity is fleshed out further elsewhere in the Aristotelian corpus:

> We saw that there are two kinds of right and wrong conduct towards others, one provided for by written ordinances, the other by unwritten. We have now discussed the kind about which the laws have something to say. The other kind has itself two varieties. First, there is the conduct that springs from exceptional goodness or badness, and is visited accordingly with censure and loss of honor, or with praise and increase of honor and decorations: for instance, gratitude to, or requital of, our benefactors, readiness to help our friends, and the like. The second kind makes up for the defects of a community's written code of law. This is what we call equity; people regard it as just; it is, in fact, the sort of justice which goes beyond the written law. Its existence partly is, and partly is not, intended by legislators; not intended, where they have noticed no defect in the law; intended where they find themselves unable to define things exactly, and are obliged to legislate as if that held good always which in fact only holds good usually; or where it is not easy to be complete owing to the endless possible cases presented, such as the kinds and sizes of weapons that may be used to inflict wounds—a lifetime would be too short to make out a complete list of these. If, then, a precise statement is impossible, and yet legislation is necessary, the law must be expressed in wide terms; and so if a man has no more than a finger-ring on his hand when he lifts it to strike or actually strikes another man, he is guilty of a criminal act according to

> the written words of the law; but he is innocent really, and it is equity that declares him to be so. From this definition of equity it is plain what sort of actions, and what sort of persons, are equitable or the reverse. Equity must be applied to forgivable actions; and it must make us distinguish between criminal acts on the one hand, and errors of judgment, or misfortunes, on the other.... Equity bids us be merciful to the weakness of human nature; to think less about the laws than about the man who framed them, and less about what he said than about what he meant; not to consider the actions of the accused so much as his intentions; nor this or that detail so much as the whole story; to ask not what a man is now but what he has always or usually been. It bids us remember benefits rather than injuries, and benefits received rather than benefits conferred; to be patient when we are wronged; to settle a dispute by negotiation and not by force; to prefer arbitration to motion [viz., litigation]—for an arbitrator goes by the equity of a case, a judge by the strict law, and arbitration was invented with the express purpose of securing full power for equity.
>
> The above may be taken as a sufficient account of the nature of equity.
>
> *Rhetoric*, Book I, ch. 13, translated by W. Rhys Roberts

The problems Aristotle raises with regard to the disparity between the hypothetical case contemplated by the legislator, and the actual case to which the law is applied, are also raised by Maimonides in the *Guide for the Perplexed*. The received opinion is that in the *Guide for the Perplexed* III:34, Maimonides, influenced by Aristotle's seminal discussion, addresses the issue of equity. Some scholars read Maimonides as totally rejecting the Aristotelian doctrine of equity, others, as unequivocally accepting it, and still others as accepting it to some degree. I maintain, however, that the point Maimonides is making in this chapter of the *Guide* is that generality is not only a hallmark of the law, but a great virtue.

The Maimonidean perspective differs from that of Aristotle (and Plato too), for whom the law's generality is a liability. They take the law's inability to cover all future cases to be a limitation of the law, and attribute it to the finitude of human understanding and the complexity of human existence. Aristotle asserts that when the judge is faced with a case not covered by the law, he must act on his understanding of how the legislator would have extended the law had he been conversant with the contingencies in question. This sentiment is totally absent from Maimonides' discussion, however, not only because the Divinity, author of the law, cannot be said to be limited, but mainly because Maimonides believes the generality of the law to be a policy adopted deliberately, as if the law were making a conscious choice, so to speak, to focus solely on the typical case. For Maimonides, the generality of the law is a virtue, not a defect. The utility of the law's generality justifies ignoring the individual case. Whereas

Aristotle speaks of the generality of the law as a problem that has to be solved, Maimonides takes the diametrically opposed perspective, and justifies the generality of the law as being of the essence of Torah law.[1]

Maimonides states his position as follows:

> Among the things that you likewise ought to know is the fact that the Law does not pay attention to the isolated. The Law was not given with a view to things that are rare. For in everything that it wishes to bring about, be it an opinion or a moral habit or a useful work, it is directed only towards the things that occur in the majority of cases and pays no attention to what happens rarely or to the damage occurring to the unique human being because of this way of determination and because of the legal character of the governance. For the Law is a divine thing; and it is your business to reflect on the natural things in which the general utility, which is included in them, nonetheless necessarily produces damages to individuals, as is clear from our discourse and the discourse of others. In view of this consideration also, you will not wonder at the fact that the purpose of the Law is not perfectly achieved in every individual and that, on the contrary, it necessarily follows that there should exist individuals whom this governance of the Law does not make perfect. For not everything that derives necessarily from the natural specific forms is actualized in every individual. Indeed, all things proceed from one deity and one agent and "*have been given from one shepherd*" (Eccles. 12:11). The contrary of this is impossible, and we have already explained that the impossible has a stable nature that never changes. In view of this consideration, it also will not be possible that the laws be dependent on changes in the circumstances of the individuals and the times, as is the case with regard to medical treatment, which is particularized for every individual in conformity with his present temperament. On the contrary, governance of the Law ought to be absolute and universal, including everyone, even if it is suitable only for certain individuals and not suitable for others; for if it were made to fit individuals, the whole would be corrupted, and *you would make out of it something that varies*. For this reason, matters that are primarily intended in the Law ought not to be dependent on time or place; but the decrees ought to be absolute and universal, according to what He, may He be exalted, says: "*As for the congregation, there shall be one statute for you*" (Num. 15:15). However, only the universal interests, those of the majority, are considered in them, as we have explained.
>
> *Guide for the Perplexed* III:34 (Pines translation)

1 H. Ben-Menahem, "Maimonides on equity: reconsidering the 'Guide for the Perplexed' III:34," 17 *Journal of Law and Religion* (2002), 25–26.

The concept of equity plays a significant role in English law. For most of its history, English law was inflexible and formalistic. From time to time, people would appeal to the king to intervene and ameliorate the harsh requirements of the law. Gradually, two jurisdictions developed, that of the regular courts, which applied the common law, and that of the king and his council, which, serving as the common law's 'conscience,' so to speak, applied principles of equity. The two systems were integrated in the nineteenth century.

Despite the semantic and conceptual commonality, there is a significant difference between Aristotelian and English equity. In England, the principles of equity were clearly laid down and defined, a task deemed impossible by Aristotle, who insisted that general principles of equity elude precise articulation.

1.1 Equity in talmudic law

The concept of equity is germane in the Jewish law context. To be sure, in contrast to the situation that prevailed in English law before the nineteenth century, Jewish law does not have two parallel sets of courts, law courts and equity courts, but it most certainly does encompass norms whose function is to refine and moderate legal rules when necessary, norms that address the very sorts of situations that were of concern to Aristotle. These norms are not themselves independent rules of the system, but rather, they apply to the rules, tempering their application. Moreover, they do not prescribe or prohibit actions, but are aspirational in nature, recommending a preferred, more noble course of action, a course of action that entails forgoing that to which one may be entitled by the law on the books. 'Equity' is not a Rabbinic concept, but a term borrowed from western law to describe aspirational norms of this kind. Recognition of the need to adjust and temper the law as written does, however, pervade the talmudic sources, and, as we will see—and as will emerge from the other chapters of this book—is a characteristic trait of the halakha.

In Jewish law, the addressee of these aspirational norms is not the courts, but the individual. The Mishnah, for example, states:

> One who pays his debt in the Sabbatical year—the spirit of the Sages is pleased with him.[2]
>
> mSheviit 10:9

2 In Hebrew, the verb *'noha'* used in the phrase "the spirit of the Sages is pleased with (*noha*) him" can have two meanings. On the one hand, it can mean 'satisfies' or 'pleases,' on the other, it can mean 'rests on' or 'resides in.' Ordinarily, the phrase is translated in line with the former sense of the verb, but occasionally, it is rendered in line with the latter sense of the verb: "the spirit of the Sages does not reside in his heart"; see *Rashi*, bBaba Kama 94b, and *Nimukei Yosef*, bBaba Kama 33b (Alfasi pagination).

According to biblical law, the Sabbatical year cancels all debts: debtors are legally exempted from settling their debts. Nevertheless, if someone paid his debt even though not legally obliged to do so, the spirit of the Sages is pleased with him.

Let us examine a similar example from the Talmud:

> Witnesses who testified [about the item] may all purchase the item, but the Sages said, 'Keep aloof from the unseemly and its like.'
>
> tJebamot 4:7 (Zuckermandel edition); bHulin 44b

According to the law, a witness who testifies as to the ownership of an object may buy it from the owner who gained title through this testimony. The acquisition is quite legal, but somehow tainted by a suspicion of collusion. The Sages therefore recommended that individuals who find themselves in such a situation distance themselves from the unseemly: perhaps it will be rumored that they testified as they did in order to buy the article.

As is evident from these examples, the Sages make recommendations as to two types of conduct, commendable conduct and reprehensible conduct. The Sages sometimes recommend that an action be taken even though there is a legal rule exempting one from the obligation to so act (for example, paying debts during the Sabbatical); and sometimes recommend that a certain action not to be taken even though there is a legal rule permitting the action (for example, purchase of an object regarding which one has testified).

In talmudic references to commendable and reprehensible conduct, a number of different expressions are used, including "the spirit of the Sages is pleased with him," "keep aloof from the unseemly and its like," and so on. Whether the differences in terminology are rooted in stylistic, historical, or geographic considerations, but convey the same principle, or denote distinct concepts, is a question that has been much discussed by contemporary scholars.[3]

Desirable conduct can be encouraged through positive or negative reinforcement, that is, through a system of rewards, or through punishment.[4] Western law generally uses the method of punishment,[5]

3 See I. Herzog, "Moral rights and duties in Jewish law," in idem, *The Main Institutions of Jewish Law* (London: 1965), 381–86; M. Silberg, "Law and equity," in idem, *Talmudic Law and the Modern State* (New York: 1973), 93–130.

4 This idea is expressed in the Tannaitic literature in the following way: "R. Shimon b. Yohai says, A loaf of bread and a stick came down from heaven intertwined; God said [to the Israelites], If you observe the Torah, here is a loaf to eat, and if not, here is a stick to be beaten with" (Sifre Deuteronomy, Ekev, 40, [Finkelstein edition, p. 83]).

5 Examples of rewarding desirable behavior in Israeli law: unclaimed lost property reverts to the finder if she deposited it with the police; laws encouraging investment; grants to encourage births; reduced taxes for those living in 'development' zones.

publicizing the penalties for violations of the code of acceptable conduct. Jewish law, on the other hand, tends to prefer reward to punishment, as in the example considered above, repayment of debts during the Sabbatical year. The conduct deemed desirable is encouraged by a declaration that one who exhibits it, that is, pays his debts during the Sabbatical year, causes "the spirit of the Sages" to be pleased with him. This exemplifies the talmudic approach, which has recourse to incentives and rewards to encourage and reinforce desirable conduct, alongside punishment of undesirable conduct.

In Jewish law, two kinds of legal norms can be said to co-exist. The coexistence within the same legal system of two kinds of norms—legal norms and equitable norms—operative at the same time within the same court, is unknown in western law. Western legal systems comprise laws setting down what is allowed or forbidden, and prescribing the proper procedure to achieve certain ends, such as drawing up a will or a contract. They do not concern themselves with recommended but non-mandatory conduct, or more generally, with ethical guidelines other than purely legal constraints.

How are we to account for the dual normative tracks, as it were, within Jewish law? If the law indeed expects a certain mode of conduct, why is it not prescribed rather than merely recommended?

Some talmudic cases where the principles of equity are adduced can, perhaps, be explained by invoking their historical context. They attest to a transitional period during which a legal norm was found wanting, but due to various historical contingencies, could not be changed.[6] In such cases, alongside the legal norm governing the matter in question, an ethical norm was introduced **as a recommendation**. This sort of historical explanation may be plausible in some cases, but cannot account for all equitable norms.

In a number of cases, equitable considerations motivated the introduction of new legislation. The provenance of these norms, which were introduced to address specific points on which there was an acknowledged gap between the demands of justice and the existing law, is thus known to us. Such norms, though different from the equitable norms that were introduced, due to historical contingencies, as recommendations alongside existing but inadequate laws, are also classified as equitable norms. A good example is the rule that "an evaluation may always be redeemed," which will be discussed below.

The fact that while in certain cases **legislation** was used to replace or circumvent laws deemed no-longer-appropriate or inimical to justice, and in others, no legislative changes were introduced, but rather, a less drastic type of intervention was employed—namely, invocation of a recommendation or moral exhortation to act in certain way—suggests that a deliberate policy was in place with respect to inculcating desirable

6 See Chapter Three above, "Exigency authority."

conduct. Before we turn to an exploration of Jewish law's equitable 'track,' let us first explore Rabbinic intervention via legislation.

1.2 Intervention via legislation

A typical example of intervention via legislation is the decree stating that a debtor whose land was seized by the court for non-payment of his debt always has the right to redeem it for the price it was valued at when taken from him.[7] This enactment is known as "an evaluation may always be redeemed." The biblical verse invoked as its exegetical justification is: "And you shall do that which is right and good in the eyes of the Lord" (Deut. 6:18). Legally, the assets transferred to the creditor belong to the creditor. However, to protect the debtor, the Sages issued an enactment granting him the right of redemption, and thereby limiting the creditor's ownership rights.

Another situation where ownership is limited by legislation, also anchored in the aforementioned verse, is the law of abutting properties. This law prescribes an order of first-refusal rights in the sale of land that overrides the owner's right to sell his property to whomever he pleases. The holder of an abutting property is given the first option to purchase the land. Even if the land has already been sold to a third party, the owner of the abutting property retains the right to buy the property from the third party for the price paid by the latter.[8] Maimonides states the reasons for this law as follows:

> This law is so, because it is said, "And you shall do that which is right and good." And the Sages said: Since the sale is the same, it is good and right[9] that this property should be bought by the abutting neighbor rather than by one from afar.
>
> *Code*, Laws concerning Neighbors 12:5

Maimonides then states the order of priority among purchasers who do not hold abutting land:

> If someone wishes to sell land, and two came, saying I will pay such-and-such an amount to buy it, but neither is an abutting neighbor—if one resides in the town and the other is a neighbor [i.e., owns a nearby but non-abutting property]—the town-neighbor [i.e., the one who resides in the town] has first priority. A neighbor and a scholar—the scholar has first priority. A relative and a scholar—the scholar has first priority. A neighbor and a relative—the neighbor has first priority, as

7 The talmudic discussion is in bBaba Metzia 35a.
8 bBaba Metzia 108a.
9 The reverse order ("good and right") is found in Deuteronomy 12:28.

> this too falls under the 'good and right' principle. If one of them came first and bought it, he has acquired it, and his fellow [the other one] who had priority rights cannot evict him [i.e., reverse the sale], for neither owns an abutting property. For the Sages did not command these priorities [but merely recommended them], for it is the way of the pious and of those of good spirit to act in this manner [i.e., sell in the prescribed order].[10]
>
> *Code*, Laws concerning Neighbors 14:5

Maimonides is thus distinguishing between situations with regard to which the Sages intervened by means of a legally-enforceable decree (as in the case of the first-refusal rights of the owner of an abutting property), and those with regard to which they intervened by recommending a course of action ("it is the way of the pious and those of good spirit to act in this manner") that cannot be enforced by the court.

The verse to which these directives refer is "and you shall do that which is right and good in the eyes of the Lord." It should be noted that the Sages' decree, at least in the first case, namely, that of the right of redemption, seeks to give concrete expression to an explicit biblical principle. Leviticus 25:25–28 states:

> (25) If your brother becomes poor, and sells some of his possession, then his next of kin shall redeem that which his brother has sold. (26) And if a man has no one to redeem it, and he becomes rich and finds sufficient means to redeem it; (27) then let him count the years of the sale and restore the difference to the man to whom he sold it; and he shall return to his possession. (28) But if he has not sufficient means to get it back for himself, then what he sold shall remain in the hand of him who bought it until the year of Jubilee, and in the Jubilee it shall go out, and he shall return to his possession.

According to biblical law, all plots of land revert to their original owners in the Jubilee year. Therefore, any sale is in essence a lease for a period of years (up to a maximum of forty-nine years if the sale is immediately after the Jubilee) until the next Jubilee.

The law of the Jubilee applies to the transfer of land for any reason. In the verses from Leviticus just quoted, land was sold due to financial difficulties. The verses state that the seller, or his kin, may redeem the property even before the Jubilee (when the land would in any event revert to him without payment) by paying for the remaining years of the lease. Scripture thus distinguishes between the sale of land due to financial

10 On the expression "the Sages commanded" as reflecting a moral obligation, see A. Hacohen, "On Maimonides' terminology in the *Mishne Torah*" (Hebrew), 14–15 *Shenaton Hamishpat Haivri* (1988/89), 113ff.

duress and a straight business deal; in the latter case, there is no right to redeem the land prior to the Jubilee year. The Sages' enactment—"an evaluation may always be redeemed"—ensures that when the law of the Jubilee year does not apply (as was already the case in the talmudic period), the spirit of the biblical law, which protects those who sold their ancestral plots due to economic difficulties, will continue to be upheld. The talmudic law does not make the scriptural distinction, and allows all land that was seized by the court for non-payment of a debt, even if incurred in a straight business transaction, to be redeemed. But it is clear that the primary motivation for the land redemption enactment is to ensure that the poor can recover land seized due to financial duress.

Above, we suggested that at least some talmudic enactments should be considered in their historical context. R. Vidal of Tolosa's *Magid Mishne* commentary on the passage from Maimonides quoted above offers a philosophical explanation for the Sages' legislative intervention, explaining why the Torah itself made such intervention necessary:

> As to the law of abutting properties—regarding the amelioration of man's character, and his conduct in the world, our perfect Torah gave [guiding] principles, by saying, "You shall be holy" (Lev. 19:2), and the meaning of this is, as the Sages, of blessed memory, said: "sanctify yourself by [abstaining from] what is permitted," so as not to be swept away by lust. And the Torah also said, "And you shall do that which is right and good" (Deut. 6:18), and the meaning of this is, that one should conduct himself [in dealings] with his fellows in a manner that is good and righteous. And it was inappropriate with regard to all of this to set out the specific details, because the commandments of the Torah apply to every season and every time and every matter, and it must be this way. But men's virtues and conduct change with the times and the individuals concerned. And the Sages, of blessed memory, wrote down a few useful details that fall under these [guiding] principles, some of which they made fully binding norms, and others they issued as recommendations and guides to the pious way. And these are all their decrees, about which it is said, "the words of our beloved are more loved than the wine of the Torah, as it is written, 'for thy love is better than wine' (Song of Songs 1:2)."[11]
>
> *Magid Mishne*, Laws concerning Neighbors 14:5

The difference between intervention via recommendation and intervention via legislation alluded to by the *Magid Mishne* can be further clarified. The former sort of intervention implies that a disparity exists between the rules of the legal system, and that which is required by the ideals of equity and justice. This disparity allows for a certain flexibility, inasmuch as the

11 Song of Songs Rabbah (Vilna edition, parasha 1, *"ki tovim dodekha miyayin,"* 2).

compliance with the recommended norms need not be universal, that is, they apply only to those who are able to live up to them. Intervention via legislation, on the other hand, when appropriate, implies that the law applies to everyone equally.

In this chapter, we will not address the issue of equity-based legislation, because in a certain sense all legislation aspires to implement principles of justice and righteousness, even if there is no explicit reference to this. Rather, our focus will be cases where the Sages recommended modes of conduct that diverge from the conduct required by law. We will also consider cases in which **courts** deviated from the legal rule. The latter cases exemplify equity as conceived by Aristotle, for in these cases the court acts to make the general law more sensitive to the circumstances of a given case.

2 Equitable norms

2.1 Commendable conduct

Consider the following passage from the Mishnah:

> One who pays his debt in the Sabbatical year—the spirit of the Sages is pleased with him. One who borrows from a proselyte whose sons were converted with him, is not to repay the debt to his sons, but if he did repay—the spirit of the Sages is pleased with him. All moveable property is acquired by drawing (*meshikha*), and whoever keeps his word—the spirit of the Sages is pleased with him.
>
> mSheviit 10:9

Obviously, the Mishnah's primary concern here is not to apprise us of the Sages' state of mind. Rather, its description of commendable behaviors—behaviors pleasing to the Sages—is intended to encourage people to choose a course of action that is desirable, but not mandated by the law.

2.1.i Settling a debt during the Sabbatical year

Deuteronomy 15:1–2 states that during the Sabbatical year, which occurs every seven years, all debts are cancelled, and creditors cannot sue for their money once the year has ended. Nevertheless, the Mishnah states that the Sages are "pleased with" someone who does not take advantage of his legal right to have his debts remitted, but pays his debts even though the Sabbatical year has cancelled them.

mSheviit 10:3 relates that Hillel, observing that due to the Sabbatical year debt-remission law, lenders were reluctant to make loans to the needy, instituted an enactment setting forth a procedure by which a creditor could demand repayment despite the Sabbatical debt-remission law. The procedure allowed the creditor, under certain circumstances, to appoint the court to collect the debt for him (*prozbul*). As the debt would then be due the court, which is not subject to the biblical injunction,[12] it had to be repaid notwithstanding the Sabbatical. Accordingly, it appears that the Mishnah stating that repayment of the loan is commendable either reflects the state of affairs prior to Hillel's enactment, or refers to a case where the said circumstances did not obtain.

2.1.ii Repaying a debt to a proselyte's heirs

> One who borrows from a proselyte whose sons were converted with him, is not to repay the debt to his sons, but if he did repay—the spirit of the Sages is pleased with him.

Upon converting, the legal connection to a proselyte's family of origin is severed, since he is considered to be newly born. His sons, even if they converted with him, are thus no longer his heirs. Hence, if one borrows money from a convert, any sons born prior to the conversion cannot legally claim the debt after his demise, and the debtor has no legal obligation to repay it. Nevertheless, the Mishnah says of one who repays such a debt, "the spirit of the Sages is pleased with him."

This interpretation of the mishnaic law raises some textual difficulties. The Mishnah says that one is not to repay a debt to a convert, which seems to imply that such a thing is forbidden. This implication would seem to be contradicted by the continuation of the Mishnah, which states that one who nonetheless pays this debt acts in a way that pleases the Sages.

Moreover, the Talmud elsewhere quotes a baraita to the contrary:

> One who borrows money from a proselyte whose sons were converted with him is not to repay the debt to his sons, but if he did repay—the spirit of the Sages is not pleased with him.
>
> bKidushin 17b

In this baraita, the first and the second statements are in harmony, the upshot of the passage being that one is not to repay a debt to a convert's sons, and if he does, "the spirit of the Sages is not pleased with him."[13] The baraita apparently reflects an early halakhic teaching that was changed by

12 See Chapter Nine below, "Charity and distributive justice," section 3.

13 Rashi maintains that the phrase "the spirit of the Sages is not pleased with him" is not intended to discourage repayment of such a debt, but is intended only to indicate that no reward will be forthcoming for doing so, implying that there is nothing reprehensible about repaying the debt. The Ran, R. Nissim of Gerona, commenting on Alfasi on bKidushin 17b, maintains that the rationale for this rule is a desire to distinguish between the status of the proselyte and that of the Israelite.

the redactor of the Mishnah via a delicate textual emendation: omission of the second "not," rendering the dictum "is pleased" instead of the baraita's "is not pleased," though retaining the "is not to repay" formula, which is now taken to mean 'is not [obliged] to repay,' that is, 'does not have to repay,' rather than, 'is not allowed to repay.'[14]

A similar example of an injunction not to repay a debt, in the 'not obliged to repay' sense, can be found in the Jerusalem Talmud, which uses the same language as the Mishnah:

> Similarly, if the deceased is the end of his family line, and he has no heir except his mother, [a debtor] is not to repay the debt [to her], but if he did repay—the spirit of the Sages is pleased with him.
>
> jSheviit 10:4 (39d)

By Jewish law, a mother does not inherit from her son; consequently she cannot collect money due her son except if the debtor assents. If the debtor agrees to settle the debt, then his action is deemed praiseworthy.

2.1.iii Keeping an oral commitment

The last part of the Mishnah quoted above reads as follows:

> All moveable property is acquired by drawing (*meshikha*), and whoever keeps his word—the spirit of the Sages is pleased with him.

Legally, a transaction is not complete unless a formal act of acquisition (*kinyan*) takes place. In the case of moveable property, one such formal act is 'drawing' (*meshikha*), whereby the buyer moves the object toward himself. As long as this act has not been performed, either of the parties may repudiate the agreement without legal consequences. Even so, the Mishnah quoted above, mSheviit 10:9, states that one who keeps his word and does not go back on a transaction is praiseworthy.

Another Mishnah states:

> If one paid money [for produce] and has not 'drawn' the produce from him, [either party] may withdraw. Nevertheless the Sages said: He who exacted punishment from the generation of the Flood and from the generation of the Dispersion,[15] will also exact punishment from one who does not keep his word.
>
> mBaba Metzia 4:2

14 The Talmud reconciles the contradiction between the two formulations by distinguishing between a child conceived and born as a Gentile, and one conceived as a Gentile, but born as a Jew.

15 See Genesis 11:1–10.

If a transaction has reached the stage of money changing hands, but has not been legally concluded by an act of 'drawing,' then either party may retract. Here, however, unlike the case where no money has yet changed hands, referred to in the previous Mishnah, a curse is placed on one who goes back on his word. If money has not changed hands, in other words, if only the bargaining stage of the transaction, in which the price and terms of sale are agreed on, has been concluded, then there is no curse. Nevertheless, as we saw, one who keeps his word is described as praiseworthy.

The Jerusalem Talmud reports a remark made by the Amora, Rav:

> Rav said, when I instruct my household to give someone a present, I never change my mind.
>
> jSheviit 10:4 (39d)

Legally, the recipient of a gift does not acquire title to it as long as he has not performed a formal act of acquisition (*kinyan*), and therefore the donor may, in the course of giving a gift, change his mind. Rav attests that despite this legal rule, he always acts in accordance with the mishnaic norm that "whoever keeps his word—the spirit of the Sages is pleased with him." The Jerusalem Talmud queries this, adducing an apparently-contradictory ruling Rav handed down on another occasion:

> A certain man paid a [partial] deposit for [a specific quantity of] salt, and the price of salt went up. [The vendor sought to retract.] They came before Rav. He said to them: either give him salt [at the contracted price] for the [value of the] deposit, or return [the deposit] and [be subject to the dictum] "He who exacted punishment."
>
> jSheviit 10:4 (39d)

In other words, here Rav rules in accordance with the legal norm that one may retract if the transaction has not been fully completed, but if he does so, he brings upon himself the "He who exacted punishment" curse. He does not invoke the mishnaic recommendation that one ought to keep one's word.

The Jerusalem Talmud then suggests a resolution of the apparent contradiction that captures the essence of the distinction we are elucidating in this chapter:

> There [i.e., in the case of the salt vendor], it was in accordance with the lawfulness criterion (*midat hadin*). [However,] Rav acted for himself in accordance with the piety criterion (*midat hahasidut*).

The conduct mandated by the mishnaic norm "whoever keeps his word—the spirit of the Sages is pleased with him" is referred to by the Jerusalem

Talmud as conduct exemplifying the "piety criterion." This reply highlights the tension between legal norms and equitable norms. The court did not enforce the norm recommended by the Mishnah. From this *sugya*, it would appear that, in the judicial context, the only norms that are applicable are legal norms, and it is only in the sphere of individual conduct that ethical norms are applicable.

This tension is further underscored in another talmudic discussion of a mishnaic ruling that addresses personal conduct:

> His loss or his father's loss—[taking care of] his loss takes precedence. His loss or his teacher's loss—[taking care of] his [own] takes precedence.
>
> mBaba Metzia 2:11

The Talmud comments, "R. Judah said in the name of Rav: All who uphold this themselves, will end up experiencing this" (bBaba Metzia 33a). Rashi explains: "Even though Scripture does not obligate one to do so, one should go beyond that which is required by the law, and not be particular and say, 'My interests come first,' if the losses in question are not serious. One who is always particular about such things casts off the burden of performing acts of loving-kindness and charity, and will end up needing assistance from others."

2.2 Reprehensible conduct

In the examples above, certain types of conduct were said to be pleasing to the Sages. Let us now consider some examples of conduct that, although legally permitted, is deemed displeasing to the Sages.

2.2.i Accepting restitution from a robber

Some recommendations to act beyond that which is required by the law are motivated by policy considerations. One such instance is described in the following passage from the Tosefta:

> Robbers and usurers who repented and [seek to] return that which they had robbed—whoever accepts [it] from them, the spirit of the Sages is not pleased with him.
>
> tSheviit 8:11 (Zuckermandel edition)

This law refers to a criminal who seeks to repent—a robber who wants to return what he robbed, and a usurer, who wants to return the interest he charged. The Tosefta advises those who were wronged to refrain from accepting their due under the said circumstances, even though legally, they are entitled to sue for their losses. Had the offender not approached them at his own initiative, they would certainly be justified in seeking restitution in court. Here, the legal right conflicts with the public interest, namely, reforming criminals by encouraging repentance. Accepting restitution from penitent criminals would raise the public's expectations of them, and those who could not afford to make amends might be deterred from changing their ways and abandoning crime. Hence the Tosefta urges victims to forgo their rights, and condemns those who accept restitution.

The Tosefta does not abrogate the robber's liability to make restitution, nor does it forbid the victim to accept restitution. Rather, it makes a recommendation as to the morally preferable course of action, though leaving the decision to the victim. Let us consider the same baraita as it appears in the Talmud:

> The Sages taught: Robbers and usurers who [seek to] return [that which they had robbed]—it is not to be accepted from them, and [as to] one who accepts it from them—the spirit of the Sages is not pleased with him.
>
> bBaba Kama 94b

What is the difference between the two versions? According to the version in the Talmud, the victim is not permitted to accept compensation. Here the phrase, "the spirit of the Sages is not pleased with him" does not refer to failure to live up to a recommended equitable norm, but to transgression of an explicit legal norm. The phrase, "the spirit of the Sages is not pleased with him" is invoked as a (general) condemnation of those who transgress the law.

The Talmud relates the historical background of the rule that restitution offered by penitent offenders is not to be accepted.

> R. Johanan said: This Mishnah was taught at the time of Rabbi [R. Judah the Prince], as it is taught: It once happened that a certain man wanted to repent. His wife said to him: 'Fool, if you repent, you'll be left without even a belt.' And this deterred him from repenting. When this happened, they said: Robbers and usurers who [seek to] return [that which they had robbed]—it is not to be accepted from them, and [as to] one who accepts it from them—the spirit of the Sages is not pleased with him.
>
> bBaba Kama 94b

It would thus seem that in some cases, social and economic conditions, on the one hand, and the desire to rehabilitate offenders, on the other, motivated the Sages to take initiative and modify accepted norms of conduct. Sometimes their intervention took the form of recommendations, other times it took the form of actual legislation. The baraita from bBaba Kama illustrates the latter form of intervention. Indeed, the Talmud itself refers to this baraita as "the penitents' enactment."

2.2.ii Disinheriting one's children

Another example further illustrates the difference between a recommendation made by the Sages, and a legal rule.

> One who assigns his property [as a gift] to others, and left out his children—what he did is done, but the spirit of the Sages is not pleased with him.
>
> mBaba Batra 8:5

Someone who sought to deprive his children of their prospective inheritance gave away his property as a gift. The transfer is valid, but the Sages are not pleased with the father's act. Here, the proper conduct is prescribed qua recommendation only. Desirable though the conduct is, it is not mandated via legislation, and hence cannot be judicially enforced.

A responsum by the Turkish decisor R. Elijah b. Haim (Raanah) explains this point. He was asked whether there was a legal means of preventing a father from violating this Rabbinic recommendation. He replied as follows:

> Since this involves a prohibition, it would seem certain that it is appropriate for any court to take steps to prevent this from being done. But in any event, I do not see any grounds whatsoever for coercing [him not to do it], since it is only said that "the spirit of the Sages is not pleased with him" … and all the more so, it cannot be coerced by imposing a ban or any other form of coercion. But rather, he must be told that he is transgressing the words of the Sages, and it is permissible to call him a transgressor.
>
> *Responsa Raanah*, 8, #118[16]

The idea that it is impossible for a court to forcibly impose compliance with equitable norms is explicitly articulated in the following talmudic passage:

> These rules were declared for the sake of peace … nets for [trapping] animals, fowl, and fish are subject to the laws of robbery [i.e., taking the creatures caught in them is robbery], for the sake of peace. R. Jose says: It is actual robbery. [Taking] objects found by a minor, one who is deaf-mute, or one who is mentally deficient, is subject to the laws of robbery, for the sake of peace. R. Jose says: It is actual robbery. One who shakes the top of an olive tree—what lies beneath is subject

16 The last part of the responsum is based on bShabat 40a: "Rava said: It is permitted to call anyone who violates a Rabbinic injunction a 'transgressor.'"

> to the laws of robbery, for the sake of peace. R. Jose says: It is actual robbery.
>
> mGitin 5:8

The common denominator of these three cases is that the disputed object (the animal, fowl, or fish in the trap; the object found by the disabled person; the olives shaken off the tree) does not belong, legally speaking, to the trap-owner, the disabled person, or the tree-shaker. By law, therefore, anyone can take these objects from them. The Sages, however, enacted—for the sake of keeping the peace—that it was forbidden to take such objects. R. Jose disagrees, asserting that these persons all do have legal title to the objects, and hence taking them is legally prohibited.

The Talmud, in bGitin 61a, explains that practically speaking, the difference between their views is that according to the Sages, the court does not compel someone who nonetheless helps himself to the objects to return what he has taken, but according to R. Jose, it does.

2.2.iii Formulation of equitable norms

We have seen that the Rabbinic recommendations are sometimes formulated in the affirmative—"the spirit of the Sages is pleased with him"—and sometimes in the negative—"the spirit of the Sages is not pleased with him." Is this merely a matter of style, or does the linguistic presentation have any substantive legal significance? If it is simply a matter of style, then if we are told that action x pleases the Sages, we can infer that not doing x displeases the Sages. So the question is, when we are told, say, that "One who pays his debt in the Sabbatical year—the spirit of the Sages is pleased with him," can we assume that the Sages would be displeased with him if he did not repay the debt?

It could, perhaps, be argued that the affirmative formulation is not simply the converse of the negative formulation, but reflects a substantively different legal evaluation of an act. On this approach, "the spirit of the Sages is pleased with him" confers merit on the moral agent who acts as recommended, yet does not bring opprobrium on one who does not act as recommended. Conversely, "the spirit of the Sages is not pleased with him" can be seen as bringing opprobrium on those who act at variance with the recommended conduct, but no special merit is conferred on those who adopt the recommended conduct. But there seems to be at least one counter-example, one instance where the two forms are used interchangeably.

> One who keeps his word—the spirit of the Sages is pleased with him.
>
> mSheviit 10:9

> One who does not keep his word—the spirit of the Sages is not pleased with him.
>
> tBaba Metzia 3:14 (Zuckermandel edition)

It could be argued, however, that the difference between the Mishnah and the Tosefta here is not merely stylistic, but reflects a different evaluation of the act concerned—keeping one's word, or breaking one's word.

Indeed, the Talmud itself struggles with the question of whether the affirmative and negative formulations are simply opposed modes of expressing the same idea, or substantively different evaluations, as is evident from yet another talmudic passage. mJebamot 2:4 uses the expression "prohibitions due to holiness." The Talmud explains that this refers to Rabbinically-enacted prohibitions against second-order incestuous relations, which were introduced as a safeguard against violation of (first-order) Torah-prohibited incestuous relations. The Talmud comments:

> Why are they called 'prohibitions due to holiness?' Abbaye said: Everyone who fulfills the words of the Sages is called 'holy.' Rava said to him: [If so, it follows that] whoever does not fulfill the words of the Sages is [merely] not called 'holy'—but is not called 'wicked' either [and surely they are called 'wicked'!] Rather, Rava said: One should sanctify himself by [abstaining from] what is permitted.
>
> bJebamot 20a

2.2.iv He is called 'wicked'

The Sages recognize a number of pejorative epithets for perpetrators of various kinds of reprehensible conduct, both with respect to matters that are 'between man and God,' and matters that are 'between man and his fellow': "transgressor," "wicked," "sinner," "abominable" and "criminal."[17] These may be used without being considered defamatory. The applicable epithet generally reflects a biblical verse regarded as relevant to the conduct in question. Let us look at one such example:

> Resh Lakish said: One who raises his hand against his fellow, even though he did not hit him, is called 'wicked,' as it is said: "He said to the wicked: why would you smite your fellow?" (Exod. 2:13). It is not written, 'why did you smite?', but rather, "why would you?" Though he did not yet smite him, he is called 'wicked.'
>
> bSanhedrin 58b

17 bYoma 72b; bBerakhot 12b; bEruvin 100b; bTaanit 11a; bNedarim 47b; bBerakhot 28a; bNida 13b.

Although the behaviors in question are harshly criticized, they are not explicitly forbidden, nor is it clear whether the objectionable conduct can be legally prevented. Indeed, the question of when there should be legal intervention in the case of conduct deemed reprehensible arises often in the halakhic discourse, particularly with regard to establishing degrees of liability. The Talmud does not provide a clear-cut answer, and it is a matter of debate among the commentators. Consider the following example:

> A poor man was rummaging [through the ashes] for a morsel of cinder-cake, and someone came and snatched it away. He is called 'wicked.'
>
> bKidushin 59a

According to Rashi. the poor man was trying to get some food from an abandoned fire, when someone came and snatched it away. Legally, the poor man had not yet taken possession of the cake, because the snatcher took it away while the poor man was poking around in the cinders. Nevertheless, the snatcher is called 'wicked.'

Would a court intervene to recover the value of the cinder-cake for the poor man? In commenting on the matter, the Ritba, R. Yomtov of Seville, quotes Rabbenu Tam, with whom he disagrees:

> Rabbenu Tam, of blessed memory, wrote that where someone is called 'wicked,' the courts will force him to repay the money. This is not so.... [the snatcher] is certainly called 'wicked,' but owes nothing to the first man.
>
> *Hidushei Haritba*, bKidushin 59a

2.3 Exempt by the laws of man, but liable by the laws of heaven

Another type of conduct that the Sages found fault with, but did not impose legal liability for, insofar as it could not be enforced by the court, is what the Talmud calls "exempt by the laws of man, but liable by the laws of heaven." Such conduct is described by Gulak as follows:

> There are certain kinds of obligations that are altogether lacking the element of enforceability, and can be fulfilled only through the good will of the obligee. By the laws of man, the obligation does not exist at all, because the inherent implication of human laws is that they are enforceable, and this element is completely missing here. This obligation exists only as a moral or religious obligation on the obligee, and hence of such an obligation it is said, "exempt by the laws of man, but liable by the laws of heaven." The courts cannot be called upon to

> address cases where one is liable only by the laws of heaven, and to enforce their fulfillment. If an obligee [by the laws of heaven] seized the property of a obligor, [that which was seized] is taken from him [and returned to the obligor]. And the obligation can never be enforced until the obligor himself seeks to fulfill his obligation, and he has a moral obligation to do so.
>
> In Jewish law, liability by the laws of heaven is invoked wherever there is even a tenuous basis for deeming an obligation legally sound, but it can only be imposed as a moral obligation that an upright person should fulfill.[18]

The Talmud, as we saw, recognizes different types of obligation, but never sets out a systematic account of the various categories. Moslem jurists, however, explicitly articulate five categories of human behavior: (1) obligatory; (2) desirable or recommended; (3) permissible; (4) shameful; (5) forbidden. From the perspective of Islamic law, this classification covers all human activity. This deontic classification scheme was known to Maimonides, as is evident from Maimonides' commentary on the mishnaic dictum: "His son Shimon says: All my days I was brought up among the Sages and I found nothing better for the body than silence" (mAvot 1:16):

> And I say that speech is to be classified, in accordance with the obligations imposed by our Torah, into five categories: obligatory, warned against [i.e., prohibited], to be kept distant, desirable, permitted.
>
> Maimonides, *Commentary on the Mishnah*, mAvot 1:16

Something like this deontic categorization was undoubtedly known to the talmudic Sages, though, as we said, they did not articulate it systematically.

3 Conduct beyond that which is required by the law

The previous examples related to conduct in specific circumstances: paying back a debt in the Sabbatical year; paying back debts to proselytes' heirs; and so on. However, in addition to the expectation that people will act in a manner that goes beyond that which is required by the law in prespecified cases, there is also a wider and more general expectation of conduct beyond that required by the strict law (*lifnim mishurat hadin*).

In the Mekhilta de-Rabbi Ishmael, which is the halakhic Midrash on Exodus, R. Eleazar of Modiin offers an exegesis of the biblical verse: "And you shall let them know the path to go upon and the things to do" (Exod. 18:20). This verse reports Jethro's advice to Moses, and serves as a foundational homiletic source in Jewish law:

18 A. Gulak, *Foundations of Jewish Law* (Hebrew), (Berlin: 1922), 2:18.

> "Let them know"—let them know the abode of their lives [studying the Torah]; "the path"—this is visiting the sick; "to go"—this is burying the dead; "upon"—this is loving-kindness; "and the things"—this is that which is required by the law; "to do"—this is beyond that which is required by the law.
>
> Mekhilta de-Rabbi Ishmael, masekhta de-amalek, 2 (Horowitz edition, p. 198)

At the end of this exegesis, a general demand is made of the individual, namely, that he must do more than that which is required by the law. The Mekhilta does not indicate when this demand is in force, nor what its scope is. In order to determine its operative meaning and application, we must examine the contexts in which it was invoked by the Talmud.

It is interesting to compare the exegesis of the verse offered by Targum Jonathan[19]:"And the things"—this is that which is required by the law; "to do"—this is beyond that which is required by the law, vis-à-vis the wicked." The Targum calls upon one to act with extreme severity toward the wicked—beyond that which is required by the law. As we are about to see, this interpretation of the notion of 'beyond that which is required by the law' differs markedly from that offered by the Talmud.

3.1 Talmudic examples

3.1.i The obligation to assist

The Torah commands us to help others in distress:

> Do not see your brother's ox or sheep straying away, and ignore it. You shall surely return it to your brother.... And so shall you do with his donkey, and so shall you do with his garment, and so shall you do with every lost thing of your brother which he has lost and you have found. You may not ignore them.
>
> Do not see your neighbors' donkey or his ox fallen down on the way, and ignore them. Raise them together with him.
>
> Deuteronomy 22:1–4

Ignoring one's fellow's plight is mentioned twice in these verses, once in the affirmative—"and ignore it"[20]—and once in the negative, "You may not ignore them."

A talmudic baraita puts forward an exegesis of the verse that is based on this duality.

19 A Palestinian Targum of the Bible, redacted not earlier that the 7th or 8th century, wrongly attributed to Jonathan b. Uziel.

20 The Hebrew Bible is not punctuated, and this clause of the verse could conceivably be read as a positive commandment to ignore one's fellow's plight.

"Ignore it"—sometimes you ignore it and sometimes you do not ignore it. How so? If the person is a priest (*kohen*) and the [lost animal] is in the cemetery, or he is an elder and it is beneath his dignity, or he is engaged in work that is more valuable than his fellow's [animal]—therefore it is said, "and ignore them."

bBaba Metzia 30a

The baraita makes use of this duality to call for two different courses of action: sometimes one must attend to one's needy fellow, at other times, one is not obligated to do so. According to the baraita, the biblical obligation to render assistance is not absolute but relative, depending on the circumstances of the case.

One of the circumstances in which the need to render assistance can be ignored, is when the lost animal is encountered by an elder. The Talmud defines the phrase "an elder and it is beneath his dignity" as follows:

Rava says: Whatever he would return for himself [i.e., if it was his own], he is also obliged to return for his fellow; whatever he would load and unload for himself, he is also obliged to help his fellow load and unload.

bBaba Metzia 30b

After presenting this definition, the Talmud proceeds to relate the following incident:

R. Ishmael b. R. Jose was walking along the road. He encountered a man carrying a bundle of dry palm branches. He put them down and rested. He said to R. Ishmael, Help me load them. R. Ishmael said, How much are they worth? He said to him, Half a *zuz*. He gave him half a *zuz* and declared the bundle to be abandoned.[21] The man then took possession of the bundle [and again asked R. Ishmael for help]. R. Ishmael again gave him half a *zuz* and again he declared the bundle abandoned. When he saw that the man was about to take possession of it yet again, he said: let it be abandoned property for everyone except you.

bBaba Metzia 30b

R. Ishmael did not proffer the money with the intention of retaining the palm branches in his possession, his sole purpose in buying them was to discharge his obligation to render assistance.

The Talmud raises the following question: R. Ishmael b. R. Jose was an old man, and it was beneath his dignity to load bundles of wood. Why did

21 I.e., declared it ownerless (*hefker*), so that others would be permitted to take it.

he regard himself as obliged to help? The Talmud gives the following answer:

> R. Ishmael b. R. Jose acted beyond that which the law required. As R. Joseph has taught: "Let them know"—this is the abode of their lives [studying the Torah]; "the path"—this is loving-kindness; "to go"—this is visiting the sick; "upon"—this is burying the dead; "and the things"—this is the law; "to do"—this is beyond that which is required by the law.[22]

In what way was R. Ishmael's action beyond that required by the law? The analysis of precedents, and particularly talmudic precedents, raises the problem of articulating the underlying principle (*ratio decidendi*). In the case before us, two contradictory principles seem to be plausible.

One way of extracting the rationale is to focus on the fact that R. Ishmael b. R. Jose could have discharged his obligation to help his fellow by actually loading the palm branches, without incurring any expense. The financial outlay was his own choice, but even were incurring this expense the **sole means** by which he could have taken action, the 'beyond that which is required' principle would not have obliged him to incur the expense. That is to say, on this reading, acting in accordance with the said principle does not mandate that one spend money.

On a different reading of the precedent, however, the *ratio decidendi* might be that precisely when one has the option of 'buying his way out' of the demeaning physical labor, acting beyond that which is required by the law obliges us to have recourse to this option and incur the expense. However, when there is no such option, in other words, where actually doing physical labor is essential, one is not obliged to go beyond that which is required by the law. On this reading, the principle applies even when it is necessary to incur an expense, but not when it is necessary to act in a manner that is beneath one's dignity.

Thus this precedent does not conclusively indicate the scope of the principle that one should act beyond that which is required by the law, and in particular, does not indicate whether the principle applies to cases where one must make a financial outlay.

3.1.ii Returning lost property

The Talmud reports the following incident:

22 This exegesis of the biblical verse: "And you shall let them know the path to go upon and the things to do" (Exod. 18:20), here attributed to the Amora R. Joseph, is identical to the exegesis in the Mekhilta of R. Shimon b. Yohai (Melamed edition, p. 133), where it is attributed to R. Eleazar of Modiin, and differs only slightly from that in the Mekhilta de-Rabbi Ishmael, quoted above. This difference in attribution is discussed below.

> R. Judah[23] carried Mar Samuel's things, walking behind him, when he went to the grain market. He said to him: If one found a purse here, what is he to do? Mar Samuel said to him: It belongs to him [i.e., he may keep it without trying to find the owner]. If an Israelite came and provided identifying marks, what then? He said to him: He must return it. How can both be the case? He [Mar Samuel] said to him: [It is] beyond that which is required by the law. As it once happened that the father of Mar Samuel found donkeys in the desert and returned them to their owners after twelve months, beyond that which is required by the law.
>
> bBaba Metzia 24b

This passage is replete with legal and textual problems. Let us consider the legal aspect first. R. Judah asks his master Mar Samuel about property found in a public place, where as a rule a large number of people are present. Mar Samuel replies that, on the assumption that the previous owner has 'despaired'[24] of finding it, the object belongs to the finder, who acquires ownership of it. R. Judah follows up with another question: If the owner turns up and identifies his property, should it not be returned? Mar Samuel replies that it indeed should be returned. This stance seems to be inconsistent: if the property belongs to the finder, then he is not obligated to return it; if it does not belong to the finder, then he should be obligated to publicize the fact that he found it. This is the meaning of the query "how can both be the case?" The Talmud resolves this by invoking the notion of "beyond that which is required by the law": legally speaking, the property belongs to the finder, but if the previous owner claims it, the finder should go beyond that which the law requires, and return it to him. To illustrate this idea, the Talmud quotes the anecdote about Mar Samuel's father finding donkeys in the desert and returning them even though the legally prescribed time for doing so had elapsed.[25]

23 R. Judah was Mar Samuel's student, and as such, he carried his master's things. While ministering to his teacher, the two were also engaged in studying the Torah. On the duty to minister to one's teacher, see H. Ben-Menahem, "Two talmudic understandings of the dictum 'appoint for yourself a teacher,'" in Robert S. Westman and David Biale (eds.), *Thinking Impossibilities: The Intellectual Legacy of Amos Funkenstein* (Toronto: 2008), 288–308.

24 A technical term meaning that he wrote it off as a loss.

25 The commentators disagree about the circumstances of this event. The Tosafists say that Mar Samuel's father returned the donkeys twelve months after he found them. After such a long time there is no obligation to return the animals, but only their value. Rashi, on the other hand, says that the animals had been lost for twelve months before Mar Samuel's father found them. In such a case, there is no obligation to return the animals or their value, because the owner certainly 'despaired' of finding them. Rashi's explanation is preferable, because as he explains the incident, in both the case of Mar Shmuel's father, and in R. Judah's hypothetical case (of finding a purse in the public domain), the object's owner has 'despaired' of finding the lost object.

Let us compare the 'obligation to assist' case (the bundle of palm fronds) with the 'found object' case (the purse found in the grain market). Both involve conduct expected of a Sage, but they nonetheless differ in three respects:

First, in the 'obligation to assist' case, one can, by helping to load the palm fronds oneself, go beyond that which is required by the law without spending money. In the case of the lost purse, however, in going beyond that which is required by the law, the finder who returns the found object incurs a financial loss, or at least forgoes a financial gain.

Second, in the case of the lost purse, our version of the Talmud does not quote the biblical or Rabbinic source for the 'beyond that which is required by the law' principle. (The commentaries of Alfasi and Asheri, which quote the Talmud, do adduce the Rabbinic source, namely, R. Joseph's exegesis, hence they must have had a different version of the 'lost property' *sugya*.) In the 'obligation to assist' case, on the other hand, the Talmud explicitly cites R. Joseph's dictum as the source for the principle.

Lastly, the lost purse case has two steps. First, a general norm is presented (lost property must be returned), then this general norm is illustrated by relating a particular case (the story of Mar Samuel's father). The 'obligation to assist' case, however, relates a particular case, and does not present a general norm.

The passage presents certain textual difficulties. At first glance it seems that the story of Mar Samuel's father is part of Mar Samuel's answer, and it is strange that Mar Samuel refers to himself in the third person. On further examination, though, it is apparent that the passage consists of two distinct parts, one Hebrew and the other Aramaic. The statement that R. Judah and Mar Samuel visited the grain market is recorded in Aramaic. Their conversation is in Hebrew. The question "How can both be the case?" is in Aramaic. Since Amoraim do not usually mix languages, it seems that this query is not part of the conversation, but rather is posed by the Talmud itself. The query is then answered by the Talmud with the story of Mar Samuel's father—also in Aramaic. On this explanation, the phrase "He said to him," which precedes the dictum "[it is] beyond that which is required by the law," is out of place. In fact, it does not appear in the Hamburg manuscript of the Talmud, which reads:

> R. Judah carried Mar Samuel's things, walking behind him, when he went to the grain market. He said to him: If one found a purse here, what is he to do? It belongs to him [i.e., he may keep it without trying to find the owner]. If an Israelite came and provided identifying marks, what then? He must return it. How can both be the case? [It is] beyond that which is required by the law. As it once happened that the father of Mar Samuel found donkeys in the desert and returned them to their owners after twelve months, beyond that which is required by the law.

Asheri explains: "The word 'both' is apt, and it is the Talmud's query. The words 'he said to him' [which, in Asheri's corrupt version of the talmudic text preceded 'How can both be the case?'] should be deleted."[26]

This reading of the Talmud is significant in two respects. With the exception of the Mekhilta, each time the expression "beyond that which is required by the law" appears, its purpose is to explain, post factum, the action of a sage that diverges from the general norm. That is, the principle is always invoked as an explanatory principle, and not as a legislative principle. If the dictum was spoken by Mar Samuel himself, this would be the only place in the Talmud where a specific behavior (returning lost property) is set down as a norm on the basis of the 'beyond that which is required' principle. On the other hand, if we assume that the 'beyond that which is required' principle was introduced to harmonize an apparent contradiction between two of Mar Samuel's statements, then the principle is simply being invoked to reconcile and explain, and not to mandate a specific conduct.

Furthermore, if we wish to ascertain the socio-historical background of a talmudic dictum, its originator must be identified, and the scope and history of its circulation determined. It would be exceedingly significant if Mar Samuel himself invoked the 'beyond that which is required' principle in the 'returning lost property' *sugya*, since, with the exception of R. Joseph, who quotes the Mekhilta, the principle is always cited anonymously, leaving us no means of ascertaining its historical background.

3.1.iii Compensation for bad advice

An expert moneychanger[27] who made a mistake in appraising a coin is exempt from paying damages. It is assumed that he was misled by some factor beyond his control, and did not act out of negligence. The Mishnah

26 Asheri is quoted by the *Shita Mekubetzet* ad loc. Differentiating between reported Amoraic conversations and the *stama* (the talmudic narrative) is a key element of research into the Talmud, which, as Shamma Friedman notes, "seeks to distinguish in every talmudic *sugya*, between the words of the Amoraim, their dicta, their disputes, and their discourse, and the later talmudic narrative that serve as a framework for interpretation of and deliberation on the Sages' discourse." See his "A critical study of Yevamot X with a methodological introduction" (Hebrew), in H. Dimitrovsky (ed.), *Texts and Studies; Analecta Judaica* (Hebrew), vol. 1 (New York: 1977), 293. The linguistic criterion was first proposed by H. Klein, "Gemara and sebara," *Jewish Quarterly Review* 38 (1947), 67–75, and expanded by Friedman. Friedman puts forward fourteen principles, the first of which is: "When Hebrew and Aramaic are both used in the same passage, the core of the passage is in Hebrew, whereas the Aramaic is the Talmud's commentary thereon. As we said, this differentiation, first suggested by Klein, assumes that the Amoraim do not mix languages" (ibid., 301).

27 Moneychangers were bankers and numismatic experts who gave advice on the value and currency of coins. Coins were appraised in accordance with their actual value, not their nominal denomination. An expert moneychanger was supposed to know the correct exchange rate and the value of all coins in use as currency.

sets down the following law: "One who has his coin certified by the moneychanger and it turns out to be worthless ... the moneychanger is exempt."[28]

The Talmud raises the following question:

> A woman went and had a dinar appraised by R. Hiya. He said to her, It is good. The next day she came before him and said to him: I showed it to others and they said that it is bad [i.e., defective] and I cannot make use of it. He [R. Hiya] said to Rav: Go and change it for her and enter it in the books as a loss.
>
> bBaba Kama 99b

R. Hiya was an expert moneychanger. Why did he compensate the woman for misleading her? The Talmud continues:

> R. Hiya acted beyond that which is required by the law, as we learned from R. Joseph:
>
> "Let them know"—let them know the abode of their lives [studying the Torah]; "the path"—this is loving-kindness; "to go"—this is visiting the sick; "upon"—this is burying the dead; "and the things"—this is the law; "to do"—this is beyond that which is required by the law.

This case adds another element to the analysis of the 'beyond that which is required' principle. Unlike the other examples, the bad advice case entails a direct financial loss, as opposed to forgoing a financial gain, as in the lost purse case. Here, going beyond that which is required by the law is impossible without sustaining an out-of-pocket loss. It follows that the obligation to act beyond that which is required by the law applies even when it entails incurring a direct loss.

Note that the 'beyond that which is required' principle is invoked in this passage too to account for the behavior of a sage.

3.2 The *ratio decidendi*

When we seek the *ratio decidendi* of a given group of talmudic precedents, how is the enterprise in which we are engaged to be characterized? There are at least two possibilities. We may be engaged in historical reconstruction, that is, we may be attempting to show that a common principle was acted on in each case, that this very principle guided the Sages in their actions and decisions. This approach is an attempt to enter into the Sages' thoughts and discover their motives. On the other hand, we may be engaging in **rational** reconstruction, that is, creative jurisprudential speculation, wherein we attempt to extract a principle that applies in all the cases,

28 bBaba Kama 99b.

without asserting that this inferred principle was in fact employed by the talmudic Sages in question. If the Talmud is regarded as a normative source of law, the latter enterprise is unavoidable, since we are seeking to formulate guiding principles for the future. The difference between the two approaches is that the former aspires to be historically accurate, and is therefore inherently limited, whereas the latter is much broader, allowing a range of principles to be read into the talmudic text.

R. Jacob of Orleans attempts to identify the underlying principle of the 'beyond that which is required by the law' *sugyot*.

> 'Beyond that which is required by the law' applies only to matters where others are liable and the person in question is exempt, as in the case involving R. Hiya [compensation for bad advice] and that involving R. Ishmael b. R. Jose [the obligation to assist].
>
> *Tosafot*, bBaba Kama 100a s.v. *lifnim mishurat hadin*

In the view of R. Jacob of Orleans, the common denominator is waiver of a special exemption, and an undertaking to act in accordance with the norm applicable to all.

This suggestion, however, fails. While it does indeed apply to R. Hiya, who is an expert money-changer and therefore exempt from compensating the woman for damage caused by his advice, and to R. Ishmael b. Jose, who was an elder sage and thus exempt from the duty of loading his fellow's palm fronds, it does not apply to the precedent of Mar Samuel's father's returning the animals, since there is a universal exemption from returning the lost property in question. And, indeed, R. Jacob of Orleans is criticized on this account by other Tosafists.

> [The view of R. Jacob of Orleans] is not well-founded, for in Baba Metzia it is stated that Mar Samuel's father acted beyond that which is required by the law when he returned the lost donkeys to their owner after twelve months, and this was a universal exemption.

In the following passage, Silberg expands on R. Jacob of Orleans' explanation so as to render it impervious to this critique. He maintains that the "distinguishing mark of the 'beyond that which is required' principle"

> is that the one who volunteers to heed it "cuts down the plants," that is to say he forgoes the qualification which relieves him, and returns to the essence which obligates him, or leaves the peripheral thought and penetrates to the central issue. Rabbi Ishmael ben Yose renounced the privilege applying to him as a "sage and it is not in keeping with his dignity" to help load a bundle of wood; Rabbi Hiya renounced the exemption granted him, in a personal way, because he was an expert

> "who did not need to be instructed" on the status of a coin; the father of Samuel renounced the presumption of a formal despair by a loser to find his lost object after twelve months.... The common denominator in all these cases is: the voluntary consideration not of the surface scene but of the substantive essence, a "bending in" of the strict law and turning it toward its central core.[29]

How does Silberg expand the rationale first offered by R. Jacob of Orleans? R. Jacob of Orleans focuses on those who are exempt from an otherwise general obligation. They may choose to waive their exemption, thereby acting in a manner that goes beyond what is required by the law. Silberg goes a step further, and focuses on any legal rule that is to an individual's advantage. By choosing to waive that advantage, the individual in question acts in a manner that goes beyond what is required by the law. This addresses the Tosafists' objection to R. Jacob of Orlean's thesis.

Above, we saw that the Mekhilta's exegesis is not adduced in the 'lost object' *sugya*. This fact, together with the distinction made by R. Jacob of Orleans, is harnessed by the Tosafists to put forward yet another thesis.[30] When an obligation devolves on all but a privileged few (as, for instance, in the 'obligation to assist' and the 'bad advice' cases), then acting beyond that which is required by the law is almost mandatory, and exegetically anchored in the Torah itself. Hence the exegesis is quoted in these two instances. But in the case of a completely universal exemption from acting in a certain way—for instance, returning money found in a public place—acting beyond that which is required by the law is less expected, and the biblical exegesis is not cited. However, this thesis is highly tenuous, since other versions of the Talmud (such as that quoted by Alfasi and Asheri) cite the exegesis in all three cases.

3.3 The addressee of the norm

In all the cases discussed, the one who acts beyond that which is required by the law is a sage, of whom a higher than normal standard of conduct is expected. Would it be correct to conclude that the principle that one should act in a manner that goes beyond that which is required by the law applies only to those who take upon themselves a higher standard of conduct?

It has been argued that this is a matter of controversy between Maimonides and Nahmanides. "The Nahmanidean position is that the imperative (whether it be legal or ethical) is addressed to Everyman, while the Maimonidean position is that it is addressed to specific elitist

29 Silberg, n. 3 above, 123.

30 bBaba Metzia 24b s.v. *lifnim*.

individuals, but not to each and every member of the Jewish community."[31]

However, a closer analysis of the sources on which this statement is based reveals that the alleged difference of opinion is far from certain, and indeed, a very different conclusion may be called for. It is doubtful whether this is even an issue of contention between the two commentators. Let us consider Nahmanides' view first. His commentary on Deuteronomy 6:18, "And you shall do what is right and good in the eyes of the Lord," reads as follows:

> Our Rabbis have a beautiful Midrash on this verse. They have said: [*That which is right and good*] refers to a compromise and going beyond the requirement of the letter of the law. The intent of this is as follows: At first he [Moses] stated that you are to keep His statutes and His testimonies which He commanded you, and now he is stating that even where He has not commanded you, give thought, as well, to do what is good and right in His eyes, for He loves the good and the right. Now this is a great principle, for it is impossible to mention in the Torah all aspects of man's conduct with his neighbors and friends, and all his various transactions, and the ordinances of all societies and countries. But since He mentioned many of them—such as, *Thou shalt not go up and down as a talebearer* [Lev. 19:16]; *Thou shalt not take vengeance, nor bear any grudge* [Lev. 19:18]; *Neither shalt thou stand idly by the blood of your neighbor* [Lev. 19:16]; *Thou shalt not curse the deaf* [Lev. 19:14]; *Thou shalt rise up before the hoary head* [Lev. 19:32]; and the like—He reverted to state in a general way that, in all matters, one should do what is good and right, including even compromise, and going beyond the requirements of the law.[32]

But Nahmanides does not discuss the issue treated in the talmudic cases in question, namely, the 'obligation to assist,' 'found property,' and 'bad advice' cases. The Talmud's focus is the gap between existing legal norms and the **higher standard of conduct** expected of those who seek to live fully in accordance with the spirit of the law. The demand that one act beyond that which is required by the law is added to the demands of the law itself.

Nahmanides, on the other hand, is interested in an entirely different situation: lacunae in the legal system, that is, instances not covered by existing legal norms. As he points out, the legal system, by its very nature,

31 S. Shilo, "On one aspect of law and morals in Jewish law: lifnim mishurat hadin," *13 Isr. L. R.* (1978), 359–69. Silberg upholds a similar thesis, but does not connect it to any controversy between the Early Authorities: "There is room to argue that the call to keep the standard of saintliness (*midat hasidut*) is directed to the hasidim [saintly] only, to one who is truly a hasid in all his ways" (Silberg, n. 3 above, 204 n. 108).

32 *Ramban (Nachmanides): Commentary on the Torah*, trans. Charles Chavel (New York: 1976), Deuteronomy, 88.

is unable to provide directives governing every conceivable case, "for it is impossible to mention in the Torah all aspects of man's conduct with his neighbors and friends, and all his various transactions, and the ordinances of all societies and countries." According to Nahmanides, "do that which is right and good" serves as a general norm that complements the legal system, filling in gaps and closing loopholes left open by its universally-applicable, and therefore inherently imprecise, norms. The norm obviously has, as its addressee, each and every individual.

Given that Nahmanides is not concerned with action beyond that which is required by the law in the sense discussed by the Talmud, he does not ground action beyond that which is required by the law in the verse adduced by the Mekhilta, but in the verse "and you shall do that which is right and the good in the eyes of the Lord" (Deut. 6:18). His sources for this exegesis are unknown.

Conversely, Maimonides uses the expression "beyond that which is required by the law" in the talmudic sense, namely, as a demand added to the requirements of the law. He does not take it to refer to obligatory conduct, but to a higher standard of conduct voluntarily undertaken, conduct referred to as meeting the 'standard of the pious' (*midat hasidut*). One who acts in accordance with this standard is called 'pious.'

> Anyone whose dispositions are all moderate and temperate is called 'wise.' One who takes it upon himself to be exceedingly meticulous, and departs somewhat from moderate dispositions, to one extreme or the other, is called 'pious.' How so? One who distances himself from a haughty heart to the other extreme, and becomes humble of spirit, is called 'pious,' and this is the standard of the pious. And if he distanced himself [from haughtiness] only moderately, and became modest, he is called 'wise,' and this is the standard of the wise. And so it is with respect to all the dispositions. And the pious men of early times inclined their dispositions from the middle path toward the two extremes. There is a disposition that can be inclined toward the far extreme, and there is a disposition that can be inclined toward the near extreme, and this [conduct] is deemed beyond that which is required by the law.
>
> *Code*, Laws concerning Ethics 1:4-5

In the next paragraph, Maimonides makes clear that the legal duty is to act moderately: "And we are commanded to go on the paths of moderation, and they are the paths that are good and straight." However, elsewhere in the *Code*, Maimonides states: "He who wishes to go on the good and straight path, and conducts himself beyond that which is required by the law — returns lost property to an Israelite if he is able to provide identifying marks [even in a public place where the owner despaired of recovering the lost object]."[33] And he reiterates: "He who takes the good and straight path, and conducts himself beyond that which is required by the law—returns lost property everywhere, even if it is beneath his dignity."[34]

Thus Maimonides **defines** the pious (*hasid*) individual as one who conducts himself beyond that which is required by the law. Conduct beyond the requirements of the law is not an obligation addressed to the elite, the view Shilo ascribes to Maimonides, but rather, those who so conduct themselves are deemed to be pious. Each and every member of the community is invited to so conduct himself.

3.4 Tension between general directives and legal rulings

We have examined the demand that one conduct himself in a manner exceeding that which the law requires in the legal context. Let us now examine how this norm is addressed in the Aggada, that is, the Rabbinic sources that are homiletic and philosophical, as opposed to legal. The Aggada provides the philosophical underpinnings of the halakha.

The Talmud quotes R. Joseph, who asserts that one must not begin the Additional Service (Musaf) prayers on the first day of Rosh Hashana until after the third hour of the day. The reason is that during the first three hours, God's rulings are stricter, and thus the individual's supplications may well be rejected. The Talmud then quotes an apparently contradictory source, which states that God spends the first three hours of the day studying the Torah, and the next three hours judging the world. The Talmud then suggests a resolution of this discrepancy, which is significant not so much with respect to its utility for establishing God's schedule, but for a distinction it highlights.

> With reference to the Torah, 'truth' is written, for it is written, "buy the truth, and sell it not" (Prov. 23:23)—God does not act beyond that which is required by the law. But with reference to judgment, the word 'truth' is not written—God acts beyond that which is required by the law.
>
> bAvoda Zara 4b

This is the only place in the Talmud where the expression "beyond that which is required by the law" is invoked in the context of the judicial procedure, albeit with reference to the heavenly court. In the other talmudic cases examined above, going beyond that which is required by the law was a norm addressed to the individual, who was admonished to forgo a legal right voluntarily. In the present context, it is a judicial norm, a norm

33 Maimonides, *Code*, Laws Concerning Robbery and Lost Property 11:7.
34 Ibid. 11:17.

applied by God when sitting in judgment, and acting beyond that which is required by the law, acquitting a defendant who is actually liable. In another Aggadic passage, bBerakhot 7a, God prays, as it were, that in adjudicating He will go beyond that which is required by the law.

This contrast between the contexts of 'Torah' and 'judgment' is significant. 'Torah,' in this context, represents the absolute and universal legal norm of 'truth,' which is not subject to qualification on the basis of personal or other external considerations. 'Judgment,' on the other hand, represents the process of applying the Torah in practice, where such considerations may indeed by admitted, and a decision 'beyond that which is required by the law' is possible. We thus observe a certain tension between the normative law, law with a capital L, and its application in practice.[35]

Similarly, in bBaba Metzia 30b, the Talmud adduces an assertion made by R. Johanan: "Jerusalem was destroyed only because they rendered judgments there in accordance with the laws of the Torah." What then, the Talmud asks, would the correct practice have been: "Were they, then, to have rendered judgments in accordance with the decisions of powerful and violent judges?" The Talmud proceeds to explain that R. Johanan was not suggesting any such thing, but rather, that his critique was in the same vein as that expressed in bAvoda Zara:

> But say thus: [Jerusalem was destroyed] because they based their judgments [solely] on the laws of the Torah, and did not go beyond that which is required by the law.
>
> bBaba Metzia 30b

The foregoing analysis will serve as a segue to a discussion of whether a human court may, in rendering judgment, also act beyond that which is required by the law. May a court hand down a ruling based on considerations that transcend what is required by the law? If so, can the court coerce the litigants to act beyond that which is required by the law?

The various considerations with respect to which the concept of acting beyond that which the law requires can be invoked are numerous and complex. Let us take, as an example, the economic status of the litigants. Is the court allowed to take a litigant's poverty into consideration, and rule in his favor?

4 Talmudic rulings on equity

Let us now examine a case much quoted in the post-talmudic literature, the case of the poor porters. The case serves as a precedent for invoking

35 See H. Ben-Menahem, "The second canonization of the Talmud," 28 *Cardozo Law Review* (2006), 37–51.

equity. It is recounted immediately after a lengthy discussion about the liability of laborers for damages they cause during their work. The Talmud concludes that laborers are liable for damages incurred due to their negligence, that is, their not taking the usual precautions mandated by their work. The employer may deduct the damages from their pay. If that amount does not suffice to cover the damages, then he may seize their belongings, as stipulated in tort law.[36]

4.1 The *sugya* of the poor porters

> Some porters broke a barrel of wine belonging to Rabbah b. Bar Hana. He seized their garments. They came before Rav. Rav said: Return their garments. He [Rabbah] asked: Is that the law? Rav said: Yes. "So that you shall walk in the way of the good" (Prov. 2:20). He returned their garments. They said: We are poor men and we exerted ourselves all day, and we are hungry and have nothing. Rav said to him [Rabbah]: Give them their wages. He said: Is that the law? Rav said to him: Yes. "And the paths of the righteous you shall keep" (ibid.).
>
> bBaba Metzia 83a

Both Rav's rulings are based on a verse from Proverbs: "So that you shall walk in the way of the good, and the paths of the righteous you shall keep."

The circumstances of the case reported in the Talmud are not altogether clear, but there is no doubt that the barrel was broken through the porters' negligence, and they were therefore liable for the loss. By law, in such a situation, the owner is entitled to seize the workers' cloaks and keep them until properly compensated, since merely withholding their wages is insufficient to cover his loss. Nevertheless, Rav ruled that the owner must return the garments and pay the porters for their work. Rav's ruling is contrary to the letter of the law, and indeed, he does not invoke a legal norm to justify his decision, but rather cites the verse from Proverbs. Rashi and other commentators identify the directives articulated in this adage—'you shall walk ... you shall keep' with the directive that one is to act beyond that which is required by the law.[37]

The case of the poor porters above is quoted from the printed version of the Talmud. There are slight textual variations in the manuscript versions, and in the versions quoted by the Early Authorities. According to Alfasi and Asheri, the owner of the barrel was Rabbah b. Rav Huna. Moreover, according to Alfasi, the word "yes" in Rav's replies is missing. What

36 See Chapter Six above, "Self-help," section 3.3.i.

37 The Tosafists, on the other hand, differentiate between the directive that we are to act beyond that which is required by the law, which in their opinion does not warrant incurring a loss as large as that suffered by Rabbah b. Bar Hana, and the 'you shall walk ... you shall keep' directive. Hence, they argue, Rav does not adduce the 'beyond the call' rubric, but offers a different prooftext; see *Tosafot*, bBaba Metzia 24b s.v. *lifnim mishurat hadin*.

conclusion can be drawn from the variant versions? According to the printed version, the implication of Rav's rely is that the ruling is in accordance with the law, though based on an equitable norm. There is no such implication according to the version that omits the word "yes" from his reply. This version underscores the equitable nature of the ruling.

Rav's ruling apparently contradicts the biblical law that a poor man is not to be given preferential treatment in the judicial process. The judge's duty is to decide the case before him on the basis of the law: "neither shall you favor a poor man in his cause" (Exod. 23:3); "you shall not favor the poor" (Lev. 19:15)

These verses are interpreted by Sifra as follows:

> "Neither shall you favor a poor man"—you should not say: This man is poor, and since this rich man [the other litigant] and I are both obliged to support him, I will rule in his favor so that he can support himself decently. Therefore it says, "Neither shall you favor a poor man."
>
> Sifra, Kedoshim, parasha 2, ch. 4 (Weiss edition)

This problem is addressed by R. Saadia Gaon, who adduces the case of the poor porters and offers the following explanation.

> Nevertheless, the conduct referred to as "So that you shall walk in the way of the good, and the paths of the righteous you shall keep" is conduct that is obligatory for all: [in this case] the owners [of the barrel], not the judge. Indeed, the judge must not add anything [to the law] in his ruling, nor subtract anything, nor corrupt the case, so that he does not distort the dictum: "You shall do no unrighteousness in judgment: you shall not favor the poor or show deference to the rich," and so on (Lev. 19:15).
>
> *Sefer Hapikadon*[38]

R. Saadia Gaon, committed to the idea that judges are enjoined not to deviate from the law, emphasizes that the directive is not a legal ruling, but rather a moral teaching that was invoked by Rav.

Silberg takes the same view, but for different reasons:

> On reading the decision given by Rav in the litigation between the employer and the porters, it appears as though Rav ruled that the employer is legally obligated to return the garments which had been seized, and to pay their wages. Such an impression is false. This was a decision given by Rav to his disciple on grounds of morality only.[39]

38 *Sefer Hapikadon*, in S. Schechter (ed.), *Saadyana* (Cambridge: 1903), XII, 40–41.

39 Silberg, n. 3 above, 120.

Silberg bases his reading of the talmudic case on the special relationship that existed between the judge and the barrel owner. Silberg prefers the version of the passage that was used by Alfasi and Asheri, mentioned above, according to which the owner of the barrels was Rabbah b. Rav Huna, who was Rav's student. Thus the directive is a moral teaching being imparted by a teacher to a student.

However, the narrative style of the case presentation indicates that it is a standard court ruling. This impression is strengthened if we examine a parallel passage from the Jerusalem Talmud, and juxtapose it to the *sugya* in the Babylonian Talmud.

4.2 The *sugya* of the potter and the porter

> It was taught in the name of R. Nehemia: A potter gave his pots to someone, who [while carrying them] broke them. The potter seized his garment. He [the porter] came before R. Jose b. Hanina. He said to him: Go and tell him, "So that you shall walk in the way of the good" (Prov. 2:20). He went and said so, and he [the potter] returned the garment. He [R. Jose] said to him: Did he pay your wages? He said to him, No. He said to him: Go and tell him, "And the paths of the righteous you shall keep." He went to him and said so, and the potter paid his wages.
>
> jBaba Metzia 6:6 (11a)

In spite of the differences between the two talmudic reports, it is reasonable to suppose that they have a common source. The elements of breaking the vessels, seizure of garments, and a ruling based on a verse from Proverbs that is not cited in any other talmudic source, indicate that the two cases are different reports of the same ruling. For our purposes, the most significant difference between the two versions is the context in which the sage was asked to intervene.

It is clear that the setting of the case as presented in the Jerusalem Talmud does not come across as a courtroom, where the presence of both litigants would be obligatory. A judge can only try a case in the presence of both litigants.[40] In the event reported by the Jerusalem Talmud, one of the litigants was absent from the court: "He said to him: 'Go and tell him....' He went and said so, and he [the potter] returned the garment." Furthermore, the porter was awarded his wages at R. Jose's initiative. This is contrary to judicial procedure, since a judge may not intervene in favor of one of the litigants during the legal process. Accordingly, it can be assumed that the Jerusalem Talmud reports an ethical directive. Conversely, the version in the Babylonian Talmud describes a properly-conducted judicial procedure: both parties are

40 See bSanhedrin 7b.

present at the time of the hearing, and the plaintiff takes the initiative throughout.

The portrayal of the case suggested by R. Saadia Gaon and Silberg, namely, that the directive issued was an ethical admonition, is only apt vis-à-vis the report of the event in the Jerusalem Talmud. By contrast, the report in the Babylonian Talmud indicates that it was a standard judicial ruling rendered by a court.[41] Some of the Early Authorities are also of the opinion that the Babylonian version of the case is a court ruling. For example, R. Mordekhai b. Hillel of Nuremburg says: "Since we see in the Talmud that the court enforced its ruling, we also coerce [a litigant] to act beyond that which is required by the law if he has the wherewithal to do so."[42]

Although the coercion mentioned in the *Mordekhai* is not warranted on the strength of the text itself, as we are about to see, the important point, for our purposes, is that it construes the episode as a court case.

4.3 Judicial coercion to act beyond that which is required by the law

This takes us back to the question of whether it is possible to impose a court ruling that mandates conduct beyond that which is required by the law. As we saw, R. Mordekhai b. Hillel maintains that such a directive can be enforced,[43] relying on the views of R. Eliezer b. Nathan (Raban, Raavan) and R. Eliezer b. Joel Halevi of Bonn (Rabia, Raavya). Others disagree. Asheri explicitly asserts: "We do not compel one to act beyond that which is required by the law."[44] Others who maintain that the court cannot coerce conduct beyond that which is required by the law include R. Joseph Caro. In his *Beit Yosef*, Caro states:

> Rabbenu Yeruham wrote on the authority of Asheri that we do not compel one to act beyond that which is required by the law, and I think this is obvious. I wonder why R. Mordekhai says in the second chapter of his book on Baba Metzia that the court can compel [litigants] to act beyond that which is required by the law.
>
> *Beit Yosef*, *Tur*, HM 12:6

A seventeenth-century commentator, R. Menahem Mendel Krochmal, seeks to harmonize the views of those who maintain that the court may

41 For a possible explanation of the gap between the versions of the case reported in the two Talmuds, see H. Ben-Menahem, *Judicial Deviation in Talmudic Law: Governed by Men, Not by Rules* (Chur, Switzerland: 1991), ch. 4.

42 *Mordekhai*, Baba Metzia, ch. 2, sec. 257.

43 Though he qualifies this with the phrase "if he has the wherewithal to do so."

44 It is interesting to observe that both R. Mordekhai b. Hillel and Asheri were students of the Maharam of Rothenburg, and while Asheri apparently upholds his teacher's view, R. Mordekhai does not; see *Responsa Maharam* (Prague edition), 4:687.

compel conduct beyond that required by the law, and those who deny it, by distinguishing between different types of coercion.

> Though Asheri says … that we do not compel one to act beyond that which is required by the law, I think he means that we do not coerce him with whips. But he might agree to the expropriation [and sale of the litigant's] property, or if even that is not permitted, we coerce by imposing a ban.… So we can well say that Asheri does not disagree with … all these authorities … who say that we do use coercion [to impose conduct] beyond that which is required by the law. And that which [Alfasi] wrote, viz., that we do not use coercion, means that we do not coerce with whips or expropriation of property, but we do coerce by imposing a ban.
>
> *Responsa Tzemah Tzedek*, #89

5 Conclusion: Is one who acts without being commanded greater than one who is commanded to act?

In the introduction, we raised the question of the enforcement of equitable norms. If the halakha deems a course of action desirable, why does it not make it compulsory? We observed that historical contingencies and constraints arising therefrom might sometimes make it difficult to change existing norms, impelling the Sages to limit their intervention to moral guidance only. Nevertheless, it stands to reason that there are also ethical considerations governing their restraint vis-à-vis legislation, and their preference for inculcating desirable norms via moral guidance. It is possible that "beyond that which is required by the law" and all the other equitable norms formulated by the Sages were guided by the desideratum of granting the individual autonomy—within predictable and defined bounds—with respect to accepting a higher standard of conduct. Voluntary decisions of this kind are conducive to the development of a refined moral sensibility, and higher moral aspirations. In other words, a noble act undertaken voluntarily is loftier than the same act undertaken due to coercion.

The proponents of the foregoing view are committed to the ethical position that voluntarily undertaking a commendable action is more praiseworthy than so acting in obedience to a command. The Babylonian Amora R. Joseph was preoccupied with this very question. R. Joseph was blind. It is debated in the Talmud whether one who is blind is obligated to fulfill religious precepts. In this connection R. Joseph asserts:

> Originally, I thought that if anyone would tell me that the law is in accordance with the view of R. Judah, that a blind person is exempt from [observance of] all the precepts, I would make a banquet for the Sages, seeing that I am not obligated and yet fulfil them. Now, however,

> that I have heard R. Hanina's dictum, that he who is commanded and fulfils [the command] is greater than he who fulfils though not commanded,[45] on the contrary, should someone tell me that the law is not in accordance with R. Judah's view, I would make a banquet for the Sages. What is the reason? Because if I am obligated to observe the precepts, my reward will be greater.
>
> bBaba Kama 87a

This tradition may explain why elsewhere, as we saw above, the Talmud quotes R. Eleazar of Modiin's teaching on "beyond that which is required by the law" in the name of R. Joseph. For this teaching is in line with R. Joseph's initial opinion that one who is blind, and thus not obligated to observe the precepts, merits greater reward than one who is obligated, because he acts voluntarily. The philosophical term for conduct beyond that which duty requires is supererogation. It may be the case that this conception of non-obligatory actions as particularly meritorious underlies the fact that the Sages did not make the norms discussed in this chapter obligatory legal norms, but preferred to leave them supererogatory.

The argument in favor of the opposite opinion ("he who is commanded is greater") is that the individual who obeys orders, and yields to authority, will "always be concerned about overcoming his impulses and fulfilling the commands of his Creator."[46] Such a person does not make his own understanding and perceptions the center of his existence, but recognizes the primacy of the commandments, and accordingly, subjects himself to them. In this vein, Robert Cover, a contemporary jurisprudential thinker, highlights the notion of obligation as the hallmark of the halakhic worldview.[47]

Another possible explanation of why the Sages did not make conduct meeting equitable standards part of the law proper, is that they recognized how difficult it might be for most people to live up to such a requirement. Their solution, therefore, was to leave these directives in the realm of the voluntary, with the recommendation that they be upheld by those seeking moral elevation.

45 This view is expressed differently in jPeia 1:1(15d): "Said R. Abun, And now, concerning that which discharges an obligation [honoring one's parents], it is written, "that your days may be long, and that it may go well with you" (Deut. 5:15)—how much more so concerning a matter with regard to which there is financial loss and danger to life!? R. Levi said to him: On the contrary, that which discharges an obligation is greater than that which does not discharge an obligation."

46 *Tosafot*, bAvoda Zara 3a s.v. *gadol.*

47 Robert M. Cover, "Obligation: a Jewish jurisprudence of the social order," 5 *Journal of Law and Religion* (1987), 65–74.

9 Charity and distributive justice

1 Introduction

One of the burning questions in the life of human society is that of social justice: what would constitute a just society, and how can this vision be achieved? This chapter will explore the position of Jewish law on the question of the just distribution of resources within society, or in short, distributive justice.

In his *Nicomachean Ethics*, Aristotle defined distributive justice as the proper division of goods and wealth among members of a society, where goods and wealth are defined broadly and include not just material resources and assets such as capital, land, labor, and so on, but even indirect benefits.[1] In contemporary societies, such indirect benefits would include tax exemptions, access to senior public positions, and the like.

The question of distributive justice engaged the thinkers, statesmen, and ordinary people of ancient times, and is no less vital today. The Cold War of the latter half of the twentieth century, for instance, can be characterized as a tension between regimes advocating opposed approaches to distributive justice. The West upheld a free market system, limited governmental intervention in economic life, private property, and the right to unlimited personal and corporate wealth. The underlying premise is that ultimately, sufficient wealth will be generated to ensure that even the less productive sectors of society live comfortably. The Soviet bloc was socialist in orientation, with a planned economy, nationalized means of production, and limitations on private property so as to achieve an equitable distribution of goods. Although the Cold War ended with the repudiation of the communist ethos, distributive justice has yet to be achieved, and it has yet to be demonstrated that capitalism can ensure a satisfactory standard of living for all. Indeed, globalization has exacerbated the distributive inequalities both within states and between developed and developing regions.

That the question of distributive justice engages many of us so passionately is due, in large part, to its immediacy. In contrast to other legal dilemmas, whose significance and relevance to the non-jurist must be explained and justified, the question of distributive justice speaks to everyone.

This chapter will explore the approach to social justice put forward in the sources of Jewish law, from the biblical period through the mishnaic and talmudic eras, with particular emphasis on the latter. As we will see, Jewish law with respect to distributive justice went through several important transformations, producing biblically-inspired concepts and institutions that became entrenched in the thought and social organization of cultures the world over, to the point where they are seen as self-evident.

In the last hundred or so years, considerable attention has been directed to the position of Jewish law on various social issues. Many of those who debated these issues interpreted the halakhic sources anachronistically, that is, in terms of the socioeconomic ideas of their own place and time. Some portrayed Jewish law as a quasi-socialist legal system,[2] others, as an individualistic proto-capitalistic legal system.[3] In reaction, some insist that Jewish law is impervious to the influence of contingent ideological or cultural trends.[4] In this chapter, sensitive to the Scylla of anachronism and

1 Book V, ch. 2, 1130b30.

2 See Joseph W. Singer, *The Edges of the Field* (Boston: 2000).

3 See J. Lifshitz, "Foundations of a Jewish economic theory," *Azure* 18 (2004), 34–36.

4 See R. Haim David Halevi, "The social approach of the Torah in opposition to capitalism and socialism" (Hebrew), *Kol Sinai* 5 (1966), 251–54.

the Charybdis of taking Jewish law to exist in a vacuum, we construe the talmudic approach to social justice as a distinctive but evolving socioeconomic orientation. From time to time, however, we will draw on the insights of contemporary 'outside' discourse on distributive justice, to sharpen our understanding of the solutions suggested in the halakhic sources.

It should be noted that our examination of distributive justice will be conducted from the **jurisprudential** perspective: we will not survey the historical realities of Jewish socioeconomic life during the periods under discussion, but rather, the principles espoused in the classic sources of Jewish law—the Bible, Mishnah, and Talmud—and the wider halakhic corpus.

Readers might wonder why the problem of distributive justice is being addressed in the legal context at all: are not the disciplines of philosophy, economics and political science more appropriate contexts within which to contemplate the most equitable distribution of a society's resources? As we will see, however, the halakhic tradition reflects the **legalization** of the problem of distributive justice and transfer of the responsibility for actions intended to benefit the weak from the political realm to the legal. It is thus apt for the directives and principles pertaining to charity to be studied in the legal context.

2 Social justice in the Bible

2.1 Biblical laws relating to social justice

Concern for the weaker groups within society—the poor, orphans, widows, strangers, slaves, and maidservants—is a central biblical theme. Numerous precepts focus on the material betterment of society and the provision of support to those in need. Many such laws are related to farming, the primary economic activity in the biblical period, and pertain to crops, stewardship of the land, and slaves, who appear to have worked chiefly in the fields. Before turning to a more detailed consideration of these precepts, we will first explain some of the relevant terms and institutions.

The Jubilee year (yovel)

The biblical precept of the Jubilee year (Lev. 25:8-13) provides that all land within the territory of the land of Israel is to be redistributed among members of the community on a set fifty-year cycle. The key to the redistribution is familial: every man returns to and gains ownership of his family's ancestral plot. The redistribution thus presupposes an initial distribution of the land according to family. In addition, within the framework of the Jubilee law, all slaves are manumitted, and return to their homes and ancestral lands as freemen.

Emancipation of slaves

The Torah provides, in effect, two separate cycles for the freeing of slaves—one personal, the other communal. The communal cycle, recurring every fifty years, is described in Leviticus 25, and occurs as part of the Jubilee year. All Hebrew slaves are to go free that year, regardless of when their term of slavery began. In addition to the Jubilee cycle, the Torah also sets down that every Hebrew slave[5] has his own personal emancipation time, six years after his entry into servitude. "When you acquire a Hebrew slave, he shall serve six years; in the seventh year he shall go free, without payment" (Exod. 21:2). The Torah adds that the slave should not be set free empty-handed, but rather, the owner is obligated to give him some of his yield: "When you set him free, do not let him go empty-handed: Furnish him out of the flock, threshing floor, and vat, with which the Lord your God has blessed you" (Deut. 15:13–14).

In contrast to the situation at the end of the communal cycle, when remaining with his master is not an option, at the end of the slave's personal six-year cycle, he is offered his freedom, but not compelled to accept it. The Torah allows him to choose to remain with his master "forever" (*leolam*): "If the slave declares, 'I love my master, and my wife and children: I do not wish to go free,' his master shall take him before the judges [lit., God]. He shall be brought to the door or the doorpost, and his master shall pierce his ear with an awl; and he shall then remain his slave forever" (Exod. 21:5–6). It is clear from the text that though the Torah allows the slave to decline to be freed, it disapproves of his doing so. The Sages, however, do not interpret the word "forever" literally, but take it to mean 'until the next Jubilee year.'

This law of emancipation is part of a more general array of precepts intended to improve the lot of slaves. These include, for example, the prohibition against working a slave too harshly in Leviticus 25:43.

The Sabbath

The commandment to rest on the seventh day—the Sabbath—is not generally thought of as falling within the Torah's social legislation. But upon scrutiny, the social justice element becomes apparent. One of the rationales the Torah offers for the Sabbath is to grant slaves and maidservants a rest their masters might otherwise deny them: "But the seventh day is a Sabbath of the Lord your God; you shall not do any work—you, your son or your daughter, your male or female slave, your ox or your ass, or any of your cattle, or the stranger in your settlements, so that your male and female slave may rest as you do" (Deut. 5:14).

5 The Torah also broadens the rights of Canaanite (i.e., non-Hebrew) slaves, but they remained less extensive than those of Hebrew slaves.

Sabbatical year release of lands

Another precept that can, on reflection, be seen to have a social justice dimension, is that of the 'release' of land every seventh year, which is referred to as the Sabbatical year. This process, as set down in Leviticus 25:1–7, has two main elements: for the year in question, the land is not worked; and whatever the fields produce may be enjoyed by anyone, regardless of ownership. In effect, private ownership of agricultural produce is suspended for the year. The primary beneficiaries of the Sabbatical year are the poor, who, during normal years, cannot enjoy agricultural produce, as they cannot afford to buy it. During the Sabbatical year, however, they can enjoy fresh produce to the same extent as their wealthy neighbors.

Nevertheless, the release of lands will not be covered in this chapter, for it does not function as an ongoing mechanism for supporting the needy. In this, it differs from the other biblical social justice laws, which, as we will see, are intended to provide effective substantive assistance to members of the weaker social strata. The precept of the Sabbatical release of lands makes only a minor contribution to this goal, as distribution of produce once every seven years has no sustained economic effect during the other six years. Release of lands seems to have a primarily religious and educational purpose, namely, to heighten awareness of the transient nature of material wealth, in contrast to the permanence and immutability of God's sovereignty over the world. The Jubilee year, on the other hand—though it, too, is a cyclical process undergone once in a set number of years—in enabling the poor to make a fresh start, has the potential to effect long-term changes in economic well-being.

Gleanings, forgotten produce, corners of the field

In fact, it is not only during the Sabbatical year that the poor are sustained by field produce; the Torah commands property owners to leave a portion of their crops—grains, fruits, olives, and so on—for the poor every year. Farmers may not harvest their entire field, but must leave a corner unharvested (Lev. 19:9). Likewise, they are forbidden to go back and gather produce that fell while being harvested or was forgotten in the field. These must be left for "the poor and the stranger" (Lev. 19:10), for "the stranger, the fatherless, and the widow" (Deut. 24:19).

Loaning money

In Deuteronomy 15:7–8, the Torah mandates that the poor must be helped not only by providing them with agricultural produce, but by ensuring their access to loans. The wealthy are obligated to lend money to the poor: "If, however, there is a needy person among you, one of your kinsmen ...

do not harden your heart and shut your hand against your needy kinsman. But you shall surely open (*patoah tiftah*) your hand unto him, and shall surely lend him (*haavet taavitenu*) sufficient for his needs, for whatever he needs" (Deut. 15:7–8).

Later in the chapter, we will examine these verses and delve into the question of why loans are emphasized, as opposed to outright donations. The lending mandated by the Bible has a markedly social character: lending on interest is forbidden. Charging interest is compared metaphorically to the lender's taking a bite out of the borrower; one biblical Hebrew term for interest is *neshekh kesef*, literally, "a bite of money." Loaning money to the poor is mandated for social reasons, not as a mechanism for advancing the lender's economic interests.

This is also evident from the laws governing the manner in which loans are to be collected, laws that protect the debtor and his dignity, for example, the prohibition against the creditor's entering the debtor's home to seize a pledged object (i.e., collateral), and the creditor's obligation to return the debtor's collateral to him every evening, if the debtor needs it to sustain himself (Deut. 24:10–13).

Remission of loans

Not only does the Torah prescribe the granting of loans; it also mandates that loans be forgiven once every seven years, at the time of the Sabbatical year. All debts are nullified and debtors can work on their own behalf rather than for their creditors: "Every seventh year you shall practice remission of debts. This shall be the nature of the remission: every creditor shall remit the due that he claims from his fellow; he shall not dun his fellow or kinsman, for the remission proclaimed is of the Lord" (Deut. 15:1–2).

Although the Torah is replete with precepts and mechanisms whose primary or secondary purpose is to care for the weaker classes within society, it nowhere considers the underlying socioeconomic philosophy. Indeed, Jewish law in general, and its biblical stratum in particular, says little about the theoretical concepts on which its various legal institutions rest. To reconstruct these concepts, we must analyze the relevant precepts, laws, and jurisprudential arrangements, and attempt to extract the relevant principles. In the following sections of this chapter, we will seek to articulate some of the socioeconomic principles that can be inferred from the Torah's social injunctions, in part, by comparing them to parallel provisions of other ancient Near Eastern legal systems.[6]

6 This comparison is subject, however, to one important qualification: the Torah, to a certain extent, represents an ideal legal system, not expressly related to the existence of an actual government with funds to distribute.

2.2 Social justice as a legal issue

A wide range of actions intended to help the weaker social strata were known in early antiquity: declaring a remission of debts, freeing prisoners and slaves, suspending taxes, and more. In some languages and at some places, measures such as these were referred to with the very rubric used in the Bible: "to do justice in the land."[7] Ancient Near East scholars have pointed out that these practices, while intended help the weak, take place within a political context. They are always effected by decree of the king and at his initiative. It is the monarch who decides whether, when, and how the weaker classes should be helped; see Appendix.

Acts intended to generate social reforms were taken when the king saw fit, or more accurately, when he saw the need or the opportunity to endear himself to his subjects and ensure the tranquility of his kingdom: on ascending to the throne, say, or at times of war.[8] Bestowing such concessions allowed the king to advance his own political interests while clothing his machinations in the rhetoric of social justice.

> Another substantial difference between the proclamation of "liberty" in Egypt and Mesopotamia and in Israel was that the motivation for this proclamation among the kings of the ancient Near East was the wish of the monarchs to win over the hearts of the people … which explains why this was usually done when they ascended the throne. While the kings ameliorated the condition of the poor by establishing "uprightness" or "freedom," their motivation for this was the wish to appear in the eyes of the people as just and upright kings, and not a genuine concern for improving the lot of the poor among their people. In ancient Greece, where this practice also took root, the tendency of the rulers to act in this way was looked upon with suspicion, for which reason the institution of cancellation of debts was a punishable offense, and anyone attempting to realize it was cursed.[9]

The biblical approach differs markedly. While the social measures legislated in the Torah were for the most part familiar—remission of debts, emancipation of slaves, restoration of property to its owners, and so on—the initiative for implementing these steps is no longer the king's, but a matter of statutory law. The Bible regularizes acts of social justice. The steps to be taken, and the timing of these steps, are no longer discretionary, but fixed and known in advance to all. The ruler cannot take such steps

7 See M. Weinfeld, *Social Justice in Ancient Israel and in the Ancient Near East* (Minneapolis and Jerusalem: 1995), 75, 84.

8 Biblical examples include Pharaoh's freeing prisoners on his birthday (Genesis 40:20), and Ahasuerus' proclaiming a tax amnesty in honor of the new queen's coronation (Esther 2:18).

9 Weinfeld, n. 7 above, 11.

whenever he finds it politically expedient, but is required to abide by the statutory schedule.

In bringing actions undertaken for the benefit of the weak under the umbrella of the law, the biblical approach to social justice was tantamount to a revolution. It ensured that the measures in question indeed served their declared purpose, and were not undertaken merely to advance the interests of the throne. To further enhance provision of social assistance, the biblical system also set in place other principles, to which we now turn.

2.3 Personal responsibility

Who bears financial responsibility for supporting the disadvantaged? On the biblical model, are those in need to seek out wealthy individuals for help, or can they seek succor from an anonymous source, such as a charity fund?

Personal responsibility is a central pillar of the Torah's social legislation. Responsibility for helping the disadvantaged falls not on public institutions, but squarely on the shoulders of the individual, who is obligated to help the poor and needy with whom he comes in personal contact. The Torah does not mandate establishment of public institutions for collecting money from the wealthy and distributing it to the poor, but rather, the transfer is accomplished directly.

This is evident, for example, in the precepts of gleanings, forgotten produce, and corners of the field. These commandments, as we saw, obligate the owner of a field to set aside a portion of his yield for the poor. This portion is transferred directly to the poor, with no mediation: "When you reap the harvest of your land, you shall not reap all the way to the edges of your field, or gather the gleanings of your harvest. You shall not pick your vineyard bare, or gather the fallen fruit of your vineyard; you shall leave them for the poor and the stranger..." (Lev. 19:9–10).

This policy of direct contact between helper and beneficiary is manifest in the formulation of the obligation to lend to the poor: "do not harden your heart and shut your hand against your needy kinsman" (Deut. 15:7). Maimonides articulates this obligation more explicitly still: "He who, seeing a poor man begging, turns his eyes away from him and fails to give him alms, transgresses a negative commandment, as it is said, 'Do not harden your heart and shut your hand against your needy kinsman.'"[10]

Note that the biblical verse Maimonides invokes terms the poor person "your kinsman," even though it is not referring literally to a member of the wealthy person's family. This device is used often in the Bible, as when fellow Israelites are referred to as "your brother" or "your friend." The family metaphor evokes social solidarity, and sends a message of interpersonal responsibility. When a needy person approaches his wealthy

10 *Code*, Laws concerning Gifts to the Poor 7:2.

neighbor for assistance, he need not hope the latter will exhibit good will and generosity, but can rely on the legal obligation imposed by the Torah. Only much later do we see the rise of communal institutions such as charity funds, that serve as intermediaries between rich and poor.

In effect, the Torah broadens the scope of the social assistance that has up to this point been viewed as the province of the ruler, requiring it to be extended to the needy by their fellows.[11] This policy is not due to a lack of familiarity with the concept of public funding, which is indeed invoked in other biblical contexts. The story of Joseph recounted in Genesis, for instance, features public funding. Joseph, serving in a public capacity in Egypt, amasses a large quantity of grain during the years of abundance to ensure the Egyptians' survival during the coming years of famine.[12] Similarly, the Israelites' construction of the Tabernacle in the desert was accomplished through a public fund that solicited valuables from the Israelites. Thus the concept of a publicly funded institution was by no means unfamiliar, and could have been harnessed to support the needy. Yet in all matters related to support for the disadvantaged, the Bible deliberately chooses to impose responsibility directly on the individual.

This policy creates direct personal contact between the two sides of the socioeconomic divide. One who has means cannot avoid his disadvantaged neighbor by telling him to direct his requests to the public authorities, but must look him in the eye and open his purse to his needs. In section 10 below, where we examine the social institutions established by the Sages, we will consider the extent to which this 'personal responsibility' principle was preserved in the post-biblical period.

2.4 Sustenance and rehabilitation

Having defined the source of funding for provision of assistance to the needy, we must consider the purposes for which this aid is provided. In what respects are the needy to be assisted, and how is the mandated assistance designed to meet those goals?

The precepts related to social justice can be divided into two groups with complementary goals. One goal can be termed 'sustaining the poor,' that is, ensuring at least a minimal standard of living: a small amount of food (through the precepts of gleanings, forgotten produce, and corners of the field[13]) and a weekly day of rest, the Sabbath. The Sabbath ensures that even someone who engages in arduous physical labor from dawn to dusk

11 Weinfeld, n. 7 above, 17.

12 See Genesis 41. The food was not provided gratis, but this does not detract from the fact that this was a publicly-run aid operation.

13 As is clear from the account in the biblical Book of Ruth, the amount of food this yields is meager, sufficient only for day-to-day survival.

is not entirely consumed by the burden of work, with no respite. Indeed, the biblical passage ordaining observance of the Sabbath sets out the social rationale: rest is the right of all, including slaves: "But the seventh day is a Sabbath of the Lord your God; you shall not do any work … **so that** your male and female slave may rest as you do" (Deut. 5:14).[14]

The second goal of the social justice precepts can be termed 'rehabilitating the poor.' The disadvantaged are not to be given goods for immediate use, but means of production that will enable them, in the long run, to attain greater financial independence. Thus in the Jubilee year, for instance, land—the primary means of production in an agrarian society—is returned to those who have lost it, and further, the freedom to work the land on his own behalf, and not for a master, is restored to the owner, giving him the opportunity to provide for his family.

Another example is the precept of manumission. As we saw, the Bible specifies that an emancipated slave must be given goods from among his master's assets: "When you set him free, do not let him go empty-handed: Furnish him out of the flock, threshing floor, and vat" (Deut. 15:13–14). This precept seeks to rehabilitate the freed slave, ensuring his short-term economic security so he can direct his attention to finding work and getting established. Were he manumitted empty-handed, he would have to spend his initial days of freedom gleaning a small amount of food and seeking shelter; before long, he might be deterred, and return to his former master. The precept mandating that departing slaves be given provisions to sustain them transforms their freedom from nominal to genuine.

Another rehabilitative precept is that concerning the seventh-year remission of loans. This measure enables those trapped in a cycle of debt—taking one loan to pay off another—to escape and start afresh. It does not provide them with goods that can be used in the short term, but rather affords them the opportunity to labor on their own behalf, and not simply to repay creditors.

A contemporary institution somewhat similar to remission of debt is that of bankruptcy. An insolvent debtor can be declared a bankrupt by the court. His debts are forgiven, and he can turn over a new leaf. But there are important differences between the two institutions. The biblical precept of loan remission is intended to provide an across-the-board social mechanism by which the vicious circle of borrowing in order to pay off debt will be preempted or dramatically reduced. By contrast, bankruptcy is intended as an ad hoc life preserver, as it were, for individual debtors who have become insolvent. Remission of loans takes place according to a regular

14 Unlike the rationale given in Deuteronomy, the rationale for Sabbath rest set forth in Exodus 20:8–10 is emulation of God's rest following His creation of the world. This is not a social rationale, and no distinction is drawn between the worker's rest and that of his employer—the precept encompasses both. There is, however, no contradiction, as the two rationales can be seen as complementary, and many so interpret them.

schedule known in advance, whereas bankruptcy comes into play only when someone can no longer pay his debts, and its occurrence cannot be foreseen.

The historical context is, of course, pertinent to understanding the institutions in question. During the biblical period, only the poor borrowed money, and they did so solely in order to provide themselves with the necessities of life. Later on, however, loans became an economic engine: people from every social stratum took out loans, often for the purpose of generating profit and increasing their earning power.

2.5 The recipient's responsibility

We have surveyed the various precepts that obligate the wealthy to provide a safety net for the disadvantaged. Parallel obligations are imposed on the needy, effectively conditioning assistance on their active cooperation. Recipients of charity must join in the effort to rehabilitate them, that is, they must help themselves.

This is manifest in the precepts of gleanings, forgotten produce, and corners of the field. Although these mandate transferring to the poor goods meant for use in the short term, the manner in which the produce is provided ensures the beneficiary's participation in the process. Farmers are obligated to give of their yield to a needy neighbor, but the Torah does not require them to harvest the grain and bring it to the recipient. Indeed, they are not even required to harvest it and leave it at the entrance to the field for the poor to come and take. Rather, the precept calls for the farmer to leave unharvested produce in the field, so the needy can actively take part in the harvesting process. The precept, in other words, commands the landowner to provide his poor neighbors with work—their wage being the produce that they gather. One who is indigent yet too lazy to go out to the field and work with the reapers will derive no benefit from the precepts of gleanings, forgotten produce, and corners of the field.

This conclusion is reinforced by the sharp contrast between the manner in which these gifts are given to the poor, and the manner in which priestly gifts (*terumot* [sing., *teruma*]) and levitical tithes (*maasrot* [sing., *maaser*]) are supplied to their recipients. Unlike the poor, the priests and Levites are given harvested, ready-to-eat produce; they need not participate in harvesting the field (Num. 18:8, 11–13). Indeed, the Sages went further, actually prohibiting the priests and Levites from participating in the harvesting process. Maimonides ruled similarly: "Priests and Levites are forbidden to serve as helpers at the threshing floor so that they can receive the gifts due them [more quickly].... The Israelite too is forbidden to allow them to help him; rather, he should give them their share with due deference."[15]

15 *Code*, Laws concerning Heave Offerings 12:18.

What explains the difference between the rule governing gifts of produce to the needy, who must participate in harvesting the field, and that governing tithes and heave offerings given to the priests and Levites, who receive their shares of the harvest ready-to-use? The priests and Levites do sacred work (see Num. 18:21), and the produce given them is compensation for this work. Accordingly, they are not required to perform any additional labor, such as working in the field, to obtain it. The needy, however, receive the produce as a donation rather than as wages, and must therefore join in harvesting the field, thereby contributing and helping themselves, so to speak.

Another instance in which the beneficiary is required to take on responsibility with respect to a donation is the precept of loaning money, an important precept that constitutes the source for the later laws referred to as the laws of charity. It is not always recognized that there is no biblical commandment mandating that money be donated—given—to the poor. The Sages derive this obligation from the passage in Deuteronomy that sets forth the obligation to loan money (interest-free, of course) to the needy:

> If, however, there is a needy person among you, one of your kinsmen in any of your settlements in the land that the Lord your God is giving you, do not harden your heart and shut your hand against your needy kinsman.
>
> But you shall surely open (*patoah tiftah*) your hand unto him, and shall surely lend him (*haavet taavitenu*) sufficient for his needs, for whatever he needs. Beware lest you harbor the base thought in your heart, saying, 'The seventh year, the year of remission, is approaching,' and are thus mean to your needy kinsman and give him nothing. And he will cry out to the Lord against you, and you will have transgressed. But you must surely give him, and your heart should not be grudging when you do so, for because of this act, the Lord your God will bless you in all your deeds and in all your undertakings.
>
> Deuteronomy 15:7–10

These verses mandate that monetary assistance be provided to the poor. The Torah recognizes that the giver may resist doing so out of concern that, due to the forthcoming Sabbatical year remission of loans, any money lent out will be forfeited, and seeks to allay these concerns by promising that all the giver's endeavors will be blessed. Clearly, then, the precept in question refers to assistance in the form of a loan, which is subject to remission, rather than an outright gift, which is not affected by the law of debt remission.

Moreover, the Hebrew verb translated as "you shall surely lend him"—*haavet taavitenu*—is derived from the root *av"t*, meaning 'collateral,' something given to the lender as a pledge that the loan will be repaid. That is, the literal meaning of the verse is "you shall take collateral against the loan you are obligated to grant him." And indeed, this is how the great medieval exegete R. Abraham ibn Ezra interpreted it: "you shall give him [something that is] yours in exchange for his collateral. And [the meaning of] *"taavitenu"* is "accept his collateral."[16]

What, then, is the essence of the assistance that is rendered to the needy by loaning them money? A loan will provide effective aid only if the borrower is prepared to keep his nose to the grindstone and use the loan productively, so that he can both repay the loan and benefit from its potential fruits. If the borrower tries to benefit from the loan immediately, it is likely that when the time for repayment comes, he will be left with nothing, or more likely, with a loan he cannot repay. Granted, a borrower struggling to repay a loan can rely on the fact that it will ultimately be remitted and thus transformed, in effect, into a donation; but this will not occur until the Sabbatical year, and does not relieve the borrower of the responsibility to work hard to pay off the loan in the intervening years. Loans, like gleanings, forgotten produce, and corners of the field, provide the needy with effective assistance only to the extent that the beneficiaries themselves actively work to reap the benefits in question.

2.6 Social stratification

We have seen that the Pentateuchal teachings on social justice seek to provide the poor with sustenance and rehabilitation, while imposing on them the responsibility of taking an active part in this enterprise. Let us now consider the formula for transferring resources to the poor and distributing these resources among them.

An important principle of the Torah's social legislation, a principle retained in the Rabbinic literature, is that assistance is provided in accordance with individual needs, which are not necessarily the same in all cases. Equality between rich and poor is not aspired to or achieved, and indeed, neither is equality among the poor themselves. In other words, the biblical outlook seeks to assist the disadvantaged classes while accepting the socioeconomic stratification that occurs naturally in every society.

Can the mechanisms outlined above, such as the Jubilee year, the emancipation of slaves, and donation of corners of the field, prevent the concentration of wealth within specific social strata? It seems not. The Jubilee year makes it impossible to accumulate vast holdings of land and slaves, and the remission of loans precludes the accumulation of large numbers of outstanding promissory notes; but the Bible does not rule out the

16 As we will soon see, this construal of the verse diverges from the Sages' exegetical interpretation of the verse. The Sages' reading of the precept is apparent in Rashi's comment: "You shall surely lend him"—if he does not want to accept it as a gift, give it to him as a loan."

possibility of accumulating other sorts of wealth known in the ancient world: silver and gold, precious stones, cattle and sheep, chattels. Nowhere is redistribution of these assets mandated. Hence one who wishes to protect his wealth, that is, remove it from the purview of the social justice precepts, can do so by accumulating precious metals, animals, and movable property. The biblical social justice directives seek to preempt the dominance of a small group over the means of production and other elements of economic independence, but not to prevent people from becoming wealthy by accumulating other goods. We see, in fact, in the patriarchal narratives in Genesis, that wealth is characteristic of those who serve God, and connotes blessedness. Although it seeks to rehabilitate the poor, the biblical text does not disparage wealth per se.

Moreover, even in the context of the social precepts intended to give the poor a chance at rehabilitation, the opportunities provided are not necessarily the same for all. Consider, for example, remission of loans in the Sabbatical year. This process affords all debtors the possibility of turning over a new leaf, but even so, it must be kept in mind that not everyone is on the same footing initially. That is, the playing field is not completely level to begin with. Remitting the debts of one who has nothing does not have the same force as remitting the debts of one who owns land or animals. For the latter, debt remission constitutes an opportunity to utilize the means of production he owns, which he can now employ for his own rather than his creditors' benefit. Remission of debts frees debtors from loans that enslaved them and prevented them from taking advantage of their own resources. Those who lack such resources remain relatively disadvantaged even after their debts have been remitted.

This is also true of the Jubilee year, when all regain the land that was their ancestral inheritance. The land one is allocated depends entirely on his family, and the redistribution is not proportionate to the holdings of one's neighbors. Thus the precept of the Jubilee year is in no sense egalitarian. A member of a large family with many heirs will receive a smaller portion than a member of a smaller family with fewer heirs to share in the ancestral holding. Clearly, then, the biblical vision of social justice sanctions socioeconomic inequities, and allows the continuation of naturally-occurring social stratification.

3 The introduction of charity laws during the Rabbinic period

The Bible's protagonists are often shepherds and farmers, and most of its social justice precepts are tied to the world of farming. The Mishnah, compiled in the land of Israel at the end of the second century CE, likewise makes laws related to agriculture the focus of measures intended to benefit the disadvantaged. The principal tractates that manifest concern for the disadvantaged are found in the 'Order' Zeraim (Seeds), which deals with the laws of agricultural produce; this concern is especially pronounced in tractate Peia (Corner [of the field]).

Various developments in Jewish society in the land of Israel during the second century CE, however, especially increasing poverty—reflected in both the number of the poor and the severity of their situation—set in motion a shift away from the primarily agrarian economy. This in turn gave rise to a need for different mechanisms to support the poor, chief among them being the distribution of money rather than produce. E.E. Urbach summarizes this transition as follows:

> The Jewish community in the land of Israel suffered greatly as a result of the wars that took place during the second century CE, and certainly did not enjoy the full benefit of the economic prosperity then prevalent in the Roman Empire. Its situation became even worse when things overall took a turn for the worse.... The harsh economic conditions and the pervasive poverty created increasing demand for individual acts of charity, and for formulation of laws of community and institutional charity. The destruction of the Temple put an end to the income the poor had earned from activities related to the sacrificial service and other Temple rituals. The dispossession of many farmers increased the rolls of the needy and diminished their income from the 'gifts for the poor' [i.e., gleanings, forgotten produce, and corners of the field] that were related to working the land; the urban population received just a small fraction of these 'gifts.' ... It stands to reason that the laws of the public welfare funds [*tamhui* and *kupa*, explained below] and the obligations of town dwellers with respect to charity were reformulated following the destruction [of the Temple].[17]

To this must be added Hillel the Elder's famous *prozbul* enactment. The Mishnah recounts how Hillel saw that the law of debt remission was doing borrowers more harm than good—lenders, apprehensive that borrowers' financial obligations would be nullified by the Sabbatical year, were unwilling to lend. In response, he devised a legal mechanism, the *prozbul*, that made it possible for creditors to continue to enforce their rights despite the Sabbatical year. The enactment was a broadening of the Rabbinic rule that promissory notes submitted to the court for collection were not nullified by the Sabbatical year. The Mishnah describes the *prozbul* as follows:

> This was one of the measures enacted by Hillel the Elder; for when he observed people refraining from lending to one another, and thus

17 E.E. Urbach, "Religious and social tendencies in the Sages' teachings on charity" (Hebrew), in E.E. Urbach, *World of the Sages: Collected Studies* (Hebrew), (Jerusalem: 2002), 106–108.

> transgressing what is written in the Torah, 'Beware lest you harbor the base thought in your heart ...' (Deut. 15:9), he instituted the *prozbul*.
>
> This is the formula of the *prozbul*: 'I declare before you, so-and-so, judges of such-and-such a place, regarding any debt due me, that I shall collect it whenever I wish.' And the judges sign below, or the witnesses.
>
> mSheviit 10:3–4

Of course, in effect, this spelled the end of debt remission, depriving those most likely to have debts—that is, the needy—of an important protective mechanism, and it became necessary to create some alternative means of providing them with assistance.

These processes herald the beginning of the laws of charity. There are a few instances where the Mishnah, in passing, discusses the obligation to give alms and provide for other essential needs of the poor. At the end of tractate Peia, for example, after discussion of the laws related to providing agricultural produce to the poor, we find a Mishnah that speaks of the obligation to provide food and shelter to the poor. This Mishnah even attests to the existence of public welfare institutions, referred to by the Sages as the "communal fund" (*kupa*) and the "soup kitchen" (*tamhui*):

> One may not give an itinerant poor person less than a loaf worth a *pondion*, when four *seah*s [of wheat cost] one *sela*. If he stays the night, one must give him the cost of what he needs for a night. If he stays over the Sabbath, he is given food for three meals. He who has the means for two meals, may not take anything from the soup kitchen (*tamhui*); and he who has the means for fourteen meals, may not take anything from the communal fund (*kupa*). The communal fund is collected by two people and distributed by three.
>
> mPeia 8:7

Elsewhere, apropos discussion of parents' financial obligations to their children, the Mishnah addresses the obligation to provide financial support to poor brides:

> If a man gave his daughter in marriage without specifying any conditions, he may give her no less than fifty *zuz*. If he arranged to have him [the groom] take her in unprovided-for [lit., naked], the groom may not say 'when I have taken her into my house, I shall clothe her with clothes myself,' but must provide her with the clothing while she is still in her father's house. So too if one gives an orphaned girl in marriage, he [the treasurer of the charity fund] may give her no less than fifty *zuz*. If funds are available, she is to be outfitted in accordance with the dignity of her position.
>
> mKetubot 6:5

The term "charity" (*tzedaka*) and the institution of "charity collectors" (*gabaei tzedaka*) are mentioned several other times in the Mishnah, always in passing and without any comprehensive discussion of the laws of charity. More extensive references to charity as an institution appear in the Tosefta, but the matter received no systematic treatment until the Gemara. It seems, therefore, that charity as an institution emerged slowly within Jewish society, in response to the waning importance of the agricultural precepts and the inadequacy of the support they afforded the needy. One of the questions that will occupy us in the next section is whether the laws of charity are a continuation of the distributive justice mechanisms established in the Bible, or should be seen as a new paradigm.

4 Charity: 'between man and God' or 'between man and his fellow'?

Social actions that are to be undertaken within the framework of a religious legal system invite consideration of their nature and purpose. Do they represent a system of norms whose purpose is societal, that is, to improve the situation of certain classes within society; or is their purpose religious, namely, to bring an individual's conduct and character closer to that prescribed by his faith? In halakhic terminology, this question can be formulated as follows: is the obligation to donate to the poor to be understood as a precept that is 'between man and his fellow,' that is, a precept whose purpose is to help one's fellow man, or is it to be seen as a precept that is between man and God, that is, intended to foster conformity between the individual and the divine will?[18]

Though the religious and social objectives of charity need not be mutually exclusive, how much emphasis is to be placed on each is not simply a theoretical question, and may have actual legal consequences. Moreover, differential emphasis may explain why the Jewish legal tradition stresses the social effects of charity—sustaining and rehabilitating the poor—whereas the Christian tradition tends to emphasize charity's inner effect on the donor's soul and character.

Indeed, we find that the obligation to give charity is understood in many different ways in the various Rabbinic sources. Some see it as a social

18 Of course, the question can be asked, not just vis-à-vis societal precepts, but about all religiously-mandated acts: we can ask of what appear to be purely ritual acts, for instance, eating matza, whether they have a societal purpose, and we can ask of manifestly rational acts mandated by biblical law, for instance, respecting one's parents and returning lost objects, whether they also have a religious role, viz., whether they are intended to bring us closer to God as are ritual precepts such as observing the Sabbath, waving the *lulav*, and eating matza. The degree to which the religious aspects of Jewish law can be separated from its more conventionally 'legal' aspects is the subject of debate among contemporary scholars, see H. Ben-Menahem, "Is talmudic law a religious legal system? A provisional analysis," 24 *Journal of Law and Religion* (2009), 379–402.

obligation, others, as a religious duty, and others still, as an ethical mandate. In Rabbinic terminology, the latter is evocatively referred to as a matter 'between man and himself.' Let us consider an example.

> R. Joshua b. Korha said: How do we know that whoever closes his eyes to [the need to give] charity is like one who engages in idolatrous worship? As it is said, "Beware lest you harbor the base (*beliyaal*) thought in your heart, saying ['The seventh year, the year of remission, is approaching,' and are thus mean to your needy kinsman and give him nothing]" (Deut. 15:9); and it is said, "some base fellows (*bnei beliyaal*) from among you have gone [and subverted the inhabitants of their town, saying, 'Let us go and worship other gods, which you have not known']" (Deut. 13:14). Just as "*beliyaal*" there refers to idolatry, so too "*beliyaal*" here refers to idolatry.
>
> tPeia 4:20 (Zuckermandel edition)

It seems that R. Joshua b. Korha emphasizes the **religious** aspect of the precept of giving charity: seeking to heighten the importance of charity, he compares the act of withholding it to idolatry, one of the gravest transgressions. But note that though he could have compared withholding charity to committing murder, another such grave offense[19]—he specifically invoked idolatry—repudiation of the Creator.

R. Joshua (to be distinguished from R. Joshua b Korha) notes the benefit received by the donor himself from the act of giving, thereby emphasizing the **ethical–educational** dimension of charity. As he sees it, the charitable act's contribution to refining the donor's character is greater than its financial contribution to the recipient:

> R. Joshua taught: More than the master of the house does for the poor person, the poor person does for the master of the house.
>
> Leviticus Rabbah (Vilna), parasha 34:8

As to the social perspective, below, we will examine laws whose purpose is to ensure that donated monies reach the proper recipients and neither remain in the hands of the funds that collected them, nor fall into the hands of fraudulent claimants. The social quality of these laws is manifest in the fact that they focus not only on the giving of charity, but also on its receipt by the needy. Moreover, the Hebrew word customarily translated as 'charity' (*tzedaka*) itself highlights the social dimension of charitable giving, as it is derived from the lexical root *tz"d"k*—to do justice. Clearly, the act of charity entails doing justice, not merely being kind or merciful.[20]

19 Such a comparison is indeed drawn by the Talmud in bSanhedrin 35a.

20 The meaning of *tzedaka* in biblical Hebrew differs from that in Rabbinic Hebrew. The Bible uses the word primarily to refer to the doing of justice and righteousness; e.g., "Thus said

In some cases, however, as exemplified by the following law from the *Shulhan Arukh,* the rationales for the mandated charitable acts are clear-cut:

> One who wishes to acquire merit for himself should subjugate his evil impulse and open his hand wide; and everything done for the sake of heaven should be done in a good and lovely way. If he builds a synagogue, it should be nicer than his home. If he feeds the hungry, he should do so from the best and sweetest foods on his table. If he clothes the naked, he should clothe him with the most beautiful of his garments. If he dedicates something [for sacred use], he should dedicate the choicest of his assets. As it is said: "All fat is the Lord's" (Lev. 3:16).
>
> *Shulhan Arukh,* YD 248:8

Clearly, this law reflects the ethical and religious objectives of the precept of giving charity. There is no social-welfare justification for giving the poor person the best of the donor's food or garments; rather, the rationale for doing so is to train one to overcome his egoism, acknowledge that his sustenance comes from God, and cultivate generosity and selflessness.

In determining the primary objective of the laws of charity, it should also be noted that the Sages took steps to ensure that the funds would reach the intended recipients, and would not fall into the wrong hands, that is, would not be diverted to the pockets of the collectors, or wind up in the hands of scammers feigning poverty. The Sages set in place a system of checks and balances to preclude such eventualities, even if this entailed reducing the net amount of money distributed to the needy, or a delay in its delivery. For example, charitable funds are to be administered by committee rather than by individuals, so that the collectors will exercise oversight over each other and preempt misappropriation of donations.

More importantly, the Rabbis also established that the credibility of those seeking charity must be investigated, to be sure that funds are not distributed to those who do not meet the appropriate criteria, though an exception is made for situations in which the urgency of the need does not allow for such investigation.

> R. Huna said: Applicants for food are investigated, but not applicants for clothing.... And Rav Judah said: applicants for clothing are investigated, but not applicants for food.... It has been taught in

the Lord: Do what is just (*mishpat*) and right (*tzedaka*); rescue from the defrauder him who is robbed; do not wrong the stranger, the fatherless, and the widow; commit no lawless act, and do not shed the blood of the innocent in this place" (Jer. 22:3). The Sages, in contrast, appropriated the word to refer to the giving of gifts to the poor.

> accordance with the view of Rav Judah: If someone says, 'Clothe me,' he is investigated, [if he says], 'Feed me,' he is not investigated.
>
> bBaba Batra 9a

The existence of such checks and balances supports the thesis that the primary objective of the laws of charity is social, namely, sustenance of the needy. Charitable donations that fall into the wrong hands make no contribution to the sustenance of the needy; they have no social value. Though such donations may indeed foster or attest to the donors' virtue and selflessness, from a social point of view they constitute an undesirable transfer of welfare funds to those not entitled to them. The law therefore seeks to minimize them. Here we can see a concrete legal consequence of the difference, noted by Urbach, between the approaches to charity underlying Jewish and Christian legal thinking. Christianity emphasized the love and kindness that are manifested in the charitable act, and therefore assigned less weight to the donation's reaching its intended recipient.[21] In contrast, the halakha focused on charity as a mechanism for social betterment, and hence conditioned discharge of the precept of giving charity on the donation's reaching its intended recipient.

5 Compulsory charity

If the system for transferring funds from rich to poor is to achieve its social goals effectively, it cannot rely solely on the good will and charitable impulses of the wealthy, who may not be responsive when the needy require assistance. It must, therefore, have recourse to coercion. It might be thought that the notion of the enforcement of charity is an oxymoron. And indeed, if the emphasis is placed on charity as a manifestation of the donor's character, the laws of charity will likely be based on voluntary giving. If, on the other hand, the primary goal is support for the disadvantaged, the laws of charity may mandate coerced donations. This notion was heatedly debated in the Rabbinic sources:

> As was stated by R. Nahman in the name of Rabbah b. Abuha ... [the collectors] can seize [his possessions] as a charitable donation even on the eve of the Sabbath. Is that so? Is it not written, "I will punish all that oppress them" (Jer. 30:20), even, said R. Isaac b. Samuel b. Marta in the name of Rav, charity collectors?! There is no contradiction: the

21 "Charity was not meant to end poverty but to manifest and arouse love.... The goal of the act of charity was not to ensure the welfare of the other and enhance his condition; it was to ensure the salvation of the donor and the redemption of his soul.... The powerful missionary spirit that drove [the Church] did not allow it to examine the sources of income of charitable donors or the actions of the recipients. It opened its hands to all who requested assistance, imposing no conditions" (Urbach, n. 17 above, 113, 118.)

one [R. Nahman] speaks of someone well-to-do, the other of someone not well-to-do; as, for instance, when Rava compelled R. Nathan b. Ami to give 400 *zuz* to charity.

bBaba Batra 8b

In R. Nahman's view, it is permissible to collateralize a charitable obligation, that is, to attach money or property that is to be contributed to the charitable fund. R. Nahman adds that this may be done even on the eve of the Sabbath—a time of feverish preparation for the approaching Sabbath, when it is least convenient for the property owner to pay his charitable obligations, especially by having his assets seized. But the eve of the Sabbath is precisely when the poor are most in need of assistance. The ruling that charitable contributions may be seized even on the eve of the Sabbath emphasizes the sweeping extent to which the laws of charity are enforced, the donor's convenience being scarcely taken into account.

R. Isaac, on the other hand, appears to reject coerced charity. Not content with simply contending that enforcement is inappropriate, he goes further and compares charity collectors to the worst of Israel's enemies: those who devour the people of Israel, fight them, prey upon them, and plunder their possessions (Jer. 30:16–20). R. Isaac's exegesis, in invoking these verses apropos charity collectors, indirectly ascribes to them an odious profile: vile and reprehensible, they are destined to be punished by God. R. Isaac is thus expressing great hostility to the institution of charity collectors. On his view, a completely voluntary system of charity, uncoerced by the communal leadership, would be preferable.

The Talmud tries to resolve the controversy between R. Nahman and R. Isaac by distinguishing one who is well-to-do from one who is not. Charity may be coerced only from the former, who clearly has the wherewithal to pay. Still, a critical reading suggests that the Talmud favors R. Nahman's approach, which upholds enforcement of the laws of charity as a matter of principle. Exempting those who lack the wherewithal to contribute is a reasonable qualification of the principle that charitable giving can be coerced, but in no way detracts from its main thrust.

This conclusion is underscored by the reference to the case of the Amora Rava, who used coercion to extract a charitable contribution of 400 *zuz* from another Amora, R. Nathan b. Ami. We know from elsewhere in the Talmud[22] that Rava was one of R. Nathan b. Ami's teachers, thus this is not merely a case of coercion, but a case of coercion of a student by his teacher; that is, coercion within the walls of the study hall, as it were. Arguably, the story recounts a dispute within the study hall over the question of coerced charity, a dispute resolved by Rava's treatment of his student.

22 bShabat 103b; bKidushin 30a.

Although the Talmud decided that charitable donations may be coerced, the post-talmudic halakhic decisors continued to debate the issue. The point of departure for their analysis was the incompatibility between the rule that charity can be coerced, and another talmudic dictum: "It has been taught, every positive commandment whose reward is explicitly stated in Scripture does not fall within the jurisdiction of the earthly court" (bHulin 110b). In other words, a precept whose reward is stated in the Torah is not subject to enforcement by the court, on the premise that the reward set out in the Torah will suffice as motivation to fulfill the precept. But if so, the decisors asked, how can the precept of charity be enforced, when the Torah explicitly states, "But you must surely give him, and your heart should not be grudging when you do so, for because of this act, the Lord your God will bless you in all your deeds and in all your undertakings" (Deut. 15:10)? The *Tosafot* suggest several ways to resolve the apparent inconsistency.[23]

One approach argues that charity is indeed enforceable, and the "every positive commandment" rule from tractate Hulin does not apply to it. Various reasons are put forward. The Tosafist R. Isaac b. Samuel, known as Ri the Elder, explains that the precept of charity comprises both a positive commandment (to give charity) and a negative commandment (not to disregard the poor), and the negative commandment, at least, can be enforced. Another Tosafist, R. Isaac b. Abraham, offers a different explanation: a court is not **required** to enforce a precept whose reward is articulated explicitly, but is **permitted** to do so if it sees fit. Both agree that it is clearly permissible to compel the affluent to give charity.

Yet another approach is that of Rabbenu Tam, who maintains that, in principle, compliance with the precept of giving charity is not to be coerced. He explains the Gemara's reference to enforcement as follows: "And this is compulsion by words."[24] The talmudic concept of "compulsion by words" refers to persuasion and verbal pressure exerted by one who is in a position of power, as opposed to physical compulsion, coercion via threatened harm, or the legal compulsion exerted by the court on parties who refuse to abide by a ruling.

Ultimately, however, the debates came to an end, and the view that charity is fully enforceable was endorsed as decided law. Maimonides even details the enforcement measures a court can have recourse to against one who refuses to pay his assessed charitable contribution:

> He who refuses to give alms (*tzedaka*), or gives less than is appropriate for him, is compelled to comply by the court, which metes out lashes for disobedience until he gives as much as the court has assessed he should give. And the court may go and seize his property in his

23 bBaba Batra 8b s.v. *akfei*.
24 Ibid.

> presence and take from him that which it is appropriate for him to give, and they can seize [his possessions] as a charitable donation even on the eve of the Sabbath.
>
> *Code*, Laws concerning Gifts to the Poor 7:10

Lashes are meted out as an *in personam* remedy, whereas seizure of property is an *in rem* remedy. The latter ensures that even if one who is affluent refuses to cooperate with the collector, the poor will not lose out.

It is important to keep in mind that the decided law on the books was not necessarily implemented in practice. R. Joseph Caro attested that, in his time, charitable giving was not coerced:

> The *Mordekhai* [R. Mordekhai b. Hillel] wrote ... no fewer than three [charity] collectors are to be appointed, and two brothers are not to be appointed [as collectors], and that is the right thing to do. Still, the practice in every place is to appoint [only] one collector. So [the *Mordekhai*] wrote.
>
> But is appears to me that since today we do not seize possessions in lieu of a charitable contribution, it is permissible as a matter of law to appoint [only] one collector.
>
> *Beit Yosef*, *Tur*, YD 256

Notwithstanding the unambiguous ruling handed down by Maimonides that charitable giving can be coerced, and his implicit endorsement of the idea that the goal of charitable giving is, in effect, a more equitable distribution of resources, that is, distributive justice, echoes of the view that the laws of charity are voluntary and unenforceable by the communal authorities, continue to be heard. For instance, R. Joseph Isaac Lifshitz, a present-day scholar, has argued as follows:

> The obligation to care for the poor stems from [a] sense of responsibility, and is expressed through the act of *tzedaka*, or charity, in which the individual voluntarily gives away the fruits of his labor out of concern for his fellow man. The Jewish concept of charitable giving does not impinge on property rights, but rather expresses the individual's moral duty as a responsible person....
>
> Despite the fact that charity relates to one's money, it does not fall into the category of civil law governing property, but of religious laws governing moral and ritual obligations.[25]

Lifshitz's view seems inconsistent with the dominant approach in the halakhic literature, on which giving charity is a mandatory obligation,

25 Lifshitz, "Jewish economic theory," n. 3 above, 52.

fulfillment of which is enforceable in the full legal sense of the term. Nevertheless, there has long been a marked gap between the law as written and the general practice, as it was often impossible for communal leaders to compel the affluent to give charity.

6 Determining the poverty line

6.1 Three tests for poverty

Thus far, we have considered philosophical questions related to the laws of charity, specifically, their essential nature, objectives and enforceability; we now turn to an examination of their substance. The first question is that of defining 'the poor,' that is, those deemed poor enough to be eligible for benefits.

To gain a fuller understanding of the Sages' views, it will be helpful to first present three theoretical possibilities for setting the poverty line.

One possibility is to draw a relative poverty line, as is currently done in many welfare states, including Israel. The rationale is that poverty is a social phenomenon and thus inherently relative; a poor person is someone at the bottom of his community's socioeconomic ladder. To apply this approach to determining the poverty line, it is necessary to select socioeconomic criteria that can be used to classify members of the society into deciles and percentiles, and then to set the point below which individuals or families will be considered poor and eligible for assistance. Such assessments can be made on the basis of income, expenditure, standard of living, personal wealth, and so on. This approach thus measures social **differences**, measuring the distance between those at the top of the ladder and those at the bottom in order to determine the extent of poverty within society.

A second possibility is to set an absolute or 'objective' poverty line. On this approach, a non-conditional definition of what is needed to maintain a reasonable quality of life must be formulated. Here too, various criteria can be invoked in formulating the definition. Those unable to procure the standard in question will be considered poor and entitled to assistance, but the size of the gap separating them from others in the community will not be taken into account.

Naturally, the unconditional criteria will indeed reflect accepted, and non-static, social norms. What were formerly considered luxuries are now considered part of the minimum required for a reasonable quality of life. Two centuries ago, indoor plumbing was available only to the very wealthy; today, its absence is, in many parts of the world, an indication of dire poverty. Even an objective poverty line, then, will be a function of time and place. Nevertheless, the relative component of this approach is almost imperceptible: the criteria are quite stable and do not fluctuate in accordance with changes in the standard of living of those above the poverty line. The absolute standard is used in countries with a capitalist orientation, such as the United States, Australia and Germany.

The third possibility is a subjective poverty line. This approach is theoretical, and not used by contemporary societies, but merits consideration. It does not define poverty relative to other members of the society, or set hard and fast objective standards for a minimally reasonable quality of life. Instead, it takes the definition of poverty to vary from person to person. Since every individual's needs and abilities differ, the definition of hardship and poverty must be variable, so that it can reflect each individual's subjective perception of his situation. It is easy to see that even if this approach has theoretical merit, it would be difficult, if not impossible, to put it into practice: a society cannot be run on the basis of subjective criteria that vary from person to person within the community.

6.2 The objective test

Let us now examine how the Sages determined the poverty line. A Mishnah in tractate Peia offers three tests for poverty, each corresponding to charity of a specific kind:

> He who has food for two meals, may not take anything from the soup kitchen (*tamhui*); and he who has food for fourteen meals, may not take anything from the communal fund (*kupa*)....
>
> He who has 200 *zuz* may not take gleanings, forgotten produce, corners of the field, or the poor man's tithe....
>
> If his property is mortgaged to his creditors or to his wife's *ketuba*, he may take [support]..... If he has 50 *zuz* and he uses it for business, he may not take [support].
>
> mPeia 8:7-9

The 'soup kitchen' (*tamhui*) was a charitable institution that distributed **daily** meals to the poor. Anyone unable to provide himself with two meals a day (the norm at the time) was eligible for soup kitchen meals. The 'communal fund' (*kupa*) was a charitable institution that distributed other necessities to the poor on a **weekly** basis; accordingly, one was eligible for such support if he lacked the fourteen meals sufficient for an entire week. Gleanings, forgotten produce, corners of the field and the poor tithe, the donations from agricultural produce discussed earlier in this chapter, were distributed **annually**. Accordingly, the eligibility threshold is 200 *zuz*, which the commentators estimated to be the sum needed at the time to live for a year. R. Ovadiah of Bartenura ad loc. explains that this sum "suffices for one year's clothing and food."

The distinction in the latter part of the Mishnah is somewhat puzzling: why does possession of 200 *zuz* that is mortgaged to a creditor or as surety for *ketuba* monetary obligations not preclude eligibility for gifts to the poor, whereas possession of just 50 *zuz* used for business dealings does? The answer appears to be that as the 200 *zuz* put aside as a surety cannot be realized until the loan is paid off, it lacks the purchasing power of 200 *zuz* that has not been attached. Accordingly, possessing this attached sum does not raise one above the poverty line. On the other hand, 50 *zuz* used for commerce may have the purchasing power of 200 *zuz* used for ongoing living expenses, given the potential proceeds to the investor. The significance of these qualifications is that the 200 *zuz* test is intended not merely as a formal condition to be met by applicants, but as a substantive indicator of an applicant's actual ability to sustain himself.

Though each of the tests is for provision of a different type of charity, the tests have a common denominator: they do not assess a person's situation relative to the community in which he lives, but only in comparison to what is deemed to be the minimum cost of a reasonable quality of life. The Mishnah does **not** set down, for example, that one who has 'about what his neighbors have' or 'more than a poor worker' may not take gleanings, forgotten produce, and corners of the field. The 200-*zuz* criterion is basically stable, varying little from community to community; and so too, the two-meal and fourteen-meal criteria.

Yet as noted, even these objective criteria are ultimately affected by empirical circumstances. At the time of the Mishnah, two meals a day were considered sufficient; today, the norm is three. The 200 *zuz* fixed by the Sages would thus not suffice for subsistence in an era, such as our own, when more than two meals were the norm, hence the decisors ruled that the 200-*zuz* figure had to correspond to relevant local conditions, and was thus subject to periodic adjustment. The Tur, R. Jacob b. Asher, articulated this view early in the fourteenth century:

> Some say that all these measures applied only in those days, when they had a communal fund (*kupa*), a soup kitchen (*tamhui*), they distributed the poor tithe annually, and the poor took gleanings, forgotten produce, and corners of the field. And therefore they estimated that one who had 200 *zuz* could not take [charity] because that amount would see him through the year, and the following year he would again be eligible [for the available resources]. But now that we do not have these [institutions], he can take until he has an amount sufficient to allow him to support himself ... and it all depends on the place and the time.
>
> *Tur*, YD 253

R. Shlomo Goren suggested a criterion for the present day:

> One who has a monthly wage, or even a daily wage, even if he has no assets, is considered affluent, as long as his work suffices for him to

> support himself. This is because the trade he plies is his principal asset, as it sustains him.[26]

Of course, if poverty is determined by applying an objective test, then in determining how charity is to be disbursed, we will be unable to take into account the feelings of the poor, and will focus solely on meeting their need for physical sustenance. Imagine a poor person who, though able to maintain a reasonable standard of living, has neighbors and acquaintances whose standard of living is much higher. If the disparity causes him distress, is there an obligation to give him charity so that he too can enjoy that standard? One contemporary authority ruled as follows:

> The precept of charity [is to be observed by donating] in accordance with what the poor person lacks ... and not his situation in relation to that of his neighbors. And even if the poor person is distressed, and jealous of those who have more than he does, he is not eligible on that account to receive charity, and any additional assistance he may receive is given as an act of kindness.[27]

The objective test comes across as cold and insensitive. It makes no attempt to address, let alone mollify, feelings of disenfranchisement that arise in the wake of income disparities and socioeconomic polarization. Where those at the bottom of the socioeconomic ladder have a reasonable minimum quality of life, but there is a huge chasm between their way of life and that of the wealthiest classes, the laws of charity do not mandate the transfer of resources from the advantaged to the disadvantaged. Yet Jewish law recognizes another test for poverty, rendering this picture more complex.

6.3 The subjective test

Above, we adduced the Mishnah in tractate Ketubot that sets out the provisions to be made for the weddings of orphaned girls.

> So too if one gives an orphaned girl in marriage, he [the treasurer of the charity fund] may give her no less than fifty *zuz*. If funds are available, she is to be outfitted in accordance with the dignity of her position.
>
> mKetubot 6:5

The Mishnah rules that a fixed minimum must be allocated to a bride who is an orphan; it sets this sum at the amount it earlier specified as the

26 R. Shlomo Goren, "Setting the poverty line according to the halakha" (Hebrew), in idem, *Torat Hamedina* (Jerusalem: 1996), 358, 363.

27 R. Naftali Bar-Ilan, "Eligibility for charity" (Hebrew), *Tehumin* 2 (1981), 459–60.

minimum a father must give his daughter prior to her marriage. But it adds that when the orphaned bride is from a household in which lavish wedding parties had been the norm, if adequate charitable resources are available, the fund's officers must allocate money for her wedding "**in accordance with the dignity of her position.**"

This Mishnah sets down a class-related criterion for an orphaned bride's entitlement (has she been outfitted in a manner befitting her family's social status?) to complement the standard allocation (the 50 *zuz* due a bride). Beyond the minimum to which **every** orphaned bride is entitled, each orphaned bride's social class is also taken into account (provided funds are available).

Another such non-universal criterion is found in a law based on exegesis of Deuteronomy 15:8: "But you shall surely open (*patoah tiftah*) your hand unto him, and shall surely lend him (*haavet taavitenu*) sufficient for his needs, for whatever he needs":

> Our Rabbis taught: "Sufficient for his needs"—you are commanded to support him, but you are not commanded to make him rich; "sufficient ... for whatever he needs"—even a horse to ride upon and a slave to run ahead of him [to escort him]. It was related of Hillel the Elder that he brought to a certain poor man from a distinguished family a horse to ride upon and a slave to run ahead of him. On one occasion he could not find a slave to run ahead of him, so he [himself] ran ahead of him for three miles. Our Rabbis taught: It happened that the people of the upper Galilee brought to a poor member of a distinguished family from Sepphoris a pound of meat every day.
>
> bKetubot 67b

According to this exegesis, some needy individuals are entitled to more substantial charitable allocations, even to the point of "a horse to ride upon and a slave to run ahead of him." These poor are from "distinguished families"—wealthy families that have fallen on hard times. This is, again, an individualized criterion: circumstances that would be considered acceptable for an 'ordinary' poor person could be such as to constitute hardship for one of distinguished birth, who would therefore be entitled to a greater allocation.

The Talmud uses the locution "distinguished family" to describe the poor person in question to emphasize that his expensive tastes were instilled in him by his family, and he did not acquire them on his own. Accordingly, he should not be castigated for pampering himself, and should be helped out in his present reduced circumstances.[28] This implies a qualification of the individualized test: if the said individual developed

28 Maharsha, *Hidushei Agadot* ad loc.

his expensive tastes on his own, he need not be afforded benefits beyond those accorded to all needy persons.

The Sages expanded on this principle, applying it to additional situations:

> If he was accustomed to clothes of fine wool, he is given clothes of fine wool; to grain, he is given grain; to porridge—he is given porridge; to a yeast loaf, he is given a yeast loaf; to being fed, he is fed; as it says, "sufficient for his needs, for whatever he needs."
>
> tPeia 4:10 (Zuckermandel edition)

One contemporary legal philosopher who has considered this sort of support for expensive tastes and extravagant personal 'needs' is Ronald Dworkin. Dworkin argues for the idea of "equality of resources," that is, providing all members of society with identical—to the greatest extent possible—conditions of economic opportunity. He rejects the competing idea of "equality of welfare," that is, providing all members of society with the same—to the extent possible—level of wellbeing. Dworkin contends that the problem of extravagant 'needs' cannot be properly addressed by "equality of welfare." As an example, he cites the case of someone who cannot fall asleep at night without having had a glass of champagne, a luxury he cannot afford to buy. If society chooses to support someone with expensive tastes, for the purpose of allowing him to sleep at night like everyone else, the patently unreasonable result, according to Dworkin, will be the subsidizing of nightly glasses of champagne for certain people. If, on the other hand, society chooses not to support expensive tastes, it will fail to attain the desideratum of ensuring equal welfare for all its members.

> Equality of welfare seems to recommend that those with champagne tastes, who need more income simply to achieve the same level of welfare as those with less expensive tastes, should have more income on that account. But this seems counter-intuitive, and I said that someone generally attracted to the ideal would nevertheless wish to limit or qualify it so that his theory did not have that consequence.[29]

Dworkin's approach differs substantially from that expressed in the Rabbinic passages just examined, which—in specific circumstances—recognize expensive tastes as legitimate 'needs' that must be supported. The Sages, apparently, did not regard equality as essential for distributive justice, much less seek to impose it, but rather accepted socioeconomic stratification as a given.

29 Ronald Dworkin, "What is equality? Part I: Equality of welfare," *Philosophy and Public Affairs* 10 (1981), 185, 228.

But though the Sages sought to augment the support provided to someone well-born who became impoverished, they did not hesitate to criticize him for his expensive tastes, which burden the community as a whole:

> A man once came before Rava [seeking charity]. He said to him, What do your meals consist of? He said to him, Fattened chicken and old [i.e., good] wine. He said to him, have you not considered the burden [this places] on the community? He said to him, Do I eat of theirs? I eat [the food] of the All-Merciful. For we have learned: "The eyes of all look to You expectantly, and You give them their food in its[30] season" (Ps. 145:15)—it is not said 'in their season,' but "in its season," teaching that the Holy One, blessed be He, provides each and every individual with sustenance in accordance with his habits [lit., his season]. Meanwhile, Rava's sister, who had not seen him for thirteen years, arrived, and brought him a fattened chicken and old wine. Rava said [to himself], What is this before me?! He said to him, I humbly concede to you, come and eat.
>
> bKetubot 67b

> *Rashi* ad loc.: "Rava said, What is this before me?!"—what is this event that has just taken place before me, for I am not accustomed to her coming here with a chicken and old wine in hand.

It is evident that this story expresses criticism, but what it targets is unclear. Rava can be understood as critical of the poor person whose expensive tastes are a burden on the public—"have you not considered the burden [this places] on the community?" Moreover, the story ends on an almost miraculous note: a coincidence enables Rava to satisfy the poor person's rarified tastes. The implication is that without this unexpected development, the said tastes would not have been accommodated, and Rava's protest would have prevailed. On the other hand, the story can also be taken as critical of Rava. On this reading, the seeming coincidence at the end of the story is in fact no coincidence, but rather an indication of the divine will, which desires that the needs of the poor, even if excessive, be satisfied.

Another critique, perhaps more penetrating, of those with expensive tastes, is found in the Jerusalem Talmud:

> A member of the Nasi's household lost his wealth and was provided food in a clay utensil; when he ate it, he threw up. The physician told him, doesn't the food itself originally come out of an [earthenware] pot? [Imagine that you] are eating directly from the pot.
>
> jPeia 8:7 (21a)

30 The pronoun here is in the third person singular, allowing the exegete to read the verse as saying "his season."

> *Pnei Moshe* commentary[31] ad loc.: "Of the Nasi's household"—someone from the Nasi's household who had lost his money and sold his elegant utensils, and was brought food in clay dishes. When he ate from them, the food repeated on him and he vomited it out, because he was of delicate constitution and unaccustomed to eating off dishes of this sort. The doctor asked him, Wasn't the food cooked in an earthenware pot? Imagine yourself to be eating directly from the pot itself, and then you won't be disgusted by the food or the clay dishes.

Though these anecdotes indeed express a critical attitude to those who are impoverished yet retain their expensive tastes, there is no need to understand them as conflicting with the directive that such individuals are to be supported by public charitable funds. The Sages take a nuanced approach, both prodding the individual to accommodate his changed circumstances by changing his habits; and imposing upon the public the duty to provide him with the costly items to which he is still accustomed as he adjusts to his new circumstances.

To limit the obligation to support such 'necessities' and extravagant tastes, and keep it within reasonable bounds, some codifiers added the following qualification:

> The Geonim, of blessed memory, wrote that all these cases of [the need to accommodate the expensive tastes of] a poor person from a distinguished family pertain to a poor person whose impoverishment is not widely known. He is treated with the honor to which he is accustomed so that [his poverty] does not become widely known. But a [formerly well-off[poor person whose impoverishment is known is treated no differently than any other poor Jew.
>
> *Shita Mekubetzet*, bKetubot 67b

The rationale here is that the only reason the poor person's subjective needs are accommodated is to preserve his self-respect. When his reduced circumstances have become public knowledge, however, maintaining his former standard of living no longer achieves this, and is discontinued.

The Sages thus proffer two tests for poverty. There is a universal threshold for poverty: anyone who cannot provide himself with a reasonable minimal standard of living is eligible for a fixed amount of charitable support. To supplement this test, a second, individualized test is applied to identify cases where those who fall under the first criterion also have additional needs. In light of the latter test, the fact that the halakha does not invoke a **relative** means-test to determine eligibility for support from charitable donations—a test that would assess the needy

31 By eighteenth century Talmudist R. Moses Margalit.

person's situation relative to his community's socioeconomic ladder—is quite striking.

The significance of this absence of a relative means-test may come to light by considering it against the background of the last of the Ten Commandments: "You shall not covet your neighbor's house; you shall not covet your neighbor's wife, or his male or female slave, or his ox or his ass or anything that is your neighbor's" (Exod. 20:14). It could be argued that the relative poverty test, and the critique of socioeconomic polarization that often goes hand in hand with it, reflect little more than a covetous desire, on the part of some classes, for that which better-off classes have.

We saw earlier that the biblical social support mechanisms combine help for the needy with preservation of naturally-occurring social stratification. The purpose of the mechanisms is to sustain and rehabilitate the poor, but not necessarily to prevent the formation of centers of wealth within society. Assistance to the poor is not premised on egalitarian principles. This conclusion seems to be consistent with the "for whatever he needs" directive, which the Sages invoked as the prooftext for helping the poor meet their individualized needs. Recourse to both standard and individualized tests ensures, on the one hand, that concrete assistance is provided to the disadvantaged, yet on the other, allows for naturally-occurring social disparities.

7 Amount to be collected

Having explained how the category of 'the poor' is to be demarcated, we must now determine the amount of goods or funds that the well-to-do are obliged to give. Here too, there is a range of possible methods for assessing the specific amounts, each reflecting a particular understanding of the duty to give charity.

The main talmudic source that addresses this question is the Usha enactment, which will be examined below. This source is relatively late. The mishnaic sources that preceded it did not address the matter, leaving it open. For example, the Mishnah from tractate Peia that sets out how much is to be given to the poor—"One may not give an itinerant poor person less than a loaf worth a *pondion*.... If he stays over the Sabbath, he is given food for three meals" (mPeia 8:7)—says nothing about how much is to be collected from the wealthy. Similarly, the Mishnah from tractate Ketubot that sets the amount to be provided to an orphaned bride says nothing about the amount to be collected for that purpose from donors.

How are we to understand this silence? It might be argued that this is indeed a legal lacuna, which could have been filled in by specifying a percentage or a fixed amount that the non-poor are to contribute, but for some reason was ignored by the Mishnah. But it could also be argued that the omission is deliberate, and the Mishnah does not define the amount of charity to be collected because the only relevant parameter is the needs of the poor. There is no need to collect charity beyond that amount, so there is no reason to specify a particular sum of money or percentage of assets or income as the amount to be donated. On this approach, the amount to be given is inherently a function of the recipients' needs.

The decisors appear to have favored the latter explanation, basing their definition of the amount of charity to be donated primarily on the needs of the poor and not the affluence of the donor. Maimonides, for instance, ruled as follows:

> It is a positive commandment to give charity to the poor, according to what is fitting for the poor, if the giver can afford it.... You are commanded to give to the poor person in accordance with what he lacks.
>
> *Code*, Laws concerning Gifts to the Poor 7:1, 3

The **practical** significance of defining the amount to be given on the basis of the needs of the poor is that when the needs of the poor are limited—when, say, an area is generally prosperous, the amount of charity to be collected will be small. Where the economic situation is not as good, however, and there is a large impoverished population, people of means will be obliged to give substantial sums.

From a theoretical perspective, defining the obligation to give charity in this manner implies that money is to be appropriated from people of means only to provide direct assistance to the needy. Possession of assets does not in itself constitute reason to tax the possessor and appropriate a specified amount or percentage of the assets. Money may be taken only in response to a specific concrete need, and no more than the amount required to address that need may be collected. This approach differs markedly from approaches—such as the contemporary institution of progressive taxation, on which the more one earns, the greater the percentage of that income she must pay as tax—that are wealth based, and seek to level socio-economic disparities rather than to simply ameliorate concrete instances of need.

Let us now turn to the aforementioned Usha enactment. Both the Babylonian Talmud and the Talmud of the land of Israel, the Jerusalem Talmud, report an enactment introduced in the town of Usha, located in the north of the land of Israel, apparently in the second half of the second century CE. This enactment addressed the question of the amount a wealthy person was obligated to set aside for charity.

In the Babylonian Talmud version, the enactment establishes a maximum contribution that no donor may exceed: one-fifth.

> R. Elai stated: It was enacted at Usha that even one who spends money extravagantly [on charity] is not to expend more than a fifth.
>
> bKetubot 67b

The decisors explain that the one-fifth in question pertains to income, not assets.

Why was the Usha enactment needed? According to Urbach, the enactment attests to a tendency in talmudic-era Jewish circles (and even more in Christian circles) to dedicate large portions of one's wealth to charity, as a means of avoiding the civic responsibilities ensuing from affluence under the Roman regime.[32] The Talmud relates several such incidents.[33] The Sages of Usha, according to this explanation, sought to ensure that donors did not themselves become needy and a burden to the community, and therefore fixed a maximum that could be donated.

As presented in the Babylonian Talmud, the Usha enactment does not fundamentally change how the requisite amount of charity is determined. The sum continues to be calculated primarily on the basis of the needs of the poor; the enactment simply imposes a cap. But the Jerusalem Talmud offers a different version of the enactment:

> They voted at Usha that one is to set aside one-fifth of his assets for [observance of] the precepts.
>
> jPeia 1:1 (15b)

The difference between the two versions of the enactment is striking. While the Babylonian Talmud speaks of a maximum percentage ("he is not to expend more than a fifth"), the Jerusalem Talmud speaks of a fixed percentage that cannot be reduced. Moreover, the Babylonian Talmud speaks of "spending extravagantly," whereas the Jerusalem Talmud speaks of setting aside a portion of one's income for "[observance of] the precepts"—a much more positive characterization. On the Jerusalem Talmud version of the enactment, one is to set aside a fifth of his income, without any connection to the immediate needs of the poor. This approach is based on assessing the donor's means, and not the recipient's needs. In other words, on the Jerusalem Talmud's version of the Usha enactment, anyone with an income must pay a charity tax, regardless of whether there are poor people in his locale.

In some respects, the Jerusalem Talmud's version of the Usha enactment is akin to progressive taxation, whereas in other respects, it is not. It resembles progressive taxation in that in absolute terms, the greater a person's income, the more he gives to charity. But unlike progressive taxation in the standard sense, the Usha enactment—or rather, the Jerusalem Talmud version of it—mandates that all are to pay the same percentage of their income. The Jerusalem Talmud's version of the Usha enactment makes more demands on citizens than does the Babylonian version, but does not take a progressively higher percentage of their income the more they earn.

32 Urbach, n. 17 above, 111.

33 See bArakhin 28a; bKetubot 50a, 67b.

The two versions of the enactment differ both in principle, and in terms of their actual legal consequences. The Babylonian version, in effect, protects those with assets, capping their charitable contributions to ensure that they themselves are not impoverished, even if the needs of the populace are immense. The Jerusalem Talmud, on the other hand, protects the interests of potential recipients of charity, ensuring that a fifth of all income is earmarked for them, whether or not there is any immediate need.

Above, we saw that in Maimonides' view, articulated in the *Code*'s Laws concerning Gifts to the Poor 7:1, 3, the needs of the poor are the sole determinant of the amount to be given. However, in deference to the enactment at Usha, he introduced an important qualification that, in essence, factors in the donor's wealth. Maimonides sets a maximum contribution, not to be exceeded; and this maximum figure incorporates the two traditions regarding the Usha enactment:

> If a poor man comes and asks for [support] sufficient for what he lacks—if the giver is unable to afford it, he gives him as much as he can afford. How much is that? [If he gives] up to one-fifth of his assets, he is observing the precept in a superior manner; up to one-tenth of his assets, he is observing the precept in an average manner; less than this—[he personifies] the evil eye.
>
> *Code*, Laws concerning Gifts to the Poor 7:5

Maimonides seems to have drawn on elements from both versions. From the version in the Babylonian Talmud, he adopted the principle that the basic criterion determining the amount of charity to be collected is the needs of the poor. The other sums cited are upper limits for contributions, which come into play only where the contributor lacks sufficient income to provide for the poor person's needs. But it seems that the Jerusalem Talmud is Maimonides' source for the principle that giving the maximum allowable is preferable to giving less than the maximum allowable. Clearly, it could not have come from the Babylonian Talmud, which simply sets the maximum and says nothing further. Overall, however, it is evident that Maimonides favored the Babylonian Talmud's version of the enactment, for he adopted, as a matter of principle, its premise that the amount to be given to charity is determined by the needs of the poor.

The practice of setting aside ten percent of one's income, referred to as a 'monetary tithe' (*maaser ksafim*) for supporting the needy, came to be accepted in Jewish communities. The decisors debated the legal basis for this obligation, the prevailing view being that the practice is a custom. For example, R. Joel Sirkes, the Bah, asserts:

> The tithe that one sets aside [for charity] from what he has earned from business dealings, monies, and other profits ... may be contributed

> [however one wishes] to charity and the redemption of captives, for he is not obligated in this regard, not biblically and not Rabbinically.
>
> *Bayit Hadash, Tur*, YD 331 s.v. *veein notnim*

The custom of giving a fixed percentage of one's entire income, regardless of the how much is needed by the poor, reflects the Usha enactment as reported in the Jerusalem Talmud.

It is instructive to consider this summary of the 'monetary tithe' laws, composed by an eminent present-day halakhic authority, R. Ezra Batzri:

- It is proper to have a special receptacle for the tithe, so that one will have coins readily available whenever he is asked to give.
- When God, may He be blessed, grants him profit, he should immediately set aside the tithe. And a merchant who sells on a daily basis should keep a special notebook, and at the end of the day, week, or month should calculate his profit and set aside [the tithe]. An official or laborer who is paid his wage at the end of a week or of a month should set aside [the tithe] as soon as he receives his wage.
- All profit is subject to tithing, whether from business, wages, brokering transactions, dividends on shares, lottery winnings, or inheritances. Even though his father tithed his assets, the son must again tithe the inheritance he receives.
- If one purchased two types of merchandise in the same transaction and profited on one and lost on the other, he deducts the loss from the profit and tithes the remainder. If he has two types of business dealings (for instance, if he has a shop and shares), and profited on one and lost on the other, his calculation of the loss is not deducted from the profit, but rather, he tithes his total profit, and absorbs the loss himself.
- One can deduct his business expenses from his [gross] profit, and set aside [the tithe] from the remainder.

Dinei Mamonot, vol. 1, gate 12

8 Sustenance and rehabilitation revisited

In examining the biblical approach to social justice, we distinguished between two goals set by the Bible: sustaining the poor, that is, ensuring their immediate needs are met, and rehabilitating the poor, that is, enabling them to be self-supporting. This duality of purpose, we saw, is reflected in the relationship between, on the one hand, gleanings, forgotten produce, and corners of the field—mechanisms for sustaining the poor—and, on the other, manumission, debt remission, and restoration of ancestral property in the Jubilee year—mechanisms for rehabilitation. Are these two distinct concerns preserved in the Rabbinic laws of charity?

Did the transition from a system where charity was collected and distributed in the form of field produce, to a system where charity took the form of monetary donations, impact which goal was emphasized?

Overall, it appears that the Rabbinic recasting of the precept in terms of monetary donations led to a reduction in the emphasis placed on rehabilitation. Giving a donation to one in need provides short-term help, but does not contribute to the beneficiary's rehabilitation. Indeed, it could have the opposite effect: those who grow accustomed to living off charitable donations may lose the motivation to be independent and reintegrate into the work force. Aware of this paradox, the talmudic Sages tried in various ways to reinforce the goal of rehabilitation within the framework of the laws of charity.

As we saw, the Bible itself does not mention a duty to **donate** to the poor, and speaks only of lending money. Only later, in the Rabbinic literature, were the verses in question interpreted as referring to outright donations. But from the perspective of rehabilitation, this is problematic, since loans clearly have greater potential than gifts for effecting long-term change. They require the debtor to use the loan wisely, so that he can repay the principal while fully utilizing the funds that have been made available to him. The Sages recognized that donating to the poor might make it harder for them to break the cycle of poverty into which they had fallen. Accordingly, they recommended the provision of charitable support in more productive forms than simple donations.

One recommendation is that the funds be used to prevent poverty in the first place. Invoking the metaphor of stabilizing a load borne by a donkey, the Midrash calls for donating to those in imminent danger of falling into poverty:

> "If your brother becomes poor and cannot support himself among you [then you shall uphold him]" (Lev. 25:35)—do not allow him to decline. To what may this be compared? To a load on the back of a donkey. While it is still in place, one person can grab hold of it and stabilize it. Once it has fallen, five people cannot put it back in place.
>
> Sifra, Behar 6:5

A second recommendation is that charitable funds be used for granting loans or creating jobs:

> R. Abba also said in the name of R. Shimon b. Lakish: He who lends [money] is greater than he who bestows charity, and he who forms a partnership [lit., puts money into a (shared) purse] is greater than all.
>
> bShabat 63a

The 'shared purse' (*kis*) is a common fund; one who invests money in it is creating a commercial partnership with the poor person being aided.

Rashi explained it as a fund into which "he invests coins and goods, intending to be rewarded with half the earnings."[34]

Why is a loan preferable to a donation and the formation of a partnership better than both? The halakhic authorities offered two explanations. The first pertains to the outcome:

> Because usually, the amounts loaned are not substantial, and it is possible that [the borrower] will earn only enough to eke out a living with the loan, and once he spends those funds on sustenance, he will have nothing left to repay it, and will default.... But if [the donor] invests in a common fund, he will certainly give him a substantial amount, so it will be possible to earn money and make a profit from it sufficient to live on and still have some of the principal of the loan left with which to pay [the investor] back.
>
> Maharsha, *Hidushei Agadot*, ad loc.

Another account explains the ranking of the different modes of assistance in terms of the embarrassment they spare the beneficiary: a loan is less demeaning than a donation, for the borrower undertakes to return the principal. Creation of a joint enterprise is even less demeaning, since the recipient becomes a partner in increasing the investor's productivity. Rashi explains it that way: "He who lends [money] is greater—because the poor person is not humiliated thereby."

Nevertheless, these endorsements of productive forms of charity are peripheral to the Sages' overall discussion of the subject, and the notion of productive charitable giving does not play a significant role in the principal talmudic discussions of charity in tractates Peia, Baba Batra, and Ketubot.

Maimonides, however, emphatically supports productive giving. On the basis of R. Abba's statement in bShabat 63a, quoted above, and other Rabbinic dicta, Maimonides set out his widely known eight-tier pyramid of charitable giving. Productive giving, which seeks to liberate the recipient from the vicious circle in which he finds himself, is at the apex:

> The highest degree [of charity], higher than which there are none, is he who steadies the hand of an Israelite who is impoverished, by giving him a gift or a loan, or entering into a partnership with him, or devising work for him, in order to strengthen his hand, until he has no need to seek aid from other people. Of him Scripture says, "You shall uphold him; as a stranger and a settler shall he live with you" (Lev. 25:35), meaning, uphold him until he will not fall into need.
>
> *Code,* Laws concerning Gifts to the Poor 10:7

34 *Rashi* ad loc. s.v. *umatil bakis.*

In the wake of Maimonides' discussion, other codifiers also placed rehabilitative forms of giving at the apex of the pyramid of charitable measures.

Thus far, we have considered rehabilitative charity from the recipient's perspective, but we should also consider it from the donor's point of view. There is no doubt that charity—at the highest level—seeks to improve the situation of the needy recipient, who can rehabilitate himself more effectively over the long run by being given a loan or a job. But we must also inquire into how charity of this sort, as opposed to a simple donation, may affect the donor. In fact, the recommended form of charity consumes less of the donor's assets, and may even increase them. Donated money is permanently given away by the donor, but money constituting the principal of a loan is destined to return to him. It is indeed possible that the poor debtor may default, but in theory, the lender will not lose the sums given as a loan. Moreover, in a case of partnership with the needy beneficiary—that is, creation of a job—the donor has an opportunity to combine charity with expanding his own financial enterprises. In this way, both parties benefit—the now-employed 'beneficiary' receives wages, and the 'donor' develops his business. Granted, creating 'make-work' jobs is not a sound business strategy for the donor (if it were, charity would not have to be mandated by the law), but it has more potential to benefit his business than does a simple donation. In other words, the recommended form of charity is not simply that which will provide greater long-term benefit to the recipient; it is also that which minimizes the financial damage to the donor's assets.

We noted earlier that the Torah seeks to sustain the poor and provide them with a real opportunity for rehabilitation, but does not seek economic leveling; it is not hostile to wealth per se. This philosophy also seems to be embodied in the fact that the mode of giving at the apex of the Maimonidean hierarchy of charity is assistance to the poor that minimizes harm to the donor's assets. As we saw, the preferred form of charity is that which has the potential to benefit donor and recipient alike. From this perspective, there is ideological continuity between the biblical outlook and Rabbinic law.

Yet though the merit of productive charity was duly recognized by many halakhic authorities, this recognition remained largely in the realm of rhetoric. The decisors, Maimonides among them, cite this highest level of giving at the end of the laws of charity, not the beginning. In practice, donations have, throughout Jewish history, played a larger role in charitable activities than did loans or job creation:

> Maimonides had written that the highest form of charity was the gift or loan or partnership designed to make the recipient self-supporting. These words were often quoted, but, as Goitein has argued, they did not shape the structure of social services in the Jewish community.

> Perhaps the poor were too numerous, the situation of the community itself too precarious, for anything more than relief.[35]

An effort to change this situation was made early in the twentieth century by R. Israel Meir Kagan of Radin, known as the Chofetz Chaim. His *Ahavat Hesed* sought to renew attention to the precept of lending to the poor, reemphasizing its position atop the hierarchy of charitable measures.

We see, then, that an attempt has been made to uphold the biblical mandate of rehabilitating the poor, a mandate less-readily implemented in the non-agrarian societies of the Diaspora than in the land of Israel in biblical times. As the focus of the social justice precepts shifted to the provision of monetary assistance, it became increasingly difficult to give substantial weight to modes of charity that rehabilitate the poor or prevent poverty in the first place. Generally speaking, the goal of rehabilitation was not actively pursued.

9 Responsibilities of the poor

Having discussed the obligations of the fortunate, let us now turn to the question of responsibilities borne by the beneficiaries of assistance. Should charity be conditional, to one degree or another, on their cooperation? Would it be proper to allow the recipient to sit back and let the responsibility for his support fall entirely on the shoulders of the wealthy or on communal charitable institutions? We saw earlier that the Torah conditions assistance to the poor—both sustenance and rehabilitation—on joining in the effort. The rehabilitative precepts, such as that of the Jubilee year, do not provide the poor with goods, but rather, with means of production, and their effectiveness requires that those to whom means of production have been restored actively cooperate in the rehabilitative process. Even the sustenance-oriented precepts, such as gleanings, forgotten produce, and corners of the field, require the beneficiaries' cooperation in gathering the produce. What is the significance of the transition to the Rabbinic donation-based laws of charity vis-à-vis the degree of active cooperation required of the poor?

Here, too, it appears that the Sages were faced with a problem. A donation is a one-sided transfer from the donor to a passive recipient; the process tends to shift responsibility away from the recipient, and place it entirely on the donor. It is no surprise that this tends to instill in the beneficiaries the conviction that they are chronically dependent and cannot support themselves. Though leery of this danger, the Sages did not forego the institution of charity in the form of donations, but sought ways to link the giving of charity to the beneficiary's active participation in improving his situation.

35 M. Walzer, *Spheres of Justice* (New York: 1983), 73.

Of course, where the charitable support is being given in the form of a loan, job or partnership, the recipient's active participation is necessary, as these measures can be effective only if such cooperation is forthcoming. But as we saw, these measures were not the principal vehicle for ameliorating poverty in post-biblical society, certainly not in practice. Hence the Sages sought to impose a genuine element of responsibility on recipients of charitable donations.

9.1 Those able to work

A basic question not addressed directly by the laws of charity is that of one who is able to work and thereby support himself, but does not do so. Is he eligible for support? That is, is he to be classified as poor, on the basis of his income, or as ineligible for charitable assistance, in view of his potential earnings? The silence of the sources is ambiguous: it could mean either that such a person's eligibility for charity is considered self-evident, or, that his ineligibility is so patently obvious that it need not be mentioned. How are we to know which of these interpretations is correct? We must work out the answer by drawing analogies.

Tannaitic sources considered a somewhat similar case, that of a wealthy person who is so miserly in tending to his needs that he becomes a burden on the community and its charitable institutions. Should such a person be supported, or should he be left to his self-imposed suffering?

> [Regarding the verse "But you shall surely open (*patoah tiftah*) your hand unto him, and shall surely lend him (*haavet taavitenu*)" (Deut. 15:8)] our Rabbis taught: "You shall lend him" (*haavet*) refers to someone who has no means, but does not want to be supported [by charitable donations], to whom [an allowance] is given as a loan, and then turned into a gift; "You shall **surely** lend him" (*taavitenu*) refers to someone who has the means, but does not want to support himself, to whom [an allowance] is given as a gift, and then repayment is taken from [his estate] after his death—so said R. Judah. And the Sages said: [As to] someone who has the means but does not want to support himself—no one need look after him. If so, how is the dictum "You shall **surely** lend him" being upheld? The Torah speaks in human parlance [i.e., the Torah speaks about the usual case, where people support themselves to the extent they are able].
>
> bKetubot 67b

According to the Sages, a person of means who does not tend to his needs is fully responsible for himself, and the community need not support him. R. Judah, in contrast, takes a paternalistic stance, contending that the community must not remain indifferent to his plight and must support him, albeit ensuring that he (or, more precisely, his estate) later bears those costs. On the one hand, he grants the person in question the right to draw on public charitable funds, on account of his **concrete** situation, though he has the potential, the theoretical capacity, to attend to his own needs. On the other hand, R. Judah instructs the community to recapture the funds from the beneficiary's estate after his death. In essence, then, this is more a simulation of charity than with the real thing. In effect, R. Judah takes the view that the community must **lend** money to him, but need not give him an outright donation. However, the law is decided in accordance with the view of the Sages:

> If . . . a wealthy man starves himself because he is so niggardly with his money that he will not spend it on food and drink, no attention need be paid him.
>
> Maimonides, *Code*, Laws concerning Gifts to the Poor 7:9

Can the case of the wealthy person who starves himself be compared to that of a poor person who is able to work but refuses to do so? Formally speaking, they differ. The wealthy person who starves himself has assets that preclude him from being classified as 'poor' (the 200-*zuz* criterion, for example); the able-bodied yet idle poor person, however, is indeed classified as poor, since he doesn't have a penny to his name. Substantively, however, it is fair to ask whether there is any reason to distinguish between assets in the form of money and assets in the form of capacity to work. Is there any real difference between a wealthy person who can deploy his assets to support himself, and one who can deploy his physical strength to support himself?

The biblical precept that one must assist someone having difficulty loading or unloading his donkey may be relevant in this context.

> When you see the donkey of your enemy lying under its burden, and would [prefer to] refrain from [helping] to raise it, you must nevertheless raise it with him.
>
> Exodus 23:5

The precept is invoked in a Mishnah apropos one who asks for help unloading his donkey, but refuses to participate in the effort himself:

> If [the owner of the animal] went and sat down, and said [to the passer-by], 'since the obligation falls upon you, if you desire to unload, unload!'—he [the passer-by] is exempt, because it is said "with him" (Exod. 23:5).
>
> mBaba Metzia 2:10

This Mishnah was adduced by R. Solomon Efraim of Lunschitz:

> This provides us with a response for some poor folk of our nation, who foist themselves on the community. They do not wish to do any work even though they are able to engage in some trade or other activity by means of which they could put an end to their families' hunger, yet complain if we do not provide them with all they need—for God did not command us to do so, but only to "nevertheless raise it **with him**." ... For the poor person should do everything he has the strength to do, and if after all his efforts, he is still unable to [support himself], every Jew is obligated to feed him, support him and provide him with all that he needs.
>
> *Kli Yakar*, Exodus 23:5

Citing this principle, other decisors also limit the obligation to give charity in cases where the needy person could in fact make a living on his own.[36]

R. Isaac of Corbeil also discusses the charity seeker who appears to be capable of working:

> [Regarding the precept] not to harden one's heart against giving charity to the poor, as it is written (Deut. 15:7), "do not harden your heart and shut your hand"—This means: "do not harden"—do not say, 'why should we support so and so; if he wanted to, he could earn more than he needs.' Scripture therefore teaches us, "do not harden"—even if you give [a donation] to him, if you have that thought, you violate [the precept] "do not harden."
>
> *Sefer Mitzvot Katan,* commandment 20

At first glance, R. Isaac of Corbeil appears to uphold a position very different from that of the *Kli Yakar*. He seems to require that charity be given to anyone lacking means, even someone who can support himself. In his opinion, a donor who gives charity but inwardly resents the fact that the recipient does not earn a living on his own thereby violates the "do not harden your heart" prohibition. A closer reading, however, reveals that R. Isaac is not addressing the question of whether a poor person able to earn a living should nonetheless be supported, but rather, the question of whether donors are entitled to suspect applicants of malingering. In other words, R. Isaac is making the point that potential donors are not to suspect the innocent without due grounds. But he would concur that where it is clear that an applicant for aid is able to support himself, he is not eligible for charitable support.

Nevertheless, in reviewing the rabbinical literature on the subject, the overall sense is that very little is said about making assistance to the poor

36 See *Derisha*, EH, beginning of sec. 71; *Beit Shmuel*, EH 71:3.

person conditional on his having exhausted his ability to earn a living, and the little that is said has no significant effect. Once the main thrust of social intervention had shifted from agricultural produce to money, and, de facto, donating rather than lending money had become the default mode of assistance, it was difficult to avoid a situation where recipients of charity ultimately became chronically dependent on public support, making no effort to work.

The aforementioned pertains to the obligation of individual donors and the community as a whole to render support to those who seek aid. But with respect to recipients of charity, the Sages explicitly and unambiguously endorsed the view—as an ethical imperative, if not a legal rule—that work of any kind, however menial, is to be preferred to taking charity. This stance is manifest in the following talmudic passage, which addresses a very different issue:

> He said to them: I received the following tradition from my grandfather's house: One is always to hire himself out to idol-worship (*avoda zara*) [lit., alien work] rather than be in need of [assistance from] his fellow creatures. And he [the speaker] thought this referred to actual idol worship. But it is not so; rather, [it refers to] work that is alien to him, as Rav said to R. Kahana: Flay a carcass in the street and earn a wage, and do not say, 'I am a great man and the thing is degrading to me.'
>
> bBaba Batra 110a

9.2 Charitable donations by the poor

Another aspect of empowering the poor person's sense of responsibility—for others as well as for himself—is reflected in the law requiring even the poor to engage in charitable giving. The law is first found in the Tosefta, which rules that someone poor is not to be required to make donations to charity, but if he wishes to make a contribution, his donation may not be rejected:

> If a poor person gave a penny (*pruta*) to the communal fund (*kupa*) or a slice of bread (*prusa*) to the soup kitchen (*tamhui*), it is accepted; if he did not give, we do not oblige him to give.
>
> tPeia 4:10 (Zuckermandel edition)

A talmudic source takes a stronger stance:

> R. Awira gave the following exposition, sometimes in the name of R. Ami and sometimes in the name of R. Asi ... If someone sees that his livelihood is meager, he should give charity from it, and all the more so if it is abundant....

> Mar Zutra said: Even a poor person who himself subsists on charity should give charity.
>
> bGitin 7a-b

The *Shulhan Arukh* rules similarly:

> Everyone is obligated to contribute to charity. Even a poor person who supports himself from charitable donations must contribute out of what he is given.
>
> YD 248:1

In obligating all members of society, including the poor, to give to charity, the Sages sought to prevent the creation of a social class that takes without giving, that is supported without providing any support to others. As Urbach observed, even if the amounts in question are slight, the poor person's obligation to donate to charity helps render him, in the eyes of the community and in his own eyes, a contributor to society.[37]

The *Arukh Hashulhan* takes the view that the rationale for requiring the poor to contribute to charity is not to maximize the amount raised, but rather, to benefit the poor donors themselves, either by affording them the opportunity to observe a precept, or by bolstering their self-image as givers and not just recipients of charity:

> And we have already explained that even a poor Jew who goes from door to door [asking for alms] and has nothing to contribute to charity is nonetheless obligated to fulfill the precept of charity once a year, as the Sages, of blessed memory, said [bBaba Batra 9a]: "One should never hold himself back from [giving] a third of a shekel [to charity] annually." And if he gives less than that, he has not fulfilled the precept of charity, and the Torah imposed this positive commandment on each and every Jew, and they must fulfill it at least once a year.
>
> *Arukh Hashulhan*, YD 249:11

10 Individual and community

Thus far, we have considered the amounts of money to be set aside to help the needy, and the circumstances in which charity is to be dispensed. But we have not yet considered how money for communal charitable institutions is to be collected. The last topic we will address in this chapter, therefore, will be that of responsibility for collecting funds for charity, or as we would say today, fundraising. Is this responsibility to be borne by individuals, or by public institutions?

37 Urbach, n. 17 above, 114.

The Bible, we saw, assumes that support for the needy will be provided by individuals. The relevant precepts—the Jubilee year, the laws governing produce of the field, remission of loans, and so on—all establish a direct connection between someone who lacks means, and someone who has sufficient means to support his needy fellow. It does not call for public funds or agencies to mediate between those with means and those without. The Rabbinic literature attests to the rise of community institutions—the communal fund (*kupa*) and soup kitchen (*tamhui*)—that provided such donor–beneficiary mediation.

10.1 Communal charitable institutions

Several considerations support the unmediated provision of assistance by donors to beneficiaries:

a. **Diminished social alienation**—Unmediated personal contact between donors and recipients helps prevent the formation of rigid classes of 'givers' and 'takers.'
b. **Meeting subjective needs**—We saw that the laws of charity seek to address not only the objective needs of the poor, but also subjective individual needs. The latter goal can be better achieved within the context of small circles in which each person's distinctive needs can be recognized.
c. **Conservation of resources**—Another factor worth noting, albeit one that may be more relevant to life in a modern state, relates to the likely waste of resources inherent in communal institutions, which necessarily incur administrative costs. In the case of charitable institutions, for instance, salaries must be paid to employees who collect and distribute funds, and run other aspects of the system (cooks in the soup kitchen, say), and costs may be incurred due to inefficiency or even corruption. Overhead often substantially reduces the amount reaching the needy themselves. Direct disbursement of charity by the affluent to the poor ensures that every cent reaches its destination.

On the other hand, a number of considerations support the institutionalization of charity:

a. **Effective fundraising**—Reliance on the good will of donors is not enough to ensure that charitable monies are, in fact, transferred from the prosperous to the needy; it is necessary to enforce charitable giving. Such enforcement is difficult when charity is given by one individual to another directly. Systematic collection of funds by the community makes it easier to identify those who are evading payment and to enforce their obligations.

b. **Equitable solicitation**—Communal charitable institutions can ensure that the burden of charity is borne equally by all those of means within the community. If the poor turn directly to those with means, they are likely to shy away from those who adamantly resist their appeals, and cluster at the doors of the more compliant. Institutionalized communal fundraising helps ensure that the kindhearted and generous do not bear a disproportionate share of the burden.
c. **Equitable distribution**—Likewise, institutionalized distribution of charitable funds helps ensure that all the needy receive what they are entitled to, and preference is not given to those who are particularly vocal in their demands, or have connections to wealthy households.

It is interesting that none of the latter factors are cited by the Sages in support of the establishment of communal charity funds. Their concern is to protect the poor person's dignity by preserving the anonymity of both sides, donor and recipient. The Sages refer to this as 'secret giving' (*matan beseter*).

To understand the Talmud's position, consider the following episodes reported in the Talmud:

> Mar Ukba had a poor man in his neighborhood into whose door-socket he used to throw four *zuz* every day. One day he said, 'I will go and see who does me this kindness.' On that day Mar Ukba stayed late at the house of study, and his wife was escorting him home. When he saw them moving the door, he went out after them, but they fled from him and [hid] in a hearth from which the fire had just been swept. Mar Ukba's feet were burning and his wife said to him: Raise your feet and put them on mine. As he was upset, she said to him, 'I am usually at home and can bestow benefactions directly.' And what was the reason for all this [i.e., their fleeing and hiding in the oven]? Because Mar Zutra b. Tobiah said in the name of Rav ... It is better that one enter a fiery oven than embarrass his neighbor in public.... R. Abba used to bind money in his scarf, sling it on his back, and place himself at the disposal of the poor. But he cocked his eye [as a precaution] against rogues.
>
> bKetubot 67b

> *Rashi* ad loc.:
> "I am usually at home"—so the poor people find me [and I give to them]; accordingly, my merit is great; "I can bestow benefactions directly"—my benefactions are ready to use, for I give them bread and meat and salt, but you give the poor coins, and they must expend effort to go buy a meal ... "he cocked his eye"—he cast his eye behind him, so that a rogue, pretending to be poor, would not come [and take the money].

These anecdotes praise Mar Ukba and R. Abba for the manner in which they contribute to charity. Mar Ukba did all he could, to the point of endangering his life, so that the poor man to whom he gave charity would not know who his benefactor was. R. Abba gave his charitable gifts in a convoluted way (in a scarf over his shoulder) to avoid a face to face encounter that could embarrass the recipients. Both stories involve attempts to devise a means by which charity could be transferred without a direct encounter that might be unpleasant or embarrassing for the recipient, the donor, or both. Elsewhere, the Talmud declares that despite the merits of the manner in which Mar Ukba and R. Abba made their donations, there was an even better way:

> It is written: "Treasures of wickedness profit nothing, but righteousness (*tzedaka*) delivereth from death" (Prov. 10:2).... What kind of charity is that which delivers one from an unnatural death? When someone gives without knowing to whom he gives, and someone receives without knowing from whom he receives. 'Gives without knowing to whom he gives'—this excludes the practice of Mar Ukba. 'Receives without knowing from whom he receives'—this excludes the practice of R. Abba.
>
> If so, how is one to act? He should put his money into the charity box.
>
> bBaba Batra 10a–b

According to this passage, if charity is contributed directly, the anonymity of the parties cannot be fully preserved. The recommended method for ensuring anonymity is the communal fund, which eliminates any chance of humiliating contact between well-off donor and poor recipient: the former does not know to whom he is giving, and the latter does not know from whom he is receiving.

In his ranking of the modes of giving charity, described in sec. 8 above, Maimonides recognizes the virtue of anonymity. After defining the highest degree of charity as that which seeks to rehabilitate the poor and prevent poverty, he sets forth the next three degrees:

> 8. Below this is he who gives alms to the poor in such a way that he does not know to whom he has given, nor does the poor person know from whom he has received. This constitutes fulfillment of a commandment for its own sake, as exemplified by the Chamber of Confidentiality in the Temple,[38] where the righteous would contribute in confidentiality, and the poor of distinguished family would draw their sustenance in confidentiality. Close to such a person is one who contributes directly to the charity fund.

38 See mShekalim 5:6.

One should not, however, contribute to the charity fund unless he knows that the person in charge of it is trustworthy, learned, and knows how to manage it properly, like R. Hanania b. Teradion.

9. Below this is he who knows to whom he is giving, while the poor man does not know from whom he has received, as exemplified by the great among the Sages who used to set out secretly and throw coins down at the doors of the poor. This is a fitting way to do it [i.e., give charity], and a commendable method if those in charge of the charity fund do not conduct themselves properly.
10. Below this is the case where the poor man knows from whom he is receiving, but the giver does not know [to whom he gives], as exemplified by the great among the Sages who used to place coins in [folds of] sheets which they would hang behind them [i.e., over their shoulder], so that the poor would come and take without any risk of humiliation.

Code, Laws concerning Gifts to the Poor 10:8–10

It is instructive to consider why anonymous charity is preferable. If anonymity is desirable because it discourages donor pride and paternalism, and fosters donor humility and generosity of spirit, the situation where the recipient knows who the donor is, but not vice versa, is preferable to the situation where the recipient does not know who the donor is, but the donor knows who the recipient is. Maimonides, however, appears to have a different reason for favoring anonymous charity: to protect the recipient's dignity and spare him the humiliation inherent in an encounter with the donor. It is more important that the poor person feel comfortable than that the donor's character be ennobled.

10.2 Dividing the burden between individual and community

Though recognizing the necessity of charity funds and publicly-run charitable enterprises, the halakha continues to ascribe importance to charity given directly to the recipients without institutional mediation. That the affluent contribute to a public charity fund does not relieve them of their obligation to help the poor directly when the occasion arises. Maimonides, while setting out at length detailed laws governing public charity funds, nevertheless upholds a separate and no less important obligation to give charity directly.

1. In every city in which Jews reside, they have a duty to appoint from among themselves well-known and trustworthy persons to serve as alms collectors, to go around collecting from the people on the eve of the Sabbath every week. They should take from each and every person whatever it is fitting for him to give and the amount assessed him. And they are to distribute the coins on the eve of the Sabbath

every week, and to give each and every poor person sustenance sufficient for seven days. And this is what is called the 'charity fund' (*kupa*).

2. They must similarly appoint other collectors to gather each and every day, from each and every courtyard, bread and other foodstuffs, fruits, or money, from anyone willing to make a free-will offering at that time. They should distribute what has been collected among the poor the same evening, and from it give to each poor person his sustenance for the day. And this is what is called the 'soup kitchen' (*tamhui*).
3. We have never seen nor heard of a Jewish community that does not have a charity fund, but as to the soup kitchen, there are some locales where it is customary to have it, and some where it is not. The custom that is widespread today is for the collector of the charity fund to go around [collecting] every day, and to distribute the proceeds on the eve of the Sabbath every week.

Code, Laws concerning Gifts to the Poor 9:1–3

He who, on seeing a poor man begging, averts his eyes from him and does not give him alms, transgresses a negative commandment, as it is said, "Do not harden your heart and shut your hand against your needy kinsman" (Deut. 15:7).

Code, Laws concerning Gifts to the Poor 7:2

Given that the halakha recognizes two distinct paths by which charity must be provided to the needy—the institutional path and the private, person-to-person path, how are responsibilities divided between them? When should someone support his needy neighbor directly, and when is he to do so through the communal institutions? And to whom is a needy man to address his plea for assistance—a better-off neighbor, or the communal charity fund? Is a private individual permitted to turn down requests for aid on the grounds that he already paid his share to the communal charity fund? Today we might ask whether payments to social security and income tax, which support the government's social welfare efforts, obviate direct contributions to the needy?

One category of charity-seekers can be eliminated from the discussion at the outset. The Sages were not sympathetic to beggars who went door-to-door on a daily basis. They sought to deny, or at least substantially limit, the right of such shameless 'professional' beggars to receive charitable funds. In the words of the Tosefta, "One who goes around from door to door—no one need look after him in any respect."[39]

This position is softened a bit at the end of the following talmudic passage:

39 tPeia 4:8 (Zuckermandel edition).

> A Tanna taught: If he goes begging door to door, no one need look after him. A certain poor man who used to go begging door to door came before R. Papa [for money], but he did not look after him. Said R. Sama the son of R. Yeba to R. Papa: If you do not look after him, no one else will look after him. Is he, then, to die [of hunger]? But [replied R. Papa] has it not been taught, If he is a poor man who goes begging door to door, no one need look after him? He said to him: We do not look after his request for a large gift, but we look after his request for a small gift.
>
> bBaba Batra 9a

According to this passage, one may not altogether deny the entreaties of a poor person who regularly goes begging door to door, but should not give him more than a token amount.

Why are the Sages impatient with beggars? The Sages see them as seeking to circumvent the communal charitable institutions by approaching householders on their own. Rashi explains it as follows: "No one need look after him—there is no need to give him money from the charity fund. Since he has learned to go begging door to door, that is enough for him." The words "that is enough for him" here can be understood in two ways: as asserting that one who begs door to door can be expected to receive enough money to cover his needs, but also as asserting that even should he fail to gather that amount, he will have to be satisfied with whatever he gets. The *Shulhan Arukh* rules that: "A poor person who circulates door to door is not given a substantial donation from the communal fund (*kupa*), but only a small one"[40]; the *Siftei Kohen* ad loc. adds that individuals, too, are "not obligated to give him a substantial donation."

i Private charity versus public charity

Having excluded the case of the inveterate door to door beggar who seeks to systematically circumvent publicly-run charitable institutions (and their assessments and limits) by begging for private donations, what kind of private assistance-seeking does the Talmud, in inquiring into the balance between institutionalized and private giving, countenance? The poor person in question is one who has run into difficult circumstances, and is trying to find a solution to his problem by approaching private donors. Are they obligated to help him, or does their having already contributed to communal welfare institutions relieve them of any responsibility to come to his aid? The question is explored in tractate Nedarim. The Mishnah there notes that if one has vowed to exclude his fellow from benefitting from his (the oath-taker's) property, the following

40 YD 250:3.

argument may be used to provide an 'opening'[41] through which the vow may be released:

> R. Meir also said: An 'opening' for him may be adduced from what is written in the Torah, and we say to him: 'Had you known that you were violating [the injunction] … "that your brother may live with you" (Lev. 25:36), or that he might become impoverished and you would not be able to provide for him [would you have made the vow you in fact vowed]?' If he replies, 'Had I known that it is so, I would not have vowed'—he is released [from the vow].
>
> mNedarim 9:4

According to R. Meir, one of the openings, that is, one of the points that, had they been taken into account by the vower beforehand, might have kept him from taking the oath, or to put it differently, one of the considerations that can be adduced to release someone from a vow, is the obligation to provide monetary assistance to one's fellow who becomes impoverished. This Mishnah thus invokes the premise—which, as we have seen, is indeed the accepted rule—that one has a personal obligation to provide monetary assistance to a fellow who is in need of assistance. In its discussion of this Mishnah, however, the Talmud questions the status of this obligation in a community that has established a charity fund:

> R. Huna the son of R. Katina said to the Rabbis: But [the vow-taker] can reply, Not all who become poor fall upon me [for support], and as for my share of the [general] obligations, I provide for him together with everyone else. They said to him [R. Huna]: It can be said: He who falls [into poverty] does not fall, first, upon the [communal charity] collectors.
>
> bNedarim 65b

R. Huna argues that the obligation to pay into the charity fund obviates, and perhaps cancels, the obligation to directly support a needy person. In his view, it is not possible to have recourse to R. Meir's suggested 'opening' for the vow-taker, that is, to adduce the argument that the oath-taker is obligated to support some impoverished person, because this obligation has already been fulfilled by his contribution to the public charity fund. The Sages respond that the public fund is only a backup solution for one who becomes impoverished, "who does not fall, first, upon the [communal

41 An opening is an argument against making the vow that the oath-taker did not consider when he undertook the obligation. If such an opening can be found, the oath-taker can be released from the vow, on the premise that had he been aware of the argument, he would not have made the vow.

charity] collectors."According to the Sages, in the first instance, the poor person turns to private individuals, who are obligated to help him.

This discussion, then, does not provide an answer to the question before us. According to R. Huna, the charitable fund is the primary vehicle for support of the needy, and they are to apply to it in the first instance. Direct charity exists, on this view, only where, for one reason or another, there is no communal fund. The Sages take a more nuanced position. They first direct one who finds himself in difficult circumstances to solicit aid from private sources. In their view, the charity fund comes into play only where the needy do not receive an adequate response from the individuals they have sought help from directly. It provides a safety net for the needy in the event that they cannot secure what they need by directly soliciting aid from affluent individuals, but does not take render void the responsibility each member of the community bears toward his fellow in need.

Assuming that there is first—that is, before the public institutions step in—an obligation on the part of individuals to give assistance to their fellows who have fallen on hard times, on whom does this obligation devolve? Is it universal, or does it apply only to the impoverished person's family and friends? The Early Authorities (*rishonim*) are not in agreement on this point.

Moreover, some decisors have argued that a progressive tax imposed by the government, whereby the wealthy pay more than others to support the poor, who do not pay the tax at all, is considered charity. For example, the twentieth-century decisor R. Isaac Jacob Weiss asserts:

> Where it is known for certain that his tax is given to charity, and to charity that the taxpayer is obligated to give, it is certainly possible to offset it from the tithe [the obligatory percentage to be donated to charity].[42]
>
> *Responsa Minhat Yitzhak* 5:34

ii Support for subjective needs—private or public?

A secondary debate among the decisors pertains to the obligation to support the subjective needs of the poor. As noted earlier, the laws of charity impose an obligation to help meet subjective needs of the poor, that is, unique personal needs fulfillment of which they perceive as essential. The Talmud illustrates the idea by adducing the case of someone from a distinguished family who has become impoverished, but needs "a horse to ride upon and a slave to run before him." But who should bear the financial burden—private individuals or communal charity funds? Is someone whose depressed neighbor asks him to help finance a therapeutic trip to the Alps, say, obligated to participate directly in funding the trip, or

42 See section 7 above.

may he refer the petitioner to communal institutions or government agencies, to which he has already contributed his share, having paid the relevant taxes and levies?

Strong arguments can be made for the claim that this sort of burden should be borne by the community, not the individual. The sums of money involved are substantial, for these are not basic needs; but idiosyncratic and costly cravings. It is unreasonable to impose such costs, or even a portion of them, on a private individual rather than the community as a whole. Yet there are countervailing considerations in favor of funding by the individual rather than the community. First, it is difficult, if not impossible, for communal agencies to assess subjective needs—to distinguish between true needs and mere luxuries, between that without which life is unbearable, and indulgences that the indolent may seek to enjoy at the expense of others. This sort of evaluation can be made only where there is direct, unmediated contact with the person making the idiosyncratic request. Moreover, even if the community could indeed carry out credible assessments of such individualized needs, the idea that a public charity fund could underwrite such diverse and expensive outlays without provoking outrage and accusations of unfairness from members of the community, is highly dubious. An individual can offer differential support to various needy parties, but a public fund would find it difficult to do so, and would invite charges of favoritism and discrimination. From this perspective, a private donor will likely be better able to look after subjective needs.

Given these opposing considerations, there is no consensus among the codifiers as to this issue. From the language of the *Code*'s Laws concerning Gifts to the Poor 7:3, and more importantly, from its juxtaposition to the "He who, on seeing a poor man begging, averts his eyes from him and does not give him alms, transgresses a negative commandment" law, which immediately precedes it, it seems that Maimonides places the burden of providing for subjective needs squarely on individual donors, and not the community as a whole.

> You are commanded to give the poor man in accordance with what he lacks. If he has no clothing, he should be clothed. If he has no household furnishings, they should be bought for him. If he has no wife, he should be helped to marry. If it is a woman, she should be given in marriage. Even if it was [formerly] the habit of this poor man to ride a horse, with a slave running in front of him, and he has become impoverished and lost his possessions, one must buy him a horse to ride upon and a slave to run before him.
>
> *Code*, Laws concerning Gifts to the Poor 7:3

R. Shabtai Rappaport, a present-day halakhic authority, interprets Maimonides' approach as mandating **private** support of subjective needs:

> There are entirely different limits for charitable burdens imposed on individuals and those imposed on the community. The rules governing individuals' charitable obligations are explained [by Maimonides,] in [*Code*, Laws concerning Gifts to the Poor] chapter 7. Charity of this sort must provide the poor person with everything he needs, as long as it does not exceed one-fifth of the donor's assets.... In contrast, charity imposed on the community, the rules of which are explained in [*Code*, Laws concerning Gifts to the Poor] chapter 9, is for the support of three needs only: food, clothing, and burial.[43]

In contrast to Maimonides, R. Moses Isserles (Rema) takes the view that subjective needs are to be supported by **public** funds. He offers the following gloss on the pertinent passage in the *Shulhan Arukh*:

> How much is given to the poor person? "Sufficient for whatever he needs." How so? If he is hungry—they should feed him. If he needs clothing—they should clothe him. If he has no household furnishings—he buys him household furnishings. Even if it was [formerly] the habit of this man to ride a horse, and he had a slave running in front of him, when he was rich, and he has become impoverished, one must buy him a horse and a slave.
>
> *Shulhan Arukh*, YD 250:1
>
> Rema ad loc: And it appears that all this refers to the charity collectors, or to [a fund contributed to by] many individuals, but an individual is not obligated to provide a poor person with whatever he needs. Rather, he informs the community of [the poor person's] straits. But if there is no organized community [fund] there, the individual must give, if he can afford it.

iii Support for relatives

The fact that there remains an obligation to provide direct charitable support for the poor even where public communal funds are in place has a further implication. The halakha tends to favor support for needy relatives over support for strangers who are needy. The Talmud, for example, offered the following explanation for the verse requiring loans to the needy:

> R. Joseph stated: "If thou lend money to any of My people, to the poor among you" (Exod. 22:24): [this teaches, if the choice lies between] My people and a heathen, "My people" take preference; the poor or the

43 R. Shabtai Rappaport, "Priorities in the allocation of communal resources" (Hebrew), in M. Halperin (ed.), *Sefer Assia* 7 (Jerusalem: 1993), 94, 100.

> rich—"the poor" take precedence; your poor [i.e., your relatives] and the poor of your town—your poor take precedence; the poor of your town and the poor of another town—the poor of your own town take precedence.
>
> bBaba Metzia 71a

Maimonides ruled in the same spirit:

> A poor man who is one's relative takes precedence over all others, the poor of one's household take precedence over the other poor of his town, and the poor of his town take precedence over the poor of another town, as it is said, "To the poor and needy kinsman in your land" (Deut. 15:11).
>
> *Code,* Laws concerning Gifts to the Poor 7:13

It must be kept in mind that preference for family members, if shown by those administering the public charitable fund, would be considered unfair bias, if not outright corruption. Moreover, strictly applying the principle that those who are closest should take precedence with respect to charitable support can leave many of the needy without sustenance and support. Only if this preference is operative in the context of direct charity, funded by private individuals, can it have a positive effect, fostering an increased sense of responsibility, solidarity and empathy. Hence the need for two channels for supporting the needy: the personal and the public. Individuals who have ample resources should indeed help maintain relatives who fall into penury, so as to enable public charity funds to better assist those who have no family, or whose relatives are not in a position to offer them sufficient material support. But it is vital to retain a proper balance between direct charity and public charity, so as to avoid a situation of overgenerous support for relatives while those without prosperous families are left unaided.

This line of thinking is manifest in a responsum by the great twentieth-century halakhic authority, R. Moses Feinstein:

> And even though [the questioners] are permitted and it is even a religious duty for them to set aside the charity from today on for their brother, so that he can marry and study Torah after being married—which is an important thing to do—still, it is not right for one to exempt himself thereby from all charity [to other people]....
>
> And he should not give all his charity to a relative to the exclusion of other [needy people].
>
> He should not exempt himself from all charities [to others in need, on the claim that he is supporting his relatives], because that would desecrate God's Name, for people would not say that he gives to his relative; they would say he is unconcerned about the precept of charity

> and the strengthening of the Torah, and it would also cause others not to give. Accordingly, they should set aside the larger share for their brother, but contribute a portion to other charities as well ... thereby fulfilling the precept properly and sanctifying God's Name.
>
> *Responsa Igrot Moshe*, YD 1:144

To sum up this section, we can say that the establishment of communal charitable institutions neither superseded nor diminished the importance of direct giving. The laws of charity mandate two distinct routes for the dispersal of charitable assistance: charity given by a donor directly to a beneficiary, and charity mediated by the community or the state. These routes sometimes overlap—and this redundancy may be the system's secret strength—but in any event dovetail neatly. The dual-track system of charity makes it possible to handle social problems that may elude publicly-run institutions. Difficult cases that might otherwise fall between the cracks, involving those in need of help yet not clearly within the categories of eligibility for public assistance, can be resolved through support provided by individuals and small circles, whether family, friends, or caring members of the community.

11 Conclusion

In this chapter, we have considered various aspects of the laws of charity, examining first the biblical social justice precepts, then the laws of charity developed by the Sages. We have attempted to identify the concepts and principles on which they rest, and endeavored to assess the extent to which the Rabbinic laws of charity reflect the distributive values implicit in biblical law.

The laws of charity did indeed preserve some aspects of the biblical principles of distributive justice, but not all. Clearly, the revolutionary quality that characterizes the Torah's seminal social justice precepts is not found in the laws of charity. We saw that the Torah mandated radical social transformations: general remission of loans, emancipation of slaves, re-distribution of land. These measures were designed to rearrange the social fabric along more equitable, less polarized lines, though not to produce a socially egalitarian society. This revolutionary spirit is not maintained in the more modest, less ambitious Rabbinic laws of charity. These laws seek to help the poor in various ways, but not to bring about a deep-seated transformation of society. This divergence between the transformative ethos of the Torah legislation and the conservative spirit of the Rabbinic laws of charity is due to the disparate contexts within which the two sets of rules were set down. The Pentateuch, which describes the Israelites' exodus from Egypt—a revolutionary event in its own right—and the establishment of an entirely new society in Canaan, has a fundamentally foundational quality. The Rabbinic sources, however, relate to an entirely different historical context: that of a nation in exile, compelled by circumstance to deal more with daily survival than with rectifying the world's ills (*tikun olam*), or instituting an ideal society. To put it differently, a foundational era—an age in which a society and sovereign state are created ex nihilo–is altogether different from an era in which most of a nation's energies are devoted to preserving something already in existence, and confronting the pressures of life in exile. The latter era is an age in which one must rest content with more modest—and realistic—social programs.

Still, even within the chastened framework of the laws of charity, the Sages retain some important social justice principles set out in the Torah.

Maintenance and rehabilitation of the poor

We saw that biblical law imposed two sorts of obligations: those intended to sustain the poor and the weak through the difficult circumstances in which they find themselves (gleanings, forgotten sheaves, corners of the field; Sabbath rest); and those intended to rehabilitate them and release them from the cycle of poverty (remission of loans, restoration of lands, emancipation of slaves, lending money). The Sages recognized the problematic nature of outright charitable donations, which run the risk of creating an ongoing state of dependency, and thus perpetuating poverty. Accordingly, they sought out various ways to direct charitable giving to more productive uses that rehabilitated the poor (preempting descent into poverty by lending money, entering into partnerships and creating jobs) rather than merely sustaining them. In this way, they implemented, to a degree, the biblical principle that merely sustaining the poor was insufficient. As we saw, however, in the Rabbinic world charity that sustained the poor predominated, as a practical matter, over rehabilitative charity.

Preservation of social stratification

The Sages sought to cultivate assistance to the poor within a framework that recognized the existence of social stratification and the need for its perpetuation. They made no attempt to create equality between the various social classes, and it may be that they did not even seek to significantly diminish the gaps between them, but only to lend assistance to the needy while preserving the existing social fabric. This accounts for the striking absence of a relative criterion for poverty in the talmudic sources, and for the emphasis, in setting the amount of charity, on the needs of the poor rather than the assets at the disposal of the rich.[44] This orientation is also reflected in the fact that the most commendable forms of charity (loans, partnerships, creating jobs) deplete

44 The Jerusalem Talmud's version of the enactment at Usha is an exception.

the donor's wealth less than do outright donations. Here too we see an interesting continuity with the biblical approach to social justice, which established mechanisms for helping the weak that were not directed at achieving social leveling.

Responsibility of the poor

The diminished emphasis on the precept of lending money in relation to that of giving charity (that is, outright donations) did not induce the Sages to relieve the poor of all responsibility for their situation. The Sages sought to divide responsibility between donor and beneficiary. They therefore mandated that charitable funds were not to be distributed to those among the poor who were capable of taking care of themselves yet chose to be supported by the public, and further, that the poor themselves were obligated, like everyone else, to contribute to charity, albeit modestly. This rule can be seen as derived from the responsibility borne by the poor in the biblical context, where, we saw, they were expected to take an active part in both the rehabilitative processes—working their returned lands, for instance—and even the provision of their sustenance, by gleaning and gathering produce left for them in the fields, as explained above.

Private and communal responsibility

In developing the laws of charity, the Sages had to establish communal mechanisms, mainly public charitable funds, that would shoulder the responsibility of attending to the needy. Such institutions were needed in order to make charitable measures more effective, but also served to protect the dignity of the poor by allowing assistance to be obtained anonymously. At the same time, the Sages were careful not to abandon the biblical principle that every member of society bears personal responsibility for easing the plight of the poor. Accordingly, they retained, alongside these public institutions, a parallel private track for charitable giving, whereby charity was given directly to the poor, especially those close to the donor, such as relatives and neighbors.

The Sages, then, devised a complex system of mechanisms for advancing social justice. It combined effective assistance to the needy with recognition of society's multi-dimensional structure, fostered the shared responsibility of weak and strong; and synergized the effectiveness of public provision of charity with the warmth and sensitivity of private beneficence.

Appendix Social justice in the ancient Near East

The following documents illustrate efforts undertaken in ancient Near Eastern societies to help the needy.

The first recounts a remission of loans ordered by King Ammisaduqa, who reigned in Babylon in the sixteenth century BCE, in an effort to ease the burden on debtors.

> Whoever has given barley or silver to an Akkadian or an Amorite as an interest-bearing loan… and had a document executed–because the king has invoked the *misharum* for the land, his document is voided; he may not collect the barley or silver on the basis of his document.
>
> If an obligation has resulted in foreclosure against a citizen of Numhia, a citizen of Emutbalum, a citizen of Idamaras, a citizen of Uruk, a citizen of Isin, a citizen of Kisurra, or a citizen of Malgium, in consequence of which he placed his own person, his wife or his children in debt servitude for silver, or as a pledge–because the king has instituted the *misharum* in the land, he is released; his freedom is effective.[1]

The second text speaks of Pharaoh Ramses IV (12th c. BCE), who, at the time of his coronation, announced several measures to be taken to benefit the needy:

> Heaven and earth rejoice, for thou art the great lord of Egypt. Those who had fled have returned to their home-towns; those who were in hiding have come forth. The hungry are sated and rejoice, the thirsty are drunk. The naked are clothed in fine linen, the ragged wear fair garments. Those who were in bonds are free again; those who were in chains rejoice. The rebels in this land are become free men once more. High Niles are come forth from their caverns and make glad the heart of the people. The widows' houses stand open once more; they let the wanderers enter.[2]

1 Translated by J.J. Finkelstein in J.B. Pritchard (ed.), *The Ancient Near East–Supplementary Texts and Pictures Relating to the Old Testament* (Princeton: 1969), 526.

2 H.S. Smith, "A note on amnesty," *Journal of Egyptian Archaeology* 54 (1968), 212.

10 Euthanasia

1 Introduction

As a result of the sophisticated life-sustaining techniques available to modern medicine, it is now possible to maintain vital biological functions in an otherwise lifeless body. The extent to which such techniques should be applied is a matter for debate. Is it obligatory, permissible, or forbidden, to apply medical technologies to sustain the life of one who is in an irreversible vegetative state, and appears to have a very minimal quality of life, if that? In making such decisions, what is the relevance of economic factors? Does the fact that hospitals have to allocate and distribute scarce medical resources justify favoring other needs over prolonging the lives of those who are terminally ill? To what extent should the family of a patient in a vegetative state bear the financial burden of sustaining the life of their loved one? These and other questions merit thoughtful and informed deliberation.

Various considerations often militate against continuing life-sustaining treatment, especially where there is no hope of recovery; these considerations include concerns about quality of life, the reliability of prognostication, pain and suffering, human dignity, and the right to refuse treatment. At the same time, terminating medical treatment is a highly charged issue, since it is often regarded as the first step in a 'slippery slope' that will eventually lead to the destruction of human life for patently immoral reasons. The dilemmas raised by the intensive medical treatment of those in a vegetative state generated heated public debate in the wake of the 1976 Karen Ann Quinlan case.[1] In its ruling that an artificial respirator could be disconnected from a patient in a persistent vegetative state, the Supreme Court of New Jersey emphasized two points: (a) expert physicians had concluded that there was no reasonable hope that Quinlan would emerge from her vegetative condition to a sapient state; and (b) her father's decision to terminate treatment was supported by the rest of the family, and the hospital ethics committee. In the aftermath of the public controversy engendered by this case, various rabbinical authorities issued responsa that addressed—from the halakhic perspective—the dilemmas raised by the Quinlan case. No unanimity was reached, but the halakhic deliberations did underscore certain central issues that constitute the conceptual framework for addressing the problem from the perspective of Jewish law. This chapter offers an exposition of this conceptual framework, as it emerges from these responsa.

These issues are as follows:

i suffering as a factor in decisions regarding the terminally ill
ii applying the halakhic categories of '*goses*' (one who is dying) and '*treifa*' (one who is mortally ill)
iii the distinction between precipitating death and removing an impediment to death
iv sacrificing one who is mortally ill to save a viable life.

2 Physical suffering as a factor in treatment of the terminally ill

Overall, Jewish law is opposed to euthanasia, views it as tantamount to murder, and punishes it accordingly. Since the precipitation of death for compassionate reasons is deemed murder, the punishment meted out to a mercy-killer is no different from that meted out to the murderer. Is this attitude based on the view that any life, even the life of one who is

1 Quinlan was in a persistent vegetative state (PVS), i.e., capable only of vegetative responses, e.g., breathing, sleeping, reacting to light. Her father sought to terminate the intensive life-prolonging medical treatment she was receiving.

moribund and suffering, is better than death? Does the halakha ever recognize a situation where the death of someone who is terminally ill and suffering is preferable to life? We will explore this question, beginning with an examination of two talmudic accounts of painful death: that of R. Hanina b. Teradion, and that of R. Judah the Prince.

2.1 The talmudic account of R. Hanina b. Teradion's death

The following account of the martyrdom of R. Hanina b. Teradion is found in tractate Avoda Zara.

> …they found R. Hanina b. Teradion sitting and occupying himself with the Torah, publicly convening assemblies, and keeping a scroll of the law in his bosom. Straightaway they [the Romans] took hold of him, wrapped him in the scroll of the law, placed bundles of branches around him, and set them on fire. They then brought tufts of wool, which they had soaked in water, and placed them over his heart, so that he would not expire quickly…. His students called out … Open up your mouth so that the fire will enter within you. He said to them, Let He who gave me [my soul] take it away, but no one should injure himself. The executioner then said to him, Rabbi, if I increase the flame and take away the tufts of wool from over your heart, will you cause me to enter into the life to come? Yes, he said to him. Then swear unto me. He swore unto him. He immediately increased the flame and removed the tufts of wool from over his heart, and his soul departed speedily. The executioner then jumped and threw himself into the fire. And a heavenly voice went forth and said: R. Hanina b. Teradion and the executioner have been called to life in the world to come. When Rabbi [Judah the Prince] heard it, he wept and said: Some acquire eternal life in one hour, others after many years.
>
> bAvoda Zara 18a

On the one hand, R. Hanina refrained from actively hastening his death by opening his mouth, but asserted, "Let He who gave me [my soul] take it away, but no one should injure himself." On the other hand, he did not object when the executioner increased the flame and took away the tufts of wool, thereby indirectly hastening his death. Furthermore, R. Hanina even assured the Roman executioner that as a reward for this action, he would be immediately admitted into the hereafter. However these contradictory responses on the part of R. Hanina b. Teradion are reconciled, it is clear that since R. Hanina b. Teradion acceded to the executioner's offer to hasten his death by indirect means, we can safely conclude that opposition to precipitating death in order to lessen suffering is not based on a principle that suffering is preferable to death.

2.2 The talmudic account of R. Judah the Prince's death

> On the day Rabbi was dying, the Rabbis decreed a public fast and offered prayers for heavenly mercy. They furthermore announced that whoever said that Rabbi was dead would be stabbed with a sword.
>
> Rabbi's handmaid ascended the roof and prayed, The immortals desire that Rabbi [join them], and the mortals desire that Rabbi [remain with them]; may it be [Thy] will that the mortals overpower the immortals. But when she saw how often he had to use the toilet, painfully taking off his tefillin and putting them on again, she prayed, May it be [Thy] will that the immortals overpower the mortals. As the Rabbis continued their prayers for [heavenly] mercy incessantly, she took a jar and threw it down from the roof to the ground. [For a moment] they ceased praying, and the soul of Rabbi departed to its eternal rest.
>
> bKetubot 104a

The Talmud does not condemn the handmaid's act, and on the contrary, appears to fully endorse it. Here again, it is clear that Jewish law recognizes that in some situations, death is preferable to a life of suffering, and in such situations, it is appropriate to hope and pray that the suffering moribund individual will die, and not go on living.

Elsewhere in the Talmud, we find that the Sages prayed for the death of colleagues undergoing great emotional torment. For instance, it is recounted of the Amora R. Johanan, who lost his mind as a result of the death of Resh Lakish, his study-partner, that the Sages prayed he would be granted heavenly mercy, viz., that he would die, so that his anguish would be alleviated.[2]

R. Isaac Liebes, a contemporary rabbinical authority, adduces the account of R. Judah the Prince's death in support of his own view that it is permissible to pray for the demise of a suffering, deathly ill individual.

> The Maharsha, in his *Hidushei Agadot*, wrote that the handmaid's taking a jar and throwing it on the ground was a hint that just as the breaking of an earthenware jar is its 'death,' so too with the human body: when it is broken and in agony, that is its death. For it cannot achieve bodily perfection in any action, as in the case of the tefillin; and see the passage. [From this incident] we see that it is permitted to pray for the death of one who is sick. Even though it is not related that the Rabbis prayed for his death, in any event, since they kept silent after Rabbi [Judah the Prince's] handmaid threw the jar, and she did pray for his death, it follows that they were content with her conduct. Also, from the fact that the handmaid's words and actions

2 bBaba Metzia 84a.

> are preserved in the Talmud, it follows that it is appropriate to act this way.
>
> *Responsa Beit Avi* , HM 2:153

R. Leibes also invokes the account of the death of R. Hanina b. Teradion in support of the view that one may pray for the demise of someone deathly ill who is suffering terribly.

2.3 Praying for a sufferer's speedy death

An important halakhic source as to the question of praying for the death of a suffering individual is R. Nissim Gerondi's commentary on bNedarim 40a, where the Talmud criticizes those who do not visit the sick:

> When R. Dimi came, he said: He who visits one who is sick causes him to live, whereas he who does not visit one who is sick causes him to die. How does he cause [this]? Shall we say that he who visits one who is sick prays that he should live, while he who does not visit prays that he should die!? That he should die!? Can you really think so? But rather, [say thus:] he who does not visit one who is sick prays neither that he should live nor that he should die.
>
> bNedarim 40a

The Ran comments:

> "He prays neither that he should live nor that he should die"—It appears to me that this means that there are times when one must pray that a sick person should die, since he is undergoing great suffering and in any case will not survive, as in the case of Rabbi [Judah the Prince]'s handmaid—"But when she saw how often he had to use the toilet, painfully taking off his tefillin and putting them on again, she prayed: May it be [Thy] will that the immortals overpower the mortals." That is to say, [she prayed] that Rabbi [Judah the Prince] would die. That is why the Talmud [in bNedarim] says that he who visits one who is sick helps him with his prayer, even to live, because [having visited,] it is a more effective prayer; and he who does not visit him, does not, needless to say, help him to live, and in cases where he [the dying person] would [due to his great suffering] take pleasure in dying, even this small joy he does not help him achieve.

The Ran connects the description of R. Judah's death to the passage from bNedarim, and concludes that in some cases it is appropriate to pray that the sick should die, so that their suffering will end. He who does not visit one who is sick is not aware of his anguish, and hence does not pray for his speedy demise; this conduct is reprehensible.

But this view is not universally accepted. R. Haim Palagi, a prominent Turkish rabbinical authority, expressed reservations about the practice of praying for a sufferer's speedy demise:

> Question: … Reuben's wife has been ill for a long time—over twenty years—and is suffering and debilitated by torment … and now she requests that they pray that she should die, and in particular, she begs her husband and sons to ask [heaven] to grant her this mercy.… If they do ask that she be granted mercy—that she should die—is there any apprehension that this violates a prohibition?
>
> Answer: In my humble opinion, it appears to me that regarding such matters, we make a compromise. If she is very severely afflicted by terrible and bitter torment, and all the doctors have said that in any event there is no cure that will allow her to recover, and they have given up on [helping] her, it would seem that despite this, her husband, sons, and relatives should not make any appeal or prayer that she die, nor should they make any prayer or appeal that she live, but rather, they should 'sit and do nothing.' For if they appeal for mercy for her, that she should die, there is concern that some will say that, as might happen, heaven forbid, in one of every thousand cases, they ask that her death be hastened in order to be rid of her and the trouble of [caring for] her, and that they have some personal interest in this, especially her husband. [There is concern] lest, heaven forbid, there is suspicion that he desired her death for his own benefit, even though he is a learned, decent, and God-fearing man.… And the talmudic account of Rabbi's handmaid is not a valid precedent, for since the Talmud says [elsewhere] that "we are like donkeys, but not like the donkey of R. Pinhas b. Yair" [i.e., we are not on the same level as the past generations and cannot simply copy their actions], we can certainly say with complete confidence that we are not on the level of Rabbi [Judah the Prince]'s handmaid.
>
> And to pray that she live is likewise difficult, since she is suffering terrible and bitter torment, and very great distress. Hence 'sit and do nothing' is the preferable option for her husband and relatives.
>
> But others, who are not related, and with respect to whom none of the aforementioned concerns arise, if they seek to pray for her so that she should die and her soul should be at rest, are permitted to do so, provided that their actions are entirely for the sake of heaven.… But if someone is dying (*goses*), then nobody should pray for him, since it is stated in *Sefer Hasidim* (§234) that "one is not to call out to him at the moment the soul departs." … Once a person becomes a *goses*, no prayers may be said on his behalf.
>
> *Responsa Hikekei Lev*, 1, YD #50, 90d

2.4 The halakhic approach to suffering

In light of the foregoing, it is clear that Jewish law recognizes that in treating the terminally ill, suffering must be taken into account, and that there are some cases where death is preferable to life. In such cases, it is permissible for the terminally ill person, and those close to him, to hope for, and even pray for, his death. This is by no means tantamount to endorsement of euthanasia, however. Three considerations weighing against acceptance of euthanasia can be found in the halakhic literature. The first is the formal halakhic consideration that every killing of a human being is considered an act of murder. Apparently, the inclination to adduce such a rigid rule reflects apprehension about the slippery slope. If we allow euthanasia in some cases, where is the line to be drawn? Second, man's soul is not man's private property, but belongs to God, hence one is not entitled to take either his own soul, or anyone else's. This point is made explicitly by R. Yehiel Mikhel Epstein in his *Arukh Hashulhan*: "even though we see that the *goses* is enduring much suffering, and it would be better for him to die, we are forbidden to carry out any act that would precipitate his death."[3] Third, euthanasia is conceived as problematic intervention in a realm governed by divine providence. This consideration, it should be noted, is rather tenuous, since any life-saving medical treatment involves such intervention.

The gap between the moral consideration that sometimes favors death to life (alleviation of suffering) and the halakhic considerations against euthanasia, is acknowledged and addressed by the decisors. For instance, R. Liebes writes:

> And I found an account in Midrash Rabbah on Deuteronomy regarding a certain woman who had become old, and came before R. Jose b. Halafta, and said to him: Rabbi, I have grown too old, and my life is now humiliating, and I cannot taste either food or drink, and I wish to withdraw from the world. He said to her: on account of what have you had such a long life? She said to him: I am accustomed that, even when I am engaged in doing something I am very fond of, I put it aside and go to the synagogue early. He said to her: absent yourself from the synagogue for three consecutive days. She went and did so, and on the third day she died. Now, had this old woman killed herself, she may very well have been treated as a willful suicide, although she did it due to the great suffering she was undergoing, even though it is not altogether clear that those who kill themselves due to suffering and pain are deemed willful suicides (*Pithei Teshuva*, YD 348:2; *Responsa Hatam Sofer*, YD #326).

3 YD 339:1.

> According to all views, however, it is clear that one who kills himself, even out of great suffering, has not acted in accordance with the standard of the pious (*midat hahasidut*).[4] But as to praying for one's own death or that of others—there are examples of the Sages doing so. It is therefore established that this does not even come close to violating the prohibition, or [even] the standard of the pious.
>
> *Responsa Beit Avi*, HM #153

R. Liebes clearly distinguishes between prayer and practice: there are, indeed, cases in which death is preferable to life, as in the incident of the old woman and R. Jose b. Halafta, and in such cases it is permitted to pray for death. But even in these cases, it is absolutely forbidden to take active steps to precipitate the death of the sufferer.

R. Liebes also alludes to a controversy among the decisors over the question of suicide due to ongoing suffering or fear of suffering that will likely ensue. This dilemma was of particular relevance during the Crusades, in the communities of Franco-Germany, when fear of the torture that would be inflicted by the crusading mobs generated a not-negligible phenomenon of suicide and the killing of one's own children. The fear was that the torment would be so great that the Jews, and especially children, would convert to Christianity.[5] It was against this background that Rabbenu Tam issued the following ruling:

> Rabbenu Tam asserts: Wherever they are afraid that the Gentiles will cause them to transgress—for example, by torturing them in such a way that they will be unable to bear it—they are commanded to harm themselves [i.e., take their own lives].
>
> *Tosafot*, bAvoda Zara 18a s.v. *veal yehabel aztmo*

3 Categories relating to the terminally ill

Despite the fact that, in clinical terms, the state of mortal illness precedes that of dying, we will discuss the concept of 'one who is dying' (*goses*) before that of 'one who is mortally ill' (*treifa*).The former concept is both more familiar and more widely used in halakhic discourse on treatment of the terminally ill. Invoking the concept of 'one who is mortally ill' in this context is still somewhat novel, and not universally accepted.

3.1 One who is dying (*goses*)

'*Goses*' (pl., *gosesim*) is the halakhic term used for someone in the throes of death; the process of dying is termed *gesisa*. Traditional symptoms include

4 See Chapter Eight above, "Equity."

5 See Y. Lichtenshtein, "Suicide as an act of atonement in Jewish law," 16 *Jewish Law Annual* (2006), 51–92.

accumulation of saliva in the throat and the onset of death rattle. There is a halakhic presumption to the effect that the *goses* is incapable of surviving for more than three days after the onset of *gesisa*. According to a ruling attributed to R. Meir of Rothenburg, the Maharam, one who is informed of the *gesisa* of a close relative must observe mourning rites starting three days after the onset of *gesisa*.[6] The basis for the Maharam's ruling is the following talmudic passage.

> MISHNAH If, when the bearer of a bill of divorce (*get*) left, [the husband] was old or sick, [the agent] still delivers it to the wife, on the assumption that [the husband] is still alive.
>
> GEMARA Rava said: This was taught only with respect to an old man who has not reached 'the years of strength' [i.e., age eighty] and one who is only sick, because most of those who are sick recover; but it was not taught of one who has reached 'the years of strength' or is a *goses*, because most of those who are dying (*gosesim*) die.
>
> bGitin 28a

The Mishnah rules that an agent charged with delivering a bill of divorce written by a sick husband can indeed deliver it, on the assumption that, at the time of delivery, the husband is still alive. The agent need not be apprehensive that the husband has died while the agent was in transit from the husband's place of residence to the wife's. In the absence of such an assumption, the bill of divorce would be invalid, since there can be no divorce if the husband is dead. In the discussion in the Gemara, Rava qualifies the mishnaic ruling, asserting that it applies only to a husband who has not yet reached the age of eighty, or is merely ill. In those circumstances, he argues, it can indeed be assumed that the husband is still alive. But where the husband is eighty or over, or not merely ill, but dying, the agent is not permitted to deliver the bill of divorce to the wife, since there is a presumption that "most of those who are dying (*gosesim*) die," and there is serious concern that after the agent received the bill of divorce from the husband and departed on his errand to deliver it to the wife, the husband passed away, rendering it invalid.

Basing himself on this *sugya*, the Maharam of Rothenburg ruled that one who heard that a close relative was dying must commence mourning three days after the onset of *gesisa*, since it can then be assumed that the relative has, indeed, passed away.

> It happened that a woman was four days' distance from her husband when some Jews came and said to her: when we left, your husband was dying (*goses*). And R. Meir of Rothenburg was consulted, and he

6 See also *Perisha*, YD 339; I. Jakobovits, *Jewish Medical Ethics* (New York: 1976), 349–418; J.D. Bleich, "Ethico-halakhic considerations in the practice of medicine," 1 *Dine Israel* (1976), 129.

> told her to mourn. For it is said in bGitin 28a, "If someone sent a bill of divorce (*get*) from abroad, and [the bearer] left [the husband] when he was sick or old, [the bearer] delivers it to her [the wife], on the assumption that [the husband] is still alive," and so on. And the Gemara explains that the Mishnah only speaks of the case where he is old or sick, but not where he was dying (*goses*), because most of those who are dying die.... If so, then most of those who are dying (*gosesim*) do not live two or three days, since most of them die.
>
> *Mordekhai*, Moed Katan, 864

A crucial question here is that of the value of *hayei shaa*, literally, life for the hour. This is the halakhic term for the brief amount of time left to one who is dying. What value, halakhically speaking, does this brief period have? Perusal of the sources immediately reveals that one whose death is imminent, that is, one who is in his death throes, who is dying (*goses*), is, despite his extremely short life expectancy, considered a living person in every respect, and anyone who causes his death incurs the penalty applicable to one who causes the death of someone healthy, namely, death. The legal status of the *goses* is summarized in tractate Semahot:

1. A dying man is considered the same as a living man in every respect. He may obligate to levirate marriage, and he may release from levirate marriage. He may confer the right to eat of the heave offering, and he may disqualify from eating of the heave offering. He may inherit property, and he may bequeath property. If a limb is severed from his body, it is regarded as a limb severed from a living person, and if flesh [is severed], [it is regarded] as flesh from a living person. The blood of his sin-offering or guilt offering may be sprinkled on his behalf. All this applies until the moment he dies.
2. His jaws may not be bound, nor his orifices stopped, and no metal vessel, or any other cooling object may be placed upon his belly until the moment he dies, as it is written: *Before the silver cord is snapped asunder, and the golden bowl shattered, and the pitcher is broken at the fountain* (Eccles. 12:6).
3. He may not be stirred, nor may he be washed, and he should not be laid upon sand or salt, until the moment he dies.
4. His eyes may not be closed. Whosoever touches him or stirs him sheds blood. Rabbi Meir used to compare a dying man to a flickering lamp: the moment one touches it he puts it out. So, too, whoever closes the eyes of a dying man is treated as though he has snuffed out his life.

Semahot 1:1-4[7]

7 *The Tractate Mourning* (*Semahot*), translated with introduction and notes by D. Zlotnik (New Haven: 1966). See Appendix for the annotated text. Tractate Semahot is also known as Evel Rabbati.

It is forbidden to do anything that will precipitate the death of a *goses*. Those in attendance must be careful not to do anything that might agitate the dying person: even small adjustments of the body position of someone in this state, such as closing the eyelids, may hasten his demise. For the same reason, funeral preparations are not to be commenced until death has been established.

As we said, hastening the demise of a dying person is, according to Jewish law, no different from killing someone healthy; the perpetrator is subject to the same penalty. A distinction is made, however, between a *goses* who is dying 'at the hand of God,' that is, naturally, and someone reduced to the condition of *gesisa* by human intervention. Before examining this distinction, we must introduce another halakhic concept, that of 'one who is mortally ill' (*treifat adam*).

3.2 One who is mortally ill (*treifat adam*)

Explication of the terms 'unfit' (*treifa*), 'dying at the hand of man' (*goses bidei adam*), and 'dying at the hand of God' (*goses bidei shamayim*)—that is, naturally—is crucial for determining the halakhic approach to treatment of different types of terminally ill and wounded patients. But as we will see below, the definitions of these terms are unclear, and this ambiguity has engendered difficulty in applying these halakhic categories to actual cases.

3.2.i The concept of *treifa*

In literal terms, a *treifa* is an animal torn by a beast of prey. In the context of the dietary laws, the term '*treifa*' refers to an animal afflicted with a fatal organic defect that makes it unfit for human consumption. Maimonides summarizes the law governing the *treifa* as follows:

> 6. Whosoever eats an olive's bulk of the flesh of a clean animal, beast, or bird which has been rendered *treifa*, is liable to a flogging, as it is said, "Any flesh that is torn of beasts (*treifa*) in the field ye shall not eat; ye shall cast it to the dogs" (Exod. 22:30). This *treifa* mentioned in Scripture refers to an animal torn by a beast of prey, such as a falcon or its like. It cannot be said that this applies only to cases where the beast of prey has not only torn the animal but killed it as well, for if it had died it would have become *neveila*. Indeed, what difference does it make whether the animal had died a natural death, or whether a person smote it with a sword and slew it, or whether a lion mauled it and killed it? Perforce, then, the reference must be to cases where the animal is torn by the beast of prey, but does not die as a result of the mauling.
> 7. If, then, a torn beast which has not died as a result of the mauling is forbidden, it might be assumed therefrom that if a wolf comes forth

and drags away a kid by its foot, tail, or ear, and someone forthwith chases the wolf and rescues the kid from its mouth, the kid should be forbidden, seeing that it is torn. That is why Scripture says expressly, "Any flesh that is torn of beasts (*treifa*) in the field ye shall not eat; ye shall cast it to the dogs," that is, it is not forbidden until it becomes fit only for a dog. **Hence you learn that *treifa* mentioned in the Torah refers to an animal so torn and crushed by a beast of prey that it is fatally wounded, though not yet dead**. And even if a person anticipates its death and performs *shehita* upon it before it dies, it is still forbidden as *treifa*, since it could not have continued to live as a result of the wound inflicted upon it.

8. From this you learn that the Torah has forbidden, first, a dead animal—which is considered *neveila*—and, second, one which is bound to die as a result of its wounds, though not yet dead—which constitutes *treifa*. And in exactly the same manner as in the case of the animal which had died—where no distinction is made between the causes of death, whether the animal had died of natural causes, or fell down to its death, or was strangled to death, or was torn and killed by a beast of prey—in the same way no distinction is made in the case of the animal which is about to die, whether a beast of prey had torn and crushed it, or the animal itself had fallen from a roof and had fractured most of its ribs, or had fallen and injured its organs, or was shot by an arrow and its heart and lungs were pierced, or contracted a disease which caused the perforation of its heart or lungs or brought about the fracture of most of its ribs, and so forth. Once the animal is about to die, it is in every case considered *treifa*, whether the cause is an act of man or an act of heaven. This being so, why does the Torah specify "torn"? The answer is that Scripture speaks in terms of what occurs most commonly. For if you should say that this is not so, you will then have to say that it refers only to an animal "torn … in the field," and that if it was torn in a courtyard you would not forbid it! Hence you learn that Scripture does indeed speak only in terms of the most common occurrence.
9. The essence of this verse is therefore that an animal which is about to die on account of its wound, and cannot survive as a result of that wound, is forbidden. Hence the Sages have enunciated the general rule that every disease which, if it afflicts an animal, makes it impossible for that animal to survive, renders it *treifa*, and in the Laws concerning Shehita [slaughter of animals for food] it will be explained which diseases render an animal *treifa* and which do not.

Code, Laws concerning Forbidden Foods 4:6–9

The physical defects that render an animal *treifa* are treated at length in the talmudic literature, and their study constitutes a major part of traditional rabbinical study.[8] The talmudic list of such defects is fixed, and no criteria can be removed or added. Maimonides states this clearly:

> 12. One may not under any circumstances add to this list of causes of *treifa*, for in the case of any other defect in an animal, beast or bird beyond those which the Sages of former generations have enumerated and to which the contemporary Israelite courts of law have given their assent, [it is assumed] that it is possible for the animal to go on living, even if our own medical knowledge assures us that it cannot eventually survive.
> 13. Conversely, as regards the defects which the Sages have enumerated, concerning which they have said that they render the animal *treifa*, even if it should appear from our present knowledge of medicine that some of them are not fatal and that the animal can survive them, one must go only by what the Sages have enumerated, as it is said, "according to the law which they shall teach thee" (Deut. 17:11).
>
> *Code*, Laws concerning Shehita 10:12–13

3.2.ii Definition of one who is mortally ill (*treifat adam*)

There is a controversy among the decisors as to the definition of 'one who is mortally ill' (*treifat adam*). Is the mortally ill person defined in precisely the same terms as an animal *treifa*? In his commentary on bSanhedrin 78a, which will be cited below, Rashi invokes two criteria from the sphere of animal *treifa* as examples of human mortal illness: having a pierced windpipe and having a pierced brain membrane. It appears that according to Rashi, a human *treifa* is to be defined in accordance with the closed list of criteria that define the animal *treifa*. Maimonides' definition of human mortal illness, however, is more general:

> If one kills another who suffers from a fatal organic disease (*treifa*), he is legally exempt from punishment by the laws of man [i.e., a human court], even though the victim ate and drank and walked about the streets. But every human being is presumed to be healthy, and his murderer must be put to death unless it is known for certain that he had a fatal organic defect, and physicians say that his disease is incurable by human agency and that he would have died of it even if he had not been killed in other ways.
>
> *Code*, Laws concerning Murder and the Preservation of Life 2:8

8 *Code*, Laws concerning Shehita 10:9.

According to Maimonides, any individual whom physicians deem certain to die of an incurable organic defect is considered 'mortally ill.' In Maimonides' view, then, the definition of 'one who is mortally ill' (*treifat adam*) is a purely medical matter, and varies with the prevailing state of medical knowledge.

Another question that arises in seeking to define mortal illness is the relevance of the twelve-month test. According to the dietary laws, a *treifa* animal will not live longer than twelve months.[9] Indeed, so strong is the presumption of death within twelve months that were an animal identified as a *treifa* to survive for twelve months, it would be permitted for human consumption on the grounds that the original diagnosis must have been mistaken.[10] Does the twelve-month limit also apply to the human *treifa*, that is, is it the case that one who is mortally ill does not live more than twelve months from the time he becomes wounded or ill? In support of the relevance of the twelve-month test, we should note that the wife of one who is mortally ill and whose whereabouts are unknown is permitted to remarry twelve months after her husband was deemed a *treifa*, even though no formal evidence of his death is available.[11] On the other hand, the *Tosafot* maintain that there is a fundamental physiological difference between animals and human beings, and that the latter may be capable of surviving with a mortal defect for longer periods.[12] The Early Authorities were divided as to the relevance of the twelve-month test, which may have bearing on the problem of releasing the agunah (chained wife).[13]

Both Maimonides and the *Tosafot* reject the twelve-month limit in relation to the concept of the human *treifa*. But if the concept of a defect that makes death inevitable, which constitutes the basis of the *treifa* category, is to have any practical application in the context of medical treatment of the terminally ill, it must be quantified and not left open and vague. That is, some temporal criterion for its use must be decided on. Such a criterion should be determined on the basis of medical knowledge, and not simply replicate the rigid twelve-month rule applicable to animals.

3.2.iii Distinguishing between *treifat adam*, *goses bidei adam*, and *goses bidei shamayim*

The punishment of death imposed by the court is meted out only to one who takes a fully viable human life. According to talmudic law, one who is 'mortally ill' (*treifat adam*) is not considered to have a fully viable life, hence someone who takes that life—that is, kills him—is exempt from

9 bHulin 57b.

10 bHulin 58a.

11 bJebamot 120b-121a.

12 *Tosafot*, bGitin 56b s.v. *venikar bemoho*; *Tosafot*, bEruvin 7a. s.v. *kegon shidra.*

13 See mJebamot 16:4, and *Tosafot Yomtov* ad loc.

liability 'by the laws of man': he cannot be punished by the court for the murder. This law may reflect a materialistic notion of the act of murder, on which murder is a kind of extremely severe blow to the human body, a blow that causes death. The killer of someone who is mortally ill, whose body is already defective, would be exempt from liability for causing death, as it was already impending. The case is analogous to someone who breaks an already-broken utensil, and is thus exempt from tort liability.

In the course of distinguishing between a *goses* who is dying 'at the hand of God'—that is, naturally—and one reduced to the condition of *gesisa* by human intervention, the Talmud articulates the difference between one who is mortally ill (*treifat adam*) and one who is dying (*goses*):

> Our Rabbis taught: If ten people smote someone with ten sticks, whether simultaneously or successively, and he died, they are exempt. R. Judah b. Bathyra said: If successively, the last is liable, because he caused the actual death. R. Johanan said: Both derive [their rulings] from the same verse: "And he who smites all the life (*kol nefesh*) of any person shall surely be put to death" (Lev. 24:17). The Rabbis maintain that "all the life" implies, [if the victim still has his] whole life, but R. Judah b. Bathyra maintains that "all the life" implies, whatever there is of life.
>
> Rava said: All agree that if he killed someone who was mortally ill (*treifa*), he is exempt; if he killed someone who was dying at the hand of God [i.e., dying a natural death] (*goses bidei shamayim*), he is liable. They disagree only regarding someone who was dying at the hand of man: one side likens him to someone mortally ill, and the other likens him to someone dying naturally. Now he who likens him to someone mortally ill—why does he not liken him to someone dying naturally? Because someone dying naturally has not been injured, but this one [he who is dying at the hand of man] has been injured. Now he who likens him to someone dying naturally—why does he not liken him to someone mortally ill? Because someone mortally ill has vital organs that are impaired, but this one does not.
>
> bSanhedrin 78a

On the question of someone "dying at the hand of man," Maimonides takes the view that though the injury inflicted is not an incurable organic defect of the sort that constitutes mortal illness, the victim falls into the same category as the *treifa* as far as criminal liability for his murder is concerned. The perpetrator in such a case is, like the murderer of a *treifa*, not subject to the punishment of court-imposed death.

> Whether one kills a healthy person or a dying invalid or even a person in his death throes (*goses*), he must be put to death on this account. But if the death throes are humanly caused, for example, if one who has

been beaten to the point of death is in his throes (*goses*), the court may not put his slayer to death.

Code, Laws concerning Murder and the Preservation of Life 2:7

3.3.iv Legal status of the killer of one who is mortally ill

Talmudic law exempts the killer of one who is mortally ill (*treifat adam*) from being punished by court-imposed death. We saw that in the course of defining mortal illness, Maimonides sought to qualify this exemption from punishment by human law by invoking divine retribution. Let us look at his ruling once again:

> If one kills another who suffers from a fatal organic disease (*treifa*), he is legally exempt from punishment by the laws of man [i.e., a human court] even though the victim ate and drank and walked about the streets. But every human being is presumed to be healthy, and his murderer must be put to death unless it is known for certain that he had a fatal organic defect, and physicians say that his disease is incurable by human agency and that he would have died of it even if he had not been killed in other ways.
>
> *Code*, Laws concerning Murder and the Preservation of Life 2:8

According to Maimonides, one who kills someone who is mortally ill is exempt from punishment "by the laws of man." This formulation indicates that on Maimonides' view, the exemption applies only after the fact. Killing someone mortally ill is forbidden *ab initio*, and one who perpetrates such a murder will be punished by heaven. This qualification of the exemption from punishment is not explicitly stated in the Talmud, and it is possible that Maimonides introduced it on the strength of a moral consideration: though by law, capital punishment is imposed only on one who takes a viable human life, from a moral perspective, it is forbidden to kill any human being, regardless of their physical condition. Maimonides invokes divine punishment to give concrete expression to this moral culpability. Indeed, Maimonides invokes the concept of 'exempt by the laws of man, but liable by the laws of heaven' with respect to other types of killings that do not incur the punishment of court-imposed death.

> If, however, one hires an assassin to kill another, or sends his slave to kill him, or ties another up and leaves him in front of a lion or another animal and the animal kills him, and similarly, if one commits suicide, the rule in each of these cases is that he is a shedder of blood, has committed the crime of murder, and is liable to death at the hands of heaven, but there is no capital punishment at the hands of the court.
>
> How do we know that this is the rule? Because Scripture says: "Whoever sheds man's blood, by man shall his blood be shed"

(Gen. 9:6), referring to one who commits the murder himself and not through an agent; "And surely your blood of your lives will I require" (Gen. 9:5), referring to suicide; "At the hand of every beast will I require it" (Gen. 9:5), referring to one who places another before a wild animal for it to devour; "And at the hand of man, even at the hand of every man's brother, will I require the life of man" (Gen. 9:5), referring to one who hires others to kill someone. In these last three cases, the verb "require" is explicitly used to show that the judgment is reserved for heaven.

Code, Laws concerning Murder and the Preservation of Life 2:2–3

Maimonides lists various kinds of homicide that do not incur the punishment of court-imposed death, emphasizing that perpetrators are nonetheless liable by the laws of heaven. Killing one who is mortally ill is, therefore, yet another category of homicide that is not punishable by the laws of man, though subject to divine punishment.

Maimonides cites Genesis 9:5–6 as the biblical source for the assertion that the prohibition against taking life applies in all these cases despite the fact that no human punishment is imposed:

5. And surely your blood of your lives will I require; at the hand of every beast will I require it; and at the hand of man, even at the hand of every man's brother, will I require the life of man.
6. Whoever sheds man's blood, by man shall his blood be shed.

According to the Talmud,[14] these biblical verses, which God spoke to Noah and his sons after the Flood, are the source for the prohibition against bloodshed, which is one of the seven Noahide laws. The seven Noahide laws constitute a universally-applicable set of legal rules that some see as the Jewish version of natural law. It appears, therefore, that Maimonides is of the opinion that the prohibition against killing in the specific kinds of homicide in question is grounded in universal natural justice.

Support for the view that killing one who is mortally ill contravenes the fundamental, universal prohibition against any form of bloodshed can be found in Maimonides' ruling that a Noahide who kills one who is mortally ill is punished by death imposed by the court, as is a Noahide who kills an embryo.

A Noahide who kills a person, even if he kills an embryo in the mother's womb, is put to death. So too, if he kills one suffering from a fatal disease (*treifa*), or ties a man with a rope and puts him before a lion, or leaves him in a famished condition in consequence of which

14 bSanhedrin 57a–b.

> the man dies of starvation, he is executed, for in the last analysis he caused the death of the victim.
>
> *Code*, Laws concerning Kings and Wars 9:4

According to the talmudic principle that the giving of the Torah at Sinai was not intended to render permissible the things that had been forbidden by the Noahide prohibitions,[15] but rather to add to them, it follows that Jewish law prohibits the aforementioned sorts of homicide, and though no criminal sanction is levied on the perpetrator, regards them as incurring divine punishment.

3.3.v Extra-legal penalties for killing one who is mortally ill

In Jewish law, both the King and the court have the authority to impose extra-legal penalties, including capital punishment.[16] Maimonides invokes this authority in a novel ruling governing those who transgress the prohibition against bloodshed in contexts where they are exempt from punishment by the court:

> Regarding any of these or similar murderers who are not subject to being condemned to die by verdict of the court, if a king of Israel wishes to put them to death by royal decree for the benefit of society, he has a right to do so. Similarly, if the court deems it proper to put them to death as an emergency measure, it has the authority to do as it deems fit, provided that circumstances warrant such action.
>
> *Code*, Laws concerning Murder and the Preservation of Life 2:4

Maimonides maintains that the killer of one who is mortally ill, though by law exempt from court-imposed punishment, can nonetheless be put to death by royal decree, or as an exigency ruling by the court.

Maimonides' underlying motivation for this ruling can, perhaps, be detected in his justification of the talmudic provision that a murderer who escapes the death penalty by virtue of technical defects in the testimony against him "is put into a cell and fed on a minimum of bread and water until his stomach contracts, and then he is given barley so that his stomach splits under the stress of his sickness."[17] Maimonides explains that such measures are not adopted against other types of offenders whose

15 Mekhilta de-Rabbi Ishmael, masekhta de-nezikin, 4 (Horowitz edition, p. 263): "Isi b. Akiva says: Before the giving of the Torah, we were warned against shedding blood. After the giving of the Torah, [is it conceivable that] instead of being made stricter, the laws were made lighter?! In truth, the Sages said: he is exempt from judgment by the human court, but his judgment is left to heaven."

16 See Chapter Three above, "Exigency authority"; E.B. Quint and N.S. Hecht, *Jewish Jurisprudence* (New York: 1980), 1:139–213.

17 *Code*, Laws concerning Murder and the Preservation of Life 4:8; and see bSanhedrin 81b.

transgressions incur capital punishment, but who cannot be convicted due to defective testimony, for "although there are worse crimes than bloodshed, none causes such destruction to civilized society as bloodshed" (ibid., 4:9). Clearly, Maimonides views the preservation of civilized society as a fundamental value that mandates recourse to extra-judicial punishment.

By harnessing exegetical and ethical arguments, Maimonides in effect eliminates the Talmud's exemption of the killer of a *treifa* from humanly-administered punishment. The Maimonidean approach has been widely accepted by subsequent halakhic authorities. Indeed, his ruling is cited in the responsa of two recent halakhic authorities, R. Liebes and R. Moses Feinstein. R. Feinstein wrote as follows:

> The prohibition against killing a *treifa* applies equally to Israelites and Noahides, since there is nothing permitted to an Israelite that is forbidden to a Noahide, and Maimonides explicitly writes, in Laws concerning Murder and the Preservation of Life 2:8, that the killer of a *treifa* is "exempt [from being punished by court-imposed death] by the laws of man," which means that he is liable by the laws of heaven, in addition to the fact that the act is prohibited. And it is as he wrote in section 2, concerning one who hires an assassin to kill his fellow, or ties him up and leaves him in front of a lion: "he ... has committed the crime of murder, and is liable to death at the hands of heaven, but there is no capital punishment at the hands of the court." Even if [Maimonides' view is rejected and] it is argued that [the killer] is exempt even from [the punishment of] death at the hand of heaven in these cases, in any event the biblical prohibition [against bloodshed] certainly applies to Israelites as well as Noahides, though a Noahide is executed for [transgressing].... And even though an Israelite is exempt from [the punishment of court-imposed] death, the prohibition applicable to him is more severe than that applicable to a Noahide.... Therefore, the Ahiezer's view[18] [that physicians may carry out a dangerous experimental therapy on a terminally ill patient] ... since he is in any case mortally ill, and moreover, an Israelite [who kills someone mortally ill] is treated more leniently [than a Noahide], is completely incorrect.
>
> *Responsa Igrot Moshe*, YD 3:36

R. Isaac Leibes takes the same position:

> Accordingly, someone suffering from a serious disease for which, according to medical experts, there is no cure, though he can go on living for a long time, is considered mortally ill (*treifa*), and one who

18 R. Chaim Ozer Grodzinski, *Responsa Ahiezer*, YD 16:6.

kills him is exempt [from punishment] by human law.... But this has no concrete bearing on our case [where it might have been assumed that the decision to terminate life-prolonging treatment would be easier than in the case of a *goses*]. From a legal point of view, the difference between liability by human law and liability by the laws of heaven is of no consequence, since in both cases the killer is called a murderer, as Maimonides wrote in Laws concerning Murder and the Preservation of Life 3:10.

Responsa Beit Avi , #153

R. Feinstein adduces Maimonides' view to rebut R. Chaim Ozer Grodzinski's contention that performing a high-risk operation on a terminally ill patient is permissible, given that one who kills a *treifa* is exempt from the punishment of court-imposed death. That is, both R. Feinstein and R. Liebes reiterate Maimonides' principled opposition to interpreting this exemption as in any way condoning such a killing, or implying that it will go unpunished.

Let us now consider a fascinating historical instance where the Maimonidean model for surmounting the Talmud's exemption of the killer of someone mortally ill from punishment by a human court is adduced. Joshua Lorki, a fifteenth-century apostate, wrote a tract slandering the Talmud. In response, R. Solomon b. Shimon Duran (Rashbash), a contemporary of Lorki, wrote a work rebutting the charges Lorki had leveled against the Talmud. One of the charges put forward by Lorki was that by talmudic law, the killer of a *treifa* is exempt from the death penalty, a law Lorki claimed was patently immoral. In rebutting this charge, the Rashbash invoked the Maimonidean position on this issue, and in addition, engaged in what might be characterized as comparative jurisprudence, citing the legal treatment meted out in Christian countries to the killer of someone mortally ill:

Since the *treifa* is damaged in such a way that he cannot live, why should his attacker die? Consequently, he is exempt from death [imposed by the court], since the Torah stated only, "he that kills a man shall be put to death" (Lev. 24:21), and the victim in this case is no longer classified as a man, for he is already classified as dead, since he will not live [long] after his injury [lit., fall]. However, if the court sees fit to punish him—they punish him. Also, they do not save him from a blood redeemer,[19] and if he is killed by a blood redeemer, [the redeemer] is not put to death.... But we do not impose the punishment of death unless there is clear evidence, and this type of case is left to

19 According to biblical law, a murder can be avenged by a "blood redeemer"—a close relative of the victim—who may kill the killer. The killer can avoid this fate by fleeing to a city of refuge, where he will be safe from the blood redeemer while the case is heard by the court; see Numbers 35:9–21, Deuteronomy 19:4–6.

> the court to deal with, and falls within its purview.... And this is better than the legal practice of the Christians, whereby the killer will incur the death penalty, but the king will pardon him ... and whoever compares the two [legal systems] will see the superiority of our holy Torah to their legal practice, as the light is superior to the darkness, provided that his scrutiny is amicable, and he thinks it through, and ponders it rationally.
>
> *Milhemet Mitzva*, 33

3.3 Applying the categories in particular cases

The tremendous strides made in the field of life-sustaining technology in recent decades have resulted in a range of physical states that seem to straddle life and death. Death itself has become a process rather than a discrete event. One can, for example, be brain-dead even though one's heart is still beating. The seminal case illustrating the impact of this technology on the law is that of Karen Ann Quinlan, in which the Supreme Court of New Jersey was asked to consider the legality of disconnecting an artificial respirator from a comatose patient in a persistent vegetative state. In the context of Jewish law, the following questions arise: What category do patients of this type fall under, that of the 'dying' (*goses*), or that of the 'mortally ill' (*treifa*)? If the former, what is the relevance of the three-day time limit? Is a respirator an impediment to death or not? If Karen Ann Quinlan is defined as 'mortally ill'—a category that encompasses the category of '*goses* at the hands of man'—what is the significance of the exemption of the killer of a *treifa* from the punishment of court-imposed death vis-à-vis those involved in the termination of Quinlan's treatment? These and related questions must be considered when applying the halakhic categories to contemporary cases.

Traditionally, the category deemed applicable to the dying has been that of the *goses*, the relevant talmudic principle being that the *goses* is to be considered a living person in every respect. This category is best suited to the context in which the critically ill person lay on his death-bed at home, surrounded by family and friends, possibly issuing final instructions and requests. Clearly, however, this model is generally not appropriate in the contemporary context, as most people today die in hospitals, under very different circumstances. The questions raised in cases such as that of Quinlan pertain primarily to medical technology, and the ramifications of terminating life support. It has been suggested that in the contemporary context, the appropriate category is not, in fact, that of the *goses*, but rather that of the *treifa*.

> For all its ambiguity, the status of *treifa* would seem virtually perfectly matched to the picture of Karen Ann Quinlan drawn at the Quinlan trial, whether or not Karen is also regarded as *goses*. The physicians were virtually unanimous in their prognosis for Karen: her

> brain was irreparably damaged, and even with the full benefit of continued mechanical respirators, high calorie nasal-gastric feeding, and antibiotic treatment to ward off infection, Karen has no more than a year to live. There was also testimony that, with some allowance for the unknown etiology of Karen's disease, there were no known cases similar to Karen's in which the results were other than fatal. Thus, insofar as the testimony is reliable, the standards relevant to a determination of *treifa* are precisely met. It follows that under Jewish law, termination of treatment impeding Karen's death, or for that matter, more active steps resulting in Karen's death, would not constitute homicide punishable by human courts.[20]

On Weisbard's analysis, someone suffering from a serious disease that has no known cure is considered mortally ill (*treifa*), even if he can go on living for a relatively lengthy period. Under Jewish law, Weisbard argues, his killer would be exempt from punishment by court-imposed death, unlike the killer of a 'natural' *goses*, who indeed incurs that punishment. In the case of a patient in a state such as Quinlan's, therefore, in ruling on the criminal culpability of medical personnel involved in disconnecting the respirator, there are grounds for leniency.

R. Liebes, too, is of the opinion that Quinlan falls under the category of 'one who is mortally ill' (*treifa*), but unlike Weisbard, he emphasizes the prohibition against killing one who is mortally ill, and the divine punishment such a killing incurs:

> Therefore, in the case of an ill person whose life is dependent on a certain machine, should someone sever the connection between him and the machine, he is considered a murderer, even in the case of a *treifa*, and not only in the case of a *goses*, for one who is liable [only] according to the laws of heaven is also considered a murderer, and disconnecting the machine is analogous to that which is described in tractate Sanhedrin: "Rava said: If one bound his fellow in the sun and he died, he is liable; but if the sun had yet to appear ... he is exempt." And see Maimonides, Laws concerning Murder and the Preservation of Life 3:10. Disconnecting the respirator is similar to binding his neighbor in the sun, since immediately after the disconnection, the patient dies, for his life and breath are entirely dependent on the machine. There is no analogy here to the removal of the woodchopper,[21] since in that case, the impediment is merely abstract, whereas in this case, the impediment removed is tangible, and directly terminates his vitality.
>
> *Responsa Beit Avi*, HM #153

20 A. Weisbard, "The bioethics of Jewish law," 14 *Isr. L. Rev.* (1979), 328.
21 This allusion will be clarified below.

According to R. Liebes, the nature of the sanction—divine or human—applied to the killer of the mortally-ill patient (*treifa*), that is, to the perpetrator of the mercy-killing, makes no difference, since in both cases he is considered a murderer. As Maimonides puts it, "the offender in each of these cases is not put to death by the court, but he is deemed a murderer, and He that avengeth blood will require blood [i.e., he will be punished by God]."[22] R. Liebes maintains that someone who disconnects a patient from an artificial respirator is considered a murderer even if the patient is classified as mortally ill (*treifa*).

R. Liebes's rejection of the leniency Weisbard suggests would be appropriate vis-à-vis those who disconnect life-sustaining devices in cases of PVS patients is upheld by other contemporary decisors.[23] From a moral perspective, it is clear that classifying a patient as falling under the category of 'one who is dying' (*goses*), where the operative assumption is that such a patient is a living being in all respects, is much less risky than classifying a patient as 'mortally ill,' with the attendant consequence that one who kills such a patient, that is, who engages in mercy-killing, is not subject to the punishment of death by the court. Apprehension about inappropriate classification of patients as 'mortally ill,' or in other words, fear of the slippery slope, may account for the reluctance of some halakhic authorities to classify patients as 'mortally ill.' In the final analysis, however, we must ask whether the moral advantage gained by not applying the *treifa* category to PVS patients is outweighed by other factors, such as the family's suffering and privation.

4 The *goses*: active versus passive euthanasia

Let us now turn to a fundamental distinction relating to the *goses*, namely, the distinction between precipitating death and removing an impediment to it. This distinction is similar to the contemporary distinction between active and passive euthanasia. Is disconnection from life-sustaining technology to be considered an instance of precipitating death, or of removing an impediment to death?

4.1 The halakhic perspective

The distinction between actively precipitating death and removing an impediment to death is articulated in *Sefer Hasidim*, the major work of the Jewish pietists of medieval Franco-Germany known as Hasidei Ashkenaz.[24]

22 *Code*, Laws concerning Murder and the Preservation of Life 3:10.
23 See *Responsa Igrot Moshe*, YD 3:36; A. Steinberg, "Euthanasia" (Hebrew), in idem (ed.), *Sefer Assia*, vol. 4 (Jerusalem: 1983), 454.
24 The work is attributed to R. Judah the Pious of Regensburg (1150–1217), but parts of it were authored by others in his circle.

> One is not to cause someone to not die quickly. If, for example, someone is dying and near that house, a woodchopper is chopping wood, and the soul cannot depart, we remove the woodcutter from the vicinity. And one is not to place salt on the tongue [of the *goses*] so that he will not die. And if someone is dying and says that he cannot die unless he is taken to a different place, he should not be moved from his present location.
>
> *Sefer Hasidim*, §723

The first sentence in this passage expresses a principle that became very influential in subsequent halakhic discussions about treatment of the dying: one is not allowed to prolong the demise of a dying person. To appreciate how radical this thesis is, we need only recall that saving life—even life that is 'for the hour' (*hayei shaa*)—is a fundamental principle of Judaism, even superseding observance of the Sabbath. The passage mentions three elements that—according to the folk-wisdom of the time—were thought to postpone death: noise (of woodchopping), putting salt on the dying person's tongue, and the place where the dying person lay on his death-bed. With regard to the first of these elements, the author of *Sefer Hasidim* rules that the source of the noise should be removed, in order that the death not be prolonged. This is not merely a dispensation to remove the source of the noise, but a directive to shorten, as much as possible, the dying person's death throes. With regard to the second element, R. Judah the Pious rules that salt should not be placed on the dying person's tongue, but his position on the removal of salt from the dying man's tongue is not clear. As to the third element, the author of *Sefer Hasidim* rules that even if the place where the dying person is lying is hindering his death, there is no dispensation to move him, even if he requests this himself. The reason for this prohibition is not stated explicitly, and in the halakhic literature, the prohibition has been explained in two different ways. Some see it as rooted in the concern that moving the dying person, or carrying him from one place to another, might cause his death, and as we saw above, according to Masekhet Semahot, moving someone who is dying, in a manner that precipitates death, is considered bloodshed. Others contend that the concern is that the dying person will be moved to a place where death will occur more rapidly, which is considered active precipitation of death, and thus prohibited.

Sefer Hasidim is not an authoritative code of Jewish law, but many authoritative texts, including the *Shulhan Arukh*, refer to its rulings on how the dying are to be treated. This reflects the fact that, prior to the modern era, it was commonly believed that certain practices were efficacious with respect to preventing death, and tension arose between these widespread folk beliefs and the normative halakha governing treatment of the dying. This tension, and more generally, the interplay of folk practices and rabbinical directives, is much in evidence in the medieval halakhic literature.

Over time, the distinction, first propounded in *Sefer Hasidim*, between causing death, and removing an impediment to it, was further elaborated on, as the following passages illustrate. *Shiltei Hagiborim*, by R. Joshua Boaz, a sixteenth-century gloss on Alfasi's code, asserts:

> There would appear to be grounds for forbidding the custom, practiced by some, in the case of someone who is dying and his soul cannot depart, of removing the pillow from underneath the *goses* so that he will die quickly. For they say that the bird feathers in the bedding prevent the soul from leaving the body. On several occasions I protested vociferously against this evil custom, but my view did not prevail, and my own teachers disagreed with me. And R. Nathan of Igra, of blessed memory, also wrote that it was permitted. Some years later I found support for my view in *Sefer Hasidim*, §723, according to which, "if someone is dying and says that he cannot die unless he is taken to a different place, he should not be moved from his present location." It is true that this statement from *Sefer Hasidim* requires careful examination, since at the beginning of the passage it says that if someone is dying and "near that house, a woodchopper is chopping wood, and the soul cannot depart, we remove the woodcutter from the vicinity," which contradicts what is written after that [i.e., it seems to indicate that one may, in fact, take steps to precipitate the death of the *goses*]. This can, however, be reconciled by saying that certainly, anything that causes the dying person not to die quickly is forbidden, such as chopping wood in the vicinity so that the departure of his soul will be delayed, or putting salt on his tongue so that he will not die quickly—all this is forbidden, as follows from what is stated there [in *Sefer Hasidim*]. And removal of every causative factor [i.e., factor causing prolongation of dying, and impeding death] is also permitted. But doing something that will actively cause a quick death and the departure of his soul is forbidden. And therefore it is forbidden to move the *goses* from one place and put him somewhere else so that his soul will depart. And therefore it is also forbidden to place the keys to the synagogue under the head of the *goses* so that he will die quickly, since this too expedites the departure of his soul.
>
> Accordingly, if there is something there that prevents his soul from departing, it is permitted to remove that factor, and there is nothing to be concerned about, since he who does so is not "touching a flickering lamp" (mSemahot 1:4) and is not performing any action. But placing something on the *goses* or moving him from one place to another so that his soul will depart quickly appears to definitely be forbidden, since it constitutes "touching a flickering lamp."
>
> *Shiltei Hagiborim*, bMoed Katan 16b (Alfasi pagination)

R. Boaz, author of *Shiltei Hagiborim*, clearly felt that the custom of removing feather pillows from under the dying person's head should be eradicated, but does not explicitly say why. He views removal of the pillow as a death-precipitating act, perhaps because it entails moving the patient's head. R. Boaz discusses the import of the declarations in *Sefer Hasidim*, and reaches the following conclusion: if an external factor, for instance, the noise of woodchopping, is prolonging the death throes of a dying person, it is permitted, and even appropriate, to remove the impediment to death. But it is forbidden to have recourse to any action believed to actively precipitate the dying person's death, such as putting the synagogue keys under his head.

The distinction between precipitating death and removing an impediment to it was adopted by the sixteenth-century Polish halakhic authority R. Moses Isserles (Rema) in his glosses on the *Shulhan Arukh*. His formulation is based on the *Sefer Hasidim* and the *Shiltei Hagiborim*:

> And so too, it is forbidden to cause the dying person to die quickly, as is the case, for instance, if someone has been dying for a long time, and his soul cannot depart. [In such a case], it is forbidden to remove the pillow and cushion from underneath him, in line with the popular saying that the feathers of certain birds cause this [the soul's inability to depart]. And the *goses* is not to be moved from where he is, and so too, it is forbidden to put the keys to the synagogue under his head so that he will depart. But if there is something that is causing a hindrance to the departure of the soul, for example, if adjacent to that house there is a knocking sound such as the chopping of wood, or there is salt on his tongue, and these are hindering the soul's departure, then they may be removed, since there is no act involved in this at all, merely the removal of an impediment.
>
> *Rema, SA,* YD 339:1

The "knocking sound" and "salt on the tongue" mentioned here are concepts that recur in the subsequent halakhic literature on treatment of the dying. They represent categories of mechanisms resorted to in order to prolong life. Below, we will see that twentieth-century halakhic analyses invoke these concepts, applying them to sophisticated life-sustaining technologies.

R. Joshua Falk Katz, writing a generation after the Rema, also weighs in on the pillow-removal question:

> And be aware that what the Rema wrote was in fact [a reiteration of] the words of the *Shiltei Hagiborim* on Alfasi, the third chapter in Moed Katan, para. 398 … and these views should be examined carefully, for it seems that even though initially R. Boaz wrote that it appeared to him that he should forbid the practice of removing feather pillows, in

> any event, in the end, he found a contradiction in *Sefer Hasidim*, and concluded—in order to reconcile the contradiction—that he had to make a distinction. It appears, therefore, that he [author of *Shiltei Hagiborim*] only prohibited moving the dying man from one place to another. But to take away the pillow from underneath him gently, in order to remove the feathers, which are a causative factor, is not prohibited. And as to that which he wrote at the beginning, namely, "there would appear to be grounds for forbidding," and so on—the implication of "there would appear to be" is that the truth, after he had reconciled the contradiction in *Sefer Hasidim*, was otherwise.
>
> *Derisha, Tur,* YD 339

R. Falk has reservations about the Rema's ruling, and maintains that according to the *Shiltei Hagiborim*, it is permitted to remove the pillow from under the head of the *goses*, since this is considered removal of an impediment rather than active precipitation of death.

Somewhat later, the seventeenth-century decisor R. Shabetai Hakohen (Shakh), in his *Siftei Kohen*, a commentary on the *Shulhan Arukh*, concurs with the Rema's ruling, but takes issue with his rationale for it:

> "And it is forbidden to remove the pillow and cushion," and so on.... since here, the prohibition is not due to the feathers, but the prohibition is grounded in the fact that it is forbidden to move the *goses*.
>
> *Shakh, SA*, YD 339:7

As noted above, the custom of removing feather pillows was fairly widespread, and a frequent source of tension between the laity and the rabbinical authorities. In the following passage, it is addressed by a seventeenth-century Turkish halakhic authority, R. Haim Benveniste:

> "And the pillow is not to be removed from underneath him," and so on. The compiler asserts: I have seen women, who, when a sick person is dying, and the pillow on which he is lying is made of bird feathers, remove the pillow from underneath him, saying that these feathers were preventing the soul from departing. In my youth, I challenged this practice, since it is counter to the baraita in Evel Rabbati ... and so too in *Shiltei Hagiborim* on the third chapter of Moed Katan, [R. Boaz] wrote that he too protested vociferously, seeking to put an end to this custom, but did not prevail, for his teachers disagreed with him, and R. Nathan of Igra wrote that it was permitted. It is therefore necessary to find a justification for those who permit this widely-practiced custom.
>
> It appears to me that what they said in Evel Rabbati, that "his jaws may not be bound," and all the other things mentioned there, do not apply except when the soul does not want to depart quickly, but there

is nothing preventing it from departing. Rather, its appointed time has not yet arrived, hence all the said things should not be done so as to hasten the death. But when the soul wants to depart, but there is something that is preventing it from departing, then it is permitted to remove the element that is preventing the soul from departing, since this is not precipitating death, for were it not for that element, it would depart. Proof for this can be found in *Sefer Hasidim*, §723, which states that "If someone is dying, and near that house, a woodchopper is chopping wood, and the soul cannot depart, we remove the woodcutter from the vicinity." And the reason for this is, as I wrote, that since the soul wants to depart, but the [sound of the] woodchopping is preventing it from doing so, we remove the impediment, and this does not constitute precipitation of death.

And regarding the other ruling in *Sefer Hasidim*, "if someone is dying and says that he cannot die unless he is taken to a different place, he should not be moved from his present location," it seems to me that the reason is that there is a distinction between doing something that is external to the body [of the *goses*], and doing something to the body [itself]. And the reason is that when one does something that is external to the body, this precipitates death, but precipitating death in this manner is permitted. But [that is different from] doing something to the body, which entails the pain caused by the movement; or alternatively, [*Sefer Hasidim* may be speaking of a case] where there is nothing that is preventing the soul from departing, but rather the soul itself is having difficulty departing, and therefore in *Sefer Hasidim*, [R. Judah the Pious] forbade moving him from his place. Accordingly, putting the keys to the synagogue under his head so that he will die quickly is forbidden.

Shiurei Kneset Hagedola, *Tur*, YD, Laws of Visiting the Sick, 4

The law on this issue was reformulated in the nineteenth century by R. Yehiel Mikhel Epstein:

The explication of [the Rema's] remark—given that earlier, it was explained that no act is to be performed that will hasten the death of a *goses*, such as removing the pillow from underneath him—is that he added that even if, in the view of those caring for the dying person, it would be meritorious to hasten his death for his own benefit, as for example, if he has been dying over a long period, and it is evident that he is suffering terribly, in any event it is forbidden to perform any act to achieve this end, since [the situation] is God's will. And needless to say, it is forbidden to remove the pillow from underneath him, an act that entails a significant moving of the head from a high to a low position, and even moving him slightly is forbidden. Even if nothing is done to his body at all, but the keys of the synagogue are simply slipped under his head without moving him at all—this is also forbidden, since in the final analysis the act is performed so that he will die quickly, even if the act is not done to the dying man's body [itself].

However, if there is something external [lit., from the side] that is preventing the soul from departing, it is permitted to remove it, for either the impediment is external, in which case, why should [the *goses*] suffer, given that the impediment is not caused by his body itself; or it is not [really] the impeding factor, hence removal will not be efficacious at all?! Furthermore, removing salt from his tongue is not considered an action, since it only involves a minute movement. Presumably it was placed there to prolong his life, hence it follows that it can be removed. Although some authorities hesitate about this, in truth, there is nothing to be apprehensive about.

Arukh Hashulhan, YD 339:4

On this reformulation of the law, if the impediment is external to the body, it may be removed, but nothing may be done to the dying person's body. Moving the body is forbidden, since it precipitates death, but removing the salt is permitted, because it entails only the most minute movement, and moreover, putting the salt on his tongue was wrongful in the first place.

4.2 Contemporary application of the distinction

R. Epstein's restatement of the Rema's ruling served as the basis for responsa on disconnecting an artificial respirator from a comatose patient in a persistent vegetative state, two of which we will quote from at length. The first was written by R. Eliezer Waldenburg, a halakhic authority on medical matters; the second by R. Aryeh Grossnass, who served on the London Beth Din after World War II.

9. … even the Rema would agree that positive steps may be taken to remove an artificial respirator, since all that is being done thereby is the disconnection of external life-support machinery, and no act at all is being done that could terminate independent functioning, since it has already been established that this has ceased.

   … Furthermore, if the respirator was removed to ascertain whether the patient still had some vitality [i.e., the ability to breathe without life-support], or it stopped working for some reason, and it became apparent that there was no longer any independent vitality, not in the brain and not in the heart, then not only is it permissible not to reconnect it to his body, but it is forbidden to do so. For it is already clear that this will not generate independent vitality, and its sole effect will be to extend the impediment to the departure of his soul. And if they transgressed and reconnected it, it is obligatory to remove it.

10. A further clarification of the Rema's words, which also supports what we have said, can be found in the explanation given by the eminent author of the *Arukh Hashulhan* . . . from which the following three points emerge:

(a) Performance of any act that will precipitate death is prohibited, even if it is not done to the body of the *goses*;

(b) To what does this apply? Where the vitality that [the *goses*] still possesses is independent vitality. But if there is doubt as to whether the vitality is due to his own body or caused by an external factor, then it is permitted to remove this causative factor [the life-support] on the strength of an 'either-or' argument (*mima nafshakh*): if the impediment [to death] is really due to this factor, then why should we let him suffer, since the vitality is not due to [the functioning of] his own body; and if the impediment is not really due to this factor, its removal will not be efficacious at all [with regard to bringing about death].

(c) There is a dispensation to remove the causative factor [the life-support] not only when it is produced by a separate apparatus external to him, but even it has been connected to his body (like putting salt on his tongue) with the goal of prolonging his life. If afterwards they see that it causes him pain, in preventing the soul from departing, the causative factor may also be disconnected from his body. There are two reasons for this. The first is that "it is not considered an action, since it only involves a minute movement." And secondly, "presumably it was placed there to prolong his life, hence it follows that it can be removed." And it appears that the *Arukh Hashulhan*'s second point is that it is permitted to remove the salt on the tongue not only because it ought not to have been put there in the first place, but because [the dying person's] vitality and continued life due to the salt is not due to his own body, and therefore terminating this kind of vitality is not considered terminating life, and it is permitted to remove it. . . .

11. It further follows that it is generally forbidden to connect [the *goses*] to anything that will cause prolongation of his life, where it is clear to us that by doing so he will not be able to live an independently-functioning life, and the vitality that will be imparted to him will not be due to his own body. Therefore, if one transgressed and connected him [to a life-support device], if he afterwards sees that he is suffering terribly, he is permitted (and perhaps obligated) to remove the device. The belief that one should not do so because 'it is God's will' is inapplicable here, since the provisional life that he still has is the result of human action alone. And not only that, but prolonging life under these circumstances is contrary to the divine will, as we saw in *Sefer Hasidim* §234:

> And one is not to call out to him at the moment the soul departs, lest the soul return and suffer terrible torment. "There is a time to die" (Eccles. 3:2). Why does Ecclesiastes have to state this? Because when a person is dying, and his soul is departing, one does not call out to him so that his soul will return to the body, since he can live only a few days more in any case, and during that time, he will suffer terribly. So why does it not say, 'There is a time to live?' Because this is not determined by man, who has no sovereignty over the day of death.

> ... It follows that no resuscitative action should be taken when it is clear to us that for the patient in question, it is already the "time to die," and the result of any such action performed on him will only suffice to retain his soul tenuously for a few days, which will be full of suffering and torment ... and it is not within the scope of the authority of any human being to maintain such a life when it is evident that this person is in a "time to die" state.
>
> *Responsa Tzitz Eliezer* 13:89

R. Waldenburg opposes sustaining life by means of machines such as artificial respirators, if the patient has lost all capacity to live on his own, and there is no possibility he will regain that capacity.

Another contemporary authority who relies on the *Arukh Hashulhan* is R. Aryeh Grossnass:

> Where a *goses* has lost all his independent vitality, and there is no medical knowledge or treatment that will allow him to live independently, but there are only external devices that impede his death, such as a knocking sound, then since he has no independent vitality of his own, this does not constitute 'life for the hour' (*hayei shaa*), and the obligation to save life does not apply here. And this is explained in *Arukh Hashulhan* (YD 339:4), which states: "However, if there is something external [lit., from the side] that is preventing the soul from departing, it is permitted to remove it ... why should [the *goses*] suffer, given that the impediment is not caused by his body itself ...?" And not only that, but there is an obligation to remove the impediment so that he will not suffer torment....
>
> To extend the life of a patient who is unable to breathe without an artificial respirator, and without which he cannot live for even an instant, is tantamount to making a knocking sound, since he has no vitality at all, only breath; and since the breath and the heartbeat are not due to his own independent vitality, this does not constitute 'life for the hour.' And it is certainly forbidden to operate such a machine on the Sabbath, since the principle that saving life supersedes the Sabbath (*pikuah nefesh*) is inapplicable here. And it may be that even during the week, one is not permitted to operate the machine, and, as

> mentioned above, there is an obligation to remove the artificial respirator, and possibly, one is duty-bound to do so.
>
> *Responsa Lev Aryeh* 2:37

R. Grossnass distinguishes between a dying person who still has some sort of independent vitality, and a dying person who has lost all such vitality. The former is regarded as having 'life for the hour' (*hayei shaa*), which one is obliged to preserve and prolong. The latter, however, does not, hence there is no obligation to prolong his life, and it may even be inappropriate to do so. R. Grossnass asserts that the principle that saving live supersedes observance of the Sabbath does not apply in the latter case, and it is therefore forbidden to operate an artificial respirator for such a patient on the Sabbath.

But R. Grossnass's argument has been critiqued:

> Dayan Grossnass suggests [that OH 329:3–4 refers to] ... someone who can live on his own bodily powers without external aid, albeit for only a short time. For such a person one is duty bound both to profane the Sabbath and to give medicines to preserve or extend his life-span even if he is in severe pain. [He argues that] Rema in YD, on the other hand, refers to someone whose natural life has already ended and who is only living by means of external factors such as salt or noise. Such a person is deemed not to have a true life at all, and although he may not be killed by positive action on his body, one can allow him to die if in severe pain, and the Sabbath cannot be profaned for him even if he is not in pain. Accordingly, [Dayan Grossness] rules that if someone has permanent lung failure he cannot be put on a respirator on the Sabbath, and says that if he is in pain, one presumably should disconnect it at all times. This distinction between intrinsically viable (although short) life and intrinsically non-viable life has its attractions, and the Dayan quotes some authority for it, but it does present difficulties. For example, what is the law where someone has permanent lung failure and is on an iron lung? Can one not profane the Sabbath for him if he is fully conscious and not in pain? And what of a patient who will always require an artificial heart valve, artery or kidney transplant? Indeed, if the basic test is whether natural life has ended and only external forces maintain it, one could not logically profane the Sabbath to give a diabetic his insulin injection or to administer dialysis for renal failure.[25]

The critique, then, is that the notion of what has been termed "independent vitality" requires considerable further elucidation if it is to serve as a helpful criterion vis-à-vis the permissibility of administering

25 G. Halibard, "Euthanasia," 1 *Jewish Law Annual* (1978), 197.

life-sustaining technologies. Defining the point at which independent vitality no longer exists is also problematic with respect to R. Waldenburg's approach. The following passage, which reports an exchange between R. Waldenburg and a physician, provides a good illustration of this problem.

> In my previous responsum, I emphasized repeatedly that a respirator may only be removed if "there was no longer any independent vitality, not in the brain and not in the heart," and so on. You ... say that these comments are not comprehensible, since if indeed [the dying patient] no longer has any independent vitality, not in the brain and not in the heart, the patient is completely dead according to all possible definitions, and it is clear that with respect to someone completely dead, there is no need to ask about disconnecting a machine or treatment.
>
> And my reply is that this is indeed the case, and my dispensation to remove the respirator is based on the principle that the patient is, indeed, considered dead. The problem in the said circumstances is that the patient manifests a certain vitality that is perceptible due to an external causative element that generates movement in his body, and also prevents the body from being overcome with signs of death—blueness, putrefaction, and so on. And regarding this point I explained and proved that such provisional life, which is generated by an external cause, is not considered real life, and the removal of this external element from the body is no more than removal of an impediment [to death]. Moreover, there is no need to be concerned with the possibility that there is, deep within the body, some spark of independent life which has thus far gone undetected [and is being maintained by the respirator], and may, over time, by the continued operation of the respirator, reveal itself and revive the entire body. As to this concern, we need only take into consideration the words of the Sages regarding the indicators of death. And since it has been established that there is no independent life in either the brain or the heart, and that without the respirator, the patient would be dead, it is permissible to turn off and remove the machine.
>
> *Responsa Tzitz Eliezer* 14:81

R. Waldenburg's reply clearly indicates the practical limitations of the 'independent vitality' criterion for the definition of death-impeding treatment. As the doctor observed, there can be no obligation to resuscitate a corpse! It is, however, important to note that R. Waldenburg's responsum was written a decade before the Israeli Chief Rabbinate recognized brain-death in the context of heart transplants.[26]

26 See section 5 below.

At the end of the first responsum by R. Waldenburg cited above (13:89), he adds a different justification for permitting disconnection of a respirator:

> I now turn to your suggestion:
>
> > Every patient brought to the emergency ward following an accident, poisoning, etc., even if their brains are crushed, should be treated with every possible resuscitative treatment, including connection to all the available [life-preserving] devices. These devices should be controlled by timers similar to those used on the Sabbath, and set for short periods, e.g., 12 or 24 hours. During this period, the doctors will be able to check all the clinical indicators, using auxiliary texts such as lab tests, x-rays, and so on, and to decide whether the patient has any chance of staying alive. Then when the devices stop, they can be immediately reactivated. Should it become clear that, for instance, the brain has been crushed, and the patient has no chance, or his spine is broken and his brain has been totally severed from his body, then when the devices stop operating, the doctor is not obligated to reactivate them.
>
> I am entirely in agreement with your suggestion, and applaud it. And in light of what I explained and elucidated above, in discussing this law, I would even say that it meets the standards of the most strictly observant, with one additional provision. After all the detailed tests are performed, as you suggested, [I would require that] when the operation of the devices is stopped by the timers, another examination be performed to determine the patient's ability to breathe independently for [a period of from] one to twenty minutes, and after repeating this test several times, if it is determined that the patient cannot do so, then the doctor will not be obligated to reactivate the machines. For we are not to budge from the words of the Sages that checking the nose for independent breathing and cardiac activity is definitive here.
>
> And it is thus evident that in the light of all this, we must say not only that the doctor will not, then, be further obligated to reactivate the device, but also that she will be forbidden to do so. Any further connection to the device will at most result only in a slight movement that does not render the patient what we would consider to be [truly] alive, and causes only immeasurable pain and suffering. And this is similar to the Rema's statement, in *Darkhei Moshe*, forbidding the placing of salt on the tongue [of a *goses*] so that he will not die quickly.... And this is in accordance with the explanation given by R. Judah Ayash, of blessed memory, in his *Shevet Yehuda*, on YD ad loc. [339], that the rationale [for the prohibition] is that [such acts] cause [the *goses*] suffering during the departure of the soul. And consult his remarks. And in the case in question, from the description you [the questioner] have provided in your letter, the pain and suffering caused by impeding the

> soul's departure is many times greater and more severe. And I can also say that we should not downplay the additional consideration you mentioned, namely, that [keeping the patient attached to the respirator] causes the family an enormous financial outlay, and very many families become impoverished, and it serves no purpose.
>
> *Responsa Tzitz Eliezer* 13:89

4.3 Limitations on the dispensation to remove impediments to death

A minority of contemporary authorities, R. Haim David Halevi being the foremost example, have upheld the classic distinction between precipitating death and removing an impediment to death without incorporating the subtle distinctions extracted by rabbis Waldenberg and Grossnass from the remarks in *Arukh Hashulhan*. Rather, they simply categorize all contemporary life-prolonging medical treatments as impediments to death, and permit their termination once it has been determined that a patient is a *goses*.

But this approach is simplistic and problematic. As we now have the technology to keep alive many patients who would formerly have died, the line between precipitating death and removing an impediment to it is an extremely difficult one to draw. Is an intravenous drip an impediment? Does the administration of a life-shortening pain-killing drug constitute an act of precipitating death? Consider the following ruling by R. Immanuel Jakobovits, a pioneer in the field of Jewish biomedical ethics and Chief Rabbi of the United Kingdom from 1967 to 1991:

> The Rema's decision, and its sources, can provide a basis for a dispensation to remove an impediment only when the patient is already dying, a state that ordinarily does not last longer than three days.... And even then, it is only permitted to withhold from the patient something that is maintaining his life temporarily, such as salt on the tongue or a knocking sound adjacent to him. And it is clear that if the death-impeding intervention consists in [supplying] food or drink, without which he cannot live, then certainly, it is forbidden to remove it, for [the Rema] mentioned only things that are not essential to life, but not food, which is an absolutely essential requirement for life.... And it is definitely forbidden to starve a *goses* in order to precipitate his death.[27]

R. Jakobovits suggests that three main restrictions be placed on the dispensation to remove an impediment, all of which are based on the examples cited by the Rema: i) euthanasia by way of removing an

27 R. Immanuel Jakobovits, "The law relating to the precipitation of death of a terminally ill and suffering patient" (Hebrew), *Hapardes* 31 (1957), 18.

impediment to death is permitted only if the patient is dying (*goses*); ii) removal of the impediment is permitted only if the impediment hinders death for just a short while ("something that is maintaining his life temporarily"). But if the impediment may hinder death for a long time, its removal is not permitted; iii) removal of the impediment is permitted only when the impediment itself is not necessary for life. For example, even though they hinder death, food and hydration cannot be withheld.

This approach was also endorsed by R. Solomon Zalman Auerbach.[28] But R. Isaac Liebes disagrees. R. Isaac Leibes too upholds the classic distinction between removing an impediment to death and precipitating death, but his conclusions differ somewhat from those of R. Jakobovits.

> A *goses* who survives for more than three days is considered as if he were already dead, since the relatives who left him [i.e., were with him three days earlier, but departed, and do not know his condition] are required to mourn for him. In any event, it is forbidden to touch him, as explained above, as long as he still has his soul, to avoid precipitating death. But medicines need not be administered to him, since [withholding them] is only removing an impediment [to death]. This is especially so in the view of those who disagree with the author of *Turei Zahav*, and rule in accordance with the Rema's view that it is permitted to remove salt from the tongue since [this requires] only a slight touch. Hence extraordinary therapies may also be withheld. And all sustenance given to him by intravenous feeding can also be withheld from him, but I want to stress that this may not be done by disconnecting the rubber [infusion] tube that is connected to his body, but only by not putting food in the tube. And in practice, thorough study of the case is required in order to determine his condition, since this is a very serious matter, and it requires rigorous study of the case, and consultation with additional doctors, and the approval of the rabbinical court.
>
> *Responsa Beit Avi* 2:153

R. Liebes, in contrast to rabbis Waldenburg and Jakobovits, permits, though somewhat hesitantly, withholding food and hydration, provided that this is done indirectly, that is, not by disconnecting a machine, but only by not refilling the tube.

Thus there is, as we have seen, a broad range of views as to the law governing the administration of life-sustaining medical treatments to one who is dying. There is also a wide range of views regarding death-precipitating and impediment-removing acts. This lack of unanimity reflects the tension between treating the *goses* "as a living person in every

28 See Abraham S. Abraham, *Nishmat Avraham, Medical Halachah for Doctors, Nurses, Health-care Personnel and Patients*, vol. 2, YD (Jerusalem: 2003).

respect" and the dispensation to remove impediments to death. Balancing these two principles is a profoundly difficult task.

5 Sacrificing one who is mortally ill to save a viable life

It is quite clear that, in the first instance, the killing of a *treifa* is a wrongful act, and the fact that it does not incur the punishment of court-imposed death does not mitigate its wrongfulness. Nevertheless, in certain contexts, the inferior status of the *treifa,* relative to one whose life is viable, as reflected in the disparate treatment of their killers, is taken into account. One such context is that of organ transplantation.

As we have seen, R. Leibes raised—but rejected—a line of argument justifying a lenient approach to the killing of a *treifa* on the strength of the killer's exemption from the punishment of death imposed by the court. This line of argument was, in fact, advanced by R. Menahem Hameiri, in relation to the talmudic case of a group of travelers faced with certain death unless one of their number is delivered up for slaughter.[29]

The Meiri makes the following suggestion with regard to the possibility of giving up someone who is mortally ill (*treifa*) in order to save the whole group:

> And there is no need to state that where a group of travelers [is threatened], and there is a *treifa* among them, that they should hand over the *treifa* and not [let themselves] be killed, since the killer [of a *treifa*] is exempt [from the punishment of court-imposed death].
>
> *Beit Habehira,* bSanhedrin 72b

According to the Meiri, "there is no need to state" that a *treifa* may be given up in order to save viable life, since his murderer is in any event exempt. A similar conclusion is arrived at by R. Joseph Babad, a nineteenth-century Polish authority:

> And it appears to me that regarding this situation [the imperilled travelers], even if a victim was not specified, that in any event if there was a *treifa* among them, it is permissible for them to hand him over and save themselves, since, as I have already written, he is not considered a 'soul' at all. For the argument, "who said that your blood is redder than that of your fellow?" [paraphrasing bSanhedrin 74a, "who knows that your blood is redder? Perhaps the [victim's] blood is redder"] does not apply, since the blood of a *treifa* is, in fact, less red than that of his fellow.
>
> *Minhat Hinukh,* commandment 296

29 See tTerumot 7:20 (Zuckermandel edition); jTerumot 8:4 (47a); Maimonides, *Code,* Laws concerning the Fundamental Principles of the Torah 5:5; *SA,* YD 157:1.

Arguably, according to R. Babad, the dispensation to sacrifice a *treifa* is applicable even if only one viable life will be saved (and not an entire group), since the talmudic principle he cites relates to weighing lives on a one-to-one basis.

This position is, however, disputed by R. Ezekiel Landau, the Noda Biyehuda, in the eighteenth century:

> And has it ever been permitted to kill a *treifa* to save someone of sound body!? We have never heard of such a thing. What difference does it make that the killer of a *treifa* is exempt [from the punishment of court-imposed death]? In any event, it is forbidden to actively kill the *treifa*, and even the strict obligation to observe the Sabbath is violated to save one who has 'life for the hour' (*hayei shaa*). As to the [general] obligation to save one who is of sound body [i.e., a viable life]—if one does not save him, he falls under the 'sit and do nothing' rubric [i.e., he does not directly violate the obligation to save life].
>
> *Responsa Noda Biyehuda*, 2nd edition, HM #59

It may be possible to distinguish between the type of case addressed by R. Landau, and that addressed by the Meiri and R. Babad. R. Landau had in mind the actual killing of a *treifa*, whereas the other two authorities were speaking about a case where the *treifa* would not actually be killed by the travelers themselves, but only handed over to Gentiles (though it is assumed that they will indeed murder the *treifa*). This distinction is suggested by R. Ovadiah Yosef.[30]

Given this distinction, it is not clear whether the Meiri and R. Babad disagree with R. Landau. However, R. Isaac Judah Schmelkes, a nineteenth-century Polish decisor, definitely takes issue with R. Landau's view:

> And behold I saw in *Responsa Noda Biyehuda* that he wrote, "And has it ever been permitted to kill a *treifa* to save someone of sound body!? Yet it would seem that we have to say that [in this specific situation] the positive commandment of saving life does supersede a negative one [in this case, the prohibition against murder, i.e., killing the *treifa*]. For it is with respect to one who is of sound body that we say "a positive commandment does not supersede a negative commandment that incurs death imposed by the court," and so on, which is not the case with regard to [killing] a *treifa*, which does not incur the punishment of [court-imposed] death, and in the view of *Minhat Hinukh*, not even a lashing is incurred. And in my view, a lashing is incurred, but he [the killer of a *treifa*] is not put to death.
>
> *Responsa Beit Yitzhak*, 2, YD #162

30 *Responsa Yabia Omer*, 4, EH #1.

R. Ezekiel Landau maintains that a *treifa* may not be killed for the sake of saving a viable life. R. Isaac Schmelkes rejects R. Landau's argument, pointing out that while the positive commandment of saving life indeed does not supersede the prohibition against killing, this is not so if the one who would be killed is a *treifa*.

There is, therefore, some basis in Jewish law for the argument that a *treifa* may be sacrificed, in an indirect manner, for the sake of saving a viable life. This point arose in the early days of cardiac transplantation. In order for a heart to be transplanted successfully, it must leave the donor's body while still beating. Clearly, this involves a violation of the prohibition against murder. If the donor is a *treifa*, however, and the donee will regain sustained viability after implantation of the donor's heart, then the operation may be permissible on the grounds that the donor's blood is "less red" than that of the donee. This argument was made by R. Judah Gershuni when the pioneering heart transplants were carried out in the late 1960s and 1970s:

> And according to the view [expressed in *Noda Biyehuda*], it would be forbidden to remove a heart from a human *treifa* who is about to die in order to save from death someone who can survive. If the donor is still breathing when doctors remove the heart from a human *treifa*, then the doctors are considered to be murderers. But later authorities who dispute the view expressed in *Noda Biyehuda* are of the opinion that the injunction against murder does not apply to a *treifa*. Hence they are of the opinion that it is permissible to save someone of sound body by killing a *treifa*, who is not considered someone who can survive.
>
> *Kol Tzofayikh*, 376–77

In effect, the entire issue has become moot since the Israeli Chief Rabbinate, in 1979, adopted brain stem death (the irreversible cessation of all independent brain stem activity) as the definition of death, and permitted heart transplants on this basis. The advantage of this definition, as far as cardiac transplants are concerned, is that the heart of an artificially-respirated patient is still capable of beating after brain stem death has been definitively established. For those who accept this definition of death, there is no longer any halakhic bar to heart transplants. R. Gershuni's thesis is, nevertheless, interesting in terms of its possible application to a wide range of contemporary bioethical dilemmas.

6 Conclusion

The treatment of the critically ill is a highly sensitive issue. As mentioned at the beginning of the chapter, some argue that any weakening of the prohibition against the taking of a critically-ill human life is the first step on a slippery slope to mass slaughter of human beings. This argument, also known as the wedge principle, is frequently advanced by opponents of euthanasia legislation, and constitutes a powerful moral challenge to any attempt to justify terminating the life of even the most critically ill of patients.

Clearly, Jewish law does not accept the wedge principle in its strong form. The concept of the *goses* constitutes clear recognition of a point at which death is preferable to life, and steps may indeed be taken to remove an impediment to the death of a *goses*. The distinction between precipitating death and removing an impediment is widely accepted in many moral and legal systems, and as noted above, is somewhat parallel to the distinction between active and passive euthanasia. Though the latter distinction has been challenged—"the bare difference between killing and letting die does not, in itself, make a moral difference"[31]—it is nevertheless widely accepted.

A more serious problem is posed by the concept of the *treifa*. This rubric can be said to reflect the recognition that in certain situations, viable life takes precedence over non-viable life, and the latter may be sacrificed to save the former. The argument that one person's blood is "less red" than another's is undoubtedly morally troubling, and is not widely accepted in contemporary religious thinking, especially within the traditions of Christianity and Islam. Indeed, the exemption of the killer of a *treifa* from the punishment of court-imposed death was cited by the fifteenth-century apostate Joshua Lorki as an example of the Talmud's immorality. As we saw, however, although the killer of a *treifa* is exempt from human jurisdiction, he is, as Maimonides makes clear, still liable to divine punishment, and subject to the king's, and the court's, authority to impose extra-legal punishments, including death. Maimonides may well have codified this law in response to the moral problem created by exempting the *treifa's* killer from human jurisdiction.

R. Solomon Duran, in defending the halakhic position, observed that the Christian policy, in cases of this nature, was to convict the killer of a *treifa*, in the knowledge that he would be granted a royal pardon, and thereby escape the court-imposed sentence. This approach is critiqued by R. Solomon Duran on the grounds that it creates the impression that justice has been subverted by an act of executive clemency. The halakhic position avoids this pitfall by declaring the killer's conduct un-punishable from the very outset.

Presumably, R. Duran is referring to cases in which there are moral grounds for sparing the killer. In this respect there is no difference between his characterization of the "Christian practice" in the fifteenth century and contemporary English law. Even today, English law refuses to recognize necessity as a valid defense for a murder charge in all but the most unusual

31 J. Rachels, "Active and passive euthanasia," *New England Journal of Medicine* 292 (1975), 79.

circumstances,[32] but is prepared to rely on executive clemency in order to pardon the accused on moral grounds.

The classic case in which this strategy was adopted was that of *R. v. Dudley and Stephens*.[33] Three men and a boy from the crew of a yacht were shipwrecked. After eighteen days in an open boat, several of them with minimal food and water, and no prospect of relief, the two accused suggested killing the boy, drinking his blood, and eating his flesh in order to survive. Two days later, Dudley killed the boy, who at this stage was very weak. The three men then fed on the boy's flesh. Four days later they were rescued. The accused were indicted for murder. The jury found that the men probably would have died within the four days had they not eaten the boy. The jury also found that the boy would probably have died before the rescue and, at the time of the killing, "there was no appreciable chance of saving life except by killing someone for the others to eat." The accused were nevertheless convicted of murder, but the death sentence was commuted to six months imprisonment by an act of executive clemency.

The accused raised the defense of necessity, but this defense was rejected by the court on the following grounds:

> Who is to be the judge of this sort of necessity? By what measure is the comparative value of lives to be measured? Is it to be strength, or intellect, or what? It is plain that the principle [of necessity] leaves to him who is to profit by it to determine the necessity which will justify him in deliberately taking another's life to save his own.

The essence of this approach to the inviolable nature of human life is captured most vividly in Justice Benjamin Cardozo's declaration that the courts will not recognize a "principle of human jettison."[34] Nevertheless, Dudley and Stephens had their death sentence commuted to six months imprisonment. In effect, the approach adopted by the common law is the following:

> When, however, all is said and done, probably the most persistent English attitude to the problem raised by the necessity plea—intellectually unsatisfying though it may be—is that hard cases are best dealt with by the prerogative of mercy.[35]

In the final analysis, therefore, English law does indeed recognize the principle of "human jettison." It does so, however, outside the judicial

32 See Re A (conjoined twins) [2000] 4 All ER 961; [2001] 2 WLR 480.

33 R. v. Dudley and Stephens, (1884) 14 Q.B.D. 273.

34 B. Cardozo, *Law and Literature and Other Essays and Addresses* (New York: 1931), 113.

35 P. Glazebrook, "The necessity plea in English criminal law," *Cambridge Law Journal* (1972), 118–19. And see Chapter Eight above, "Equity."

framework. Jewish law incorporates this principle within the system, and is prepared to recognize exceptions to the supremacy of human life within the context of substantive criminal law. The Jewish system also possesses a range of sanctions beyond those of the positive criminal law, which the common law does not offer. Given this range of human, divine, and extra-legal sanctions, it can be argued that the moral risk accepted by Jewish law, in exempting the killer of a *treifa* from human jurisdiction, is not as great as that which would be incurred by English law were it to recognize necessity as a widely-available defense against a murder charge.

It appears that where the indirect termination of the life of a mortally-ill patient (*treifa*) would save a viable life, Jewish law, in principle, supports saving the viable life, as in the case of organ transplants or the allocation of scarce medical resources. In this chapter, we have tried to show that, in dealing with delicate end-of-life scenarios, the halakhic system has more nuanced instruments than the general legal language of prohibitions and obligations.

Appendix *Masekhet Semahot*, ch. 1, 1–4

From: *The Tractate "Mourning"* (*Semahot*), (Regulations Relating to Death, Burial, and Mourning). Translated from the Hebrew with Introduction and Notes by Dov Zlotnik, Yale University Press, New Haven 1966.

CHAPTER I

1. A dying man is considered the same as a living man in every respect. He may obligate to levirate marriage, and he may release from levirate marriage. He may confer the right to eat of the heave offering, and he may disqualify from eating of the heave offering. He may inherit property, and he may bequeath property. If a limb is severed from his body, it is regarded as a limb severed from a living person, and if flesh, as flesh from a living person. The blood of his sin-offering or guilt offering may be sprinkled on his behalf. All this applies until the moment he dies.
2. His jaws may not be bound, nor his orifices stopped, and no metal vessel, or any other cooling object may be placed upon his belly until the moment he dies, as it is written: *Before the silver cord is snapped asunder, and the golden bowl shattered, and the pitcher is broken at the fountain* (Eccles. 12:6).
3. He may not be stirred, nor may he be washed, and he should not be laid upon sand or salt, until the moment he dies.
4. His eyes may not be closed. Whosoever touches him or stirs him sheds blood. Rabbi Meir used to compare a dying man to a flickering lamp: the moment one touches it, he puts it out. So, too, whoever closes the eyes of a dying man is treated as though he has snuffed out his life.

NOTES

1 See Introduction (pp. 9f.) for a discussion of the legal status of the *goses*, and for the Midrash that precedes our text in several MSS and printed editions.

"obligate to levirate marriage." The widow of his childless brother may marry only him, or else perform the *halisah* ceremony [release from levirate marriage] (Deut. 25:5–10; cf. below, vii, 18; and Nid 5:3).

"release from levirate marriage." If his father dies without leaving any other children, the goses releases his mother from the obligation of marrying his uncle (*ibid.*)

"right to … heave offering." If his deceased father was a priest, the goses confers upon his mother the right to eat of the heave offering (Num. 18:8 ff.; Yeb 9:5).

"disqualify from … heave offering." If his deceased father was an Israelite, and if his mother is the daughter of a priest, the goses disqualifies his mother from sharing in the heave offering of her own father's house (Lev. 22:13: Yeb 9:6; MT, VIII, III, vi, 12).

"He may inherit," etc. If the mother of the goses dies, he is her heir, and upon his death—if he leaves no issue—her property falls to his paternal brothers. Had not the goses been considered a living person, he could not have inherited, and the property would have immediately reverted to his mother's nearest kin.

"limb ... flesh." A limb from a living person causes ritual uncleanness when touched, carried, or overshadowed in the manner of a tent, provided it is severed *in toto*; if a part of this limb is cut off, that part no longer defiles. On the other hand, a piece of flesh even the size of an olive would defile if it were cut from the severed limb of a corpse or directly from the corpse itself (Ed. 6: 13).

The homoioteleuton in A, "and if flesh ... person," has been filled in on the basis of the other MSS (SmH, 98, line 5).

"The blood ... may be sprinkled." If the owner of an offering dies, the animal may not be sacrificed. If it is a sin-offering, the animal must be left to die (Tem. 4:1; MT, VIII, VII, iv, I [YJS, *12*, 316]); if it is a guilt offering, the animal is sent out to pasture until it develops a blemish that releases it for common use (MT, *ibid.*, iv, 14 [YJS, *12*, 319]).

"Until the moment"—*'ad sa'at se*. Professor Kutscher suggests that this construction seems to be identical with phrases like *mekom aser*, "the place where," in Biblical Hebrew and *'al menat le*, "on condition that," in Mishnaic Hebrew.

2 The jaws were tied to prevent the mouth from falling open. The orifices were stopped to prevent air from entering the body. A heat conducting object was placed on the belly to inhibit swelling, the verse being interpreted as proof that a corpse's stomach swells and bursts (B. Shab. 151 b, and see Rashi, *ad loc.*; below, note to xi, I). All these are post-mortem practices, and are forbidden in the case of a goses because, being premature, they might hasten his death.

In the process of putrefaction, corpses exhibit a general distention of body cavities, the gas formation causes a ballooning of the face, neck, and trunk, and especially a swelling of the abdominal and chest cavities (T.A. Gonzales, M. Vance, M. Helpern, and C.J. Umberger, *Legal Medicine: Pathology and Toxicology* [New York, 1954], pp. 59–70). I am grateful to Dr. Donald Gribetz for directing my attention to this work.

"as it is written," etc. Except for A, all the MSS, the *editio princeps*, H, and the Giustiniani edition of 1550 include this verse. Cf. also the citations in HG p. 215, and HP, p. 174. Note that although the entire verse is translated here, it is only the first part that is cited in the variants; the remainder, as a matter of course, is left for the reader to fill in (SmH, *ibid.*, line 7).

3 Shab 23:5 and early citations of Sm (SmH, 233, line 4; cf. SmK, p. 16,

n. b) indicate that the corpse was "anointed and washed," i.e., it was first smeared with oil to remove the dirt and then washed to cleanse it of the oil (A. Buechler, KJV, 36–54). It is difficult to understand how this practice could have been cited as a basis for the conjecture that Jews during the Hellenistic period embalmed their dead (TA, *I*, 234, n. 244; 2, 55, n. 415, discussed by Buechler, *loc cit.*), a process that necessitated cutting open the body, when the Mishnah itself states: "provided that no limb of the corpse is stirred."

"sand or salt." TH omits "salt" and reads "clay and earth" (15d; cf. SmH, p. 233, line 6. and SmK, *ibid.*, n.d). The corpse was placed upon sand or salt in an effort to stay the rapid decomposition that would take place in a warm climate (Shab 23:5; cf. *ibid.*, 4:1; Albeck, 2, 424; *Aruch*, 5, 289, *s.v. mtn*).

Cf. the explanations given by Rabbi Aaron Berechiah, *Ma'abar Yabbok* (Wilno, 1880), p. 203. In contrast, note the custom of the Germans of placing a dying man on the ground in the belief that a person should die on the earth from which he was fashioned, cited by J.L. Zlotnik, *Mahbarot*, published as a supplement to *Sefer ha-'ittim*, ed. J. Shor (New York, 1959), p. 21.

4 See Introduction, pp. 18f.

"closed"—*me'assemin*. Cf. variants (SmH, 98, lines 10 and 12), and see B. Shab 77b, and MLM, *I*, 281. In the reading of A, the Mishnaic Hebrew verb *'amas* may have been changed to conform to the Biblical idiom *'asam* (on this tendency, see E.Y. Kutscher, *H. Yalon Jubilee* Volume [Jerusalem, 1963], p. 247, n.7a).

"Rabbi Meir"—as a master of parable, see Sot 9:15, and cf. below, viii, 10.

Private law

11 Agency

1 Introduction

Agency is a fundamental legal institution. It enables one individual (the principal) to be assisted by another (the agent), who carries out legal actions for him and in his name, though the principal does not physically participate in the said actions and is not even present when they are carried out. This is so despite the basic legal principle that one's actions govern his own legal status, and not that of his fellow. For example, the sale of a property is usually valid only if carried out by its owner, and not a third party; but will be valid if the seller is the owner's agent. Similarly, if a betrothal was carried out vis-à-vis woman A, ordinarily, the betrothal will bind woman A, unless woman A serves as a proxy for woman B, in which case woman B has indeed been betrothed.

Legal agency has two aspects, one internal, the other external. On the one hand, the laws of agency govern the relationship between the principal and his agent. In this context, various matters must be regulated, such as creation of the principal–agent relationship, the agent's duty to his principal, and so on. On the other, the laws of agency regulate the relationship between the principal and his agent, and a third party, with whom the agent has dealings. Here the matters to be regulated include the circumstances that create the legal relationship between the principal and the third party, the nature of the rights and obligations that agency generates between them, the nature of the agent's responsibility toward the third party, and so on.

The centrality of the institution of agency is attested to by a number of phenomena. First, all contemporary legal systems recognize this institution, which is not specific to any one system. Second, agency is present in almost every branch of the law, from tort law to private law, commercial law, and marital law. Third, the rapidly increasing scope, sophistication, and complexity of contemporary commerce and economic life has been accompanied by parallel developments in the institution of agency. Today, personal transactions that in the past would have been transacted personally are carried out by proxies of various sorts (sales representatives, trade union negotiators, brokers, and so on). This is equally true of dealings between ordinary individuals, and dealings between institutions and professionals.

Conceptually, if the institution of agency is juxtaposed to the fundamental legal principle of personal autonomy, it is soon apparent that, paradoxically, they are both antagonistic and complementary. There is clearly antagonism between them, since on the principle of personal autonomy, the individual controls his legal affairs, and only he can initiate changes in them, if he so desires, yet within the framework of agency, others can take actions on one's behalf, as, for example, when a man finds himself betrothed to a woman his agent has betrothed on his behalf. But agency and autonomy also complement each other, inasmuch as agency is the summit and quintessential expression of the principal's wishes. The principal desires that the law recognize and ascribe to him actions taken—at his behest—by someone else. This tension finds concrete expression when, for instance, a properly-appointed agent, in carrying out the assignment, acts, upon encountering circumstances not covered in the directives he received initially, in accordance with his own judgment, which is not necessarily in harmony with the principal's wishes given the changed circumstances. Is this a realization of the agent's individual autonomy, or its negation?

It is hardly surprising that the institution of agency was unknown in antiquity, and is not explicitly mentioned even in the Bible. The ancient legal systems were not aware of agency, as it requires a relatively high degree of abstract legal thinking. In Roman law only a partial form of agency is recognized, and even this comes only at an advanced stage of its development. Indeed, legal historians find it difficult to reach a consensus as to precisely when it was that the institution of agency came to be recognized.[1]

Against this background, it is striking that in the world of the Tannaim, agency was a well-known institution of broad scope. In the Talmud, there are significant discussions of its theoretical basis. Agency is invoked extensively in the Mishnah, sometimes in the classic legal spheres and sometimes with regard to non-legal—that is, ritual—matters. The governing principle is that "one's agent is like oneself."[2]

This chapter will provide an introduction to the basic issues pertaining to the laws of agency in Jewish law, with an emphasis on talmudic sources. After setting out some of the principles of agency, we will survey the talmudic *sugya* that discusses the origins of agency, from which we will endeavor to draw conclusions about the historical roots of agency and its talmudic rationale. We will then address two foundational questions. First, what theory best accounts for the doctrine of agency as it is understood in the halakhic sources? And second, what is the scope of the institution of agency in Jewish law? What kinds of acts can be consigned to an agent, and what kinds cannot? We will end our study of agency by reflecting on the connection between these two questions.

2 Agency in Jewish law

Before beginning our jurisprudential analysis of the institution of agency, we will first set out some of the core laws of agency.

2.1 Actions within the scope of agency

The institution of agency is invoked, in Jewish law, with respect to both ritual obligations and ordinary legal matters. That is, it governs such matters as the appointment of agents for the separation of heave offerings and tithes from agricultural produce, as well as matters such as the laws of buying and selling produce by proxy. From this perspective, the mishnaic ruling regarding "one who says to his agent, acquire some vegetables for me" (mNedarim 7:1) need not be differentiated from that regarding "one who says to his agent, go and bring my heave-offering" (mTerumot 4:4).

Nevertheless, we can expect to find a distinction between two kinds of ritual obligations: some religious precepts require, for various reasons, the

1 See M. Kaser, *Roman Private Law*, 2nd ed. (London: 1968), 58.
2 mBerakhot 5:5.

physical presence of the person who is discharging them, for instance, when the very thrust of the act is the **experiencing** of its result. It stands to reason that these precepts cannot be performed by an agent. Precepts that do not require the presence of the person discharging them, however, can be carried out by an agent. Some precepts are such that they encompass elements of both types, that is, elements whose thrust is experiential, and elements where physical performance of the act in question is not the essence of the precept. For example, fastening the knot of the phylactery (*tefilin*) and winding the straps around the arm of the principal can be carried out by an agent, since the person donning the phylacteries does not have to put them on by himself to discharge the precept, but the precept is not discharged if the phylactery is put on the arm of the agent.

In this spirit, R. Moses Sofer (the Hatam Sofer) distinguishes between precepts that can be carried out by an agent, and precepts that cannot be delegated:

> It is, indeed, in regard to precepts that must be **personally discharged** that we say that one's agent is like oneself, but this is not so regarding precepts involving his [actual physical] body. For example, the Holy One, blessed be He, wanted ... the [children of Israel] to be circumcised, and it is the father's religious obligation to circumcise [his son], and [here] his agent is like himself. And so too we are to tie phylacteries to our arms. And this tying can be performed by an agent, who can tie my phylactery onto my arm for me, and it is as if I tied it myself. But had the agent tied it onto his own arm or circumcised his own foreskin intending that it would be as if the phylactery was on the principal's arm, or as if the principal's foreskin was removed—this does not [discharge the precept]. We are thus compelled to say that in cases where the precept is discharged **through** the principal—one's agent is like oneself, but not in cases involving the principal's [actual physical] body. An agent cannot be appointed to pray [in place of his principal] unless he [the principal] hears the prayer as well, as in any event the agent's moving his lips cannot be regarded as if the principal were doing so, because prayer is a precept involving one's actual [physical] body.
>
> *Responsa Hatam Sofer*, OH #201

Later on, we will consider an additional category of precepts, with regard to which it is of absolutely no importance who carries out the precept—a given individual or his agent—since all that matters is that a certain result is achieved, not **how** it is achieved. These precepts can be carried out by someone else even without invoking the mechanism of agency. We will also inquire into whether the institution of agency is relevant in the context of material actions, that is, physical as opposed to legal acts.

2.2 Appointing an agent

According to Tannaitic law, there is no particular formal method for appointing an agent. To generate an agency relation, it suffices for the principal to indicate his intention to appoint an agent. In the Mishnah, this indication is usually verbal, that is, the agency relationship is usually generated by a verbal appointment. For example, when the Mishnah discusses appointing an agent to bring the paschal sacrifice, it describes the creation of the agency relation via speech, without any additional formal procedures: "[It happened that] a group lost its paschal sacrifice and instructed one [of their number], 'go and seek [an animal to sacrifice], and slaughter it on our behalf.'"[3]

To be sure, in a few instances, non-verbal indication of the principal's intentions is sufficient. Regarding someone who lost his power of speech and wished to divorce his wife, the Mishnah states:

> If he became mute, and when they said to him, 'shall we write a bill of divorce for your wife?', he nodded his head, they test him three times [i.e., with three questions]. If he says no when no is the right answer, and yes when yes is the right answer, then they write the bill of divorce and give it [to her].
>
> mGitin 7:1

Apparently, at a later stage it became customary to appoint agents by a formal process, including a symbolic act of acquisition (*kinyan*). For this reason, many decisors felt a need to make it clear that to appoint an agent, no formal appointment process was necessary. Maimonides explains:

> There are many things that do not require an act of acquisition, and with respect to which an act of acquisition makes no sense. For example … one who divorces his wife or appoints an agent … or forgives his fellow's debt or [releases] a deposit he is holding, and all such things. In most places it is customary to perform an act of acquisition for some of these or similar things, and say 'We have acquired it from A, who made B his agent, or forgave B an outstanding debt' … even though it is not necessary. This act of acquisition that has become customary in such matters has no effect at all, except to announce that he is not speaking in jest, but decided on [the appointment] beforehand and only afterwards spoke. Therefore, if he wholeheartedly said, I have decided to do this thing—there is no need for any other procedure at all.
>
> *Code*, Laws concerning Sales 5:11–13

3 mPesahim 9:9.

2:3 Who can appoint an agent?

Assuming that the actions in question can be carried out by an agent, each of the sides to a transaction involving two parties may have recourse to an agent, and indeed, the transaction can take place without either principal being present, as long as each is represented by his agent. We can conclude this from the following mishnaic dictum: "A man may betroth a woman himself or through his agent; a woman may be betrothed by herself or through her agent."[4]

On the basis of this and similar mishnaic rulings, the decisors do not restrict recourse to agency to the vendor or buyer, the debtor or creditor. Maimonides, for instance, states: "One who told his agent: 'Go and sell land or chattels on my behalf, or buy for me'—the agent sells and buys and carries out his assignment, and all his actions are legally valid."[5]

This law raises some interesting questions. For example, can an agent simultaneously be both the groom's agent and the bride's, or the agent of the seller as well as of the buyer? A further question is whether one of the sides to a transaction can be the agent of the other, and in effect conclude the transaction with himself, as, for instance, in the case of someone sent to sell a property who seeks to buy it for himself. These questions will be discussed below when we explore theories of agency in Jewish law (section 5.2).

Is anyone competent to serve as a principal or agent? With regard to the former, the accepted rule is that one must himself be competent to carry out the action he seeks to delegate to an agent. One cannot appoint an agent to carry out an action that one cannot carry out oneself. The Talmud states the following principle: "There is nothing that we ourselves are unable to do and our agents are able to do."[6] Elsewhere, the Talmud notes, for example, that an old or infirm priest who is unable to offer sacrifices by himself cannot appoint an agent to offer them in his name, since "If ... he is not able to perform the service, how can he appoint an agent?"[7]

This principle raises a number of questions. Can one appoint an agent for an action that he himself is unable to perform due to some technical-legal reason, though he is essentially competent to do so? Can one appoint an agent to perform an action that one cannot carry out at present, but will be able to carry out in the future? For instance, suppose someone is interested in marrying a woman who is about to get a divorce. Since he cannot marry her now (because she is still married), he wants to appoint an agent to betroth her for him as soon as she is divorced. Since the principal himself is at present precluded from carrying out the act of betrothal, but will be able to do so in the future, is his appointment of the agent valid? These questions, too, will be addressed below in our discussion of theories of agency in Jewish law.

4 mKidushin 2:1.
5 *Code*, Laws concerning Agents and Partners 1:1.
6 bYoma 12b.
7 bBaba Kama 110a.

2.4 Deviation from, or error in carrying out, assigned tasks

Sometimes the agent does not carry out his task fully in accordance with the instructions given him. In such cases, the usual outcome of the mission assigned him—the ascription of rights and obligations to the principal—is not achieved, since the agent did not carry out his mission in accordance with his mandate. The laws of agency have to determine the degree to which the consequences will be borne by the agent himself, the degree to which they will be borne by the principal, and the status of any third party vis-à-vis transactions carried out with the agent who deviated from his mandate.

The law distinguishes between an agent who deviated from the mandate given him, and an agent who carried out his mission incorrectly. If an agent deviates from the mandate given him, his act is void, because he is deemed to have "overstepped his [principal's] instructions."[8] Maimonides rules that "An agent who overstepped his principal's instructions has accomplished nothing."[9]

On the other hand, if the agent performed his mission incorrectly, the principal has the right to decide whether to void or uphold the action, in line with the talmudic principle: "I sent you to improve my position, not to worsen it."[10]

Obviously, these rules are subject to a wide range of qualifications. In this context the decisors took into account the balance between the interests of the principal, whose instructions were not carried out, those of the agent, who deviated from his mandate, and those of the third party, who suddenly finds himself in a problematic situation, given that the agent with whom he dealt turns out to have deviated from his appointed mandate.

2.5 The agent's fiduciary duty

The agent's obligation is not merely to obey his principal, that is, to fulfill his instructions and to execute the appointed task, but also to be loyal to him. He must act faithfully for the benefit of his principal. These obligations are not necessarily identical. Below, we will consider some situations where even if the agent carries out to the letter the instructions of his principal, there may be concern that he has not done so with sufficient loyalty. Such concerns may arise in cases where the agent has a responsibility to his principal that goes beyond, and hence is not discharged by, merely fulfilling his instructions to the letter.

Incidentally, this is the difference between the principal–agent relationship and the relationship between parties to a contract. In the contract law context, many legal systems require parties to a contract to act

8 See bKetubot 98b.

9 *Code*, Laws concerning Agents and Partners 1:2.

10 bKetubot 99b.

in good faith. They must not only act in their own interests, but also take into account, to a certain extent, the interests of the other party. The agent's obligation of loyalty is much broader: the agent must act **only** in the interest of his principal, and not in his own interest.

For example, the agent has a special duty to report to his principal on the progress of his mission. This obligation can be inferred from the following talmudic case. Someone was sent to purchase something, but when he approached the seller, discovered that the seller refused to sell to the principal. In such a case, the agent may make the purchase for himself, since his mission cannot be carried out. But before doing so, the agent has a special duty to inform the principal that the mission cannot be carried out, and that he therefore intends to buy the merchandise or property for himself. The Talmud presents the scenario as follows:

> Rabbah b. Bar Hana gave money to Rav [and] said to him, Buy this land for me. He went and bought it for himself. But did we not learn, 'What he did is done, but he has behaved like a swindler toward him'? It was a stretch of land belonging to violent men; they showed respect for Rav, but did not show respect for Rabbah b. Bar Hana. Then should he not have informed him? He feared that in the meantime someone else would come and buy it.
>
> bKidushin 59a

On the basis of the Talmud's position, Maimonides rules as follows:

> One who gave money to his fellow to buy him land or chattels, and the agent put the money aside, and proceeded to buy it for himself with his own funds—what he did is done, but he has behaved like a swindler toward him.
>
> If the agent knew that the seller liked and honored him and would sell to him, but not to his principal, he is permitted to make the purchase for himself, after informing the principal. But if he fears that [in the meantime] someone else will come, and will buy it before he can do so, he may buy it for himself [first] and inform the principal afterwards.
>
> *Code*, Laws concerning Sales 7:10–11

Another constraint on the agent that many see as arising from the obligation to be loyal, is that he cannot serve as the agent of both parties at the same time. If he is the agent of the vendor, he cannot serve as agent for the buyer, and vice versa. A question about this is raised in the following *sugya*:

> A certain man sent a bill of divorce to his wife, and the agent went and found her sitting and kneading [dough]. He said to her, here is your bill of divorce. [Her hands being full of flour,] she said to him: Take it [for me].
>
> bGitin 63b

The Talmud rules that the validity of the divorce is doubtful, since it may be that there is no valid agency when an agent represents both parties at the same time. Rashi explains the nature of the bar to recognizing a divorce carried out under these circumstances:

> An agent who changed over and became the agent of the party to whom he was sent, has dissociated himself from the first assignment before having had the opportunity to report back to his principal and say, 'I have completed my mission.' And agency wherein the agent cannot report back and inform [the principal about how the mission is going] is not [valid] agency.
>
> *Rashi*, bGitin 63b

In other words, the agent has, at the end of his mission, a responsibility to report to his principal that the mission has been carried out, and this may be thwarted if at some stage he begins to serve as the agent of the other party.[11]

The same restriction was applied by the Shakh to an agent sent to carry out a business transaction:

> Where one person gave another something to sell, and someone else told the agent, 'Be my agent and buy it from him' … the validity [of the transaction] is doubtful, for the burden of proof is on the one who seeks to take that which is in the possession of his fellow.
>
> *Siftei Kohen*, *SA*, HM 185:1

Below, we will discuss the restrictions placed on an agent's carrying out his mission via a transaction with himself: he is not to buy for himself a property he was appointed to sell, or to buy for himself a property he was appointed to acquire for the principal.

The agent's obligation to be loyal to his principal, a few aspects of which we have just explored, underscores the importance of ascertaining whether a relationship that has some, but not all, elements of agency is indeed to be defined as an instance of agency, or is, rather, an ordinary contractual relationship. Classifying such a relationship as a principal–agent relationship may significantly increase the appointee's responsibilities vis-à-vis his appointer. This will be discussed below in section 3.4.

3 The scope of agency: material actions and legal actions

3.1 Introduction

Demarcation of the scope of the institution of agency has received much attention in the halakhic literature. In what contexts, and with respect to

11 Other halakhic authorities explain the restriction differently, seeing it as rooted in the law of acquisitions, according to which the agent cannot serve as both buyer and seller at the same time.

what actions, is agency germane? Are there any actions performed for someone by someone else that are nonetheless not deemed to exemplify agency, inasmuch as agency is irrelevant in the contexts in which such actions are carried out? These questions are important not only for understanding the scope of the institution of agency, but also for understanding its nature and development. The answers are by no means obvious, and indeed, different legal systems have given different answers.

> Agency in Jewish law embraces more than in other ancient and modern legal systems. It would seem that all actions by proxy that have direct or incidental legal implications, come under the framework of agency—and there is virtually no act that has no indirect legal implications. In our opinion, the problem in Jewish law is not to identify the actions that fall within the rubric of agency, but rather, to identify those that do not. What are the characteristics of actions that do not fall within the legal concept of agency? There are situations that, in our opinion, Jewish law regards as exemplifying agency, yet it is highly doubtful they would fall under the laws of agency in other legal systems.[12]

The crux of the issue is whether every action performed via someone else is an instance of agency in the strict sense that would render it subject to all the laws of agency. An important distinction with respect to the question of the scope of agency, is that between legal actions and material actions. This distinction is not always easily invoked in practice.

A legal action is an act that seeks to change the legal status of the party who performs it. Examples include signing a contract, taking a loan, making a will, betrothing a woman, and so on. Conversely, a material action seeks to change the physical status of either the party who performs it or the object of the action, and any attendant changes in legal status are at most incidental. Like legal actions, material actions can be performed by someone on behalf of someone else. Typing a letter is a material action, as is giving a speech, whether or not one does so on behalf on someone else who is unable to be present. More complex examples of material actions carried out for someone else would be the following: an insurance agent filling out a form for his client; a committee investigating a matter for those who appointed it; a solicitor transferring his client's monies to a third party. In all these cases, the 'agent' performs an action in the name of someone else, but the legal outcomes of the actions, if any, are purely incidental.

There are also ambiguous cases where there is no consensus as to whether they should be regarded as legal or material actions. These are actions that do not seek to bring about a legal change, but such a change is

12 S. Shilo, "Basic issues in the law of agency: a comparison of Jewish and Israeli law" (Hebrew), 9 *Dine Israel* (1978/1980), 113–26, 117.

definitely a direct and predictable outcome of the actions in question. For instance, suppose someone asks a friend to take construction material that is the property of someone else and use it to build him a house. The **intent** of this action is not purely legal, but material: to build a house. So on the face of it, this should be classified as a material action. On the other hand, the **outcome** of the action is definitely a change in the legal status of both the builder and the owner of the material, so it would seem that it ought to be deemed a legal action.

To what extent can agency be meaningfully applied to material actions? Is a courier carrying money from a creditor to a debtor to be regarded as the creditor's agent? In what way is a courier different from a postman, who, we intuitively think, ought not be considered the agent of those who wrote the letters he is delivering? Contemporary legal systems, particularly those from civil law as opposed to common law jurisdictions, tend to answer these questions in the negative, rejecting the idea that the institution of agency applies to material actions. Having someone perform an errand does not make that person an agent in the legal sense. A distinction is made between an **agent**, who is sent to carry out legal actions, and a **messenger** (*nuntius*), who is sent to perform material actions; the laws of agents are not applicable to messengers. The problem for these legal systems is how to define the ambiguous cases—actions the primary goal of which is material, but the direct and predictable outcome of which is legal.

The distinction between legal actions and material actions allows us both to further refine our understanding of the institution of agency, and to better delineate the scope of the laws of agency. The distinction underscores the idea that the essence of agency is conferral of the principal's legal powers on the agent (the mechanics of this conferral will be discussed later in the chapter). This accounts for the relevance of agency to legal actions, which require special legal powers, as well as its irrelevance to material actions (such as a courier's conveying money from one person to another), which do not require any particular legal powers, as evidenced by the fact that they could, in theory, be successfully executed even by trained animals. And the distinction between legal and material actions is also important for determining the boundaries of the scope of the laws of agency. If, for instance, there is a presumption that an agent has a special legal responsibility toward both his principal and the third party involved in the relevant (trans)action, this raises the question of whether a courier performing a material action has a similar legal responsibility. The answer may shed light on disparities between the applicability of agency to legal actions and material actions.

As we will see, agency has broad scope in Jewish law, applying, in differing degrees, to a wide variety of actions, not all of which are defined as legal actions. Though fully applicable to legal actions, agency is only partially applicable in the context of material actions.

3.2 Agency with respect to material actions

The institution of agency is relevant only with respect to actions that have a legal outcome, however small or indirect. But as the Hatam Sofer explains, it is of no relevance with respect to actions that have no legal implications:

> One's agent is like oneself obviously does not apply to mundane [i.e., non-legal] matters. Were one to say to another, 'Sit,' 'Go,' 'Speak,' and so forth, so that it would be as if he himself was sitting, going or speaking [i.e., so that the acts would be attributed to him]—it would achieve nothing. The dictum only addresses such matters as precept observance, or transgressing, or buying and selling, in the context of which an agent's act of 'pulling' to take possession [of a purchased item] is regarded as if it were the principal's, and so too an agent's *hazaka* [demonstrating ownership of real property by fencing it in], purchase, barter, and so forth.
>
> *Responsa Hatam Sofer*, OH #201

Nevertheless, it is not yet clear whether there can be recourse to agency vis-à-vis every action that has some legal effect, however indirect, or only vis-à-vis manifestly legal actions. The above quote from the *Hatam Sofer* seems to imply that agency is limited to manifestly legal actions (observing precepts, buying, selling), but a number of talmudic *sugyot* and responsa indicate that its scope extends to actions we would consider material:

i In a *sugya* about the competence of an agent to serve as a witness to the mission he carried out, bKidushin 43a, the law is decided in accordance with the view that agents can serve as witnesses. The Talmud notes that this law applies to agency in the contexts of betrothal, divorce, and commerce. As an example of agency in the latter context, where, as we said, the law that an agent can serve as a witness applies, the Talmud cites the case of someone sent by a debtor to pay back a loan to the creditor. The Talmud argues that even in this case, the rule governing agents serving as witnesses applies, and the agent can testify in court about his mission, just as agents can testify in the contexts of betrothal and divorce. Although transferring money from a debtor to a creditor is not a legal action, but the classic example of courier service, the Talmud regards it as an action within the scope of agency law.

ii We see a similarly broad construal of the scope of agency in a *sugya* that addresses the laws of Sabbath boundary markings (*eruv tehumin*):

> R. Johanan said: ... If one placed it [the parcel of food required to create an *eruv*] on an ape, which took it to the right spot, or on an

elephant, which took it to the right spot, and had told someone else to receive it from the animal, this constitutes a valid *eruv*. Does this not prove that the agency has been executed?

bMeila 21a

The Talmud draws an analogy from the case of the animal to that of those with no legal capacity, such as the deaf-mute, the mentally deficient, and minors. Actions they carry out are nonetheless valid and have legal effect, for they are viewed as having been performed at the principal's behest. This is the situation with regard to transporting foodstuffs for the Sabbath boundary markings (*eruv tehumin*), which can be done by an elephant or an ape.[13] R. Johanan argues that an *eruv* can be set up via the agency of those who are not generally competent to serve as agents, such as minors and even animals. Setting up an *eruv*, which appears to be a material action–taking foodstuffs from one place to another—is referred to by the Talmud in terms of "agency," and can be carried out even by animals.

To be sure, it is possible that use of the term "agency" here is merely hyperbole or metaphor, and not intended to denote agency in the precise legal sense of the term. But as we are about to see, while it is not certain that the Rabbis of the Talmud had the legal sense of agency in mind with respect to material actions, the Early Authorities did use the term "agency" in its true legal sense in the context of unequivocally material actions.

iii The Rashba, R. Solomon b. Adret, was asked whether a Jewish court that had sentenced someone to death could employ a non-Jewish executioner. The question presupposes that carrying out a death sentence is an act that falls within the court's authority, hence it is not clear whether someone who not only is not a member of the court, but is not even obligated to observe the precepts (viz., a Gentile), can perform it. The inquirer, R. Joseph de Santiche of Acre, notes: "It does not seem to be proper to say that taking a life will be carried out by Gentiles, for where else do we find that the obligation to perform a positive commandment can be discharged via Gentiles?" The Rashba answered that even though carrying out the execution was a religious precept to be discharged by the court, it could, like other precepts, be carried out by appointing an agent: "Upon your life, sir, I contend that the court may instruct the Gentile to throw the wick into his mouth. The Gentile is only the court's agent, and a

13 It is not clear whether the Talmud meant that the ape and the elephant are fully competent to place the *eruv*. It is so implied by most of the textual witnesses for this *sugya*. But other sources seem to hold that the placement of the foodstuffs for the *eruv* is a legal action (see the discussion of bEruvin 31b below). These sources thus require that the animal's actions be overseen by a human, who would be considered the *eruv* maker (*Tosafot*). Others require that the animal's action be restricted to transporting the food from the person seeking to establish the *eruv* to the person who will set the food down in the proper spot (Maimonides).

death sentence imposed by the court does not have to be physically carried out by the court itself."[14]

The Rashba, it seems, is arguing that although handing down a death sentence is part of the court's duty to administer justice, which is, indeed, a religious obligation, implementation of the death sentence, that is, actually carrying out the sentence and putting the offender to death, is not an inherent element of the precept. Hence, it can be carried out by the agency of a non-Jew. Now the execution itself is, it would seem, a material, not a legal action. It is a physical act, and does not change the rights and obligations of the person who carries it out, namely, the executioner. There are, indeed, changes to the legal status of the executed criminal, such as the transfer of his estate to his heirs, and so on, but they are only indirect legal consequences. Nevertheless, the Rashba regards an execution as an act that can be carried out via agency.

iv Yet the status of material actions is not unequivocal. Some later sources indicate that there is a consensus that agency is applicable vis-à-vis manifestly material actions. Our next example deals with the case of a non-Jewish worker who builds a parapet. Putting up a railing around rooftops is a scriptural commandment, the objective of which is the preservation of life: "When thou buildest a new house, then thou shalt make a parapet for thy roof, that thou bring not blood upon thine house, if any man fall from thence" (Deut. 22:8).

There is a special blessing for performing this precept, which can only be recited by one who erects the parapet on the roof himself, not one who has others erect it for him. R. Efraim b. Aaron Navon, an early eighteenth-century decisor in Constantinople, was asked whether someone who hired a non-Jewish craftsman to put up the parapet for him could say the blessing. Is the act of erecting the parapet ascribed, from the halakhic perspective, to the homeowner himself, enabling him to recite the blessing? Or is it ascribed to the craftsman, precluding the homeowner's reciting the blessing? R. Navon approached the question from two directions: in terms of employer–employee relationships in Jewish law, an issue of no relevance to the present discussion, and in terms of the laws of agency. In addressing the latter issue, the question of whether the laws of agency apply to material actions, such as building a parapet, is of particular salience. If they do apply, then it is possible to ascribe to the principal, that is, the homeowner, the act carried out by the agent (the craftsman); if they do not apply, then the craftsman will be deemed to have put up the parapet himself.

R. Navon maintains that erecting a parapet is not an action that falls within the scope of the laws of agency. Erecting a parapet is a commonplace physical undertaking that seeks to ensure the safety of those who will be on the roof, a goal that can be achieved regardless of who

14 *Responsa Rashba*, 1, #357.

builds the parapet. It is thus achieved if carried out by someone other than the homeowner, without any recourse to agency. It thus makes no difference whether the person who puts up the parapet is a Jew or a Gentile: if the homeowner does not erect the parapet himself, he cannot say the blessing.

> I considered another argument for saying that he is permitted to recite the blessing, even though it was made by the Gentile, and Gentiles cannot serve as agents, namely, that [the Gentile's competence to serve as an agent is restricted only] where it is a matter of agency for [bringing] the heave offering and similar acts. But where it is not a matter that calls for agency, anyone can perform the act and it will be valid, such as in our case—if someone put up a parapet for someone else without his consent, it is [still] satisfactory—so if a Gentile put it up, we would regard it as if it had been put up by a Jew.... But this argument alone does not suffice except to establish that [the act of putting up a parapet] is effectively carried out ... by the Gentile, since this act is not a matter that calls for agency.... But to consider that which was carried out by the Gentile to have been carried out by the homeowner himself, so that he can say the blessing?! For even if a fellow Jew put it up, it would not be considered as if [the homeowner] himself had done so, so that he would be the one obliged to make the blessing. For ... such things as building a parapet do not call for agency, and the homeowner does not say the blessing, but rather, the craftsman who put it up says the blessing. For since agency is not required for this type of action, only the person who actually puts up [the parapet] is considered to have fulfilled the precept.
>
> *Mahane Efraim*, Laws of Agents and Partners, sec. 11

3.3 The distinction between agency for material actions and agency for legal actions

Though on the whole the sources indicate that the institution of agency is germane to material actions, this does not mean it is germane to material and legal actions to the same degree. The Talmud makes a number of distinctions that highlight the complexity of this issue.

One such distinction is found in a *sugya* regarding the laws of the *eruv*. The Mishnah states:

> If someone sends [the foodstuffs for] his *eruv* by the hand of one who is deaf-mute, mentally deficient or a minor ... this is not a valid *eruv*. But if he told someone to receive [the foodstuffs] from him [i.e., from one who is deaf-mute, mentally deficient or a minor], this indeed constitutes a valid *eruv*.
>
> mEruvin 3:2

As we said above, those who are deaf-mute, mentally deficient or minors, are not deemed to be legally competent, and cannot serve as agents. Hence an *eruv* they are sent to set up cannot be recognized as valid. The Talmud is uneasy about this law, as it contradicts another source, which recognizes the capacity of a minor to serve as an agent for setting up an *eruv*.

> A minor is not [competent to set up an *eruv*]?! Did not R. Huna state: A minor may gather [the foodstuffs] for the *eruv*? This is not a difficulty, since the one ruling refers to an *eruv* for boundaries (*tehumin*), whereas the other refers to an *eruv* for courtyards (*hatzeirot*).
>
> bEruvin 31b

The Talmud distinguishes between two kinds of *eruv*. The minor is competent to serve as an agent for setting up one kind, namely, that enclosing courtyards, but not the other, namely, that which extends boundaries. Rashi explains that making an *eruv* for courtyards is not a legal but a physical action, and therefore it can be carried out through the agency of a minor. The activity in question, placing food for a joint meal for all the neighbors sharing the courtyard, does not preclude its being carried out by a minor. The case of the *eruv* for boundaries is different. Its goal is to shift one's place of residence to the edge of the space that can be traversed on the Sabbath (2000 cubits), so that the boundary will be extended another 2000 cubits. As Rashi puts it, "it enables us to transfer possession for [the purpose of] staying [within the Sabbath boundaries]." This is considered a legal action, and therefore it cannot be performed through the agency of a minor.[15]

R. Menahem Hameiri articulates this distinction: "The majority of the authorities say that an *eruv* for boundaries is like acquisition of a house, and a minor has no capacity to acquire a house for someone else, but the *eruv* for courtyards is simply a partnership without acquisition."[16]

If we accept the opinion of Rashi and other Early Authorities who followed him as to this matter, we can conclude that this *sugya* makes a

15 It is interesting to compare this *sugya* with that in bMeila 21a (see section 3.2 above), which also discusses the appointment of someone who is deaf-mute, mentally deficient, or a minor. In both cases a baraita is quoted about the *eruv* for boundaries; the conclusions of these *baraitot*, however, are opposed. The Early Authorities noticed this contradiction and accounted for it in various ways. They argued that the baraitot address different events, and seem to suggest that there is a distinction between setting up the *eruv*, which is a legal act that cannot be performed by an ape or an elephant, and the physical setting down of the foodstuffs, which is a material act, and can be carried out even by the legally incompetent. It might well be that the contradictory baraitot represent different conceptions of the *eruv* for boundaries. On one conception, it is an act of acquisition, but on the other, it is not really an act of acquisition, but merely the setting down of an object, which is then interpreted as marking the abode of the individual who made the *eruv* (or sent someone else to do so for him).

16 *Beit Habehira*, bEruvin 31b s.v. *ze shebiarnu*.

clear distinction between agency in the context of legal actions, where minors are not deemed competent, and agency in the context of material actions, where minors are deemed competent. The explanation for this, it seems, is that legal actions require transfer of the principal's legal powers to the agent (the theoretical basis for this transfer is discussed in sections 5.1.iii and 5.2.iii below), and this is impossible in the case of a minor. But material actions, which do not require legal powers, can be carried out through the agency of a minor.

This distinction, originating in the Talmud, was developed by the Early Authorities, and further elaborated by the Later Authorities. They used it to validate a number of actions performed by agents who do not legally qualify to serve as agents, arguing that the said actions do not require agency in the strict legal sense, but a limited kind of agency which we have called 'agency with respect to material actions,' or in their terminology, 'merely the action of an ape.' Such material actions, which do not require any legal competence whatsoever, can, at least in theory, be performed even by an ape. Let us consider some examples.

As we said, Jewish law does not recognize the agency of non-Jews appointed by Jews to serve as their agents. Hence though one may appoint an agent to convey a bill of divorce to his wife, the divorce is not valid if the appointed agent is a non-Jew. The Rosh, R. Asher b. Yehiel, was asked whether a husband can give a bill of divorce to a non-Jew to take to his duly competent agent, who will then convey it to his wife:

> Reuben lives in Tiberias and sent a bill of divorce to his wife in Sepphoris via an Arab, with a valid affidavit, and appointed Shimon, who lived in Sepphoris, as his agent to convey the bill of divorce to his wife. And those in Sepphoris are acquainted with the signatories to the affidavit and the signatories to the bill of divorce.
>
> *Responsa Rosh*, 18:12

Asheri replied that although Gentiles are not deemed legally competent to serve as agents for conveying a bill of divorce, the act of taking the bill from the principal to his agent is no more than an act of mechanically moving it from one place to another (what the Talmud calls 'merely the action of an ape'), or what we have characterized as an act of couriering the document. As such, it is not halakhically problematic, and does not invalidate the divorce.

The law was decided in accordance with Asheri's view: "A bill of divorce sent via a Gentile to deliver to a Jew, the latter having been appointed by the husband in writing to be an agent for conveying the bill of divorce to the wife, is valid, because the Gentile's act has been no more than 'merely the action of an ape.'"[17]

17 *Shulhan Arukh*, EH 141:35.

Several centuries later, R. Jacob Lorberbaum expressed essentially the same view in the context of civil law. He discusses a case in which someone made a contract to sell something to someone else, and utilized the services of a third party to take the object from him to the buyer. Since this third party does not enter into a contract in the name of the seller, but only delivers the item, there is no impediment to this courier's being someone not deemed competent to serve as an agent:

> But if the vendor gave the object to a minor or a Gentile to take it to the buyer, and through this party said or wrote to the buyer to 'pull' on the object so as to acquire it from the vendor, it is a valid transaction ... for in carrying over the things that the seller told the buyer to 'pull' on and acquire ... the Gentile's act is 'merely the action of an ape.'
>
> *Netivot Hamishpat*, 182:2

The following ruling aptly illustrates the distinction between agency with respect to a legal action and agency with respect to a material action in the context of a commercial transaction:

> If he sent it via someone not deemed competent to serve as an agent, such as one who is deaf-mute, mentally deficient, a minor, or a Gentile, whether this person was sent to buy or sent to sell or to conduct any other transaction—he has done nothing, even if there was a formal act of acquisition and witnesses—since they are not deemed competent to serve as agents.
>
> Nevertheless, if the vendor sent the object with them and wrote to the buyer, 'pull' on it and buy it—the buyer has acquired it by pulling on it. Similarly, if the buyer sent such persons with money to buy it, the sender acquired it when the seller received the money, because the act was not concluded by the messengers, and their act is no more than 'merely the action of an ape.'
>
> *Arukh Hashulhan*, HM 182:14

R. Jacob Lorberbaum goes even further, ruling: "Also, if the vendor said to the agent: Sell to whoever gives you such-and-such a price ... he is certainly able to announce this, even through someone who is not deemed competent to serve as an agent, so that the buyer will pay the said amount and 'pull' [on the object] and acquire it."

R. Lorberbaum extends the concept of a material action. In the case at hand, the vendor's representative does not serve merely as a messenger who delivers an offer from the seller to the buyer, but rather, publicizes a general offer to anyone interested. In practice, the vendor's representative, in announcing the price at which the article will be sold, is selecting the buyer and conveying an offer to him. But since, from the legal point of view, the vendor's representative only conveys the offer, and the act of buying is carried out by the buyer himself, there is nothing to prevent the vendor's representative from being regarded as having performed no more than 'merely the action of an ape'—that is, a material action. This renders the transaction legally valid despite the fact that the said individual is not deemed competent to serve as an agent. Above, we invoked the metaphor of the messenger to convey the concept of agency for material actions; the vending machine might be an apt metaphor for the extended concept of such agency.

3.4 Significance of the distinction between agency for material actions and agency for legal actions

Though it is clear that Jewish law distinguishes between agency for material actions and agency for legal purposes, this distinction warrants further inquiry. These are, in fact, two distinct kinds of agency: agency in the wider sense and agency in the strict sense. Agency in the wider sense encompasses actions—for instance, settling a debt or delivering an object—that are not what we have called legal actions, whereas agency in the strict sense relates only to legal actions, such as buying, selling, and discharging religious obligations. What are the practical implications of this distinction? Generally, where agency in the strict sense is concerned, the laws of agency **apply in full**, whereas with regard to agency in the wider sense, only **some** of these rules apply, namely, those rules that are appropriate for the non-legal arena. When the laws of agency apply in full, the principal's legal powers are conferred on his agent, so that actions he carries out can be attributed to the principal. When the laws of agency apply only partially—that is, in the case of agency for material actions—no legal powers are conferred on the agent, as none are needed for the successful completion of the actions in question, which are by nature physical. To be sure, such an agent is responsible for his actions to a certain extent, mainly with respect to the obedience and loyalty he owes to his principal. Some of these duties were discussed in section 2.5 above, where the agent's obligation to be loyal to his principal was explored. We noted that these duties do not apply in ordinary contractual relationships. Hence, although agency for material actions does not confer legal powers, it does confer legal obligations, even on those not deemed legally competent to serve as agents proper.

Thus the status of an agent for a legal action is unlike that of an agent for a material action, though even the latter is indeed sometimes referred to as an agent in Jewish law. The former has the legal power to represent his principal, whereas the latter only performs a physical action at his principal's request. The difference comes to the fore in a number of contexts:

a **Blessings** When one appoints an agent to discharge a religious duty requiring legal powers, he may recite the blessing when the agent fulfills his mission. Even though the principal has not carried out the action himself, but only through his agent, it is regarded as if he has observed the precept. Take, for example, the precept of circumcision, where the laws of agency apply in full. Even though circumcising his son is a duty incumbent on the father, he may appoint an agent to do it in his stead, and recite the blessing for the circumcision carried out by the agent, because it is as if the agent's action has been carried out by the father. In contrast, when one appoints an agent to carry out a religious precept that does not require legal powers, as it consists of a purely physical action, he cannot say the blessing when the agent performs the action. This is exemplified by the case of the parapet: as we saw, R. Efraim Navon argued that the homeowner cannot recite the blessing when the parapet is built by a craftsman.

But on the basis of what criterion are the two types of precept—those discharge of which requires legal powers, those discharge of which does not require legal powers—to be distinguished? We can infer that the criterion is the need for the obligated party's consent. When a precept, or more precisely, the obligation to observe a precept, cannot be discharged without the consent of the obligated person, its observance constitutes a legal action. Discharging the obligation to observe a such precept via an agent therefore necessitates that the agent be endowed with legal powers. On the other hand, when a precept can be discharged even without the consent of the obligated party, its observance only constitutes a material action. Discharging the obligation to observe this sort of precept via an agent therefore does not necessitate that the agent be endowed with legal powers.

b **Voiding an agent's action** The most significant consequence of the distinction between the two kinds of agency—agency in the strict sense and agency in the wider sense—has to do with the possibility of voiding an agent's action. There are situations in which the laws of agency assert that an agent's action is void; upon examination, we see that this occurs only with regard to legal actions, and there is absolutely no possibility of voiding an action that is material and not legal. One situation where an agent's action is deemed to be void is when the agent deviated from his mandate. Maimonides articulates the rule as follows:

> As to an agent who made a purchase or a sale, and told someone that he was acting as an agent in this regard—even if he 'pulled' on the item or had the buyer 'pull' on it [i.e., even if he completed the transaction], if it turns out that he overstepped his principal's directive, the transaction is void and the [goods or money must be] returned.
>
> *Code*, Laws concerning Agents and Partners 2:4

c Nevertheless, agency for material actions is not altogether meaningless. Although, as we said, it does not entail conferral of legal power, it has other implications, particularly with respect to the agent. In the context of material agency, there is no bar to validating an action performed by one person for another, even if the former is not deemed competent to serve as an agent, for instance, if he is a minor or a non-Jew. Taking a bill of divorce from the husband to his agent is a simple courier service, and there is no reason to deny those deemed incompetent to serve as agents the opportunity to perform it. At the same time, a courier is not totally devoid of any agential status, and there is no reason to exempt him from the obligation to be loyal to the person who sent him. Thus even one sent to carry out a material action bears responsibility for any deviation from his mandate. Moreover, it seems that such an agent is not only responsible for carrying out his mandate to the letter, but also obliged to carry it out with loyalty to his principal. This is the rationale underlying a ruling handed down by the Rashbatz in a case involving a cloak supplied by a debtor to his creditor with the instruction that it was to be taken to a specific vendor, who would sell it so that the proceeds could be transferred to the creditor. The creditor instead sold it himself. Though the task in question is a material action, the Rashbatz ruled that in selling the cloak himself, the creditor, qua agent of the debtor, had failed to carry out his mission of taking the cloak to the said vendor to execute the sale: "he has violated the directive of his principal, and if [the latter] incurred a loss, [the creditor] must pay for it."[18] His rationale is that the laws of agency that govern the responsibilities of an agent in the strict sense are equally appropriate to the kind of agency that is in play here, and there is no justification for excluding material actions from their purview.

It must be kept in mind that, as we said, in the context of agency, the obligation of loyalty is considerably greater than that imposed by the laws governing ordinary contractual relationships. Thus ascribing to someone the status of agent, as opposed to merely the status of courier or messenger, is significant, since it may well impose on him broader obligations to the principal.

It is important to note that legal systems in which the institution of agency is not taken to be applicable to material actions may reach this same conclusion, though indirectly. They may draw an analogy between acts of agency and material actions such as serving as a courier, and on the strength of the analogy apply the laws of agency to the latter despite the fact that generally, material actions are not governed by the laws of agency in the strict sense. Jewish law does not need to rely on analogies, since its concept of agency has, from its inception, been broad enough to encompass material actions in various contexts.

3.5 Concluding remarks on the applicability of agency to material actions

Jewish law takes agency to be applicable to a wide range of actions, even those that are purely material, that is, in the language of the Talmud, those

18 *Responsa Tashbetz*, 2, #96.

that are 'merely the actions of an ape.' Yet the broad applicability of agency does not obscure the differences in how it invoked in the various legal spheres where it is utilized. The application of agency to legal actions, such as agency for buying and selling, differs from its application to material actions such as delivering a bill of divorce or conveying payments to a creditor. The specialized laws of agency, including restrictions on who is deemed competent to serve as an agent, the transfer of legal powers, and the legal identification, to one degree or another, of agent and principal, do not apply to material actions, but the obligation to be loyal, and its attendant responsibilities, most certainly do.

Why did Jewish law extend the scope of agency to material actions rather than limiting it to legal actions, and only extending it, as needed, to other actions in an indirect manner, relating to them as exceptional, rather than viewing them as integral to the rubric of agency? This cannot be explained by presenting a purely historical account of the development of agency in Jewish law. For historically, it is reasonable to suppose that agency for material actions arose **before** agency for legal actions. A primitive society that does not have specialized legal structures and abstract legal institutions would be more likely to feature agents in the material sense, to shepherd the flocks of wealthy kinsmen, hunt for other members of the tribe, draw water from the well for those too weak to do so, and so on. Agency for legal actions presupposes the existence of the sort of legal system that would only emerge at a later stage of development. It would seem, therefore, that at the outset agency applied to material actions, and only later was it extended to legal actions, rather than vice versa. And only after the development of the legal apparatus had reached an even higher and more abstract plane would the conceptual distinction between legal and material actions be internalized to the point where the latter would be deemed foreign to the institution of agency, and explicitly excluded from its purview. It is thus significant that Jewish law, which was, as we noted, aware of the profound distinction between the two kinds of actions, nonetheless chose not to exclude material actions from the rubric of agency, but to retain them, albeit only in specific contexts, and not across the board. Hence the historical perspective contributes little to an understanding of the development of the institution of agency in Jewish law, and the explanation must be sought elsewhere.

4 Origins of agency

The legal institution of agency is not explicitly mentioned in the Bible. Its development in the Tannaitic period, however, is of particular importance. This calls for an investigation of two main questions: the historical origins of agency, and its halakhic rationale. The former investigates how the institution of agency emerged, and the sources from which it drew. Did it develop within a specific sphere of the law? Can we identify the period when this development took place, and the factors that brought it about? The second question is that of the halakhic rationale for agency, that is, the normative source on the basis of which Jewish law recognized the institution of agency. These are entirely different questions, though, as we will see, in some ways they are interconnected.

4.1 Historical roots of agency

Asher Gulak, one of the founders of contemporary research in Jewish law, showed that the historical roots of the laws of agency can be found in the realm of religious precepts which are carried out by proxy, particularly in the Temple services:

> Even during the early stages of the Jewish legal doctrine, the institution of agency was already developed to a considerable extent … the observance of the precepts that can only be performed in the land of Israel, or the precepts that could only be discharged in the Temple, led to the need to use agents, who could take the place of the principal. For this reason, that is, to enable recourse to agents for religious needs and observance of the precepts, agency in Jewish law has a religious, sacramental character that has been preserved throughout its history.[19]

This calls for explanation. As noted, Scripture itself does not mention agency. All the religious and legal actions it mandates are actions to be carried out by the individual observing the precept in question. But there is one exception that is fairly close to the institution of agency, though not explicitly described as such by Scripture, namely, the priestly service in the Temple. The Israelites were commanded to fulfill numerous precepts in the Temple, but they do not perform them themselves, but rather, through the priests. It should be noted that the precepts in question are not incumbent upon the priests, but on the Israelites themselves; they are, however, carried out by the priests.

In the relationship between the Israelites and the priests that develops around the Temple service and its sacrificial offerings, we can discern the first expressions of the incipient concept of representation, of the notion that an action carried out by one person is credited to another. The Talmud, in attempting to clarify the legal basis for the priestly service, ponders the question of whether the priests are agents of God, or agents of the people of Israel. "They pondered the following problem: are the priests our agents, or agents of the Heavenly One?"[20] Whatever the answer, this clearly indicates that in the view of the Talmud, the priests do not act on their own behalf, but on behalf of someone else, either the Israelites or God. The fact that agency played an important role in the Temple service, may, Gulak

19 A. Gulak, *Foundations of Jewish Law* (Hebrew), (Berlin: 1922),1:42.
20 bNedarim 35b.

contends, explain the talmudic rule that the laws of agency are only applicable to Jews.

Indeed, in the talmudic *sugya* on the legal origins of the institution of agency, which we are about to discuss in detail, the view is expressed that the sacrificial service is the legal source for all the laws of agency in the Torah.

> R. Joshua b. Korha said: How do we know that one's agent is like oneself? Because it is said, "and the whole assembly of the congregation shall kill it [the Passover sacrifice] at dusk" (Exod. 12:6). Does the whole assembly really slaughter it? Surely, only one person slaughters it. Hence it follows that one's agent is like oneself.
>
> bKidushin 41b

In the context of prayer, a relationship similar to that between the people of Israel and the priests exists between the congregation and the prayer leader (*hazan*). Here too, we have a religious precept incumbent on the entire congregation, yet in practice, it is discharged by only one of them. The halakhic term for this function, '*shaliah tzibur*'–agent of the community–renders the connection to the institution of agency explicit. Interestingly, the 'one's agent is like oneself' principle is first mentioned in connection with the prayer leader: "If one prayed and made a mistake, it is a bad sign for him. If he is a prayer leader for the congregation (*shaliah tzibur*), it is a bad sign for those who have commissioned him, because one's agent is like oneself."[21]

Of course, it remains to be seen whether the prayer reader is indeed an agent in the legal sense, or is so described as a metaphor. Here, however, the important point is that the religious construct of precepts incumbent on the entire community being carried out by one of its members reflects a quasi principal–agent relationship.

4.2 Legal source and rationale for agency

Beyond the historical aspect, which by its very nature is an external view of the law, it is important to examine the institution of agency from the internal viewpoint of Jewish law itself. What is its halakhic source? A fascinating talmudic *sugya*, bKidushin 41a–42a, is devoted to this issue. Although it is presented as an inquiry into the seemingly straightforward technical question of the legal source of the institution of agency, this question turns out to be highly significant for understanding how the talmudic Sages perceived the nature and origins of agency.[22]

21 mBerakhot 5:5.

22 Before examining this *sugya*, we should note its location within the Talmud, namely, in tractate Kidushin, which deals with the laws of marriage. Though the Mishnah and

The starting point of the *sugya* is the mishnaic law that either the bride-to-be, or the groom-to-be, can be represented at their betrothal by an agent. The Talmud then poses the question, "Whence do we know the principle of agency?", that is, what is the legal basis for the institution of agency? The answer presented in the *sugya* is complex and multi-faceted; here we will only mention the main points. On the one hand, the Talmud does not adduce a specific legal source to anchor the institution of agency systematically, but surveys various legal contexts where agency is invoked, and regarding each one seeks to identify a separate legal source: a source for agency in divorce, a source for agency in betrothal, and a source for agency with respect to heave-offerings and tithes. Yet on the other hand, the Talmud also appears to put forward an inclusive source for the institution of agency:

> R. Joshua b. Korha said: How do we know that one's agent is like oneself? Because it is said, "and the whole assembly of the congregation shall kill it [the Passover sacrifice] at dusk" (Exod. 12:6). Does the whole assembly really slaughter it? Surely only one person slaughters it. Hence it follows that one's agent is like oneself.
>
> bKidushin 41b

R. Joshua b. Korha bases the validity of agency on a biblical law that allows the Temple's sacrificial service to be performed via an agent. On this interpretation, the priests, in performing this service, represent the people of Israel, who are regarded as having presented the sacrifices, even though they have not done so in person. "Hence it follows that one's agent is like oneself." Whereas up to this point in the *sugya*, the Talmud seeks a separate legal source for each of the actions (divorce, betrothal, heave-offerings) surveyed, R. Joshua b. Korha seeks a legal source for the institution of agency in general. He sees the above-quoted scriptural verse

Talmud mention the laws of agency numerous times, there is no special tractate or even chapter devoted to these laws, nor is there any one place in the talmudic corpus where they are listed together. Rather, they are scattered throughout the Talmud in the context of laws governing a range of legal actions that can be performed via an agent. One such action is betrothal (*kidushin*). The Mishnah declares: "A man may betroth [a woman] himself or through his agent; a woman may be betrothed by herself or through her agent." The Talmud utilizes this mention of the laws of agency in the context of betrothal as an opportunity to introduce the question of the legal source for the institution of agency. This would seem to indicate the absence of a long-standing tradition (namely, a tradition from the mishnaic period) regarding the conceptualization of agency, and in particular, a tradition of viewing it as a distinct legal institution. Centuries later, the situation changed and the laws of agency came to be discussed as a subject unto themselves. The culmination of the process whereby agency came to be recognized as an independent legal institution can be seen in the Book of Acquisitions in Maimonides' *Code*, which presents the laws of agency together under the heading "The Laws of Agents and Partners."

regarding the paschal offering as the basis for the legal principle that "one's agent is like oneself."

But even after quoting this passage, the Talmud is not convinced that it can serve as a general source for the institution of agency. It may well be, the Talmud argues, that it is a context-specific rule, applying only to Temple-related matters and sacrifices, and no inferences should be drawn from it with respect to other legal spheres. After analyzing the legal sources adduced for agency in the aforementioned specific contexts, the Talmud concludes that each such source is insufficient, by itself, to serve as a general source for agency, as it can only be associated with a single sphere. But conjoining them does yield a structure that, taken as a whole, constitutes the legal foundation of the institution of agency.

What can we learn from the talmudic debate in this *sugya*? A number of important conclusions seem to follow. First, it appears that in the talmudic period there was a considerable disparity between the practical level, at which the presence of agency is conspicuous in various legal spheres, and the theoretical–normative level. The Mishnah invokes the institution of agency in many legal spheres, yet when the Talmud seeks the legal basis for this institution, it finds that such a foundation is lacking. In response, it takes upon itself the task of providing theoretical support for agency.

Second, the Talmud is in no hurry to present the institution of agency as an independent entity, but is inclined to regard it as ancillary to other legal institutions. For this reason, it prefers to find a separate legal source for agency in each area of the law: one source for agency in divorce, another for agency in betrothal, yet another for agency with respect to heave-offerings. Only after assessing these contexts does the Talmud put forward the notion of agency as an independent, non-context-specific institution: "One's agent is like oneself."

The concept of agency seems to have developed 'bottom-up' rather than 'top-down,' that is, from practice rather than theory. At its inception, it appears as a response to certain practical needs that arose with respect to carrying out specific legal acts, such as betrothal, divorce, and so on, in the principal's absence. The legal and conceptual basis for the institution of agency was developed later. The various exegeses offered by the Talmud as sources for the laws of agency serve as 'sustaining exegesis' (*midrash mekayem*), that is, exegesis that provides a legal explanation for a familiar practice and anchors it in well-known normative sources.[23]

It is noteworthy that the parallel *sugya* in the Jerusalem Talmud is constructed quite differently.[24] In answer to the question, "How do we know that one's agent is like oneself?", the *sugya* in the Jerusalem Talmud does not seek a separate source for each context where agency plays a role (sacrifices, betrothal, divorce, and so on). Rather, from the outset, it invokes

23 As opposed to 'creative' exegesis (*midrash yotzer*), which creates new laws.

24 jKidushin 2:1 (62b).

the laws of the Temple sacrifices, with a view to regarding them as a general source for agency. That is, it adduces, as the legal rationale for the institution of agency, the sphere that, as we saw, seems to have been the historical source of agency.

5 Theories of agency

5.1 Introduction

Like their counterparts in general law, students of Jewish law have long contemplated the theoretical foundations of agency. The 'one's agent is like oneself' rule is unequivocal. It means that the action of an agent vis-à-vis a third party obligates or confers rights on the principal, whereas the agent who carried out the action is no longer a party to it. This is the normative **outcome** of the rule. But it still remains to understand the **substance** of agency, that is, the theoretical explanation of both the rule, and its efficacy: how does the rule bring about the aforementioned outcome? Such an explanation will define the rule's operative parameters, and will thus be of great importance in interpreting and applying the rule, especially to ambiguous or borderline cases. As an eminent social scientist once noted, "there is nothing more practical than a good theory"![25]

But the importance of the theory of agency is not limited to its practical implications. Perhaps its greatest contribution is the fact that it enables us to elucidate the conceptual difficulties built into the institution of agency. A man betroths a woman but does so on behalf of someone else, namely, the principal who appointed him to be his representative. This third person, that is, the principal, finds himself a party to a contract with the said woman, or even her husband, even though he did not betroth her himself. This outcome seems to conflict with the principle of personal autonomy, on which the individual is solely sovereign over his property and personal status, and only he can change them, if that is his wish. Appointing an agent creates a situation where another party—the agent—controls changes to the principal's legal status. Furthermore, sometimes the agent may act without regard for the wishes of the principal, or even contravene them (for instance, if the principal sought to terminate the mission, but was unable to do so before the agent carried it out).

i Identity theory

Three main theories of agency have been suggested by scholars. One of these theories contends that in the wake of the principal's having authorized the agent to act for him, the law identifies the agent with the principal. Hence the actions of the agent are regarded as tantamount to actions of the principal. On this approach, it is not correct to say that the actions of the

25 Kurt Lewin, *Field Theory in Social Science: Selected Theoretical Papers* (London: 1952), 169.

agent (for example, signing a contract with someone) bring about an outcome that is **attributed to** the principal himself (for example, entering into a contractual relationship), since from the legal point of view it is as if the principal himself carried out the act of entering into a contractual relationship. In this context, the talmudic dictum "one's agent is like oneself" is apt, as are the Latin maxims "*Qui facit per alium facit per se*" (One who acts through another is deemed to act for himself) and "*Qui mandat, ipse fecisse videtur*" (One who gives an order is seen as having acted himself). Metaphorically, the agent is seen as the extended arm of the principal.

The principal's autonomy is not infringed on by the agent's action, since the latter's wishes and actions are regarded as those of the principal himself. This theory is obviously based on a legal fiction, which is, perhaps, essential. The agent is not, in reality, the extended arm of the principal: their actions are not identical, and their volitions may diverge considerably.

We should note that this theory is not an explanation, but a description. It describes the substance of agency, but does not explain it. The question for which we seek an answer is how and why the law attributes the actions of the agent to the principal. Even if we adopt the identity theory, the question of how and why the law identifies the agent with the principal remains unanswered.

ii Contract theory

Another approach situates the theoretical basis for the institution of agency in contract law. The contract is an instrument whereby the two parties enter into a relationship, and make a consensual decision to change the configuration of their respective rights and duties. On this basis, it is argued that agency rests on a contractual agreement between the principal and a third party, with whom the agent comes into contact. Although it is in fact the agent who actually carries out the contracted action, legally speaking, the real parties to the contract are the principal and the third party; the agent is but a courier who takes the offer and its acceptance from one party to the other. For example, when a principal appoints an agent to sell his car to x, this is to be regarded as an offer made by the principal and conveyed by the agent to x. When the said x expresses his acceptance of the offer, a contract between the principal and x, the buyer, is entered into directly. In the words of a noted proponent of this view:

> Let us never forget that our law of agency does not say that the agent makes a contract and that by some process of transfer the rights and duties thus executed are transferred to the principal ... on the other hand it does not regard the contract as made by the principal through the agent, the agent being treated only as a medium of transaction. It is the mind of the principal which meets the mind of the third party,

just as much as where the medium of conversation is an agent, or where, for example, it is a letter.[26]

This approach invites two criticisms. First, in many situations the wishes of the principal are not identical to those of the agent. Sometimes the intentions of the principal have not really crystallized, and in practice he is relying on the agent's decisions. Moreover, sometimes the wishes of the principal have crystallized, but the agent's mandate enables him to deviate from these wishes and act at his discretion. Thus to regard the agent as one who merely **conveys an offer** to a third party is problematic. It seems more satisfactory to distinguish between the express wishes of the principal, which relate to the agent's mission, and authorize him to carry it out, and the express wishes of the agent vis-à-vis the third party, which—within the boundaries of his assignment—are a matter for his own discretion.

A second criticism of the contract theory is that there can also be agency for actions where there is no third party, that is, unilateral actions for which the principal appoints the agent. This will be the case, for instance, if we take agency to apply to material actions with direct legal consequences, such as building with materials that are someone else's property. If it is possible at all to appoint an agent in such cases, it cannot be explained on the basis of contract law, since there is no third party with whom to make a contract. In Jewish law there are more common examples, such as agency for conveying a bill of divorce. Divorce, it must be kept in mind, is not a contractual relationship between the husband and wife, but rather the husband dispatches the bill of divorce of his own volition. Another example is agency for the discharge of religious obligations, which by their very nature are unilateral.[27]

iii Conferred powers theory

Another approach argues that agency is not grounded in the identification of the principal with the agent, or any contract between the principal and a third party, but in conferral of the principal's powers on the agent. This conferral is possible because it reflects the will of the principal, who has sovereignty over his own legal rights, and is compatible with the legal principle that recognizes the autonomy of the individual's will. Just as the principal is able to effect changes to his rights, so he is able to authorize someone else to act for him, and change the principal's rights and obligations. That is, he is able to confer some of his powers on an agent, so that the latter can act to change the principal's rights and obligations.

26 Cook, "Agency by estoppel: A reply," 6 *Col. L.R.* (1906), 34.

27 There are also more sophisticated versions of the contract theory of agency, e.g., the 'transferred contract' theory, but these theories are inapplicable to Jewish law.

This conferral of power by the principal is described by Dowrick as "a reproduction of the power possessed by the [principal] to alter his own legal position ... the power conferred by the law on the agent is a facsimile of the principal's own power."[28]

The uniqueness of this approach is that it does not explain agency in terms of other legal concepts. The contract theory invokes the institution of contract, the identity theory invokes the fiction that there is identity between agent and principal. On the conferred powers theory, agency is a manifestation of the principal's will, which is cannot be reduced to a more basic concept.

This approach does not explain away agency altogether. As we have seen, identity theories trivialize the essence of the act of agency—an act carried out for someone by someone else—by identifying the agent with his principal. The doctrine of conferred powers, on the other hand, recognizes that the situation created by agency is generated by the principal's desire that someone else act on his behalf. Agency is conceived as a transfer of power from the principal to the agent in such a way that the results of the agent's actions will be attributed to the principal.

Yet the conferred powers theory does not **explain** the substance of agency, but merely **describes** it. It does not offer any new insight, but rather describes the process of agency in legal terms. This is not necessarily a weakness, however; indeed, it may well be the theory's strong point. It does not compare agency to other legal institutions, but captures its uniqueness.

5.2 Theories of agency in Jewish law

Two main theories of agency can be discerned in the sources of Jewish law: the doctrine of identity and the doctrine of conferred powers. We must now clarify the weight and scope of these theories in Jewish law. Various talmudic *sugyot* have been adduced by scholars to elucidate and argue for one or the other of these theories; some of the connections are manifest and direct, others indirect and circuitous. We will examine a few of the *sugyot* that clearly reflect the dilemma as to the most fitting theoretical analysis of agency, beginning with a *sugya* that is difficult to classify.

i Case study: Can an agent become a witness?

The dilemma as to which theory of agency is most apt in the halakhic context comes to the fore in the debate over whether an agent may testify in court about the actions he carried out in executing his agency. For example, can an agent who was sent to betroth a woman to his principal give testimony in a rabbinical court that the couple has married? On the one hand, according to Jewish law, one is not deemed competent to be a

28 F. Dowrick, "The relationship of principal and agent," 17 *Mod. L. Rev.* (1954), 24–40, 37.

witness to his own actions, because he is an interested party. And this being so, this rule must also apply to his agent, who is, we saw, deemed to be 'like' his principal. On the other hand, the agent has acted for someone else, not for himself, and this action has not changed his own personal status. Why, then, is he not considered reliable enough to testify as to the act he carried out?

In a discussion of agency for betrothal, a controversy over this point arose among the Amoraic Sages.

> It was stated: Rav said: An agent can become a witness; the school of R. Shila said: An agent cannot become a witness.... Rav said: An agent can become a witness, for he strengthens the matter [i.e., having taken part in the action being attested to, his evidence is particularly strong]. The school of R. Shila said: An agent cannot become a witness, since it is said: One's agent is like oneself—he is tantamount to his [principal's] own person.
>
> bKidushin 43a

The Talmud decides in favor of Rav and against the school of R. Shila: "The law is that an agent can become a witness." The tradition adduced by R. Shila holds that the "one's agent is like oneself" rule signifies the complete identification of agent and principal—"he is tantamount to his [principal's] own person," and since the principal is not deemed competent to serve as a witness at his own marriage, the agent is not competent to serve as a witness to that event either.

R. Meir Simha Hakohen of Dvinsk explains the Amoraic debate as a debate over the nature of agency. There is a significant parallelism between the aforementioned two theories of agency—the identity theory and the conferred powers theory—and the two Amoraic views:

> Their disagreement is that R. Shila is of the opinion that an agent becomes tantamount to the principal himself, and Rav is of the opinion that only the agent's action is attributed to the principal and is as if it was carried out by the principal himself, but the agent is not an interested party who would be disqualified from testifying.
>
> *Or Sameiah*, Laws of Divorce 2:15[29]

Another account of the Amoraic dispute, that of R. Arye Leib Heller, denies that it is a controversy over the nature of agency. Rather, he says,

29 This explanation originates in remarks by Rabbenu Nissim (Ran): "And we conclude that the rationale of the authority who says that an agent cannot become a witness is 'Since it is said: One's agent is like oneself—he is tantamount to his [principal's] own person' [bKidushin 43a]. But we do not uphold that view, but rather, an agent can become a witness" (*Ran*, bKidushin 17b [Alfasi pagination] s.v. *itmar*).

both Amoraim accept the identity theory, but still disagree as to whether the agent can testify. R. Heller argues that whereas one cannot be a witness for himself because he is an interested party, and his testimony may gain him some personal advantage, this is not so with regard to the agent, to whom it makes no difference if the woman is betrothed to the principal or not. Hence here, his testimony is acceptable, even though legally he is considered the 'extended arm' of the principal, who is deemed incompetent to testify.

> It is clear that ... even though the agent is tantamount to the principal himself, [nevertheless,] since he is not an interested party vis-à-vis this matter, he can be a witness. And R. Shila is of the opinion that since he is tantamount to the principal, even though he is not an interested party, he is disqualified.
>
> *Avnei Miluim* 35:1

We can thus assume that the Sages accept the notion that one's agent is like oneself in the sense of the identity theory; their disagreement has to do with whether this identification of agent and principal disqualifies an agent from becoming a witness. On one opinion, the moment he is formally identified with his principal, the agent is rendered incompetent to testify as to his mission, just like his principal. Others are of the opinion that despite the legal identification, competence to serve as a witness is a substantive, as opposed to a formal, question, and if it is found that the agent does not stand to gain any personal advantage, there is no reason to disqualify him from serving as a witness.

This line of thought took an interesting turn in a responsum by the late fourteenth-century Spanish decisor, R. Isaac b. Sheshet Perfet, the Ribash. He was asked about someone who had been sent to betroth a woman in another town. After some time, the agent and the woman returned from that town and declared that the mission had been carried out and the woman was betrothed to the principal. But they had no evidence to corroborate this. The question was whether, given that there was no clear corroborating evidence of the betrothal apart from the agent's and the woman's testimony, the couple should be recognized as betrothed.

> You asked: Reuben appointed an agent to betroth a woman in another town, and the said agent duly betrothed her for Reuben in accordance with the law. For there is a legal presumption that an agent carries out his mission, and they recited the betrothal blessing. And the woman came with the agent to Reuben's town to marry him. The woman and the agent say that she was betrothed to Reuben by the agent. Is Reuben required to betroth her again himself, and to recite the betrothal blessing a second time, himself, before standing under the wedding canopy with her [i.e., marrying her], or not?
>
> ...

Answer: There is no doubt that since both the agent and the woman say that she was duly betrothed to the principal, she is betrothed to him, and another betrothal is not needed, even though no witnesses to the betrothal came before us. Think about it yourself: A man and his wife arrived from abroad, and we do not know them. He says, 'This is my wife,' and she also says, 'This is my husband.' Would anyone entertain the idea of separating them from each other until the witnesses to their marriage came before us, or other witnesses testified that she was his wife? So too in this case, the agent takes the place of the husband, for one's agent is like oneself, and it is as if the husband himself said that she was betrothed to him.

Responsa Ribash, #82

The Ribash identifies an exception to the general rule that one may not testify in a case in which he is an interested party. The exception is testimony as to one's own personal status. Although here the witness is testifying about himself, he is viewed as the best source for the relevant information. Jewish law recognizes the reliability of an individual's testimony regarding his own personal status, as, for instance, when he acknowledges his progeny, or asserts that he is married (provided there is no good reason to disbelieve him). In essence, the Ribash is claiming that the Amoraic controversy over whether agents can become witnesses is about testimony regarding someone else, as opposed to testimony regarding one's self. As we saw above, according to one opinion, an agent is identified with his principal, he is thus an interested party with respect to the matter about which he is testifying, and hence his testimony is inadmissible. According to the other opinion, the agent is not completely identified with his principal, and we do not consider him an interested party, hence there is no bar to accepting his testimony. But with regard to testimony as to personal status, where one may testify as to himself, all agree that the agent can serve as a witness, because one's agent is like oneself, and the testimony of the agent is tantamount to that of the principal.

To complete the picture, the talmudic *sugya* (bKidushin 43a) notes that under certain circumstances, when there is reason to suspect that the agent has a personal interest in the matter, he is disqualified from serving as a witness. But this is not due to his being identified with the principal (who is deemed incompetent to testify, as he is an interested party regarding his own affairs), but because the agent himself is an interested party. For example, the Jerusalem Talmud records the following opinion:

Apparently the agent can serve as a witness only if he betrothed her by way of a document, but if it was by a monetary gift, he is an interested party vis-à-vis his testimony.

jKidushin 2:1 (62a)

The testimony of an agent who betrothed a woman with monies belonging to his principal may raise various questions about the agent's discharge of his responsibility for the funds entrusted to him. Therefore, on this line of thinking, he is deemed incompetent to testify about the betrothal; not because he is identified with the principal, but because he himself is an interested party.

As we said, even though the law was decided in accordance with the view that agents can serve as witnesses—a ruling that can be interpreted as supporting the theory that agency is the conferral of the principal's powers on the agent, and rejecting the identity theory—the latter does not entirely recede from view, and from time to time is invoked by prominent Early Authorities, an example being the ruling handed down by the Ribash.

ii *Sugyot* reflecting identity theory

a The vendor's agent who purchases something for himself

Someone was appointed an agent to sell a certain property, but no instructions were given as to who to sell it to. Can this agent buy the property for himself while he is representing the vendor? This question was presented to R. Solomon b. Adret, who answered in the negative, for the following reasons:

> The agent cannot buy it for himself ... because he was appointed an agent for selling the property to a buyer, but he cannot transfer the rights to himself and acquire it, because one cannot transfer rights to oneself. For a sale constitutes a transfer of ownership, but the property will not leave the seller's ownership, because he [the agent] stands in for the principal.
>
> *Responsa Rashba attributed to Nahmanides, #44*

The Rashba clearly and unequivocally invokes the theory of identity here: the agent is tantamount to the principal, hence he cannot buy the property for himself since, "one cannot transfer rights to oneself." The Rashba's source for this ruling is the *sugya* in tractate Ketubot about someone with whom assets belonging to orphans had been deposited, apparently so that he could sell them. In the end he bought them himself. The Talmud is inclined to disqualify the sale.

> A certain man, with whom coral belonging to orphans had been deposited, went and had it appraised, on his own behalf, at 400 *zuz* [and purchased it]. And later, when its price rose to 600 *zuz*, he appeared before R. Ami [to determine who was entitled to the profit], who said to him, Who authorized you to make the appraisal?
>
> bKetubot 98a

The man sold the orphans' coral to himself at what turned out to be a low price. R. Ami annulled the sale, arguing that the agent had no right to get the coral appraised. This ruling is invoked by the Talmud in discussing a similar case concerning a widow who, acting as guardian of her orphaned children, had bought their property for herself.

Rashi ad loc. explains the meaning of the argument: 'Who authorized you to make the appraisal?' as follows:

> From whom did you receive this property? Not from the court and not from the orphans. Therefore [the property] did not cease to be owned by the orphans. Had you sold it to someone else, [the transaction would have been valid], since the property would have ceased to be owned by the heirs.

Rashi identifies the agent with the owner. In this particular case, the owners are the orphans, and the agent is the woman. Since she sells it to herself, the property, on this interpretation, has not changed hands.

The Rashba apparently had this sort of interpretation in mind when he ruled that the agent could not sell the property to himself because the property "did not leave the [seller's] ownership, because [the agent] stands in for the principal." The Rashba did not see such cases as exceptional, as cases where the judge acted 'beyond the letter of the law' in order to be solicitous of the orphans' interests, but rather, he saw them as expressing the normative rule that an agent cannot execute a legal action 'with himself.' The Rashba's position was adopted by other Early Authorities, who can thus also be taken to uphold the identity theory of agency.

But this is not the only possible interpretation of the *sugya*. It could be argued that the impediment is not the fact that the property has not changed hands, but rather, apprehension as to a possible conflict of interest. A bailee who sells the property of a depositor to himself is suspected of selling at a price that is favorable to himself and unfavorable to the depositor. The same consideration applies to agents: an agent who sells the principal's property to himself has a similar conflict of interest. It is likely no coincidence that the price at which the bailee sold the orphans' property was lower than the market price shortly thereafter. The bailee's and agent's obligation to be loyal to the depositor and principal, respectively, does not permit them to carry out legal transactions (purchases, sales, and so on) involving assets entrusted to them, with themselves, as opposed to third parties. This has nothing to do—on this interpretation—with what theory of agency we uphold, but is a matter of the agent's obligation to be faithful to his principal and the conflict of interest to which it gives rise in the said circumstances.

Indeed, R. Yomtov of Seville, the Ritba, elucidates this *sugya* as follows: "And the Geonim, of blessed memory, explained: 'Who authorized you to make the appraisal?'—Perhaps you made an imprecise appraisal ... since it was for yourself."

Contemporary legal systems also tend to forbid self-dealing—legal actions executed by an agent with himself. Their rationale for doing so is not the principal–agent identity theory, but rather, the agent's duty of loyalty to the principal. On this understanding, the agent's conflict of interest precludes his performing, on behalf of his principal, legal actions to which he is a party.

> Unless otherwise agreed, an agent is subject to a duty not to deal with his principal as an adverse party in a transaction connected with his agency without the principal's knowledge.[30]

The official explanation of this paragraph stresses that the rationale for this rule is the desire to prevent the agent from involvement in a conflict of interest:

> The rule stated in this Section is not based on the existence of harm to the principal in the particular case. It exists to prevent a conflict of opposing interests in the minds of agents whose duty it is to act solely for the benefit of their principals. The rule applies, therefore, even though the transaction between the principal and the agent is beneficial to the principal.

Other legal systems, such as the Italian Civil Code, stipulate that in exceptional cases, where it is proven that the conflict of interest was not detrimental to the principal, legal actions carried out by the agent with himself can be recognized as valid:

> Self-contracting has either to be authorised by the principal or to regard contracts the content of which has been pre-defined by the principal in such a way as to exclude even the possibility of conflict of interest. [31]

b Sub-agency

We can learn more about the theory of agency and its implications by briefly considering the institution of sub-agency. By 'sub-agency' we mean

30 Restatement (Second) of Agency, §389 (1958). Cf. German Civil Code (*Bürgerliches Gesetzbuch*): "An agent may not, without leave, enter into a legal transaction in the name of his principal with himself in his own name, or as agent of a third party, unless the legal transaction consists exclusively in the fulfillment of an obligation."

31 Article 1395; see Luca Enriques, "The law on company directors' self-dealing: a comparative analysis," 2 *International and Comparative Corporate Law Journal* (2000), 297–333, 304 n. 37.

any instance where an agent authorizes someone else to carry out the assigned mission in his stead. This raises two questions: first, is the first agent indeed permitted to transfer his mandate to someone else, and if he is, what is the status of the sub-agent: is he the agent of the principal or of the primary agent (or of both)? And what legal consequences follow from this?

Most of the classic sources of Jewish law on sub-agency discuss it in the context of agency for delivering a bill of divorce. They express a wide range of views, as is characteristic of the halakhic literature generally. R. Joseph Caro summarizes these views as follows:

> Regarding one who is sending a bill of divorce to his wife, and said to [the agent], 'You are to convey this bill to my wife,' or said to him, 'You are to convey it'—the agent cannot send it via someone else, unless he fell ill or was under duress, or [the principal] told him explicitly that he could appoint another agent, and the [second] agent could appoint another agent—even several times.
>
> But there are some authorities who dispute this, saying: If he said in a general way, 'Convey it,' then the agent can send it with someone else even if he did not fall ill. But if he said, 'You are to convey it'—the agent must not send it via someone else, unless he fell ill, or [the principal] told him explicitly that he could appoint another agent.
>
> *Shulhan Arukh*, EH 141:38

This suggests the following question: are the laws of sub-agency in the realm of monetary law different from, or the same as, those of divorce law? The Ribash discusses this question at length. He is perhaps the first, and one of the few, to discuss the question of sub-agency vis-à-vis a realm other than divorce law.

> It seems that in all [realms] of the law [lit., the Torah], an agent can appoint another agent, even if the principal did not explicitly tell him so, unless there is a particular complication ... since it is so in divorce law ... we apply it to other things as well, because we derive it from divorce law.
>
> *Responsa Ribash*, #228

The Ribash is thus of the opinion that in any area of the law, an agent may appoint another agent without the explicit consent of the principal. He bases his ruling on the analogy with the laws of divorce, but also adduces an additional rationale:

> We derive the 'one's agent is like oneself' rule from the verse concerning the paschal sacrifice, "and the whole assembly of the congregation

> of Israel shall kill it" (Exod. 12:6). We infer that the agent is fully tantamount to [his principal], for Scripture refers to the agent as representing the entire congregation. And if so, then the agent is tantamount to the principal in all respects.

According to the Ribash, we infer that an agent can appoint another agent from the very essence of agency—the identity between principal and agent—as set out in Scripture. An agent can appoint another agent because he is truly tantamount to his principal, and since the principal can appoint an agent, his agent, who is like him, can as well. Here the Ribash is explicitly stating that he upholds the identity theory, and is applying it to the issue at hand.

But it is not altogether certain that the identity theory provides the best account of the agent's power to appoint another agent. The Rashbatz arrives at a similar conclusion about sub-agency on the basis of concepts taken from the conferred powers model of agency; his argument will be discussed below. He asserts:

> Let it be known that.... even though it is not explicitly stated, an agent can appoint an agent, for with the very power to be an agent that the principal conferred on him, with that very power, he can appoint [someone else as] an agent.... This is the power of agency: either he or his agent can carry out the mission.
>
> *Responsa Tashbetz*, 1, #25

Like the Ribash, the Rashbatz derives his conclusion from his view as to the nature of agency: the powers conferred on the agent suffice to enable him to appoint another agent to carry out the mission.

But the Rashbatz's argument is inconclusive. The conferred powers theory need not be understood as conferring **all** the principal's powers. The fact that power to act on behalf of the principal was conferred on the agent does not necessarily imply that the specific power to appoint a sub-agent was among the powers conferred.

Their respective theories of agency, though different, lead both the Ribash and the Rashbatz to the same conclusion: an agent may appoint a sub-agent, either because, being tantamount to the principal, who can appoint an agent, he can do so himself, or, because the capacity to appoint a sub-agent is inherent in the power of agency that was conferred on him.

We should also note that even if the inherent nature of agency supports the notion that an agent can appoint another agent, this authority is subject to the presumed wishes of the principal. In a case where there is reason to suppose that the principal wants the mission to be carried out by the agent in person, it is clear that the authority granted the agent is inherently limited.

iii *Sugyot* reflecting the conferred powers theory

The second theory of agency found, explicitly and implicitly, in the Jewish legal sources, is the conferred powers theory. On this theory, the foundation of agency is the principal's conferral on the agent of power to act on the principal's behalf. The principal's power to carry out an action is thus bestowed on the agent, who henceforth acts by virtue of the powers conferred on him by the principal. This explains how and why the agent's action brings about a change in the legal status of the principal. But what is the legal basis of the principal's power to confer his powers on the agent? The law creates a 'virtual' legal reality—essentially, the power to delegate power is a legal fiction.

Is the doctrine of conferred powers an apt description of the laws of agency in Jewish law, and in harmony with the different halakhic sources and opinions? In our view, a strong case can be made for the claim that it is, although the identity theory cannot be dismissed out of hand, and must be reckoned with. While, as we saw, the identity theory is upheld by many halakhic authorities, others find it objectionable, though they generally do not articulate the reason for their discomfort. The conferred powers theory allows us to articulate what it is about the identity theory that these authorities find problematic, and provides an adequate theoretical basis for agency.

Consider, for example, the Amoraic dispute over whether an agent can become a witness, a *sugya* explored above. The view that an agent cannot become a witness is explained in terms of the agent–principal identity theory, but the theoretical basis for Rav's view—that an agent **can** become a witness—is not explained in the *sugya*. It seems abundantly clear, however, that the conferral of power model meshes well with Rav's view that an agent can serve as a witness, since on this model, the agent is fully distinct from the principal.[32]

There is no explicit reference to the concept of conferred powers in the Talmud, but it finds expression in the works of the Early Authorities. For example, the Rashbatz, as we saw above, permits an agent to appoint a sub-agent "even though it is not explicitly stated," that is, even when the principal has not expressly authorized the agent to do so. In support of this stance, he argues that this capacity is inherent in the nature of agency: "for with the very power to be an agent that the principal conferred on him, with that very power, he can appoint [someone else as] an agent." This is without any doubt an expression of the idea that agency is the conferral of the principal's powers on the agent.

32 Granted, this is not the only possible explanation that can be offered for Rav's position: it could still be argued that Rav upholds, not the conferred powers theory, but the identity theory, but does not apply it to the laws of evidence, invoking it only with respect to the laws of agency.

The concept of conferred powers is expressed more clearly by some Later Authorities, one of the more prominent advocates being R. Yomtov Lipmann Heller.

> The 'one's agent is like oneself' dictum does not mean that every single detail of this action [viz., the agent's mission] is regarded as if it was carried out by the principal, and their persons are identical. [Rather, it means] only that the agent has the power to carry out this action just as the principal does.
>
> *Responsa Oneg Yomtov*, #113

In addition to these explicit references to the doctrine of conferred powers in the halakhic literature, there are also indirect references, mostly in connection with the rule that one cannot appoint an agent for a task he himself cannot carry out at the time of the appointment. This rule, formulated in the Talmud, was subsequently developed by both the Early and the Later Authorities.

a Appointing an agent for an action one cannot carry out

Among the laws of agency is the rule that one cannot appoint an agent for a task he himself cannot carry out at the time of the appointment.[33] This rule is more in line with the conferred powers theory than the identity theory. Let us examine two talmudic *sugyot* that discuss this rule, and their implications for agency theory.

The first *sugya* is about the freeing of a slave via a bill of manumission. In the opinion of R. Shimon b. Eleazar, a slave cannot be freed by receiving a bill of manumission from his master. A bill of manumission is only valid if it leaves the master's domain, which does not happen if he gives it to his slave, since the slave is legally his possession (lit., "the hand of the slave is regarded as the hand of his master"). Rabbah raises a question about this: "According to R. Shimon b. Eleazar, can he appoint an agent to accept his bill of manumission from his master?" Rabbah answers in the affirmative. The Talmud then asks:

> R. Huna, son of R. Joshua, said: These priests are agents of the All-Merciful, for should you think they are our [agents], is there anything that we ourselves cannot do whereas they can do it for us?! Is that indeed so? What of a slave, who cannot accept his bill of manumission himself, yet can appoint an agent [to accept it on his behalf]?!
>
> bKidushin 23b

33 See H. Ben-Menahem, "The judge–agent analogy in the Talmud," in H. Ben-Menahem and N. Hecht, *Authority, Process and Method: Studies in Jewish Law* (Amsterdam: 1998), 33–58; M. Wygoda, "On the relationship between the capacity to perform a legal task and the capacity to appoint an agent to perform it," 14 *Jewish Law Annual* (2003), 315–50.

R. Huna's remarks relate to the status of priests performing the Temple service, a point discussed in section 4.1 above. He assumes that they perform their sacrificial service in the Temple as agents, since they offer up not only their own personal sacrifices, but those of others too. But whose agents are they? R. Huna thinks they should be construed as agents of God, not agents of the Israelites, since the Israelites are not deemed competent to offer up their sacrifices at the Temple themselves, and as such, are not competent to appoint agents to do so on their behalf. This argument is grounded in the law that one cannot appoint an agent to do something one cannot do himself. The Talmud then wonders how to reconcile this argument with Rabbah's conclusion that a slave who himself is not competent to accept a bill of manumission is deemed competent to appoint an agent to accept it. To resolve the contradiction, the Talmud distinguishes between the two cases:

> But that is not so: an Israelite has no connection at all to the laws of sacrifices, whereas a slave has a connection to bills of manumission. For it was taught: It appears to be the case that a slave can accept his fellow's bill [of manumission] from his fellow's master, but not [his own] from his own master.
>
> bKidushin 23b

In other words, the fact that a slave cannot accept his own bill of manumission is not a substantive defect in his ability to accept his freedom via a bill of manumission. The problem is different, namely, the fact that upon being accepted by him, the bill of manumission has still not left his master's domain. The slave does in principle have the power to accept a bill of manumission, but cannot exercise this power in practice by receiving it directly from his master. Although this impediment is not temporary, it is nonetheless considered a technical difficulty, rather than a status that precludes his receiving legal documents. The slave is thus deemed competent to appoint an agent to accept the bill of manumission for him from the master.

On the other hand, Israelites have "no connection at all to the laws of sacrifices." That is, they lack the power, and are not deemed competent, to perform the sacrificial service in the Temple. Hence it is impossible for the priests to be considered their agents for doing so. This passage teaches us that in order for someone to be able to appoint an agent, he must have the legal power to perform the action himself.

A similar idea is expressed in another talmudic *sugya*. The case has to do with the appointment of an agent to betroth a currently-married woman after she receives her divorce. The betrothal cannot, of course, be performed while she is still married, but the agent is appointed to wait until the divorce has been executed, and then betroth her for his principal. The Talmud does not accept the validity of the appointment. "One can appoint an agent only for something he can do now, but for something he cannot do now, he cannot appoint [an agent]."[34]

The principle here is the same as in the previous case, but the circumstances are reversed. Whereas the slave could not get his bill of manumission from his master before surmounting a legal technicality, here the impossibility of a married woman's being betrothed to someone else is a substantive impediment. The principal himself lacks the power to betroth her at present, since the betrothal of a married woman is null and void; hence, he cannot appoint an agent to perform this act (even though the principal's intention is for the agent to betroth her only after she is divorced).

The underlying principle here seems more in line with the conferred powers theory than the identity theory. Making the appointment of an agent subject to the condition that the principal must be able to perform the action himself, and particularly, focusing on his ability to perform the action at the time the appointment is made, as opposed to his ability to perform it at the time the mission is carried out, reflects the idea that agency is a form of conferring the principal's power to do something on someone else. If he lacks this power at the time he is making the appointment, how can he confer it on someone else?

A clear account of this analysis of the cases, with due emphasis on the principle of conferred powers in agency, is presented in an eighteenth-century commentary on the *Shulhan Arukh*:

> R. Huna's remarks rest on the argument that one who has no power is not able to confer it on his agent, since he himself does not have this power. The Talmud takes it for granted . . . that the principal must have powers to confer at the time of appointing the agent, for what good will power acquired by the principal after having appointed the agent do, and what will it change?
>
> Since we see that a slave is able to accept the bill of manumission on behalf of his fellow, we understand that his inability to receive his own bill [of manumission] from his master is not due to some defect in his status, but to the lack of a domain of his own. As to R. Huna's conclusion that the priests are agents of the All-Merciful—this conclusion is based on the assertion that Israelites are not connected in any way to the laws of sacrifices, from which it follows that they lack the power to offer sacrifices.
>
> R. Meir Posner, *Beit Meir, SA*, EH 119:6

6 Conclusion

We have explored the scope of the institution of agency in Jewish law—the kinds of actions that fall under the rubric of agency—as well as the leading

34 bNazir 12b.

conceptual analyses of agency. We can now draw some conclusions regarding the connection between the question of the scope of agency, and that of its conceptual analysis, in the Jewish law context. But let us first review the main conclusions arrived at thus far.

The contract theory does not seem to provide a suitable account of Jewish law's approach to agency, given that a large number of the halakhic sources and laws concerning agency deal with cases that cannot be explained in terms of contractual relations. This is most evident with respect to the realm of the ritual precepts, which, we saw, likely constitutes the source of agency in Jewish law. The idea of a contract, which is based on a meeting of minds with regard to the transfer of rights and obligations, is inappropriate for explaining the essence of agency for discharging religious obligations. And this is also the case regarding other instances of agency in Jewish law, such as an agent's conveying a bill of divorce. The contract model is also inappropriate in light of the problematic status of obligatory contracts in Jewish law: Jewish law is reluctant to recognize the binding validity of obligatory contracts, as is explained elsewhere in this volume.[35] To be sure, solutions to this problem have been found, and Jewish law indirectly recognizes the validity of such contracts, but it would be difficult to adduce contract law as the theoretical basis for agency in Jewish law, since the status of the former is far more precarious than that of the latter.

The two theories of agency relevant to Jewish law are the identity theory and the conferred powers theory. On the former, the agent takes on the legal identity of the principal, and the actions of the agent, who is regarded as the principal's 'extended arm,' discharge obligations of, and obligate, the principal. In contrast, the doctrine of conferred powers asserts no such identity, but regards agency as conferring the principal's powers on the agent. Since the talmudic era, the halakhic authorities have pondered the legal rationale for agency, as it undoubtedly has implications for how the law is applied. In bKidushin 43a, the Talmud discusses the question of whether an agent can become a witness in terms of the underlying rationale for agency. As we saw, other questions, such as whether an agent appointed to sell an asset can purchase it for himself, are also tackled in terms of this foundational issue.

Jewish law also makes a distinction, familiar from other legal systems, between two kinds of actions: legal actions, that is, actions that have a legal outcome, and non-legal actions, actions that have no legal outcome. This distinction has important halakhic implications. The distinction between the two kinds of actions is already found in the Talmud, in the context of the laws of Sabbath boundaries, and was elaborated on by the Early Authorities. The Hatam Sofer, we saw, formulates it as a general principle, distinguishing between 'the way of the world,' that is, actions that have no

35 See Chapter Twelve below, "Employee and independent contractor."

legal effect, and actions that do have legal effect, such as discharging religious duties, assuming a (financial) obligation, and selling.[36]

The primary import of this distinction, much discussed in the halakhic literature, has to do with the validity of the agency of those deemed legally incompetent to serve as agents, such as Gentiles and minors. If the action carried out by the agent is not of a legal nature, but is something like transporting an object, then it is valid and attributed to the principal. On the other hand, if it is a legal action, such as a signing a contract or making an acquisition, the action is void if performed by someone deemed incompetent to serve as an agent.

Yet as we saw, the distinction has other, less familiar, legal implications, the most salient of which has to do with the possibility that an agent's action is legally ineffective. The laws of agency define the cases in which the agent's action has no legal effect. Obviously this is relevant only with respect to legal actions, but not material actions such as delivering an object or making a payment.

We therefore distinguished between two kinds of agencies: agency in the strict sense, and agency in the broad sense. Agency in the strict sense only encompasses legal actions, whereas agency in the broad sense also encompasses actions that are of no legal effect. The laws of agency apply in full only to acts of agency in the strict sense, whereas only some laws of agency, those that are appropriate for the sorts of actions in question, apply to agency in the broad sense. To illustrate this, we considered the question of how much responsibility an agent who deviated from his mandate bears with respect to compensating his principal. The standard laws governing the agent's responsibility to his principal, we saw, are also perfectly appropriate with respect to material actions, and hence the agent who deviates from his mandate vis-à-vis a material action is subject to these laws. This explain why, in the halakhic sources, the laws and terminology of agency are applied even to actions such as conveying repayment of a debt from the debtor to the creditor.

Moving on to the question of the connection between the scope of agency and its conceptual analysis, we can cautiously conclude that there is indeed a connection between the theory of agency upheld by a legal system, and its stance on the applicability of the laws of agency to material actions. On the conferred powers model of agency, the scope of agency is limited to legal actions. It is meaningless to analyze material actions in terms of agency, since the agent is not carrying out an act that requires legal powers. Agency, on this model, is irrelevant in the context of physical actions, such as delivering goods from the seller to the buyer, that do not require legal powers, but are 'merely the action of an ape.'

When we explain agency in terms of the identity theory, however, it may be meaningful to speak of agency for material actions. If we understand

36 *Responsa Hatam Sofer*, OH #201.

the 'one's agent is like oneself' dictum 'maximally,' that is, as asserting that not only the outcome of the mission is attributed to the sender, but even the actions and perhaps the person of the agent are identified with the principal, we can take an integrated view of the actions carried out through agency, encompassing both legal and material actions. That is, if we regard the agent as the 'extended arm' of the principal, the boundary between the stages of an agent's mission where the actions performed are material actions, such as making a delivery, and those where the actions performed are legal actions, such as signing a contract, may be blurred.

Granted, the maxim 'one's agent is like oneself' can indeed be interpreted in a more limited manner, as applying only to legal actions, but the interpretation of broader scope, which encompasses material actions as well, is evident in the Talmud.

We can reformulate the doctrines we have discussed at an even higher level of abstraction. In essence, the doctrine of conferred powers reflects the principal's utilization of his personal autonomy to perform legal actions—actions he himself has the power to carry out—through the agency of another. On this analysis, agency reflects an individual's transferring his legal rights to someone else so as to achieve his goals, and constitutes a means of realizing the principal's wishes.

The identity theory, which, as we noted, is manifest in some of the halakhic sources, can also be reformulated more abstractly. Agency can be understood as a form of close cooperation between principal and agent, a cooperation by means of which they achieve a common goal. The law recognizes the individual's ability to extend his legal person and to join it, for certain purposes, with the legal person of another. This model of agency fully exploits the principle that 'one's agent is like oneself.'

The identity theory is usually regarded as reflecting the initial stage in the development of agency, whereas the doctrine of conferred powers is taken to be more abstract, and thus to represent a later stage of legal thinking. But since, as we have seen, it is possible to take both theories as instances of more abstract models, it is conceivable that the two theories do not represent different levels of conceptualizing agency, but rather, complementary understandings of agency.

12 Employee and independent contractor

1 Introduction: the employee–contractor distinction

This chapter will explore the laws governing employees and independent contractors in Jewish law, and the validity of agreements they enter into. As we will see, the employee–contractor distinction raises a fundamental question that will engage us throughout the chapter: what is the legal foundation of the employment agreement? And what is the underlying philosophical and jurisprudential basis for the legal status of agreements entered into by employees and contractors? We will argue that the employer–employee relationship in Jewish law was initially based on an **acquisition** model, but later came to be modeled on the concept of **obligation**. This distinction has important implications for the nature and scope of the obligations and rights created by such agreements, and even broader implications for labor law and employer–employee relations more generally in Jewish law.

1.1 General law

Before addressing the employee–contractor distinction itself, some general remarks about labor law and its historical evolution will be helpful. It is accepted today that employment contracts are to be differentiated from other contracts and dealt with separately under the rubric of labor law. The primary reason for this distinction is the high degree of protection that the worker usually requires in the course of his relationship with his employer, protection that cannot be secured by standard contractual rules. Typically, workers are perceived as financially vulnerable, relative to their employer, and therefore subject to manipulation by the employer, who can wield the threat of bad, and even intolerable, working conditions.

At present, in most countries workers are protected by two kinds of labor laws: laws governing collective bargaining, which regulate the delegation of the power to negotiate agreements, intervene in labor disputes and so on to unions and labor organizations; and laws that protect the rights (to breaks, vacations, minimum wage, severance pay, and so on) of individual workers directly.

During the Middle Ages, the highly stratified feudal society in many western European countries differentiated between different strata of workers and artisans on the basis of the work that they were able or allowed to do, through the institution of the guild. The modern period, that is, the period beginning in the eighteenth century, by contrast, was characterized by the rise of new principles governing labor, such as 'freedom of contract' and 'laissez faire.' These principles reflect the transition from a class-based society to a contract-based society.[1] In other words, the modern period ushered in the philosophy that individuals could define their legal status themselves by means of the contracts they concluded, and in particular, the labor relations specified therein. Their social standing was now defined, not by the work they were able or allowed to do, but by the kinds of **contract** they could enter into. Later on, various historical processes that gained momentum at the end of the nineteenth century and beginning of the twentieth, such as industrialization and capitalism, returned the focus to the plight of the workers as a class. In the wake of these developments, there was increasing recognition that workers required protection beyond that which they could negotiate

1 See H. Maine, *Ancient Law*, 10th ed. (London: 1984), 172–74.

on their own, giving rise to the enactment of labor laws of both the aforementioned types.

It is against this background that the importance of recognizing a category of employees—as distinct from independent contractors—becomes manifest. Clearly, not everyone who agrees to provide a service to someone else is considered the latter's employee and, as such, entitled to the special protection of labor laws. It is unreasonable, for example, to view taxi drivers and restaurant owners as employees of their customers, from whom they are entitled to receive social benefits (e.g., healthcare, unemployment insurance, pensions, maternity leave, disability allowances, daycare, vacation pay, and severance pay).

A number of legal distinctions between employees and independent contractors are widely accepted today. Among them are the following: (1) protective labor law applies to employees and not to independent contractors; (2) whether a worker is an employee or an independent contractor will impact the employer's responsibility for injury incurred by the worker (or a third party injured by the worker); (3) whether a worker is an employee or an independent contractor will impact the tax obligations of both the employer and the worker; (4) the ownership of creative ideas developed in the course of employment depends on whether the work was done by an employee or an independent contractor; (5) the type of legal tribunal authorized to adjudicate legal disputes in which a worker is involved varies depending on whether he is an employee or an independent contractor.

The employee–independent contractor distinction also has significant social implications. Indeed, classifying a worker as an employee or an independent contractor has implications that transcend the employment context, and in some sense defines her social status more generally. Furthermore, it can influence not only the worker's own self-perception and the esteem in which the worker is held by others, but also the resources society invests in the worker's protection—and thus, ultimately, in his well-being. The greater the extent to which a worker is defined as an employee, the more he will be covered by protective labor laws that are paternalistic in nature and cannot be opted out of. In contrast, the greater the extent to which a worker is defined as an independent contractor, the more he will be governed by principles that respect his personal autonomy, such as freedom of contract. The employee–independent contractor distinction, the focus of this chapter, lies at the very heart of labor law.

How, then, are we to distinguish between a worker and an independent contractor? Both the employer–employee relationship, and the employer–contractor relationship, are consensual relationships formed for the purpose of getting work done. That there is an important distinction between these two relationships is universally recognized, but there is also general agreement that it is difficult to arrive at a precise definition of the distinguishing features. In the words of Lord Denning, one of England's greatest jurists: "It is recognized by all that there is a difference between a laborer and a contractor, though they are unable to point out exactly the cause for this distinction."[2]

Everyone instinctively grasps the obvious difference between a bus driver who works for the company that employs her, and an independent taxi driver who is not working for the customer sitting in his cab, but rather, works for himself. Nevertheless, the distinguishing feature is difficult to identify. Lord Denning suggested the following characterization:

> It is often easy to recognize a contract of service when you see it, but difficult to say wherein the difference lies. A ship's master, a chauffeur, and a reporter on the staff of a newspaper are all employed under a contract **of** service; but a ship's pilot, a taxi-man, and a newspaper contributor are employed under a contract **for** services. One feature which seems to run through the instances is that under a contract of service, a man is employed as part of the business, and his work is done as an integral part of the business; whereas, under a contract for services, his work, although done for the business, is not integrated into it but is only accessory to it.

Many different parameters for distinguishing between employees and independent contractors have been suggested in the legal literature. Some of the more plausible are the following:

i Control: can the employer tell the worker how to carry out the work?
ii Integration: is the worker systematically integrated into the employer's operations, or does he work independently?
iii Personal involvement: is the worker obligated to complete the work himself, or can he have someone else do it in his place?
iv Corporate status: is the worker a corporation? If so, can it be assumed that he is a contractor and not an employee?
v Exclusivity: does the worker provide the service to one employer, several employers, or to anyone who requests it?
vi Sophistication: how sophisticated is the work? It has been suggested that employees perform simple tasks and contractors, more complex and sophisticated work.
vii Intention as defined in the contract/agreement: what does an analysis of the contract/agreement reveal about the work relationship?
viii Social benefits: does the employer provide social benefits or not? The payment of social benefits generally implies that the worker is an employee.
ix Salary calculation: is the salary calculated on an hourly/daily basis, or for an extended period of time?

2 *Stevenson, Jordan and Harrison v. Macdonald and Evans* [1952] 1 T.L.R., 101, 111.

x Compensation for expenses and risk: does the employer compensate the worker for expenses and risks incurred during the course of his work? If so, this is generally taken as an indication that he is considered an employee.
xi Term of contract/agreement: is the commitment for a short or long period of time? The longer the term of the contract/agreement, the greater the likelihood that the worker is an employee.
xii Determination of work hours: can the worker set his own hours? If so, this is generally taken as an indication that he is considered a contractor.
xiii Determination of work venue: can the worker determine the location where the work is to be carried out, or is he required to work in a specific location?
xiv Work tools: does the employer or the worker supply the tools needed to do the work? Generally, an independent contractor brings his own tools, whereas an employee's tools are supplied by his employer.

Other criteria have also been proposed, but those listed suffice to establish that no one criterion provides an unassailable distinction between employees and contractors.

An eminent Israeli legal scholar has expressed pessimism about the very possibility of formulating a satisfactory definition:

> It is not possible to establish clear criteria—either formal/technical or qualitative—that capture the essential distinctions between hired workers and contractors. Qualitative criteria ... merely re-describe the categories in different terms, leaving unanswered the question of how to distinguish them. In every legal system, these criteria serve only as a rhetorical device for concealing the impossibility of establishing clear criteria for the said demarcation.[3]

1.2 Jewish law

From the perspective of Jewish law, the employer–employee distinction is particularly significant. As is widely known, the Jewish legal system has clear and well-established principles protecting workers, such as the Sabbath as a day of rest, severance rights, and so on. But Jewish law also addresses the rights of employers. One scholar encapsulated the halakhic approach to labor law as follows:

> The principle of protection for the worker in Jewish law is consistent with the ancient traditions of the Torah, which tended to protect the

3 Eyal Zamir, "On the distinction between an employee and an independent contractor" (Hebrew), 22 *Mishpatim* (1992), 113–68, 166.

> weaker elements of society—the proselyte, the orphan, the widow, and the poor—so that they would not be exploited by the stronger. . . . Along with protection of the worker by setting down certain presumptions (both as a matter of law, and beyond what is required by law), Jewish labor law also concerned itself with the just rights of the employer, demanding of the worker that he faithfully fulfill his obligations to him.[4]

While the protection afforded employees by labor laws constitutes an important reason for specifying with exactitude the legal definition of an employee, this specification has added significance in the Jewish law context, in that the validity of these relations depends on the validity of contractual obligations in general. As we will see, Jewish law does not recognize the validity of a contract that creates the obligation to carry out or desist from specific tasks in the future, yet does grant acquisitional or quasi-acquisitional rights in the present. Hence a contract between an employer and an employee for the completion of a specific task raises two concerns: in addition to the need to protect the employee's rights, the very possibility of validating such a contract must also be addressed.

The lack of clarity as to the distinction between an employee and an independent contractor afflicts Jewish law no less than general law. A survey of the constraints that gave rise to this vagueness will not only afford us deeper insight into the different categories of worker–employer relationships, but also afford us a better understanding of labor law in the wider sense.

As was stated above, in this chapter we will seek to demonstrate that the employer–employee relationship in Jewish law was initially based on an **acquisition** model, and in some ways similar to slavery, but later evolved, coming to be modeled on the concept of **obligation**. It is our contention that the (quasi)validity of contracts was not accepted by the Jewish legal system until the post-Maimonidean period, that is, until the thirteenth century. We will explore how this transition impacted the legal distinction between employee and contractor at both the theoretical and the practical levels. We will also consider some of the social implications of the different modes of employment, and see how they were addressed by the halakhic authorities. As we will see, ironically, the transition from the acquisition model to the obligation model did not necessarily improve, and perhaps even worsened, the employee's actual status.

To begin, let us consider a case that came before the Tel Aviv Rabbinical Court.[5] It involved a taxi driver whose employment was terminated by his employer. The driver claimed from his employer a number of payments

4 Shilem Warhaftig, *Jewish Labor Law* (Hebrew), vol. 1 (Tel Aviv: 1969), 2, 5.

5 File No. 2535/19 Rabbinical Court (TA) Kiserman v. R. Alexander Direnfeld, 3 PDR 272 (Isr.) [1959]. See Appendix 1.

that, in his opinion, the employer was obligated to pay. This claim required a clarification of the nature of the legal relationship between a driver and his employer: was the driver an employee or a contractor? A careful reading of the court's ruling (see Appendix 1), and the opinions brought before the court as to the position of Israeli law on the matter, sheds light on the problem of articulating the employee–contractor distinction.

The halakhic authorities who addressed the employee–contractor distinction have endorsed two basic criteria, which we can call the 'degree of subjection' criterion, and the 'basic of renumersation' criterion. The 'degree of subjection' criterion examines the nature of the worker's relation to his employer; the 'basis of remuneration' criterion examines the basis used for calculating the worker's remuneration. Let us take a closer look at these criteria.

i 'Degree of subjection' criterion

Among the issues determined in the aforementioned ruling was the following point:

> We do not concur with the defendant's representative in determining that the claimant was employed as a contractor, given that there is no disagreement over the fact that the claimant's work caused him to be tied up for a specific length of time at specific hours of the day: the school bus driver is not in a position to choose at what times the children are driven to school, as these are fixed times, and it was stated [in the contract] that he could not come early or be late.... In light of all that has been said, it is clear in our case that since the claimant worked as a driver at specific times, corresponding to the times students had their scheduled classes at the Talmud Torah, the law deems him an employee ... and not an independent contractor.

One member of the court, R. S.B. Werner, elaborated on the reasoning behind the ruling in a scholarly article published some years later. In his comments, he refers to the law that an employee is allowed to unilaterally break a contract, whereas a contractor may not do so. This law will be considered in greater depth below. Here we will just focus on the criterion R. Werner suggests for distinguishing between an employee and a contractor, namely, the degree to which the worker is free to set his work hours:

> As we said, a contractor is independent, as if he were working for himself, and his work does not involve a sense of bondage even if he cannot withdraw in the middle of his work. Therefore, he may not withdraw... since he has privileges and relative comfort in terms of his work conditions, in that he may work when he wishes and [when] it

> is convenient for him. Therefore, he is not regarded as subjugated to his employer, as if he were a slave who could not withdraw from his commitment. As to a salaried employee, however, whose conditions of work are more difficult, insofar as he cannot work schedules and hours that are convenient for him—were he unable to withdraw in the middle of his work, he would seem like his employer's slave, and the Torah said, "they are My slaves" (Lev. 25: 55).

It is the feeling of bondage, not bondage itself, that makes the difference. As R. Werner explains:

> The worker who hired himself out for a certain time has, so to speak, placed his person at the disposal of the employer, and to a certain extent resembles a slave whose person is subject to control by others.... In contrast, although a contractor took it upon himself to do a certain job, this fact does not negate his bodily independence or render his person subject to control by others in any way. And with regard to him it is not said "they are My slaves."... He is not a slave, and is not entitled to withdraw.

What is the connection between the issue of setting the worker's work times and that of the worker's affinity to the slave[6]? Why would it be mistaken, in this context, to take into consideration the question of whether the worker has a say in determining the type of work he will do? It is obvious that neither an employee nor a contractor can determine the type of work he will do, as both are hired to carry out a specific task set by the employer. It seems that the only feature of the work through which a worker's independence can be gauged is the determination of its pace and hours. Hence whoever controls the determination of the pace and time of work controls the employee. If the worker receives a fixed work schedule he must abide by, he is considered an employee, that is, he is like a slave. If the worker is allowed to set the pace or hours of work, that is, if he is in charge of his work schedule, he is considered an independent contractor. In the words of the Maharam of Rothenburg:

> The employee is not permitted to be idle ... but a contractor, who took upon himself to harvest a field or to weave cloth, is allowed to be idle if he wishes to do so.
>
> *Responsa Maharam* (Prague edition), #477

In one of his rulings, Moshe Silberg, an Israel Supreme Court Justice and scholar of halakhic jurisprudence, came to the following conclusion:

6 In Hebrew, the words 'worker' (*oved*) and 'slave' (*eved*) share the same lexical root, highlighting the basic affinity between a worker and a slave.

> There is, ultimately, just one question: Who does the man work for, himself or others? Did he agree to work for someone else, in which case he obviously owes this employer the products generated by this labor, or does he work for himself, and in serving himself, as it were, prepare the final product, the complete finished project, which he owes to the employer?[7]

It is clear that the extent of the worker's independence is that which distinguishes between an employee and a contractor. Unfortunately, Silberg does not provide a clear standard that allows us to determine whether the worker works for himself or for his employer. R. Werner's criterion—the extent to which the worker is free to set his own work hours—can successfully fill this void.

ii 'Basis of remuneration' criterion

Another approach to distinguishing between an employee and a contractor examines the basis used for calculating the worker's remuneration. When the salary is calculated on the basis of the hours worked, the worker is generally considered an employee, whereas when the remuneration is per project—viz., for completion of the job he has undertaken to do, regardless of how long it takes—the worker is generally considered a contractor.

R. Abraham Borenstein of Sochatchov, a nineteenth-century authority, defined the 'basis of remuneration' criterion as follows:

> The difference between an employee and a contractor resides solely in the nature of the obligation to the employer. The employee's obligation is to do work for the employer, and it makes no difference what this work consists of. This is not so with respect to the contractor, whose obligation is to fix up whatever he committed himself to fixing. And were he able to fix the object in an instant, without any work at all, [his obligation would be discharged and] he would have no further obligation. Thus, his obligation is unlike that of the employee.
>
> *Responsa Avnei Nezer*, HM #52

In holding this view, he is following R. Abraham b. David (Rabad):

> The wage [of the employee] is solely a function of his exertion, and whoever does not exert himself does not get paid. But the contractor's wage depends solely on completion of his work, and whenever it is completed, whether by him or by somebody else, he gets paid.
>
> quoted in *Beit Yosef*, *Tur*, HM 334:4

7 Justice Silberg, CA 47/48, Agoshevitz and others v. Futerman, 5(4) PD 12 (1950).

What is the difference between the criterion suggested by the Rabad and the 'degree of subjection' criterion suggested by R. Werner? According to the Rabad, the primary question is not whether the employer or the worker sets the work hours, but whether the salary is paid on the basis of the number of hours worked, or per project, regardless of how long the project takes. This differs from the 'degree of subjection' criterion, on which the important parameter is whether the work hours are set by the employer or the worker.

A contract may sometimes set down a complex formula for a worker's wage, and how it is to be paid, making it difficult to determine whether the basis of remuneration is indicative of employee or contractor status. For example, it would be difficult to categorize an agreement that specifies an all-inclusive amount to be paid for the completion of a certain job, but stipulates that it will be paid in installments at fixed intervals, for instance, weekly. And so too in the case of a work agreement that sets out a daily wage, but only on condition that the worker meets specific daily output targets.

One halakhic authority who endorsed the 'basis of remuneration' criterion tried to deal with such complex cases:

> This is the difference between an employee and a contractor: An employee's wage depends on the time [he puts in], a contractor's wage depends on the completion of his work.... And even though it is possible that a time-limit has been set for the contacted job, say, a year or more, this is no more than a secondary proviso, and not a substantive and essential element of the agreement; it is akin to stipulation of the place where, or means by which, the work is to be carried out... and it does not change the main thrust of the contract. And one is an employee only if the payment for the work is associated with a specific duration ... daily, weekly, monthly, and so on. But if they made payment for the work dependent on its completion, then that is a contracting arrangement. Conversely, if they agreed on the daily wage, and the employer told the worker to stay until the field was harvested or the cloth woven, he is still considered an employee paid a daily wage and the completion of harvesting the field or weaving the cloth is but a secondary condition agreed on between them....
>
> Even if [the contractor] is paid weekly or monthly, it is only an agreement as to the terms of payment, which is but a secondary condition. It is like [the case of] a builder who undertakes to build a house for an agreed sum, and [he and the one who engaged him] decided on a payment schedule, [such as] that he would pay him a specific sum every week or every month. And it is clear that the builder remains a contractor nonetheless, because his pay does not depend on his weekly or monthly output, but on finishing the entire job, and [the

> agreement that he would be paid in weekly or monthly installments] is only a secondary proviso setting out the terms of payment.
>
> *Responsa R. Yekutiel Asher Enzil*, #15

In the final analysis, then, R. Ensel applies the 'basis of remuneration' criterion as a **substantive** rather than a formal test. Hence it might well happen that even though a contract formally articulates the remuneration in terms of specific amounts paid at specific time intervals, examination of the contract from a substantive perspective leads to the conclusion that the payment is in fact an overall amount for completion of the work without regard to its duration.

There appears to be a weakness in R. Ensel's explanation, namely, its circularity. To establish whether a condition pertaining to calculation of the remuneration is central or secondary, it is necessary to analyze all of the communications between the two parties so as to determine whether the worker is an employee or a contractor. In other words, the definition of the worker's status depends on the interpretation given to the contractual provisions governing calculation of the remuneration, but the interpretation of these provisions may depend on how the worker is classified.

2 Legal basis of the employer–employee relationship

To fully understand the nature of the tension between the two categories of workers, 'employee' and 'contractor,' we must be attentive to the legal foundations of labor relations in Jewish law. The fundamental question is that of the legal foundation which imparts validity to the employer–employee relationship.

As noted above, two opposed approaches to this question can be identified in the corpus of Jewish law. On the older of the two approaches, which can be called the 'acquisition' model, someone who hires himself out as another person's employee is actually selling himself to the employer. Just as he can sell an article he owns to his employer, so he can sell himself for the purpose of doing a specific job at a specific time. The wages paid him are considered to be payment for the purchase of his capacity to work. On the second approach, which we will call the 'obligation' model, the relationship between the employer and the employee is to be viewed as simply a relationship of obligation. The employee is obliged to work, and the employer is obliged to pay the agreed-upon wages.

It might seem odd and even superfluous to devote time to studying the 'acquisition' model, in view of the indisputable primacy of the 'obligation' model in modern legal thought. As we will see toward the end of this chapter, at some point the 'obligation' model also came to be dominant in Jewish law. Given that today slavery in any form is considered despicable and indefensible, what value can there be in exploring a model that views the employee as the employer's property? Yet understanding the tension between the acquisition model and the obligation model is important from a number of standpoints. For one thing, it clarifies the earlier stages of labor law, and the ways in which it evolved into the legal structures known to us today. More importantly, the acquisition model can serve as a critical standard for evaluating the obligation model's success in differentiating between employees and contractors. Coming to grips with a model so fundamentally different from that upheld today gives us an opportunity to examine anew premises taken to be axiomatic in contemporary legal thought.

This task would be easier if the Jewish legal sources were wont to reveal the basic assumptions upon which they are based. The primary sources of Jewish law, however, are not obliging in this respect, and do not tend to articulate these abstract legal structures, which must therefore be deduced from the laws themselves.

3 The acquisition model

3.1 Talmudic source

A well-known *sugya* in the Babylonian Talmud that addresses the question of the status of workers, bBaba Metzia 10a, may help dispel doubts as to their status. The *sugya* discusses an employee who finds a lost object in the course of his work. The question that arises is who takes ownership of the object, the employee or the employer. To fully understand the *sugya*, a brief introduction will be helpful.

In mEruvin 7:11, the following principle is set down: "One can benefit someone without his knowledge [that is, without his actually having consented, as he was not present; this is so because we can presume that he consents to be benefited], but one cannot obligate someone without his knowledge."[8] According to this principle, one can carry out a beneficial legal transaction on behalf of someone else, and it will be credited to this other person even if the one carrying out the transaction is acting without prior authorization. One of the restrictions on this law is that the transaction in question may not harm others. Thus, for example, if Reuben finds out that he can collect a debt for Shimon from his debtor Levi, he may do so even without prior authorization from Shimon. This, however, is on condition that Levi has no other creditors who would, as a result of Reuben's collecting Shimon's debt, be rendered unable to collect their debts. Another example would be the case where someone finds a lost object and wants to take possession of it on behalf of someone else. In this situation, taking the lost object would harm the interests of others who might be interested in taking the lost object for themselves.

8 See also mGitin 1:6.

In light of this principle, the *sugya* discusses the case of an employee who finds a lost object. The question is whether it is the employer who acquires the object, and if so, how this differs from the case just mentioned, where, we saw, one who picks up a found object with the goal of acquiring it for his fellow cannot in fact acquire it for his fellow. The discussion brings to the fore fundamental questions regarding employer–employee relations in talmudic law.

> Both R. Nahman and R. Hisda say: If someone picks up a found object for his fellow—his fellow does not acquire it. Why so? Because it is like one who seizes [a debtor's property] on behalf of a creditor, where [the debtor] has other creditors. And one who seizes [a debtor's property] on behalf of a creditor, where [the debtor] has other creditors—does not acquire it. Rava queried R. Nahman: [Is it not the law that] anything found by a worker belongs to him? What does this apply to? Cases when the employer said, 'Weed for me today' or 'Hoe for me today.' But if he said to him, 'Do work for me today'–[anything found by the employee] belongs to the employer. [R. Nahman] said to him: This case of the employee is different, for the hand of the employee is like the hand of his employer. But didn't Rav say: 'A worker may withdraw [from his work] even in the middle of the day'? He [R. Nahman] said to him: As long as he has not withdrawn, his hand is like the hand of his employer. For the right to withdraw has a different rationale, as it is written: "For unto Me [the children of Israel] are slaves; they are My slaves" (Lev. 25:55)—not slaves of slaves.
>
> bBaba Metzia 10a

To recapitulate, R. Nahman claims that a lost object taken by an employee becomes the property of the employer, because the hand of the employee "is like the hand of his employer." Rava objects, arguing that this is incompatible with the employee's right to withdraw from a work agreement at any time. R. Nahman replies that even though there is a conflict between the two laws, and the employee's right to withdraw is based on a biblical verse, nevertheless, as long as the employee has not withdrawn, his hand is like that of his employer.

Some background is helpful here. The institution of slavery existed throughout the ancient world, and biblical law accepted this as an established fact. Nevertheless, within the context of ancient Near Eastern law, the Bible broke new ground in seeking to mandate humane treatment of slaves, who were to be related to as people, and not merely the property of their masters. With regard to Hebrew slaves, the Bible is even more demanding, seeking to limit the institution of slavery, and to some degree, eliminate it altogether.[9] It establishes set intervals at which masters are

9 See Chapter Nine, "Charity and distributive justice."

obligated to free their slaves, and even in the course of their bondage, masters may not work their Hebrew slaves "with rigor." The Hebrew slave is also referred to as "your brother" in the Bible. Guiding biblical law in this regard is the idea that the enslavement of another individual is wrong, since it perverts the natural order of things, and man, instead of being subservient to God alone, becomes subservient to his fellow man: "For unto Me the children of Israel are slaves; they are My slaves whom I brought forth out of the land of Egypt: I am the Lord your God" (Lev. 25:55).[10]

In the *sugya* under discussion, this principle grounds a cardinal labor law, namely, the law that an employee has the right to "withdraw even in the middle of the day," that is, to break the work agreement before the end of the agreed-upon period of employment. The Talmud maintains that the employee's right to withdraw from the work agreement is necessary to emphasize that the work agreement is free of any element of slavery.

On the strength of the principle that as long as the employee does not invoke his right to withdraw, "his hand is like the hand of his employer," the Talmud established the law that a lost object acquired by an employee (while he is working) belongs to the employer. R. Abraham Karelitz, the Hazon Ish, explains this dictum as follows:

> The employer has acquired the worker, so to speak. And even though the employee can withdraw, so long as he has not withdrawn, the employer indeed has acquisitional rights in him.... And R. Nahman replied that, since the employee may withdraw, the relationship is not that of bondage, but as long as he has not done so, it is indeed the case that he has been acquired—with regard to this matter—by his employer, and if the employee picks up a found object, the employer acquires it *eo ipso*, because acquisition of anything found is [one of the] work conditions stipulated by the employer, for the hand of the employee is like the hand of the employer.
>
> *Hazon Ish*, Baba Metzia, Likutim, sec. 20, 10a

Similarly, R. Meir Simha of Dvinsk explains:

> The hand of the employee is like the hand of the employer, that is, the employer hired the hands of the employee with respect to any benefit they may confer, and it is as if the employer has acquired all rights to whatever [the employee] may produce or find.... He can transfer to his master his hands and whatever they find, just as a palm-tree and its forthcoming fruit [can be sold].
>
> *Or Sameiah*, Laws of Hiring 9:11

10 See I. Mendelsohn, *Slavery in the Ancient Near East* (New York: 1949), and Z. Falk, *Hebrew Law in Biblical Times*, 2nd ed. (Winona Lake IN: 2001), 114–21.

Thus the employer has acquired a right in the body of the worker. As the Rashba, R. Solomon b. Adret, puts it, "the body of the worker is bonded for the purpose he was hired for, just as if one has leased a field or vineyard from his fellow, and their produce belongs to him."[11] Hence if a worker finds something and takes possession of it, the acquisition is made on behalf of the employer.

Yet this fact that a worker is tantamount to a slave acquired by his employer is obscured by the worker's right to break off the relationship at will. In the continuation of the responsum cited above, the Admor of Sochatchov offers an **ideological** explanation for the employee's right to withdraw from the work agreement halfway through the day. On his view, this right derives from the Torah's fundamental opposition to the concept of slavery. He contends that it is precisely because the employee is indeed like a slave that, at any moment, he is permitted to sever the bonds that enfetter him:

> First the employee becomes a slave, since [in agreeing to take the job], he expressed a desire to be a slave. Even though the virtue of the Jews is that they are slaves of the Holy One, blessed be He, and not of other slaves, the Torah nonetheless gives this person the prerogative of eschewing this virtue and becoming a slave.... But when he [changes his mind and] does not want to be a slave any more, he reclaims this virtue, and the acquisition is terminated.

3.2 That which is not yet in existence

It might be argued that certain employer–employee work agreements are inherently problematic, inasmuch as they can be construed as transactions in 'futures,' things not yet in existence. Talmudic law does not recognize the validity of such transactions. According to the halakha, an agreement wherein someone sells the fruit that will be on his trees at the end of the season, is inherently invalid, since the fruit did not exist at the time of the agreement. Similarly, we might think that if a worker is hired to find something for his employer, or a wet-nurse is hired to nurse the employer's child, the transaction is invalid because it involves something not yet in existence, viz., the lost property was not yet found, let alone acquired, by the worker, and, in the case of the wet nurse, her breast milk.

Let us consider the implications for labor law of non-recognition of the binding validity of obligations incurred through transactions involving 'things not yet in existence.' Non-recognition of the validity of a transaction involving 'things not yet in existence' could undermine any possible foundation for labor law, since labor law seems to address transactions involving actions not executed on the spot, but in the future. Without some

11 *Responsa Rashba*, 2, #72.

sort of recognition of the binding validity of obligations undertaken by workers vis-à-vis their employers, and vice versa, the labor market could not have emerged. This outcome is not feasible, as no society in which employer–employee relations lack binding validity is sustainable. Thus it seems that one way or another, every legal system must recognize the binding validity of work agreements, even those that refer to future actions.

The problem of transactions in 'futures,' or as the Talmud puts it, 'things not yet in existence,' can, however, be resolved by attending to the basic premise of the acquisition model, namely, that the employee's person is, in effect, acquired by the employer when the work agreement is entered into. The object of the transaction in these cases is not the object yet to be found or the milk yet to be suckled, but the persons of the worker and the nurse, respectively, which were acquired for particular purposes pertaining, admittedly, to future events. Yet since the worker and the nurse are already in existence, we can adduce the Rashba's position that "concerning hiring, we do not argue that the thing is not yet in existence."

> Hence in the case of an employee hired to do whatever work is given him by his employer, including finding lost property, whatever he finds belongs to the employer even if, at the time he took the lost property, he indeed intended to acquire it for himself—as long as the employee has not actually withdraw from the work agreement.
>
> *Responsa Rashba*, 2, #72

This understanding of the acquisitional dimension of employer–employee relations also explains the difference between the legal results of an act carried out by an agent and those of an act carried out by an employee. An agent who wishes to make an acquisition for his principal can do so, but if he did not intend to make an acquisition on behalf of his principal, the latter has not made an acquisition.[12] Where the acquisition is made by someone's employee, however—as opposed to his agent—then under the same circumstances, viz., where the acquiring employee does not intend to acquire the object for his employer, the employer nonetheless acquires it. The explanation for this disparity between an agent and an employee lies in a crucial difference in their legal status. The agent is independent, his relationship to his principal being merely that of representation. In other words, the agent is authorized to act for his principal with regard to specific matters. This power of representation does not negate the agent's power to act for himself, as he remains, at the same time, his own master. Hence the ownership of a lost object that is picked up by the agent depends solely on his intention when picking it up–did he intend to acquire it for himself or for his principal? By contrast,

12 See *Mahane Efraim*, Laws of Agents and Partners, sec. 11.

during the work day the employee is not independent, but rather his power to acquire 'belongs' (as long as he has not withdrawn) to his employer. This being so, the employer acquires a lost object that the employee has picked up, regardless of the employee's intentions.

3.3 Problems raised by the acquisition model

The acquisition model solves the problem of acquiring 'that which is not yet in existence,' which arises in the context of labor law, but nevertheless raises other difficulties. Conceptualizing the worker as a slave, and the employer–employee relationship as an acquisition, raises questions that emerge from the gap between slavery in the full sense of the word, and the state of being in someone else's employ. One difficulty manifests itself with regard to termination of the relationship. On the slave model, we would expect termination of employment to be a complicated procedure along the lines of manumission. A second difficulty is that the prohibition against selling oneself into slavery would appear to imply a parallel injunction against hiring oneself out as an employee. Let us examine these problems more closely.

i Termination of employment

The Talmud sets down that a slave can acquire his freedom only through a writ of manumission. A verbal declaration on the part of the master that he is freeing the slave does not suffice. From this, the Amora Rava deduces the following principle:

> The body of a Hebrew slave belongs to his master; hence if the master waives the remainder [of the slave's term of bondage], the remainder is not waived.
>
> bKidushin 16a

The master's waiver of the remainder of the slave's term of bondage does not take force, since the slave, not having received a writ of manumission, remains the master's property. Property rights cannot be terminated by waiver: there must be an act of acquisition for ownership to be transferred.

The Maharam of Rothenburg applied this principle to the employer–employee relationship in the case of a labor dispute between a tutor and his employer:

> A tutor started teaching, and his employer said to him, 'Go away from me, I do not want you.' And the tutor agreed [to this]. And then the employer once again changed his mind and wanted him to stay. And the tutor said, 'You have waived my subjection, and I do not want to

> teach for you any more.' It seems to me that the subjection cannot be waived by mere speech.
>
> *Responsa Maharam* (Prague edition), #77

The Maharam's ruling follows from the acquisition model, on which an employee can only be released from his work agreement in a manner paralleling that by which a slave is released from his bondage. Just as a slave is only freed by means of a writ of manumission, so too, according to the Maharam, the employer's verbal statement to the tutor cannot terminate the legal relationship between them. Hence the teacher is still obligated to work for the employer.

R. Joseph di Trani (Maharit) was asked a similar question about a tutor who had committed himself, by a work agreement, to teach a certain group of students. Another group of students enticed him to come and teach them instead, and even convinced him to swear that he would leave his job and teach this second group. Subsequently, the teacher regretted the oath he had sworn and his desire to breach his obligation to the first group. In one of several questions he posed to the Maharit, he claimed that the oath had no validity, since by law he was unable to breach his obligation to the first group. The Maharit replied that although an employee may generally withdraw from his work agreement halfway through the day, he may not do so if it causes a loss to the employer. Since cessation of the teacher's work is considered a loss of the said type, he is forbidden, by law, to breach the work agreement with the first group. The Maharit points out that denial of the employee's right to renege on his commitment to work where this will cause a loss to the employer demonstrates that the employee belongs to the employer. In establishing this principle, the Maharit mentions the Maharam's aforementioned assertion that an employer cannot terminate a work agreement by means of a verbal statement alone:

> Since there is a loss involved [and hence he may not withdraw], it is regarded as if his body were bought, and his subjection cannot be waived verbally. We do not invoke [here] the rule that a worker may withdraw halfway through the day. And we do not say that although, where there is a loss, the employer may engage another worker for the sum of the first worker's wage, he [the employer] may waive his right to [avoid] that loss and say, 'I do not wish to use the Rabbinic enactment that was enacted for my benefit'.... Rather, in the opinion of the Maharam, where there is a loss involved, the person of the worker is bonded, in accordance with the law regarding the Hebrew slave, and such subjection cannot be terminated verbally.
>
> *Responsa Maharit*, 2, YD #50

The Maharit concludes that the tutor's oath to the second group is not binding, since, given that his person belongs to his employer, an employee cannot swear an oath to leave his ongoing place of employment where a monetary loss will be incurred [by his employer] thereby. Furthermore, since the worker is subject to the employer, in any financial disagreement between them, the burden of proof falls on the employee, as the employer is regarded as 'the one in possession.'[13]

Clearly, then, applying the acquisition model to employer–employee relations greatly complicates the process of terminating an employee's employment.

ii The prohibition against selling oneself into slavery

A further difficulty arises from the talmudic dictum '"they [the children of Israel] are My slaves" (Lev. 25:55)—not slaves of slaves.'[14] If so, how is it permissible to seek employment at all, since in so doing—on the acquisition model—one transgresses the prohibition against selling oneself into slavery (the law of the Hebrew slave)?[15] The Maharam suggests the following solution:

> For up to three years, he is regarded as an employee, and not a slave, since it is written, "For he has given you double the service of a hired servant" (Deut. 15:18)—that is, six years. Therefore, he may hire himself out for one, two, or three consecutive years, but no more, because up to three years he is considered an employee and not a slave.
>
> *Responsa Maharam* (Prague edition), #72[16]

3.4 Significance of the employee's right to breach the work agreement

We saw that the Talmud anchors the employee's right to withdraw at any time, and cancel his work agreement with the employer, in the biblical verse: "For unto Me the children of Israel are slaves; they are My slaves." The Rabbis interpreted the latter clause to mean: "they are My slaves"—not slaves of slaves." Two features of this right are noteworthy. First, this

13 According to the halakhic laws of evidence, in disputes over property that is in the possession of one of the sides, the burden of proof falls on the other side, viz., the side seeking to change the situation. Hence the Maharit's statement that the burden of proof falls on the employee, who wishes to change the situation vis-à-vis his employer's stake in his person. Note that were it not for the fact that the employee is considered to be in the employer's possession, another evidentiary rule, more favorable to the employee, might have been applicable: "the burden of proof is on he who seeks to take something from his fellow."

14 bBaba Metzia 10a.

15 See bKidushin 22b.

16 However, this is not a satisfactory solution, since the *sugya* about the lost object that is found by a worker applies to all workers, regardless of the length of time they are hired for: the hand of the employee is always considered to be "like the hand of his employer."

right is not often encountered in the contractual arrangements of any legal system. Second, the importance of this right resides in the fact that it guarantees the employee's prerogative to regain his freedom whenever he chooses. This explains why the Sages deemed it imperative to anchor this right in a verse from the Torah, and thereby emphasize its significance.

The Sages were apprehensive lest the employee end up a slave, a concern arising from the fact that the employee is subject to his employer, who has the authority to decide for him how, when, and where he will work. The fact that the legal foundation of the employer–employee relationship is the employer's proprietary rights vis-à-vis the employee may have heightened this concern. They therefore granted the employee the right to realize his potential freedom at any time by escaping his 'bondage' and leaving his place of employment, a right differentiating him from the slave proper. This prerogative gives the employee full protection against any withholding of wages for work already performed, even if completion of the job by a different worker will cost the employer more. The Sages, sensitive to the inherent inequity of the employer–employee relationship, saw fit to restore a kind of balance, and gave the employee the right to withdraw without incurring a penalty. Otherwise, he would never be able to actualize his right.

4 The obligation model

4.1 Introduction

There is another approach to employer–employee relations in Jewish law, an approach that seeks to account for the relationship without invoking the laws of acquisition. According to this approach, the legal foundation on which the employer–employee relationship rests is the contract they have concluded. This approach is first articulated in writings of the twelfth century halakhic decisors, although allusions to it can already be found in the Talmud. The blossoming of this approach as an alternative to the acquisition model is readily apparent in the medieval halakhic authorities' interpretive analysis of the talmudic laws of fraud.

First, however, some background information is called for. The Torah states: "And if you sell anything to your neighbor, or buy from your neighbor's hand, you shall not wrong one another" (Lev. 25:14). From this verse, the Tannaim derived the prohibition against transactions at exaggerated prices, that is, selling an item for more than its market value or purchasing an item for less than its market value. The Tannaim also set forth the recourse available to someone who has been cheated; these laws of fraud are codified in Maimonides' *Code*, Laws concerning Sales, chapters 12-13.[17] One mishnaic limitation on the scope of the laws of fraud is

17 See Appendix 2.

expressed by Maimonides as follows: "These are the things with respect to which the laws of fraud do not apply—land, dispositive legal documents (*shtarot*), slaves, and objects dedicated to the Temple. Even if he sold something worth one thousand dinar for one dinar, or vice versa—the laws of fraud do not apply."[18]

The Babylonian Talmud raises the question of whether the laws of fraud apply only to sales, or also apply to rental transactions. Abbaye concludes that the laws of fraud apply to rental transactions too, because in effect, renting is acquisition for a limited time. As Abbaye puts it: "On its day, it is a sale."[19]

In this context, the Early Authorities discussed the question of whether the laws of fraud also apply to the labor market, that is, when workers earn more than the going rate or, as is more common, less than the going rate. They concur that the laws of fraud do not apply to workers' wages. But beginning around the twelfth century, we find that the decisors adduce two very different rationales for this conclusion. These disparate rationales are rooted in different understandings of the legal foundation of the employer–employee relationship. We will examine these opposed understandings as represented by, on the one hand, Maimonides, and on the other, R. Yomtov of Seville (the Ritba).

4.2 Applying the laws of fraud to employees' wages

As we said, the laws of fraud do not apply to land sales. Upholding the conception that renting out property reflects a temporary sale of partial rights in a property, Maimonides concludes that the laws of fraud do not apply to rentals of land either:

> Just as the laws of fraud do not apply with respect to [the sale of] land, so they do not apply with respect to renting land, even if one has rented a huge palace for a dinar a year, or a little shed for a dinar each day—the laws of fraud do not apply.
>
> *Code*, Laws concerning Sales 13:14

Similarly, Maimonides concludes that just as the laws of fraud do not apply to the sale of slaves, so too they do not apply to hiring workers:

> If one hires a worker to work with him, whether on the land or with movables—the laws of fraud do not apply, for it is as if he purchased him for a [temporary] period, and the laws of fraud do not apply to slaves.
>
> *Code*, Laws concerning Sales 13:15

18 *Code*, Laws concerning Sales 13:8.
19 bBaba Metzia 56b.

The method by which Maimonides arrived at the above conclusion can be reconstructed as an argument leading to the determination that the laws of fraud do not apply to hiring workers.

1 Rental is like a short term sale, and therefore, the laws of fraud apply to it (bBaba Metzia 56b).
2 The laws of fraud do not apply to the sale of slaves (mBaba Metzia 4:9).
3 Hiring an employee is like acquiring a slave, just as renting property is like buying (acquiring) it.

Conclusion The laws of fraud do not apply to the hiring of employees.

Subsequent Early Authorities disagreed with Maimonides' reasoning regarding fraud as it relates to employees. Nahmanides states:

> We say that the laws of fraud apply to the rental of animals, tools and so on. But the laws of fraud do not apply to the lease of land or of slaves, because rental is acquisition for a limited time. With regard to the hiring of an Israelite, as when someone hires **workers**, some say that the laws of fraud do not apply, for **it is not a sale, and the same applies to a contractor**.
>
> bBaba Metzia 56b s.v. *ha deamrinan*

The Ritba takes a similar view:

> It is obvious that in the case of [both] work contracted out and hiring a worker, the laws of fraud do not apply, because Scripture explicitly spoke of a "sale," and in these contexts **there is no sale at all**.
>
> bBaba Metzia 56b s.v. *baei rabi zeira*

They thus deny that there is a difference between the employer–employee relationship and the employer–independent contractor relationship in this respect. Neither agreement is regarded as a sale, hence both are valid even in cases of over-charging or under-charging.

Thus whereas in the view of Nahmanides and the Ritba, a contractor, or the side to a contract that claims to have been unfairly treated because the remuneration in question was significantly lower, or higher, than the going rate, has no legal recourse, Maimonides maintains that he does. This is reflected in an innovative law set down by Maimonides:

> It appears to me that the laws of fraud do apply to the contractor. How so? If the contractor agrees to weave a garment for ten *zuzim*,[20] or to sew a cloak for two *zuzim*, he is covered by the laws of fraud.
>
> *Code*, Laws concerning Sales 13:18

20 1 *shekel* = 1 *sela* = 4 *dinar* (also called *zuz*).

4.3 Does a contractor have a right to breach the work agreement?

We saw that the disparate views upheld by Maimonides and the Ritba have concrete legal consequences vis-à-vis the question of whether the laws of fraud apply to a contractor. Another issue with concrete legal implications is the question of whether a contractor can withdraw from his work agreement. We saw that an employee is permitted to withdraw from a work agreement even at midday. We can go back to the definitions of 'employee' and 'independent contractor' suggested at the beginning of the chapter to see if the principle that an employee may withdraw at midday—that is, whenever he wishes—applies to the contractor as well. As will become clear, the answer hinges on the different explanations of the employee's status offered by Maimonides and the Ritba.

According to Maimonides, an employee may quit in the middle of the day on the basis of the injunction: '"they are My slaves"—not slaves of slaves.' But the contractor's right to withdraw is justified even without this injunction. Maimonides rules:

> If the employee commenced his work and then he withdrew, even halfway through the day–he may withdraw, as it is said, '"for the children of Israel are My slaves"—not slaves of slaves.' And what is the law with regard to an employee who began but then withdrew? They estimate the [value of the] work done, and he is paid for it. But if he is a contractor, they estimate the [value of the] work he was going to do [but left undone], [and it is subtracted from his wage].
>
> *Code*, Laws concerning Hiring 9:4

In other words, in Maimonides' view, there is apparently no difference between an employee and a contractor with respect to the fact that they may withdraw from the work halfway through the day. The difference between them is that the employee must rely on the special right bestowed on him by the Torah, but the contractor may withdraw from the work contract because any contract to do something in the future is, according to Maimonides, invalid and hence retractable.

Other Early Authorities do not concur with Maimonides' view. Consider the views expressed by two eminent medieval commentators, Rabbenu Tam and R. Bezalel Ashkenazi. Rabbenu Tam writes as follows: "Only an employee, of whom it is written, 'They are My slaves—not slaves of slaves,' can withdraw, but not a contractor."[21] And R. Bezalel Ashkenazi writes: "One who is hired neither by the day nor by the hour, is not a slave but a contractor."[22] Hence, he may not withdraw from the contract, for he cannot invoke the biblical verse.

21 *Tosafot*, bBaba Metzia 48a s.v. *veha baei*.

22 *Shita Mekubetzet* ad loc. See also *Mahane Efraim*, Laws of Hiring Workers, sections 4–5.

The relationship between the positions taken by the halakhic authorities on the question of whether the laws of fraud apply to a contractor, on the one hand, and on the question of whether contractors have a right to withdraw, on the other, is paradoxical. Let us begin with Maimonides. As we saw, Maimonides regards the employer–employee relationship as that of acquisition, and thus maintains that the laws of fraud do not apply to an employee, who is tantamount to a slave. On the other hand, Maimonides rules that the laws of fraud do apply to a contractor, who is not akin to a slave. This being so, we would expect Maimonides to rule that the contractor is not permitted to withdraw from a job at midday, since the rationale for the right of withdrawal is that "they are My slaves—not slaves of slaves." Since the contractor is not akin to a slave, this rationale ought not to apply. Yet Maimonides rules that a contractor is permitted to withdraw from a job in the middle!

The second opinion, it will be recalled, contends that the laws of fraud apply to neither an employee nor a contractor, for the same reason—in both cases, their engagement by the employer is not a sales transaction, and the laws of fraud apply only to sales. On this approach, which does not distinguish between an employee and a contractor, we would expect that just as the employee can withdraw from the work agreement at midday, so too the contractor. However, the ruling is precisely the opposite: the contractor may not withdraw!

To understand and resolve this apparent paradox, we must examine yet another central issue in Jewish law–the question of the binding validity of contractual agreements.

One of the foundations of modern contract law is recognition of the legal validity of contractual agreements: *pacta sunt servanda*—contracts are to be fulfilled. As was explained above in section 3.2, this fundamental principle is not necessarily accepted in Jewish law. Jewish law distinguishes between obligations incurred through transactions that go into effect immediately, such as sales, which do have binding legal validity, and obligations incurred through transactions with respect to things not yet in existence, which will have to be fulfilled sometime in the future. As the status of such transactions is problematic, the said obligations are not deemed valid by Jewish law.

Maimonides regards a contractor as someone who takes it upon himself to do a specific job for someone else, a job he promises to do in the future. That is, he suggests an unambiguous criterion for differentiating employees from contractors: an employee sells himself to his employer, whereas a contractor does not sell the employer anything, but rather, promises to complete a job. Hence the employee is subject to his employer, and would be unable to withdraw were it not for the explicit biblical dispensation granted him, the specific intent of which is to ensure that the employee does not become a slave in the full sense of the term. The contractor, however, is not like a slave, and may withdraw even without the biblical dispensation, just as one cannot be forced to fulfill any other promise one makes.

According to Maimonides, then, a promise to work is not binding, and one may break this promise without recourse to a special dispensation. This view is stated explicitly in the *Mishne Torah*:

> How so? One who sells a house to his fellow or gives it to him as a gift, stipulating that he must accompany him on a journey to Jerusalem on a certain day, and meanwhile the buyer took possession—he acquires title when he accompanies him to Jerusalem on the said day, but if the day passed and he did not accompany him, he does not acquire title. But if the vendor made it a condition, saying to him, If you accompany me to Jerusalem on a certain day, or if you bring me a certain thing, I will give you this house, or sell it to you for a certain sum, and he accompanied him on the said day, or brought him the thing requested, then even if [the promisee] had the house in his possession after fulfilling the condition, he has not acquired title, because this was a mere *asmakhta* (promise). And it is so in all similar cases.
>
> *Code*, Laws concerning Sales 11:3

Maimonides' position is based on that of the Geonim, who in turn based their stance on clear indications to this effect in the Talmud.[23] This approach categorically rejects the validity of future obligations, including, obviously, the obligation to carry out a job for someone in the future. The only way to make such an undertaking binding is by formalizing the transaction in the present, as, for instance, by becoming an employee who transfers his personal powers to the employer. This transaction, as opposed to a future obligation, is valid.

At this point in our discussion, let us define Maimonides' stance on the difference between the employee's and contractor's respective rights vis-à-vis withdrawal from a job at midday. The employee has a right to withdraw from a job **despite** the fact that he has committed himself to a work agreement, and **despite** his status as an employee. His status as an employee obligates him to fully complete his work, but the halakha grants him a mechanism by which he can exercise his freedom though he has not completed the job. In contrast, the contractor's right to withdraw is inherent in his legal status. That is to say, from the outset there is nothing that requires the contractor to work, since an agreement based on 'things not yet in existence' is not binding. Consequently, it is his undeniable right to breach the work agreement at any time, since it was never binding in the first place.

Other Early Authorities, we saw, do not extend the laws of fraud to the employer–employee relationship, because "there is no sale at all." On this

23 See B. Lifshitz, *Asmakhta–Obligation and Acquisition in Jewish Law* (Hebrew), (Jerusalem: 1988).

view, a worker is not acquired, but rather takes upon himself the obligation to work. As one of the Provençal authorities says, "the extent of this barber's obligation is that he took upon himself the obligation to shave someone."[24] But if obligation is understood in this way, what renders it legally binding? Is it not merely "a transaction by words," that is, a promise, the validity of which is rejected by the Talmud?[25]

What is the difference between an employee's promise to work and a promise to divide a courtyard? This question is not asked by any of the Early Authorities, hence we have no explicit answer. It was raised, however, by some of the Later Authorities, such as the Hazon Ish, who asserts:

> There are two kinds of agreements with workers. One: a verbal agreement (*psikat dvarim*) that he will come and do his work. This agreement has no force at all—it is merely verbal.... The second: an agreement in which he makes his body subject [to his employer] or makes his property subject [to his employer].
>
> *Hazon Ish*, Baba Kama, sec. 21

That is to say, according to the Hazon Ish, only if the worker makes his person or his property subject to his employer has he entered into a binding work agreement with him. If not, it is merely a promise (*kinyan dvarim*) that lacks any binding validity.

Nevertheless, there is a tendency to recognize the employee's obligation, a tendency that is, we contend, part of a more general trend, among the post-Maimonidean Early Authorities, to recognize various obligations as binding. This tendency, the existence of which cannot be denied, conflicts with the earlier tradition, and some of the difficulties it has engendered remain unresolved. On this approach, both the employee and the contractor are obligated to complete any work they agree to do for the employer, and may not breach this commitment, which is considered binding.

5 Implications of the obligation model

The approach favored by the post-Maimonidean Early Authorities had two significant legal consequences: diminution of the employee's right to

24 *Hidushim Hameyuhasim Laritba*, bBaba Metzia 48a s.v. *ha deamrinan*.

25 bBaba Batra 3a. The issue in this *sugya* is an agreement between partners to divide a courtyard that does not meet the requirements for being divided at the demand of only one of the partners. The Talmud asks how the partners' agreement can be binding, and first gives the answer that an act of acquisition (*kinyan sudar*) was made (see n. 26 below). But it goes on to ask: "What of it? It is merely a transaction by words [i.e., a promise]." The Talmud concludes that the arrangement does not involve merely a promise to divide the courtyard, but an immediate transaction with respect to the parts of the yard each partner is acquiring.

breach the employment agreement, and blurring of the employee–contractor distinction.

5.1 Diminution of the employee's right to breach the employment agreement

The Ritba, on the authority of his teacher R. Aaron Halevi, espouses the following view:

> [The rule that] an employee may withdraw applies only if he hired himself out verbally, as per the Torah law of the worker. But whoever subjected himself by a *kinyan sudar*,[26] did so in order to improve the contract, so that he cannot withdraw.
>
> *Responsa R. Aaron Halevi*, #117[27]

According to the Ritba, the work agreement has the force of a valid contractual obligation. In his opinion, the Torah did indeed specifically assert that an employee is permitted to withdraw from the work agreement, but the employee can choose to waive this right, and such a waiver is valid if formalized with a *kinyan sudar*. From the Ritba's remarks, it seems that even when the employee does not explicitly forego his right to withdraw, he can nonetheless lose it: his performing the said formal act (*kinyan sudar*) at the start of his employment would be construed as waiving this right.

Needless to say, in light of the Ritba's innovative ruling, every employer will make certain to execute a *kinyan sudar* with his employees, and thereby utterly deprive them of their right to withdraw from the job at midday, in breach of their work agreement. Ironically, then, the Ritba's approach to employment law, which sought to bolster the employee's status by construing his relationship to his employer as reflecting obligation rather than acquisition, did the reverse, worsening the employee's status by severely curtailing his most significant privilege, the right to withdraw at midday. Ironically, on the Ritba's position, the employee's status is more accurately characterized as that of a slave, and it therefore would have been appropriate for him to retain the capacity to free himself on the strength of the injunction, "They are My slaves—not slaves of slaves."

26 *Kinyan sudar* is a formal legal act that gives validity to business transactions and relationships. It is performed by lifting a certain object, though the precise details of the procedure are the subject of controversy. Some see the *kinyan sudar* as a formal act that is based on an acquisition through exchange (*kinyan halifin*). A *kinyan halifin* is effected by performing an act of acquisition with one object as a means of effecting acquisition of the other. On this explanation of the *kinyan sudar*, the seller makes an act of acquisition with the *sudar* (lit., scarf), which can be any mundane object designated for this use alone, as a means of procuring the property for the purchaser. The *kinyan sudar* is used as a means of effectuating a variety of legal relationships.

27 See also *Hidushei Haritba*, bBaba Metzia 75b s.v. *hapoalim*.

R. Shabtai Hakohen, author of the *Siftei Kohen* commentary on the *Shulhan Arukh*, objects to this understanding of labor law. He argues that the right to withdraw is not subject to being overridden via stipulations on the part of the worker, and thus should apply even to someone who has committed himself not to withdraw.[28] The reasoning here is that even if we accept the claim that the employee's obligation is contractual and not rooted in acquisition, his having carried out the said formal act (*kinyan sudar*) turns him into a kind of slave, who is now in need of the additional protection afforded by the right to withdraw. Paradoxically, the contractual nature of the employer–employee relationship that enables the employee to waive his right to withdraw renders his status akin to that of the slave, and reawakens the need for legal protection.

5.2 Blurring of the employee–contractor distinction

The second consequence of the obligation model is erosion of the basis for differentiating the employee from the contractor. On the acquisition model, an employee was defined as someone who sold himself, and a contractor, as someone who promised to do a job, reflecting an unambiguous 'ontological' distinction between an acquisition and a promise. The distinction can also be characterized as follows: an employee is conceived as tantamount to a slave to his employer, whereas a contractor is a slave "only unto himself," as Rashi aptly puts it.[29] But by taking the employee, too, to be defined as someone who promises to do a job, the distinction between employee and contractor loses its rationale.

We may now be in a better position to understand the roots of the controversy, discussed at the beginning of the chapter, over the criterion for distinguishing between an employee and a contractor. It will be recalled that one side favors the 'degree of subjection' criterion, namely, whether the employee can set his own work hours. On this approach, a worker who sets his own hours is considered a contractor, whereas a worker whose work hours are set by the employer is considered an employee. The other approach favors the 'basis of remuneration' criterion, that is, whether the salary is calculated by time worked, or by completion of the specified job, regardless of how long it takes.

In light of our discussion, it should now be apparent that the 'degree of subjection' criterion gauges whether, and to what degree, a worker is subject to his employer's control—a status evocative of slavery—or, on the other hand, works independently, and is, in effect, his own master. Using this criterion for determining whether a given worker is an employee or a contractor thus in some sense presupposes the acquisition model, which is, as we have seen, well-grounded in the talmudic literature and the

28 *Shakh*, *SA*, HM 333:14.
29 *Rashi*, bBaba Metzia 10a.

writings of the Early Authorities. In contrast, the obligation model does not view the employee as the employer's property, but from the outset takes the employee to be independent, just as a contractor is. Hence on the obligation model, the 'degree of subjection' criterion is useless for distinguishing between an employee and a contractor. Rather, a worker's status is determined by the nature of the obligation he has undertaken, that is, by the basis on which his remuneration is calculated. If he is paid on the basis of the number of hours he works, he is an employee, if he is paid on the basis of whether a specific task has been completed, he is a contractor.

6 Displacement of the acquisition model by the obligation model

It is interesting that the contemporary scholarly literature, though aware of the acquisition model, does not recognize that this model is indeed upheld by the Talmud and other authorities. Here is the account offered by Gulak:

> Business transactions whereby workers are hired ... are transactions whereby the actions of one person are purchased to meet the needs of another. They create a relationship of obligation between the parties: they impose on one side the obligation to act, and on the other, the obligation to pay for these actions. According to our laws, a transaction whereby actions are purchased establishes a weak obligation relationship. The formal reason for this is that the actions thus purchased are only potential, and have no real substance (*davar sheein bo mamash*) to which the laws of acquisition could apply, and there is no other concrete entity here that could constitute the object acquired by concluding the agreement....
>
> Hiring someone does not, therefore, confer any acquisition vis-à-vis the body of the hired person, and involves no more than a relationship of obligation between free men.... On this point, the decisors deviated somewhat from the talmudic principle that the action of a hired worker is always voluntary, and never forced or obligatory, and created the fiction that the worker's body is, as it were, subject to the employer, and this body is the concrete entity that could be acquired.[30]

This is, however, a distortion of the stance taken by the Talmud, the Geonic literature, Maimonides, and others who conceived the employer–employee relationship on the model of the master–slave relationship.

Shalom Albeck, too, seeks to downplay or recast the talmudic acquisition model of the employer–employee relationship by formulating it in terms of acquisition of the employee's **tools**:

30 A. Gulak, *Foundations of Jewish Law* (Hebrew), (Berlin: 1922), 2:178.

> Workers and craftsmen are hired by the act of acquiring their work tools. The obligation of these workmen to work for their employer is only contractual, and there are no rights of acquisition vis-à-vis their person at all.[31]

Indeed, Albeck does not differentiate between an employee and a contractor.

It appears that, consciously or not, these scholars are intent on presenting Jewish labor law solely in terms of the obligation model, and therefore systematically downplay any traces of the acquisition model. It may well be that their motivation is apologetic. That is to say, the approach that construes the employer–employee relationship as one of acquisition is likely to be considered primitive and inhumane, insofar as it appears to establish that one individual is the property of another.

Another contemporary scholar, though aware of the basis of the employer–employee relationship, struggles mightily to reduce its significance:

> Though labor law is a branch of the general laws of hiring, employment contracts, according to Jewish law, belong to the realm of acquiring the services of a person, as opposed to transactions whereby [material] things are acquired. The object of the transaction is not the body of the worker (unlike the case of purchasing a slave, whose body is acquired by the purchaser), but his actions; they alone are hired.[32]

Yet the suggestion that "[actions] alone are purchased" is no solution, since according to Jewish law, actions are intangible and cannot be acquired per se.

Having noted the fact that recent scholarship barely recognizes the doctrine of acquisition, let us return to the halakhic literature proper, and inquire into the explanation for the displacement of the acquisition model by the obligation model. No explicit and unequivocal answer to this question was put forward by the halakhic authorities, who did not articulate this question directly. Nor has it been addressed in the scholarly literature.

When we discern an apparently unwarranted attitudinal shift with respect to a jurisprudential question in Jewish law—a shift that makes it necessary to interpret key legal sources in a strained way, and is incompatible with the general structure of the legal norms embedded in these texts—it would seem that the explanation for the change must be sought in changes in the wider social context. In the case at hand, it would

31 S. Albeck, *The Law of Property and Contract in the Talmud* (Hebrew), (Tel Aviv: 1976), 122.
32 Warhaftig, n. 4 above, 1–2.

seem that repudiation of the view that a worker is acquired by his employer developed against the backdrop of a society where the feudal system, though still entrenched, was starting to erode and evolve. The feudal system was a regimented social order based on human bondage and servitude of various types, in particular, serfdom and vassalage. As it fell apart, these forms of bondage were modified, the most notable transition, from our perspective, being that from fief to indenture, that is, from a feudal to a non-feudal contract. These emerging institutions reflected an ethos that acknowledged the importance of human liberty. Slowly, personal bondage was mitigated by gradually increasing liberties.[33]

Influenced by these socio-cultural currents, the halakhic authorities of the thirteenth and fourteenth centuries began to view as non-slaves, as individuals whose bodies were only nominally the property of their masters, those formerly (and often still) regarded by the surrounding society as tantamount to slaves. They were aware of the gap between the obsolete terms in which the legal institution of the employer–employee relationship was articulated–terms connoting slavery and subjection—and its essence, namely, the exchange of labor for remuneration.

This state of affairs was welcomed as natural by those who viewed the institution of slavery as antithetical to the spirit of the halakha, an attitude reflected in the talmudic dicta: "They are My slaves" and "He who buys a Hebrew slave—it is as if he bought himself a master."[34] As we saw, the talmudic Sages, invoking the "they are My slaves—not slaves of slaves" principle, sought to protect workers, introducing the requirement that they were allowed to withdraw even at midday.

The aforementioned external influences gaining momentum in the surrounding society were viewed by the rabbinical authorities as validated by their compatibility with the spirit and teachings of the halakha, and their halakhic rulings were indeed influenced by these social trends. The simple acquisition model, based on the rights of masters over their slaves, gradually fell into disfavor. At the same time, construal of employer–employee relations as the acquisition of future commitments, previously unheard of in Jewish law, which had until then classed labor relationships under the rubric of acquisition of the worker, was also coming to be seen as valid. Before long, the acquisition model of the employer–employee

33 See Marc Bloch, *Feudal Society* (Chicago: 1961).

34 bKidushin 20a. Jewish law imposes on the master a broad range of responsibilities vis-à-vis his slave. The master must provide the slave with food, drink, and all his other needs. This is established by a baraita in bKidushin 20a: "'because he fares well with you' (Deut. 15:16)—he should be with you in food and with you in drink: you should not eat white bread and [your slave] black bread, you should not drink old wine and [your slave] new wine, you should not sleep on a feather bed and [your slave] on straw." Paradoxically, then, in light of these obligations, "He who buys a Hebrew slave—it is as if he bought himself a master." On the rights of a slave vis-à-vis his master, see chapter 1 of Maimonides' *Code*, Laws concerning Slaves, in Appendix 3.

relationship waned to the point that the halakhic authorities could declare that "there is no sale at all" in the hiring of a worker.

The growing conviction that Jewish law rejects any acquisitional relationship between employer and employee seems to have led modern researchers in Jewish law to view the acquisition model as entirely irrelevant. Gulak, for instance, presents the following account of its demise:

> In earlier times one man's need for the labor of another was fulfilled by purchasing, as private property, someone who had the potential to provide this labor, and he became a slave, whose body, productive capacity, and handiwork were acquired to be used by others. As humanity advanced, personal liberty increased and slavery gradually disappeared. Man's legal status was elevated to that of a free individual, and his body was no longer classified as a negotiable object that could be bought and sold on the market. If the labors of one man are required to fulfill the needs of another, only these actions themselves can be the object of bargaining and negotiation, and they alone are hired—without limiting the personal liberty of the individual carrying them out. So slavery was superseded by a more elevated and suitable form of labor, namely, the free labor that is purchased by hiring a worker.[35]

Gulak maintains that the transition from slavery to free labor took place in the talmudic period: "In a number of places in the Talmud where it says that someone pledged himself, it means that he mortgaged his assets."[36] This is, however, a clear distortion of the plain meaning of the Talmud, which is unquestionably speaking of a pledge of the body itself.

7 Critique of the obligation model

Although it might seem that the obligation model underscores the worker's freedom and personal autonomy, its adoption actually led to a diminution of personal liberty, because workers lost the freedom not to be bound by promises to carry out work, that is, work agreements. Once future obligations were recognized, a worker's future rights and obligations were no longer an empty canvas, but pre-determined by commitments undertaken earlier. This can be termed the paradox of freedom. Indeed, it has been explicitly addressed by philosophers and legal theorists. Isaiah Berlin, the preeminent political philosopher, noted the paradoxical fact that the endorsement of liberty, autonomy and democracy may not be inimical to the state of enslavement:

35 Gulak, n. 30 above, 2:180.

36 Gulak, *History of Jewish Law: Talmudic Period*, vol. 1, Law of Obligation and its Guaranties (Hebrew), (Jerusalem: 1939), 30–31.

> In an essay comparing the liberty of the moderns with that of the ancients he [Benjamin Constant] said that an equal right to oppress—or interfere—is not equivalent to liberty. Nor does universal consent to loss of liberty somehow miraculously preserve it merely by being universal, or by being consent. If I consent to be oppressed, or acquiesce in my condition with detachment or irony, am I less oppressed? If I sell myself into slavery, am I the less a slave? If I commit suicide, am I the less dead because I have taken my own life freely?[37]

And a general labor law theorist expressed similar conclusions with respect to purportedly liberating legal developments:

> Standard contracts in particular could thus become effective instruments in the hands of powerful industrial and commercial overlords, enabling them to impose a new feudal order of their own making upon a vast host of vassals. This spectacle is all the more fascinating since not more than a hundred years ago, contract ideology had been successfully used to break down the last vestiges of a patriarchal and benevolent feudal order in the field of master and servant. Thus the return back from contract to status which we experience today, was greatly facilitated by the fact that the belief in freedom of contract has remained one of the foremost axioms in the whole fabric of the social philosophy of our culture.[38]

In this chapter, we have discussed a variant of this 'paradox of freedom.' The model of employer–employee relations that denies the worker independence, viewing him as his employer's property, nonetheless endows him with considerable freedom, insofar as it enables him to withdraw from the work agreement at midday. Conversely, the model that affirms the worker's independence, seeing him as an autonomous individual who obligates himself to work, nonetheless restricts his freedom. Although independence and freedom might seem to be complementary concepts, here they are zero-sum concepts: one can be realized only by losing the other.

It appears that the notions of 'independence' and 'freedom' are not interchangeable, and may even be incompatible. Admittedly, in many situations, one who lacks independence also lacks freedom. The slave is the paradigm case of one who has neither freedom nor independence. Yet under certain circumstances, independence can actually undermine freedom. An independent person is often forced to yield his freedom to someone else, and thus of his own free will loses his freedom. This is true

37 Isaiah Berlin, "Two concepts of liberty," in idem, *Four Essays on Liberty* (London: 1969), 164.

38 F. Kessler, "Contracts of adhesion—some thoughts about freedom of contract," 43 *Columbia L.R.* (1943), 629–42, 641.

in the case of one who enters into a long-term work agreement. Such an individual has the independence to choose his future, and chooses to forfeit his freedom—the freedom to determine what hours he works, say—to his employer. On the obligation model, this is precisely what transpires vis-à-vis an employee: once the employee is deemed to be a free agent who obligates himself to the employer, he has no need for the protection formerly offered to workers deemed to be the employer's personal property, viz., the right to withdraw at midday. Similarly, it is possible for lack of independence to foster freedom. On the acquisition model, it is the very dependence of the employee that renders it imperative for the law to step in and enshrine a degree of inalienable personal freedom.

In talmudic law, the paradox of freedom was solved by another paradox. Conceiving the employer–employee relationship as an acquisition created a balance between liberty and bondage by establishing a space for liberty within bondage. This balance was reached by bestowing on the employee the right to withdraw in the middle of the day. In essence, this solution regards the employee as a hybrid: in certain respects an object (*res*) and in others, a legal person (*persona*).

The employee may stop working at any time. His decision to go on working despite his right to sever the relationship with his employer reflects an ongoing freedom of choice—it is he who can decide whether or not to forego his freedom by making himself subject to his employer. He thus **retains the freedom to relinquish his freedom**, and temporarily 'deposit it,' as it were, with someone else, reserving the right to end this relationship at will. This prerogative can be invoked, at least in theory, at any given moment.

It was precisely the ascription to the employee of the status of 'mere' property, that is, ascribing to the worker the status of a slave, and recognition of the implications of this status, that brought about the development of a mechanism for ensuring that the employee retained significant freedom. Conversely, it was the repudiation of the master–slave relationship and its redefinition in terms of obligation that brought about the negation of that freedom, and the emergence, as Kessler noted, of what is in essence a new feudal order, wherein union-members have virtually no power to negotiate their work conditions. The assumption that autonomy and liberty are to be preferred to enslavement is so natural and so 'politically correct' in contemporary jurisprudential thought, that the causes of the neo-feudal order are hardly recognized, let alone addressed.

In the final analysis, the criteria used to distinguish between an employee and a contractor mesh well with the traditional, acquisitional definition of the employer–employee relationship. Adoption of the obligation model, however, makes it difficult to provide an explication of the employer–contractor distinction.

Jewish law recognized at a relatively early point that the status of the employee was similar to bondage, and precisely because it recognized this, afforded the employee a significant freedom. The responsiveness of Jewish law to the social problem of protecting the worker seems prescient and ahead of its time. How might this be explained?

The halakha's relative isolation from the full weight of the social, economic, and political forces constraining the surrounding society—though, as we saw above, a certain degree of indirect influence certainly existed—enabled it to be more progressive vis-à-vis the worker. In the surrounding society, the tensions generated by shifting political and economic theories and regimes hindered the emergence of the process in question—recognition of the fact that the worker's status is akin to bondage, and thus must be cushioned by affording the worker some elements of liberty and enshrining them as law—suppressing it for extended periods. Ultimately, of course, concerns about the need to protect the worker could not be ignored, and emerged as a salient consideration in western law. In the world of the halakha, it was far easier for the concept of liberty to penetrate the legal system. The early textual sources were given readings that highlighted the 'newly discovered' notion of personal freedom. As noted above, this process was facilitated by the fact that this notion lay at the very heart of these sources, and was a foundational principle of Jewish labor law even prior to the encounter with the late medieval critiques of vassalage and embrace of freedom of contract.[39]

39 See B. Lifshitz, *Employee and Independent Contractor—Acquisition and Obligation in Contrast* (Hebrew), (Jerusalem: 1993), 116–17.

Appendix 1 File No. 2535/19 Rabbinical Court (TA) Kiserman v. R. Alexander Direnfeld, 3 PDR 272 (Isr.) [1959]

In this case, the claimant, a professional driver and owner of a passenger van, was hired beginning in the year 1955 on a part-time basis—about 4 hours daily—by the Belz Talmud Torah Institution, to transport its students from their homes to school and back. The claimant's wages were paid on a per student basis. In recent years, it was agreed between them that a monthly salary would be paid; recently, the salary came to 385 Israeli pounds per month. This sum included 150 pounds for fuel and other expenses. According to the claimant, he and the defendant had agreed that the Institution would pay for the van's fuel, and hence the salary fluctuated in accordance with fluctuations in the price of fuel. This year, in the month of Kislev, the defendant informed the claimant that his employment at the Institution was being terminated because the Institution was acquiring its own transport vehicle for the said purpose, and that as of the 14th of Kislev, the claimant would cease to drive the students.

The claimant proposed to the employer that he work for the Institution as a salaried driver [of the Institution's vehicle], but the proposal was not accepted by the defendant, and another driver was hired in his place.

In a complaint that was presented to the rabbinical court, the claimant seeks, in view of his having been terminated, to obligate the defendant to pay severance in the amount of 2025 Israeli pounds. This amount includes compensation based on four months of salary, according to the customary calculation—one month's salary for each year of employment. The claimant also seeks to obligate the defendant to pay one month's full salary [as termination pay], inasmuch as he was unemployed for approximately one month beginning on the 14th of Kislev, when he stopped working at the Institution. In addition, for the period beginning the 14th of Tevet [the month following Kislev] until the end of the school year, he is asking for 100 Israeli pounds per month for unemployment compensation. Although he did have some work during that time, he was not successful at this new work and earned only 60 pounds per month during the said months.

The claimant asserts that his status at the Institution was that of a salaried employee and not an independent contractor, since in recent years he had received an annual paid vacation, and he was therefore entitled to receive compensation from his employer upon the termination of his employment.

The claimant also claims that upon hearing that the Institution intended to acquire a passenger van, he approached the defendant to ascertain whether this was correct, so that he could get a contract with another institution before the start of the school year, but the defendant did not confirm it, and claimed that in his opinion nothing would come of it in practice. The claimant therefore argues that the defendant's advice caused him a loss, and that he [the defendant] should pay damages over and above the accepted payment of one month per year of employment, in accordance with the halakha as decided in the *Shulhan Arukh*, HM 333.

Counsel for the defendant responded that the legal status of the claimant was that of an independent contractor and not an employee, that he worked only part-time for the Institution and was left with time to do other work, and that the claimant in fact worked at another institution and also did moving, and other such work. Proof of this is the fact that the claimant did not receive an annual vacation as part of his salary, except in rare instances when the Institution employed him during the vacation to do moving. Therefore, the claimant is not entitled to compensation, inasmuch as he worked as an independent contractor, and especially since the claim targets a non-profit charitable institution which should in any case not be required to pay compensation. [The defendant] adds to his response that the claimant has not yet proven that any harm was caused him, and the burden of proof is on him, in line with the legal principle that "[the burden of proof falls on] the one who seeks to take that which is in the possession of his fellow."

Included in the file is a letter replying to the defendant's request, addressed to the Ministry of Labor, for a clarification of the claimant's legal status, on the basis on the facts as described above by the defendant. It states: "The relationship between you and the school was not that of an employee and his employer, but of an independent contractor. Hence there is no legal foundation for your claim to be an employee." In his conclusion, the claimant requests that the Ministry of Labor's confirmation letter be disregarded since the opinion was issued on the basis of the defendant's description of the facts, which is not consistent with the real situation.

A witness—Mr. Israel Gottlieb, an official at the trade unions department of the Hapoel Hamizrahi organization—appeared before the rabbinical court. In his testimony, included in the file, the said witness affirms that in determining an employee's compensation, one must take into account the salary criterion—that is, whether a worker's wages are monthly or daily is a factor in establishing the existence of an employer–employee relationship, even if the work is part-time and he has free hours left to take on additional work at another institution. It is understood that the amount of compensation and vacation days paid out is calculated in accordance with the work and the monthly salary.

A second witness, named Eliyahu Rozovsky, a trade unions official of the Poalei Agudat Yisrael organization, affirmed in his testimony that the monthly wage is not a benchmark for establishing whether someone is an employee or an independent contractor. In his opinion, the relevant criterion is the means of production—that is, if the means of production belong to the employer, then he is an employee. Moreover, the way in which the income tax authorities relate to the worker has substantial importance in determining the compensation, and from it a conclusion can be drawn as to whether he is considered by law to be an employee or an independent contractor. The witness affirmed that since there is no one law governing the payment of compensation, decisions on such matters were left to the discretion of the relevant trade union The witness stated that, among other things, if a worker is bound to work at specific hours of the day, that would be a factor in relating to him as a salaried employee. However, his occupation during the rest of the day should be taken into account.

A fundamental question stands before the court: determining whether the law regards the claimant as an employee or an independent contractor. In a similar situation, the Jerusalem Talmud, in tractate Baba Metzia, chapter "*Hasokher et hapoalim*" [jBaba Metzia 7:1 (11b)] states: "This means that custom overrides the law that [the burden of proof is on] the one who seeks to take that which is in the possession of his fellow." But we have not yet heard from a reliable source what the prevailing custom vis-à-vis part-time workers is, so that we can—in accordance with this custom—draw a conclusion in our case. Even hearing the witnesses has not proved too helpful to us, since their testimony is based on the theories and judgments of the official handling the case, and their approaches and professional assessments do not coincide. And thus it is not surprising that the [testimony of the] witnesses who appeared before the court was, to a considerable degree, not identical, since, as was stated, it is a matter of judgment (*shikul daat*), and each one is free to express his own opinion. Thus, the disagreements are not about establishing the facts, but about how we are to reach a conclusion as to this matter.

Therefore, since we do not yet know the prevailing custom of the land as to a worker such as the claimant, we must first determine his status from the point of view of the halakha, and in accordance with that determination, reach a conclusion as to this matter.

Appendix 2 Maimonides, *Code*, Laws concerning Sales, chapter 12, 1–5

1 It is forbidden for a seller or a buyer to defraud each other, as it is said: "And if you sell anything to your neighbor, or buy from your neighbor's hand, you shall not wrong one another" (Lev. 25:14). And even though he [who overcharges] transgresses a negative commandment, he is not punished by flogging, inasmuch as repayment can be made. And regardless of whether he defrauded him maliciously or he did not know that the sale was fraudulent, he must repay it.

2 How much does the fraud [overcharging or underpaying] have to amount to, to render he who committed it obligated to repay it? A sixth of the article's value. Thus, if one sells an article worth six *dinar* for five, or worth seven for six, or worth five for six, or worth six for seven, this constitutes fraud. And the transaction is valid, but the defrauder has to repay the entire difference to the defrauded party.

3 If the fraud amounts to anything less than that, as when one sells something worth 60 *dinar* for 50 *dinar* and a *pruta*, the defrauder is not obligated to repay anything, because it is the universal practice to excuse fraud amounting to less than a sixth.

4 If the fraud amounts to anything more than a sixth, as when one sells something worth 60 *dinar* for 50 *dinar* less a *pruta*, the transaction is void and the defrauded party may return the object and not buy it at all. But the defrauder may not go back on the deal if the injured party consented to it. Even if the transaction is void, the defrauder is not obligated to repay [the difference] unless the fraud amounts to more than a *pruta*. Even if it amounts to one *pruta* exactly, he does not have to repay [the difference], for fraud involving only a *pruta* is not considered fraud.

5 How long does the injured party have to go back on the deal and claim the amount of the fraud or cancel the deal? As long as it takes him to show the object to a merchant or to his relative. If he waits longer, even if he bought something worth 100 *zuz* for 200, he may not go back on the deal.

Appendix 3 Maimonides, *Code*, Laws concerning Slaves, chapter 1, 5–9

5 One who sells himself [into slavery] or is sold by the court, is not to be sold publicly on the sale block or in an alley, as slaves are customarily sold, for it is stated: "they shall not be sold as slaves are sold" (Lev. 25:42). He should rather be sold discreetly and with dignity.

6 It is forbidden to work any Hebrew slave with rigor. What constitutes work with rigor? It is work that has no fixed limits and unnecessary work that is done only for the purpose of keeping [the slave] working, so that he will not be idle. Hence the Sages said that the master should not tell his Hebrew slave: 'Hoe beneath the vines until I arrive,' for he has not given him a fixed limit. Rather, he should say to him: 'Hoe until a certain time or up to a certain place.' So too, one should not say to him: 'Dig up this place,' when [the master] has no need for it. Nor should he command him even to warm or cool a drink for him if he does not need it. Doing so is forbidden, and constitutes transgression of a negative commandment, as it is said: "You shall not rule over him with rigor" (Lev. 25:46). Hence, [the Hebrew slave] does for his master only work that has fixed limits and for which there is a need. Likewise, if the heathen to whom he is sold works him with rigor, Israelites are commanded to prevent this. If they let [the heathen do so], they transgress a negative commandment, as it is said: "He shall not rule over him with rigor in your sight" (Lev. 25:53). But we are not obliged to enter the premises of the heathen and check that he does not work the Hebrew slave with rigor, as it is said, "in your sight," meaning, when you see it.

7 It is forbidden for an Israelite who buys any Hebrew slave to make him perform menial tasks that are relegated to slaves only, such as making him follow him to the bathhouse carrying [the master's] things, or take off his shoes, as it is said: "You shall not work him like a slave" (Lev. 25:39). He must treat him only as a hired man, as it is said: "As a hired servant and as a settler, he shall be with you" (Lev. 25:40). But it is permissible for [the Hebrew slave] to cut the master's hair, wash his garment, and bake his dough. But the master should not make him an attendant at a public bath or a public barber or a public baker. However, if that was his trade before he was sold, he may do it. But initially, he should not be taught a new trade, but allowed to work at the same trade that he plied before. To whom does this apply? It applies only to a Hebrew slave who feels humiliated at having been sold [into slavery]. But it is permitted to have an Israelite who was not sold [into slavery] do the work of a slave inasmuch as he does the work of his own will and volition.

8 It is permitted to treat those who do not act properly very harshly, and even enslave them. If a king decrees that he who does not pay the tax

assessed on each and every one of his subjects shall be enslaved to he who pays the tax for him, it is permitted to the latter to make [the delinquent] do more work than usual, but not work him like a slave. And if he does not act properly, it is permitted to have him do the work of a slave.

9 The master must treat every Hebrew slave, male and female, equally with regard to food, drink, clothing and shelter, as it is said: "Because he fares well with you" (Deut. 15:16); you should not eat white bread and [your slave] black bread, you should not drink old wine and [your slave] new wine, you [should not] sleep on a feather bed and [your slave] on straw, you [should not] reside in the city and [your slave] in the country—or you [should not] reside in the country and [your slave] dwells in the city, as it is said: "He shall go out from you" (Lev. 25:41). Hence the Sages said: "He who buys a Hebrew slave—it is as if he bought himself a master." And one must treat [his Hebrew slave] as a brother, as it is said: "And over your brethren the children of Israel" (Lev. 25:46). Nevertheless, the slave must conduct himself in a slavish manner when doing the work that he does for his master.

13 Unjust enrichment

1 Introduction

1.1 Preliminary remarks

In the framework of private law, it is customary to distinguish two kinds of personal obligations: consensual obligations, which arise from voluntary actions of the parties concerned, and tort obligations, which arise by force of law when damages have been inflicted.[1] That is, there must be a legal basis, whether mutual agreement, or the need to compensate someone for losses suffered at the hand of another, in order for a monetary obligation to exist. But this classification of obligations is far from exhaustive, and meets neither society's needs nor its expectations. For the law is intended to regulate the entire range of interpersonal relationships, and these extend beyond consensual obligations and liability for damages. And indeed, the law recognizes obligations that do not fall under either of these categories.

Let us consider some examples.

1. Farmer A was unexpectedly hospitalized for a lengthy period. His neighbor, B, fed his livestock and tended his fields. Is B entitled to compensation for his work and expenses?

1 A third category of legal obligations, those arising from family relationships, e. g., the obligation to maintain one's children, falls outside the scope of the discussion here.

2. An individual abandoned his family without funds, and the social welfare system provided for their maintenance. Is the welfare system entitled to reimbursement from the absconder?
3. The city of Detroit contracted the services of an eminent ecologist to devise a strategy for lowering the emissions of a power station in the city. Is the city entitled to claim part of the consultant's fee from the city of Windsor, Ontario, which borders on Detroit and benefits equally from the project?
4. An impecunious student moved into an empty cabin in a rural area. One of the locals noticed this and informed the owner of the property. The owner in turn told the squatter to pay a month's rent and leave at once. Is the owner entitled to make these demands?
5. A tenant sublet an apartment for more money than she was paying as rent. Is her landlord entitled to the difference?

Common to all the examples is that one party **benefits at the expense of another**. In some of the cases, it intuitively seems that the former should compensate the latter. It seems unfair, for example, that one who has gone out of his way to look after someone else's farm should sustain a loss for doing so. It does not seem right for someone to desert his family without making any provision for them, leaving his responsibilities to the social welfare system. We may have doubts, however, about whether rent is in fact called for in the case of the vacant cabin, or with regard to the landlord's right to her tenant's profit. Various legal mechanisms have evolved to deal with such cases, which, in English and American law, are referred to as cases of 'unjust enrichment.'

The concept of unjust enrichment is an ancient one. It was already mentioned by Aristotle.[2] Cicero considered such profiteering destructive to the very fabric of society, and held that there was no rule as vital as that intended to prevent unjust enrichment.[3] It has been claimed that in Roman law no ethical principle appears as often, and in more diverse contexts, than the prohibition against unjust enrichment.[4] Indeed, even the writings of Karl Marx reflect a negative attitude to unjust enrichment.[5] Over the past century, various general theories as to the development of unjust enrichment law were formulated, and there is no doubt that the institution of unjust enrichment is presently entrenched in both common law and civil law.

Liability, in the area of unjust enrichment, exists when the following three elements are present: (1) enrichment of the beneficiary; (2) at the expense of the (unwitting) benefactor; (3) without legal claim.

2 *Nicomachean Ethics* 1132a–b.
3 Cicero, *De off.* III, 5.21.
4 C. Allen, *Law in the Making* (Oxford: 1964), 396.
5 J. Dawson, *Unjust Enrichment* (Boston: 1951), 3.

1.2 General attitude to unjust enrichment in Jewish law

Above, we sketched what was in essence a tripartite classification of obligations. Such a classification is more formally set out in the following account, from one of the pioneering works of academic Jewish law:

> An obligation may arise in three ways: by an explicit undertaking based on a contract and the mutual agreement of both parties ... by causing damage ... and by benefitting another while sustaining a loss, e.g., one who forsakes his own property and saves the imperiled belongings of another—the latter is obliged to compensate the former for his loss.[6]

As we will see, however, this definition of the third category does not cover all the cases that fall under the rubric 'unjust enrichment.'

Research into the position of Jewish law on a given subject must take into account the difficulties posed by its casuistic nature—its being based primarily on cases rather than general formulas and principles. It must therefore be studied inductively, and great care must be taken in identifying and characterizing the general principles implicit in the source material.

This problem arises in our context as well. The sources of Jewish law do not explicitly articulate the notion of unjust enrichment. Nevertheless, these sources recognize monetary obligations that arise from events such as the hypothetical examples adduced above. Even so, it remains to be seen to what extent we will be able to infer and classify the general principles underlying these sources without being unduly influenced by classification schemes from other legal systems. Students of jurisprudence often assume that the legal categories they have come to take for granted are universal, and that which applies in, say, common law, applies equally in the halakhic context. But as readers of this book should now be aware, there is no necessary correspondence between the concepts and categories of Jewish law, and those of western law.

1.3 Classification and terminology

By analyzing how a benefit was generated, we can identify three different categories of unjust enrichment. This is the standard analysis of unjust enrichment, and can be fruitfully applied in the context of Jewish law.

6 I. Tzuri, *Talmudic Law* (Hebrew), (Warsaw: 1921), 5:1. See also See H. Dagan, *Unjust Enrichment: A Study of Private Law and Public Values* (New York: 1997); J. Blass, "Halakhic altruism: a critique of H. Dagan's 'The law of unjust enrichment: between Judaism and liberalism,'" 15 *Jewish Law Annual* (2004), 3–11; Irwin Haut, "Unjust enrichment revisited," 15 *Jewish Law Annual* (2004), 41–56.

i Passively-gained benefit

Sometimes there is some benefit to one party without the active participation of either party. The Talmud offers the following example: An animal belonging to A consumes fruit belonging to B under circumstances in which A is exempt from paying damages. But A has derived a profit from B, because he does not have to feed his animal, which is no longer hungry. Is A obliged to compensate B for this passively-gained benefit, namely, the worth of the animal's meal? This type of case is discussed in section 2.

ii Benefitting someone else

Unlike the first example, here the direct action of a benefactor is the cause of the benefit. This category includes the following cases, which serve as prototypes: (1) 'one who scares away a lion from his fellow's property' (abatement of a nuisance); (2) 'one who settles someone else's debt'; (3) 'one who entered his fellow's field and planted there' (improving someone else's property).

A number of questions merit consideration. We must determine whether these actions should be regarded as purely voluntary and altruistic, and free of any implicit obligation; we must also consider the significance of the distinction between abating a nuisance and actively conferring a benefit. Another question is whether the beneficiary's response influences the extent of his liability—whether he may refuse a benefit that generates an obligation to compensate the benefactor. These questions are considered in section 3.

iii Benefitting from someone else

Here, the benefit is created by direct action on the part of the beneficiary, who gains something without depriving the other party of his rights, for instance, reading someone's newspaper over his shoulder, or being a stowaway on a vessel. This category includes the talmudic case of 'one who lives in someone else's courtyard without his knowledge' (the squatter). We will have to determine whether the benefit to one party must exceed a minimal amount, and whether this must be a loss to the other. These issues are discussed in section 4.

Consider the following case:

> [Regarding] someone who leased a cow from his fellow, and lent it to someone else, and the cow died a natural death: the lessee* must swear that the cow died a natural death, and the borrower** must pay [the

* One who leases something is not responsible for mishaps due to force majeure, such as natural death.

** One who borrows is liable for damages regardless of the circumstances.

> value of cow] to the lessee. R. Jose said: How can this person do business with someone else's cow?! The [compensation for the] cow must be returned to the owner.
>
> mBaba Metzia 3:2

Sometimes a benefit accrues to an agent in the course of his agency, giving rise to the question of who the unexpected benefit belongs to. For example, if an agent is instructed to sell an item at a certain price, but in fact receives a higher price, who is entitled to this additional sum? Although unexpected profit does not fall under the rubric of unjust enrichment, we will address this issue in section 5, because halakhic sources that have analyzed the issue have sometimes employed terminology ordinarily associated with unjust enrichment.

2 Passively-gained benefit

In this section we will discuss the first type of unjust enrichment—passively-gained benefit. Here, the benefit is gained without the intentional intervention of any of the parties involved.

2.1 Talmudic sources

The Mishnah states:

> An animal is considered prone to do damage[7] with respect to eating fruit and vegetables.... Where does this apply? In the domain of the injured party. But in the public domain, its owner is exempt. However, if the animal benefited, its owner must pay compensation for the benefit incurred.
>
> mBaba Kama 2:2

It is normal for an animal to eat fruit and vegetables. Hence, the Mishnah asserts, if an animal trespasses and eats fruits or vegetables, its owner is liable to pay damages. But if the animal has eaten fruit or vegetables in a public place, its owner is exempt. Under the circumstances, the owner of the fruit should have assumed that animals were likely to nibble at it, and taken appropriate precautions. The Mishnah rules that the owner of the animal is exempt from paying for the damage, but liable for the value of his benefit.

7 It is assumed that such an animal will eat fruit to which it has access, and therefore, its owner is liable for negligence. Were such an animal to eat a spare tire, with respect to which it is considered 'innocuous,' there would be no liability, because there was no reason to anticipate that it would behave in this manner.

2.2 Assessment of liability

While assessment of the value of the fruit eaten by the animal is relatively simple, evaluation of the benefit to the animal's owner is more complicated. The Talmud records the following debate:

> Rabbah said, the value of the sheaves; Rava said, the value of the cheapest barley.
>
> bBaba Kama 20a

As Rashi explains, the basis of the assessment, in the opinion of Rabbah, is the cost of fodder (sheaves), the animal's usual diet. The kind of produce actually consumed is irrelevant, since the animal's owner can argue that he would never have fed the animal expensive food. His benefit is assessed, therefore, as the amount of fodder saved, the cost of which he is obliged to pay to the owner of the fruit. Rava, Rabbah's student, disagrees. The basis for the assessment, he argues, should be the actual benefit that accrued to the animal. If the fruit consumed by the animal is of a kind usually eaten by the species, the assessment should be based on the worth of the fruit even though the owner would not have fed the animal this particular food. However, it is assumed that the owner would have purchased the fruit at the lowest current market price, and hence, this is the amount he is obliged to pay.

The Mishnah can be summarized as follows: liability for damages is determined by the actual damage caused; liability for passively-gained benefit is less than the actual damage, and is equivalent to the value that the beneficiary gained. In the case of the animal, it is equivalent to the value of the feed the animal's owner saved.

2.3 Liability for damages and liability for benefits

Let us examine another talmudic example, 'the confiscated crop,' which makes explicit the difference between liability for damages and liability for gains made at someone else's expense.

> One whose crop was forcibly seized by the king's officer–if it was for arrears, he must tithe it, if it was confiscated, he is exempt from tithing it.
>
> bHulin 131a

Priestly tithes are due on all crops. If the grain was seized in lieu of a debt to the king, the owner must give to the priests an amount equivalent to the tithe owing on the crop that was seized, because the grain that would have been the priests' tithe went toward his debt. But if the grain was illegally seized, the owner is exempt from having to compensate the priests for the tithe they lost. The Talmud explains that in the former case, the owner benefited, because his debt was settled. But this benefit was gained, in part, at the expense of the priests, who lost their tithe, and thus must be compensated by the owner of the grain. In the latter case, the owner does not benefit from the seizure of his grain.

The passage allows us to infer that liability for damages is assessed from the point of view of the party who suffered the damages, while liability to pay compensation for benefits is assessed from that of the beneficiary: if there is no benefit, there is no liability to pay compensation, even if the other party has suffered a loss.

A further example of this talmudic distinction is the hypothetical case in which someone stole food and forcibly fed someone else.[8] Since the person who was force-fed did not steal the food, nor did he willingly partake of it, he is not held responsible and is exempted from paying damages. Nevertheless, he is obliged to pay for the bodily benefit (sustenance).[9]

2.4 The distinction between bodily benefit and property improvement

We will examine only one of the numerous other examples of passively-gained benefit discussed by the Talmud. In bBaba Kama 101a, the Talmud describes a scenario in which cloth absorbs dye that is adjacent to it. Is the owner of the dye entitled to compensation? As described in the Talmud, this instance of dyeing is an "ape-like" process, the talmudic term for an action for which the agent bears no legal responsibility, and thus cannot be sued. The owner of the dyed cloth did not steal the dye, and cannot be sued for theft. The question is whether he can be sued for the value of the dye absorbed by his cloth.[10]

The Tosafists raise the question of whether the owner of the cloth can be sued for the passively-gained benefit of his cloth's being dyed at someone else's expense. From the fact that the Talmud does not consider this point, they conclude that the owner of the cloth is not liable to pay for this benefit. The Tosafists express bewilderment at the apparent incompatibility between this ruling and those mentioned above, and propose to resolve the apparent contradiction by limiting the scope of a beneficiary's liability:

> We have to differentiate, since the benefit in our case was not generated by acts carried out by the beneficiary or by an act of his animal, whereas in the case of one who is forcibly fed, even though [the benefit] is not [generated by] his acts, his body benefits nonetheless.
>
> *Tosafot*, bBaba Kama 101a s.v. *o dilma*

8 bKetubot 30b.

9 Cf. *Rashi* ad loc. s.v. *shetahav*.

10 See I. Warhaftig, "Unjust enrichment in Jewish law," 9–10 *Shenaton Hamishpat Haivri* (1982/83), 187–92.

The Tosafists limit liability for passively-gained benefit, concluding that one does not have to pay for such a benefit unless he or his animal caused it, or he himself gains some bodily benefit. But there is no liability to pay for a monetary gain incurred without any action on the part of the beneficiary or his animal. The latter type of benefit is not considered unjust enrichment.

Apparently, the Tosafists believe it can be assumed that one is willing to pay for the enjoyment of a bodily, as opposed to a monetary, benefit that he does not set out to attain. Such an individual can plausibly argue that he was not interested in the latter. The Tosafists' conclusion here conflicts with that of 'the confiscated crop.' There, although the benefit came about passively, and was not bodily benefit, the beneficiary is liable nonetheless.

Indeed, the Tosafists make another suggestion as to how to reconcile the different cases, arguing that the dye does not increase the value of the cloth, but "just makes it prettier," hence, the benefit has no monetary value.

3 Benefitting someone else

Section 3 addresses the second type of unjust enrichment, in which benefit accrues to someone as the result of direct action by someone else, whom the beneficiary did not ask to take that action, and without his prior knowledge. Does such action constitute an act of altruism that need not be remunerated, or does it create an implicit obligation to the benefactor?

3.1 Talmudic sources

i Settling someone else's debt

One who maintains his fellow's wife

> A man went abroad and someone else came forward and supported his wife. Hanan says: He lost his money. The sons of the high priests disagreed with him, and said: He declares his expenses under oath, and he is reimbursed. R. Dosa b. Hyrkanos [said]: It is as they say. R. Johanan b. Zakai says: Hanan spoke well: he placed his money on the antlers of a deer [i.e., he forfeited his outlay].
>
> mKetubot 13:2

It is a husband's obligation to maintain his wife, and he is indebted to his wife for the amount of her maintenance. One who supports an abandoned family is in essence settling the absent husband's debt without consulting him first. The Mishnah records a debate, which took place during the Second Temple period, over whether the husband must reimburse him for his outlay. Hanan and R. Johanan b. Zakai say he is exempt, whereas the sons of the high priests and R. Dosa say he is liable.

ii Improving someone else's property

One who entered his fellow's field and planted there

> It was stated: [Regarding] one who entered his fellow's field and planted it without permission, Rav said: We estimate it, and he is at a disadvantage. And Samuel said: We estimate how much someone would willingly spend on planting a field such as this.
>
> bBaba Metzia 101a

A trespasser planted trees on someone else's property, thereby improving it. In Rav's opinion, he is entitled to recoup his expenses only if they do not exceed the worth of the improvement. If the improvement is worth less than he invested, he is only entitled to the amount of the improvement. In the opinion of Samuel, he is entitled to his expenses and reasonable compensation for his work, without regard to the value of the improvement. We will examine this case in detail below. For the time being, it is sufficient to state that according to both opinions, the planter is entitled to restitution, the debate being over how the restitution is to be calculated.

Why is this case different from 'one who maintains his fellow's wife,' where the law is decided in accordance with the view of Hanan? In the *Tosafot*, the following distinction is made:

> In the case of 'one who entered his fellow's field and planted there,' the improvement is tangible (*shevah baein*), hence it is fitting for him to be reimbursed. But here, in the case of 'one who maintains his fellow's wife,' he did not make any improvement to [the husband's] property, but rather, he saved [the absconding husband] from his creditor [i.e., his wife]'s collecting [what he owed]. But he did not give him anything. This is like abating a nuisance [lit., scaring away a lion] on his fellow's property, where even though [the benefactor] causes him a benefit, he [the beneficiary] does not thereby incur an obligation, as the Talmud concludes in bNedarim 33a–b.
>
> bKetubot 107b s.v. *hanan*

In bNedarim 33a–b, the Talmud rules that one who settles someone else's debt is not entitled to compensation, since he is like one who "scares away a lion from his fellow's property." The meaning of this expression will be discussed in section iii below.

The *Tosafot* state that from the point of view of the beneficiary, there are two distinct kinds of benefit: improved property, where the benefit is concrete and manifest, and must be paid for, and benefit derived from the abatement of a potential danger to property, where there is no tangible profit. This latter type of benefit does not create any obligation.

iii Abating a nuisance on someone else's property

On the basis of the talmudic ruling in bNedarim 33a–b, the Tosafists equate settling someone else's debt with the abatement of a nuisance, neither of which entitles the benefactor to restitution. We will now consider the question of whether this is so in every case, that is, whether in every case where benefit is created by prevention of a loss, the benefactor is not entitled to restitution. This will help us to clarify the concept of abatement of a nuisance, or in talmudic parlance, "one who scares away a lion from his fellow's property."

The Talmud stipulates that abatement of a nuisance does not warrant restitution when the following conditions are fulfilled: the abater acted voluntarily; and the abater sustained no loss by his action.[11] Whether these conditions are conjunctive or disjunctive, that is, whether both conditions must both be fulfilled, or only one, remains to be seen.

On the view that both conditions must be fulfilled, it would follow that only in the case of abatement of a nuisance that was voluntary and caused no loss to the benefactor is restitution not required. But if so, how could the Talmud in bNedarim compare abatement of nuisances with settling someone else's debt, a case in which the benefactor takes a loss? On the view that only one condition need be fulfilled, however, the talmudic comparison makes sense.

On the other hand, the hypothesis that fulfilment of either condition suffices to preclude restitution clashes with several talmudic precedents, cases where one who voluntarily acted to save someone else's property at a loss to himself was deemed entitled to compensation. For example, one who hired shepherds to protect someone else's herd from wolves was entitled to have his outlay reimbursed by the herd's owner.[12] Similarly, one who returned lost property was awarded compensation in the amount of what he would have earned in the time he expended on returning the lost property.[13]

3.2 Reconciling the talmudic sources

i Volunteering

The Tosafists attempted to harmonize the conflicting talmudic sources. They state that according to the letter of the law, the beneficiary of an action that prevents a loss (such as abatement of a nuisance, settling a debt, maintaining someone else's wife) is exempt from having to compensate his benefactor. One who voluntarily saves someone else's property is entitled to compensation for his outlay only in special cases:

11 bBaba Kama 58a.
12 bBaba Metzia 93b.
13 bBaba Metzia 31b.

> According to the strict law, he is certainly exempt ... but [in the case of one who voluntarily returns lost property], the Sages issued an enactment that he is to be compensated [to encourage] people to return their fellows' lost property, and so too, if he confronts [the lion] with [hired] shepherds and sticks ... so that they will scare away the lion.... but settling someone's debt, or coming forward and supporting his wife[14]—why do we need an enactment for this!?
>
> bKetubot 107b s.v. *hanan*

In the opinion of the Tosafists, the conditions mentioned above are disjunctive: satisfaction of either one is sufficient to exempt the beneficiary from compensating the volunteer. However, the Sages issued an enactment that in cases where the voluntary benefactor spent money or lost work days, and it is in the public interest that his activities be encouraged, the beneficiary must compensate him for his outlay.

On this view, one who abates a nuisance on someone else's property, and in so doing incurs expenses (e.g., the cost of hiring a shepherd) or sustains a loss (e.g., lost wages), is entitled to be compensated for this outlay or loss by the beneficiary. But the beneficiary is exempt from compensating him for the effort itself, just as the beneficiary is exempt from paying someone who returns lost property for doing this good deed. The Tosafists' opinion is based on the assumption that voluntarily helping someone else does not entitle the volunteer to any compensation for his effort and expenses. The individual is expected to extend help to others when doing so does not cause any loss, and such conduct requires neither encouragement nor reward. Sometimes, however, rendering assistance must be encouraged, namely, in cases where the volunteer cannot render assistance without expenditure or direct loss. In such cases, there is concern that people will refrain from helping those in need. To address this concern, it was enacted that volunteers are entitled to compensation for their costs and losses.

Reimbursement for expenses incurred during rescue

The concept of encouraging people to help those in distress, and providing for the reimbursement of expenses incurred in offering such aid, is reflected in a responsum by R. Asher b. Yehiel. It deals with a case in which family members who had paid the medical expenses of a mortally ill relative sought reimbursement from his heirs after his demise. R. Asher b. Yehiel ruled as follows:

> It is a routine practice that when someone falls ill and cannot help himself, his relatives endeavor to help ... and even other persons [who

14 An abandoned wife has other options: she may be able to support herself, or borrow money, which her husband is legally obliged to repay. There is no need for special enactments to encourage people to support abandoned families.

> are not relatives].... It seems to me that they ought not lose ... since this was a life-threatening situation, and whoever acts promptly is praiseworthy.
>
> *Responsa Rosh*, 85:2

Providing aid to save a life is unquestionably desirable, and a duty incumbent on all. It might be thought that when such an urgent matter—saving a life—is at stake, no allowance is made for the inconsequential issue of expenses and material losses. Asheri informs us that this is not so, and the volunteer lifesaver must be reimbursed by the beneficiary or his heirs, even if it is not absolutely certain that his life was saved by the voluntary action, as in the instance in question. Mandating compensation ensures that all will unhesitatingly extend life-saving assistance, and reduces loss of life due to delay and qualms about extending the needed assistance.

Asheri takes the same approach in commenting on the following *sugya*:

> How do we know that one who sees his fellow drowning in the river, dragged by beasts, or attacked by robbers, has a duty to save him? Scripture teaches, "Neither shalt thou stand idly by the blood of your neighbor" (Lev. 19:16).
>
> bSanhedrin 73a

The Talmud rules that the duty to save a life applies even if the rescuer has to exert himself, or hire help and equipment, but does not discuss the question of whether the rescuer is entitled to reimbursement from the saved party. Asheri addresses this point:

> And the one who was saved is obliged to compensate his rescuer for his outlay, for one is not obliged to save his fellow's life at his own expense if the rescuee has money [with which to compensate him].
>
> *Rosh*, bSanhedrin 73a

Apropos this issue, let us consider a concrete case. In medieval Germany, a Jew was taken prisoner. Members of the community raised the ransom needed to secure his release. Are they entitled to a refund from the released prisoner? This very question was addressed in a responsum by R. Meir of Rothenburg, see Appendix 1.

ii Causal linkage

Elsewhere,[15] the *Tosafot* adopt a different approach to harmonizing the conflicting talmudic passages dealing with reimbursement of expenses

15 *Tosafot*, bBaba Kama 58a. Contradictory opinions expressed by the Tosafists in commenting on different tractates of the Talmud are not unusual, since the *Tosafot* commentaries

incurred in proffering aid voluntarily. On this view, to justify a claim for reimbursement, a causal connection must be established between the benefactor's help and the benefit incurred through prevention of an otherwise inevitable loss. If it is beyond doubt that the acts of the volunteer prevented an otherwise certain loss or damage, then the beneficiary of the act must make restitution to the volunteer. But if the volunteer's actions merely abated a potential nuisance, the beneficiary is exempt from having to make restitution.

The beneficiary's exemption from having to compensate the volunteer for acts of 'scaring away a lion' is due to the absence of certainty that the lion was about to attack the beneficiary's herd. Similarly, the debtor whose debt was settled by someone else can argue that he could have reached an agreement with his creditors for a lesser amount, or that his friends would have put up the money for him. The same argument applies to 'one who maintains his fellow's wife': the absconder can argue that his wife would have been able to manage well enough without outside interference. On the other hand, in all the cases where the volunteer is entitled to reimbursement, the situation was such that, without the act of the volunteer rescuer, loss or damage would have been inevitable.

> And the opinion of R. Isaac[16] is that the rubric of one who scares away a lion and does not receive any payment applies only when it was not certain that a loss was imminent; for instance, if the lion was far away, and he only saved him the anxiety and fear that the lion would attack. But if it is certain that a loss will be incurred and the lion will ravage him ... he certainly receives payment, as in the case of 'the river that swept away someone's donkey' [referring to bBaba Kama 117b]
>
> *Tosafot*, bBaba Kama 58a s.v. *i nami*

The causal connection criterion is not articulated in the Babylonian Talmud, but is implied by the Jerusalem Talmud in its discussion of the mishnaic debate over 'one who maintains his fellow's wife' (mKetubot 13:2). With regard to the right of reimbursement, the Jerusalem Talmud distinguishes between one who maintains his fellow's wife and one who settles someone else's debt. It asserts that the different opinions in the mishnaic debate relate only to 'one who maintains his fellow's wife,' or in other words, that even the sons of the high priests (who award compensation to one who maintains his fellow's wife) would concur that one who settles someone else's debt is not entitled to reimbursement. The debtor

have no one author or editor. "In various places we find contradictory *Tosafot*, the reason being that in one place the opinion of Rabbenu Tam is quoted, in another, the opinion of Rabbenu Isaac or Rabbenu Isaac b. Asher, or others, who disagree with him" (*Yad Malachi*, rules for interpreting the *Tosafot*, sec. 20).

16 R. Isaac b. Samuel of Dampierre (12th c.), known as Ri (the Elder).

whose debt was settled can argue, 'I could have appeased [the creditor], and he would have waived [the debt],' an argument that can be put forward even if the creditor holds a pledge or has started proceedings against the debtor, though in these circumstances the debtor's plan has little chance of success. Nevertheless, the benefactor cannot claim reimbursement. In the words of the Jerusalem Talmud:

> R. Ba b. Mamal asked: One who redeems his fellow's promissory note without his knowledge, is this [also] a matter of controversy between Hanan and the sons of the high priests? [Should we say that this question is linked to the mishnaic controversy between Hanan and the sons of the high priests?] Said R. Jose: The rationale of the sons of the high priests [is as follows]: It never occurred to the absconder that his wife might starve to death [and he surely consents to someone else's supporting her, and will repay that outlay]. But in this case the man argues, 'I could have appeased him, and he would have waived [the debt].'
>
> jKetubot 13:2 (35d)

Rabbenu Tam's view

Unlike the Jerusalem Talmud, Rabbenu Tam extends the principle of causal connection to 'one who settles someone else's debt.' He rules that the benefactor is entitled to reimbursement, since it can be assumed that the debtor's chances of reaching a favorable settlement with his creditors are negligible.

> And Rabbenu Tam explains that this [the mishnaic rule about one who maintains his fellow's wife] only applies to supporting a wife [whose husband has absconded], and hence the husband is exempt [from repaying the benefactor] because it was not certain that he would have had to pay any maintenance at all; perhaps he could have evaded it, or his wife would have spent less had she not had someone funding her.... But with regard to a promissory note, even Hanan agrees that the benefactor does not forfeit his outlay [i.e., he must be compensated], because he conferred a definite benefit, since the debtor could not have avoided paying in any event.
>
> *Tosafot*, bKetubot 108a s.v. *ha mani*

Rabbenu Tam is not troubled about holding an opinion contrary to that expressed in the Jerusalem Talmud, and maintains that the Babylonian Talmud, in bKetubot 107b–108a, disputes the Jerusalem Talmud's stance on this point, distinguishing between settling a debt and maintaining someone's wife. According to Rabbenu Tam, the Babylonian Talmud asserts that one who settles someone else's debt is entitled to reimbursement because he saved his beneficiary from a virtually inevitable loss, since there was no other realistic possibility for the debt to be settled, hence the benefit was incontrovertible. But in the case of one who comes forward with money to support someone else's wife, there are plausible scenarios on which the absconding husband might not have had to pay, hence the benefit was not certain. Therefore the husband need not compensate the benefactor.

Rabbenu Tam's approach is, in effect, adopted in the contemporary Israeli legislation on unjust enrichment. Section 4 of the *Unjust Enrichment Law, 5739–1979* states:

> A person who pays another person's debt without being under duty towards him to do so is not entitled to restitution unless the other person had no reasonable cause to object to the payment of the whole or part of the debt and not beyond the amount paid.

See Appendix 2 for the law in its entirety.

3.3 Settling someone else's debt involuntarily

i One who is forced to settle someone else's debt

The Talmud distinguishes between one who scares away a lion voluntarily, and one who does so though he is not inclined to do so voluntarily.[17] The Talmud is referring to a case mentioned in the Mishnah where a sheep accidentally fell off a raised path into a garden, and was saved by landing on vegetation, which was destroyed. In such a situation, the owner of the crop is entitled to reimbursement for the damage. The same conclusion can also be reached on the basis of 'the confiscated crop,' in which, as we saw, the authorities seized grain, including portions that had been set aside as a tithe for the priests, thereby causing the priests, against their will, to settle part of the crop-owner's debt. The Talmud rules that the priests are entitled to reimbursement from the owner of the grain.

This appears to contradict the position taken on this point in the Jerusalem Talmud, which rules that one who is forced to pay someone else's debt is not entitled to be reimbursed, except if he paid either the property tax (*arnon*) or the poll tax (*gulgolet*).[18] According to this ruling, only in the case of payments in remittance of these specific taxes is a benefactor is entitled to reimbursement. Now these taxes are fixed taxes incurred by all, as opposed to private debts run up by individuals. The Jerusalem Talmud maintains, it appears, that one who is forced to pay someone else's private debt is not entitled to reimbursement.

17 bBaba Kama 58a.
18 jKetubot 13:2 (35d).

The Babylonian Talmud, as we saw, does not make this distinction, and in the 'confiscated crop' case rules that someone forced to settle his fellow's debt is entitled to reimbursement.

But there may be another rationale for the Jerusalem Talmud's ruling: reimbursement is restricted to debts that are incurred legally. *Arnon* and *gulgolet* exemplify such legally-incurred debts, settlement of which entitles the benefactor to reimbursement. But if a debt arose illegally, for example, as a result of extortion by local officials,[19] the beneficiary is exempt from having to reimburse one who was forced to pay the debt. If indeed this is the rationale, the ruling in the Jerusalem Talmud accords with the 'confiscated crop' *sugya* in the Babylonian Talmud. Restitution must be made for the repayment of someone else's legally-incurred debts ("if it was for arrears"), but not where the debt was incurred illegally ("if it was confiscated").

ii Guarantors, partners, and guardians

Sometimes there is a legal relationship between benefactor and beneficiary, such that the former's involvement is warranted; in these instances, he is not considered a volunteer. We will consider three cases of this type.

a Guarantors

If a debtor is insolvent, his guarantor must assume responsibility for the debt upon the creditor's demand. The debtor, on his part, implicitly assumes the obligation to repay the guarantor. If not otherwise stipulated, the guarantor's obligation only arises if the creditor presents the debtor with a demand for repayment that he cannot meet. But what is the law regarding a guarantor who redeems a debt before payment is demanded from the debtor, without any prior agreement between the guarantor and debtor as to what should be done in such a scenario?

Maimonides rules that such a guarantor falls under the category of 'one who settles someone else's debt,' and the beneficiary need not reimburse his outlay.[20]

R. Abraham b. David (Rabad) states that Maimonides' ruling is "preposterous and an insult to the intelligence," but brings no argument for this assertion.[21] R. Joel Sirkes suggests that if a legal relationship existed between the benefactor and the beneficiary, it cannot be assumed that the benefactor acted voluntarily, that is, altruistically; he is therefore entitled to reimbursement.[22]

19 See bHulin 131a, and see Chapter Three above, "Exigency authority," section 4.4.
20 *Code*, Laws concerning Creditor and Debtor 26:5.
21 *Rabad* ad loc.
22 *Bayit Hadash*, *Tur*, HM 130:2.

b Partners

The nature of the obligation is similar in a case in which a loan was extended to two partners who are jointly and separately liable for the whole sum. This type of partnership is regarded as a binding relationship by Asheri, who rules:

> Two who borrowed jointly and became guarantors for each other ... since by law the creditor could collect the whole amount from either of them, the partner whose debt is paid must reimburse the other partner, since the 'one who settles his fellow's debt has forfeited his money' rule only applies where someone paid someone else's debt voluntarily and on his own initiative, without being obligated to do so, for he is like one who scares away a lion.
>
> *Responsa Rosh*, 73:9

c Guardians and relatives

A guardian is appointed to administer the affairs of those incapable of looking after themselves—orphans, minors, the mentally deficient, and so on. What is the law regarding a guardian who paid his ward's debt and claims reimbursement from the ward's assets? Asheri rules on a case in which a widow settled her late husband's debts in order to keep the estate intact: "She is entitled to reimbursement because, without being officially appointed, she acted on behalf of the orphans, as a guardian."[23]

3.4 Improving someone else's property without permission

i Introduction

This section, like the previous one, deals with the acts of someone who benefits someone else without the latter's knowledge, that is, cases in which a benefactor, at his own initiative, bestows some benefit on the beneficiary. 'One who entered his fellow's field and planted there,' in tractate Baba Metzia, is the prototype of this kind of case.

'One who entered his fellow's field and planted there' differs from 'scaring away a lion' and 'settling someone else's debt,' discussed above, because in the case of 'one who entered his fellow's field and planted there,' the 'meddler' **improves** the beneficiary's property—planting his field, renovating his building, and so on—whereas in the other cases, the benefactors' actions save the beneficiaries from sustaining a loss, but do not cause them a net enrichment.

23 *Responsa Rosh*, 87:4.

Cases on the model of 'one who entered his fellow's field and planted there' usually involve a craftsman (or one who aspires to that status) who intends to receive payment and does not intend to donate his services. The meddler usually acts in the owner's absence, on the assumption that the latter will, post factum, accept the fait accompli and pay him, at the going rate, for the work he has put in.

ii English and Israeli law

'One who entered his fellow's field and planted there' must not be confused with the case in which one entered his fellow's field and planted there **at the owner's request**, but did not stipulate his wage in advance.

English law differentiates between the two types of cases. If the laborer acted at the owner's request, but without agreeing on a wage in advance, the relevant principle is that of *quantum meruit*—fair market value of the work done—and the laborer gets paid for the work he did at the usual rate. Israeli law is similar:

> An obligation to make, for a commodity or service, a payment the amount of which has not been agreed upon, shall be fulfilled by paying an amount which, according to the circumstances at the time the contract was made, it would have been appropriate to pay.[24]

This law covers cases where the liability is based on a contract. In the case of one entered his fellow's field and planted there **at the owner's request,** but did not stipulate his wage in advance, the contract is incomplete, but we complete the contract according to our estimation of the intentions of the parties concerned.

On the other hand, according to English law, someone who entered his fellow's field and planted there for reasons of his own, and not at the owner's request, is not entitled to payment even if his action generated a profit. As an Israeli jurist explained, according to English law, the meddler has no valid claim, because a stranger cannot be permitted to interfere in the affairs of someone else and force business decisions on her. "Undoubtedly, the general principle is that work performed and moneys expended on preserving or improving someone else's property do not create any lien on that property, nor do they create an obligation to reimburse the outlays. We cannot impose obligations on those who were not present, just as we do not impose benefits on them against their will.[25]

On this point, apparently due to the influence of Jewish law, Israeli law differs from English law. Section 5 (a) of Israel's *Unjust Enrichment Law, 5739–1979* states:

24 Contracts (General Part) Law 5733–1973 27 LSI 117, 46 (1972–1973) (Isr.).
25 Cheshin J., quoting M. Silberg, in CA 138/55 Cohen v. Sibirsky, 9(3) PD 1457, 1833 (1955) (Isr.).

> Where a person, in good faith and reasonably, does any act to protect the life, physical integrity, health, honor or property of another person without being under duty towards him to do so, and in that connection incurs or undertakes to incur any expenses, the beneficiary shall indemnify the benefactor for his reasonable expenses, including obligations incurred by him towards a third party, and if damage is caused to the property of the benefactor in consequence of the act, the Court may order the beneficiary to pay compensation to the benefactor if it considers it just to do so in the circumstances of the case.

Our intention here is not to analyze the differences between Israeli law and Jewish law, but the comparison is useful inasmuch as it highlights the different approaches that can be taken to the question of reimbursement for expenses incurred by one who voluntarily acts in someone else's interest.

iii Jewish law

We have already noted, in section 1.2 above, that the relevant general principle in Jewish law is that if one benefits at the expense of another, the beneficiary must make restitution unless there is a specific reason for exempting him from this obligation. We have discussed two such reasons: purely altruistic intent on the part of the benefactor; and the absence of causal linkage between the benefactor's action and the benefit accrued.

These considerations do not apply in the case of the 'one who entered his fellow's field and planted there,' which, we saw, concerns a business relationship, in which the benefactor invested physical labor, or spent money, to improve someone else's property. It is difficult to conceive of this as a voluntary, altruistic act. Furthermore, since an actual improvement has been made, the property-owner cannot claim that he has not benefited from the benefactor's action, or that the benefit would have been incurred even without the benefactor's act. In other words, the causal connection cannot be denied. The only line of argument open to the property-owner is to say that he was not interested in the benefit. This line of argument will be discussed after we review the pertinent talmudic sources.

iv Fields earmarked for planting, and those not earmarked for planting

The Talmud rules that one who enters and sows someone else's field without permission is entitled to payment. Regarding the amount of payment, the Talmud distinguishes between two kinds of fields: (a) those earmarked for planting; and (b) those not earmarked for planting, and hence, though improved by the act of planting, not optimally improved.[26]

> It was stated: [Regarding] one who entered his fellow's field and planted it without permission, Rav said: We estimate it, and he is at a disadvantage. And Samuel said: We estimate how much someone would spend on planting a field such as this. R. Papa said: They do not disagree: one [speaks of] a field earmarked for planting, the other [speaks of] a field not earmarked for planting.
>
> bBaba Metzia 101a

That is, Samuel is referring to cultivation of fields earmarked for planting, and Rav, to cultivation of fields not so earmarked. Cultivation of fields earmarked for planting entitles the meddler to higher payment than cultivation of fields not so earmarked. In the latter case, payment is warranted only if the land's value has been increased. Let us specify how the two scenarios play out.

a Fields earmarked for planting

The prototype here is a field that has been tilled and prepared for planting. The meddling planter merely plants there before the owner has a chance to do so himself. In this case, the value of the planter's work must be estimated. The planter is entitled to be paid at the usual rate for such work, as if he had been properly contracted.

b Fields not earmarked for planting

In this type of case, the owner claims that he did not intend to plant anything, but does not deny that the value of his property has increased as a result of the planting. The planter is not entitled to payment at the usual rate, but rather, "We estimate it, and he is at a disadvantage." Rashi explains Rav's rather cryptic statement as follows: 'If the improvement is greater than his outlay, we reimburse his outlay, but if the outlay was greater than the improvement, we award him only the value of the improvement.'

v The beneficiary's response

In some cases the beneficiary reacts as soon as the meddling benefactor's unsolicited action comes to his attention. Sometimes this reaction is positive, implying assent, in other instances it is negative. The beneficiary's reaction may have some bearing on the extent of his liability.

26 E.g., consider the case where someone plants grape vines on a vacant lot in Manhattan, which, if tended, will yield fifty bushels of grapes, at $50 a bushel.

a 'Take back your timber and masonry'

We noted that English law denies the meddler any rights at all: one cannot be forced into a business decision without prior consultation. Against this, it could be argued that if the beneficiary indeed wishes to reject the benefit he has incurred due to the meddler's unsolicited efforts, he should not make any use of the improvement, but rather order the meddler to restore the *status quo ante*. The right to make this demand is not articulated explicitly in the Talmud, though the Talmud recognizes the meddler's right to recover his investment—'I am taking back my timber and masonry'— if an agreement as to compensation for his outlay and effort is not reached. But Alfasi, and other authorities in his wake, award the owner the corresponding right to have the unsolicited improvements removed:

> If the property owner says: 'Take back your timber and masonry, because I do not want this building'—this scenario is not discussed by the Talmud. But this ruling was issued by the Academy[27]: Just as the one who built is entitled to say, 'I am taking back my timber and masonry,' so the property owner is entitled to say, 'Take back your timber and masonry.'
>
> *Alfasi*, bBaba Metzia 101a (Alfasi pagination)

The Early Authorities disagree over the extent of the owner's right to have the *status quo ante* restored and be exempted from reimbursing the meddler. Some rule that it applies only to land not earmarked for planting, where the improvements do not generate optimal profits for the beneficiary.[28] But with regard to fields earmarked for planting, they maintain that the owner cannot deny that the profit he is earning from the improved land is not less than that he expected to earn, and his not having given prior consent makes no difference. They maintain that the owner does not have the right to have the *status quo ante* restored, and he must reimburse the meddler for his outlay. Other Early Authorities rule that the owner is always within his rights to refuse to reimburse any outlay that was forced on him, and register strong reservations about any external interference in one's business affairs: "If it were not so, anyone could force his fellow to plant fields, make a garden or courtyard, or build houses."[29]

b Pre-emptive protest

If the beneficiary was aware of the meddler's intention to bestow an unsolicited benefit, and registered a protest in advance, then if the meddler

27 The Babylonian talmudic academies of the Geonic period.

28 E.g., *Magid Mishne* on *Code*, Laws concerning Robbery and Lost Property 10:5.

29 This remark was made by students of R. Solomon b. Adret, quoted in the *Beit Yosef*, *Tur*, HM 375.

goes ahead and makes reversible improvements, he is exempt from having to compensate him. R. Solomon b. Adret rules: "There is unanimous agreement [that in this case] he can tell [the meddler], 'Take back your timber and masonry,' in order to prevent people from forcing their fellows to plant or to build."[30] This ruling prevents unwanted liabilities from being incurred, but does not provide a solution for cases in which the previous state of affairs cannot be restored, and the meddler's investment cannot be recovered. Though the property owner did indeed protest beforehand, has he not also, in the final analysis, profited?

c Expression of approval

Sometimes the beneficiary acts in a manner indicating that he is pleased with the benefactor's efforts. In such a case, the beneficiary must compensate the benefactor. The Talmud describes just such a case: someone entered his fellow's field and planted there without permission, following which the property-owner fenced the field in.[31] By this action, the property-owner indicated that he was content with his field's having been planted; accordingly, he was ordered to pay the benefactor for his work.

3.5 Provision of accommodations or meals without a contract

Thus far we have discussed the case of one who entered and planted another's field in the context of a business transaction. We now consider this type of act in the context of ordinary interpersonal relationships. The classic case is that of one who confers a benefit on someone else by offering him room and board, without stipulating at the outset that he expects to receive payment in return—for example, someone who raises a orphan in his home, or invites a relative or friend to stay with him for a while. Is the benefactor entitled to payment?

This situation is not analogous to settling someone else's debt, or abatement of nuisances, for here the benefactor does not save the beneficiary from possible harm, but confers a direct benefit on him. The salient characteristic of the cases discussed in the previous section ('improving someone else's property without permission') is that the benefit is conferred within the context of a business relationship, where it is clear that the benefactor intended to receive payment. In the cases we are now considering, however, the beneficiary is under the impression that the benefit was extended out of the goodness of the benefactor's heart, and the benefactor had no intention of exacting payment, whereas the benefactor argues that

30 *Responsa Rashba*, 4, #54.
31 bBaba Metzia 101a.

from the outset, he intended to be paid for the benefits that accrued to the beneficiary.

In a case where payment is not an expressly stipulated condition, the question is that of the benefactor's intent at the time the benefits were conferred: is the benefactor to be regarded as one who intended to give a gift, or as one who extended credit? That is, it must be decided whether the case is analogous to that of 'one who entered his fellow's field and planted there' or to that of 'one who settles someone else's debt.' There is no direct reference in the Talmud to this type of case, nor is it treated systematically by the halakhic authorities. R. Ezekiel Landau describes the law on this point as "opaque."[32]

Alfasi

In the opinion of Alfasi, the situation in question is analogous to that of 'one who settles someone else's debt.' One of his responsa deals with a case in which someone who had raised an orphan in his household sued for reimbursement of his expenses upon the orphan's coming of age. The orphan argued that at the outset, the man took him in as an act of benevolence, and had only now, after the fact, decided to ask for payment. Alfasi rules as follows:

> By law, this Reuben cannot take anything from the orphan, because while he maintained him, he did not tell him that his outlay was intended as a loan.... therefore [the maintenance] was surely provided as an act of benevolence, as we learned ... "one who went abroad and someone came forward and supported his wife," and so on [citing bKetubot 107b].
>
> *Responsa Alfasi* (Leuter edition), #116

R. Shimon b. Tzemah Duran (Rashbatz) rules similarly. He exempts one who lived in his fellow's courtyard, at the latter's invitation, from paying rent.[33]

R. Solomon b. Adret and R. Moses Isserles

R. Solomon b. Adret (Rashba) sees the case in the light of 'one who entered his fellow's field and planted there.' He infers from it that anyone who confers a benefit on someone else intends to be paid for it.[34] On the basis of the Rashba's ruling, R. Moses Isserles (Rema) rules:

32 *Noda Biyehuda*, 2nd edition, HM #34.

33 *Responsa Tashbetz*, 1, #174.

34 The Rashba's ruling is quoted in the Ran's commentary on bNedarim 33b.

> And so it is with anyone who acts for, or confers a benefit on, someone else. [The beneficiary] cannot argue, 'You did this for me gratis, since I did not ask you to do it,' but is obliged to pay him.
>
> *Rema*, *SA*, HM 264:4

Yet R. Moses Isserles appears to contradict this ruling at HM 363:10, where he accepts the position taken by Alfasi and the Rashbatz: "One who invites his fellow to live in his courtyard—the latter does not have to pay him rent." Some halakhic authorities subsequently suggested that this contradiction between the Rema's rulings reflects the fact that the law on this point is open to doubt–or in the words of R. Ezekiel Landau, "opaque"—and hence the beneficiary's liability is also in doubt.

4 Benefitting from someone else

4.1 Introduction

We have discussed the liability of one who gains a benefit passively (section 2), and one who gains due to the action of a benefactor (section 3). In this section, we consider benefits that someone actively and intentionally derives from someone else's property, on his own initiative. At first glance, such cases might seem to entail robbing or otherwise causing harm to the benefactor, for what other way is there to derive a benefit from someone else's property? However, it is possible to use someone else's property without robbing him or causing him damage. One who parks his car on someone else's property is not guilty of theft, since "land cannot be stolen,"[35] nor has he caused any damage to the land.

Furthermore, even if damage has been caused to the unwitting benefactor, the benefit may exceed it. If so, it must be decided whether the beneficiary is liable to pay for this benefit, in addition to being liable for the damage. The problem can be stated more generally: in addition to his liability for the robbed goods, does a robber bear liability for the benefit he has gained from them while they were in his possession?

4.2 Talmudic source: one who lives in someone else's courtyard without his knowledge

The talmudic model for this problem is the case of the squatter, one who lives in someone else's courtyard, that is, on her premises, without her knowledge. It is assumed that the squatter does not damage the property. The question is whether he is liable to pay for his benefit; whether he can be charged rent for use of the property. The talmudic passage reads as follows:

35 bBaba Kama 117b.

> R. Hisda said to Rami b. Hama, You were not with us last night at the study hall when we probed an important matter. He asked, What important matter? He said to him, One who lives in someone else's courtyard without his knowledge—does he have to pay him rent, or doesn't he?
>
> What is it all about? If the courtyard was not going to be rented out, and [the squatter] would not have rented it, then one did not benefit and the other did not lose. If the courtyard was going to be rented out, and [the squatter] would have rented it, then one benefited whereas the other lost. It must therefore apply to a courtyard that was not going to be rented out and [a squatter] who would have rented it. How do we rule?
>
> bBaba Kama 20a

There are two variables in this problem, one related to the property, the other to the squatter. The property may or may not be intended to be rented out, and the squatter may, or may not, be someone who would rent such a property. If the property is not intended to be rented out, and the squatter would not rent it in any event, then the squatter does not save any rent, because he has other options,[36] and the owner does not lose any rent, because he never intended to rent out the property. This is a case in which "one did not benefit and the other did not lose," so the squatter bears no liability to pay the property owner for living there.

If the property is intended to be rented out, and the squatter is an individual who would have rented it, then "one benefited whereas the other lost," and the beneficiary is surely liable for paying rent. Hence the Sages who deliberated the matter at the study hall were discussing a third permutation of the two variables, where the owner did not intend to rent out the property, but the squatter is someone who would have paid rent. This is a case in which 'one benefited, but the other did not lose.' The squatter benefited because he had a place to live without paying rent, but the owner did not lose because he did not intend to rent out the property.

The Talmud concludes that in a 'one benefited, but the other did not lose' situation, the beneficiary is exempt from paying for the benefit: "one who benefited, but the other did not lose, is exempt."[37] Therefore one who lives on someone else's property without the latter's knowledge does not have to pay rent if the property-owner had no intention of renting out the premises.

36 *Rashi* ad loc., explains that the squatter might have other free alternatives, such as another dwelling where he can live rent-free, or even his own place.

37 bBaba Kama 20b.

On the basis of this talmudic conclusion, Maimonides rules:

> [Regarding] one who lives in someone else's courtyard without his knowledge—if the said courtyard is not going to be rented out, he does not have to pay any rent, even though his usual practice is to rent a place for himself, because one benefited but the other did not lose. If the courtyard is going to be rented out, the squatter has to pay rent, even if his usual practice is not to rent a place for himself, because he caused [the owner] a monetary loss.
>
> *Code*, Laws concerning Robbery and Lost Property 3:9

Israel's *Unjust Enrichment Law 5739–1979* embodies a principle similar to the talmudic principle that 'one who benefited, but the other did not lose, is exempt.' After establishing liability in section 1, section 2 of the law states: "The Court may exempt the beneficiary from the whole or part of the duty of restitution under section 1 if it considers that the receipt of the benefit did not involve a loss to the benefactor or that other circumstances render restitution unjust." The difference between the talmudic principle and that adopted by Israeli law is the role of the court. Israeli law leaves the exemption to the court's discretion, whereas the talmudic exemption is absolute.

4.3 'One who benefited, but the other did not lose, is exempt'

i Underlying rationale

Various justifications can be adduced for the 'one who benefited, but the other did not lose, is exempt' principle:

(a) If the benefactor loses nothing, he can be presumed, as long as there is no evidence to the contrary, to have waived his monetary rights vis-à-vis the beneficiary.[38]

(b) The presumption of waiver applies even against the benefactor's protestations to the contrary. A waiver not based on factual evidence that the benefactor indeed waived his right to payment is a 'constructive waiver,' that is, a waiver inferred by the law, and acted upon accordingly. That is, under certain circumstances, the law does not permit the individual to fully exercise his legal rights, but exhorts him to show compassion, lest he be like the evil inhabitants of Sodom and Gomorrah. In talmudic parlance, "we compel him not to act in accordance with the ethos of Sodom."[39]

(c) As long as the benefactor has lost nothing, there are no grounds for holding the beneficiary liable; one is not obliged to pay for a benefit

38 *Mahane Efraim*, Laws of Robbery, 10.
39 bBaba Batra 12b; and see R. Jacob Joshua Falk, *Pnei Yehoshua*, bBaba Kama 20b.

> incurred if it was not gained at someone else's expense. Can a restaurateur charge passers-by for the smell of his food?

Note that the 'one who benefited, but the other did not lose, is exempt' principle is applied to exempt the squatter from having to pay rent after the fact, but does not mean grant permission to break into the property of others. R. Joseph Habiba, the Nimukei Yosef, reviews the opinions of other halakhic authorities and concludes: "But [the Sages] certainly did not say that one may make use of the property of another, because were we to say that, there would be no one who didn't engage in extorting his fellow."[40]

ii Protest on the part of the property-owner

As noted above, the principle that one who benefited without causing a loss to his unwitting benefactor is exempt from having to pay restitution only addresses the situation ex post facto. It does not restrict the owner's right to protest and demand that the squatter vacate his property. And indeed, if the squatter ignores the owner's protests and stays, he is obliged to pay for the use of the premises. The *Shulhan Arukh* rules: "One who lives in someone else's courtyard without his knowledge, and [the owner] told him to leave and he did not leave, must pay him the full rent."[41] R. Moses Isserles adds:

> Even though in cases where 'one benefited but the other did not lose,' we compel him not to act in accordance with the ethos of Sodom, this only applies where the benefactor could not have benefited even had he wanted to. But in this case the courtyard-owner could have benefited and profited by renting out his courtyard had he wanted to, but he did not want to, and he cannot be forced to do it gratis.
>
> *Rema, SA*, HM 363:6

The Rema distinguishes between two scenarios where the benefactor does not lose: instances where the benefactor cannot make any use of the property, and instances where the benefactor can put his property to use, but chooses not to do so. The Rema maintains that in cases that fall into the first category, not only is the beneficiary exempt post factum, but the property-owner can be legally compelled, *ab initio*, to permit someone to enjoy the benefit, since otherwise he is acting like the evil inhabitants of Sodom. In cases that fall into the second category, post factum the beneficiary is exempt from paying for his benefit, but the property-owner may prevent him from continuing to enjoy the benefit, as he can reserve the right to generate a profit from his property.

40 *Nimukei Yosef*, bBaba Kama 9a (Alfasi pagination).
41 HM 363:6.

There is no incompatibility between the opinions of R. Joseph Habiba, R. Joseph Caro, and R. Moses Isserles. All would concur that the property-owner can tell the squatter to leave, since in principle he is able to use his property to generate a profit.

iii Minimal loss

In the talmudic debate over the liability of "one who benefited but the other did not lose," the following baraita is quoted: "R. Judah says ... Even one who lives in someone else's courtyard without his knowledge must pay him rent."[42] The Talmud asks whether we can infer from this the principle that 'one who benefited, but the other did not lose, is **liable**.' It rejects this inference, saying that the baraita can be interpreted as applying to a specific situation: "There, it is because he blackened the walls." In other words, since the squatter caused damage to the property by dirtying the walls, he has to pay rent. This talmudic explanation of the baraita is the basis for a law that does not itself appear in the Talmud, but was set down by the Early Authorities. The *Nimukei Yosef* commentary asserts: "According to the Rosh and the Ritba, of blessed memory, even though he only caused a very small loss, he has to pay him for the benefit in its entirety."[43]

On this view, any loss caused to the owner as a result of the squatter's benefit triggers full liability.[44] The squatter's exemption from liability for restitution is conditional on the benefactor's incurring no loss whatsoever. In the words of the *Shulhan Arukh*:

> Some say that even causing a small loss, such as blackening the walls of a new house, renders the squatter liable to pay for the benefit in its entirety, though the damage wrought by the blackening is but small.
>
> *Shulhan Arukh*, HM 363:3

Given the damage, however minor, caused to the property-owner, the case does not fall under the rubric 'but the other did not lose,' and the 'one who benefited, but the other did not lose, is exempt' principle does not apply.

iv Expression of approval

In the context of determining the extent of the beneficiary's liability, another talmudic case presents an important principle:

42 bBaba Kama 20b.

43 bBaba Kama 9a (Alfasi pagination).

44 On some views, the squatter is only liable for the actual damage. R. Meir b. Todros Halevi Abulafia, e.g., is quoted by *Nimukei Yosef* as stating that the squatter must repaint the walls.

> Where someone's property surrounds a neighbor's property on three sides, and he fenced in the first side, the second side, and the third side, the neighbor cannot be compelled [to participate in the expenses]. R. Jose said: If the one who was surrounded fenced in the fourth side, this renders him obligated to contribute to the [costs of erecting the] entire fence.
>
> mBaba Batra 1:3

Reuben and Shimon own neighboring lots. Reuben's lot surrounds Shimon's on three sides. Reuben made a fence around his own lot, thereby incidentally building a fence for Shimon on three sides. At present, Shimon derives little benefit from this fence, because the fourth side of his lot is open. He is not obliged to contribute to Reuben's expenses. R. Jose adds that if Shimon encloses the fourth side, he must participate in the expense of fencing in the other three sides as well.

The Tosafists raise the following objection: this case is similar to that of the squatter, that is, 'one who benefited, but the other did not lose.'[45] Reuben erected the fence for his own purposes, and why should Shimon have to share the expense after Reuben had already built his fence? The Tosafists then reply that by enclosing the fourth side, the surrounded neighbor revealed that he was willing to invest some money in a fence, but the squatter gave no indication that he would be willing to live in the benefactor's courtyard if he would have to pay any rent at all.

On the basis of these remarks in the *Tosafot*, the *Shulhan Arukh* rules that if the beneficiary indicates willingness to pay for enhanced benefit, the 'one who benefits, but the other does not lose, is exempt' principle no longer applies, and he is obliged to pay for his benefit in full.[46]

4.4 Use of someone else's chattels

Thus far we have discussed benefits derived from real estate. Let us now consider the case of a robber who derived benefit from an object he robbed. According to the Talmud, liability for robbery is incurred at the time of the robbery, and the deemed value of the robbed article is its value at that time. "All robbers pay [restitution] according to the [value at the] time of the robbery."[47] Thus a robber must return the original value of the robbed object even if it has been damaged, destroyed, stolen, or has ceased to exist.

This principle usually works in the owner's favor, because it ensures that his right to restitution is not diminished by events that take place after the robbery. But a side effect of this rule is that since his liability is fixed at

45 *Tosafot*, bBaba Kama 20b s.v. *taama*.
46 HM 63:8.
47 bBaba Metzia 43a.

the time of the robbery, the thief does not have to pay for the benefit he gets from using the robbed article, as long as this use does not cause it to depreciate. The robber is held responsible for the full value of the robbed article, but he may treat it as if he were its owner. It follows that, like an owner, he is permitted to use the article.

It is thus necessary in every case to ascertain whether use of someone else's chattels without his permission is considered robbery. For taking an object without intent to commit robbery—if, for instance, the person who takes it is under the impression that he is the rightful owner—is not considered robbery, and therefore the one who takes an object under these circumstances is liable to pay for the benefit he gets from using it.

Before we continue to analyze the case of a robber who rents out the robbed items, it will be helpful to understand the talmudic distinction between direct and indirect benefit, as it is presented in another *sugya*, to which we now turn.

4.5 'How can this person do business with someone else's cow?!'

We can distinguish two kinds of benefits that can accrue from someone else's property: direct benefits, such as those we saw in the case of the squatter, or benefits incurred by utilizing a legal arrangement, such as subletting a rented apartment at a higher rent. The legal significance of this distinction is debated by the Mishnah in the *sugya* of the 'borrowed cow,' to which we now return.

The Case of the Borrowed Cow

> [Regarding] someone who leased a cow from his fellow, and lent it to someone else, and the cow died a natural death: the lessee must swear that the cow died a natural death, and the borrower must pay [the value of cow] to the lessee. R. Jose said: How can this person do business with someone else's cow?! The [compensation for the] cow must be returned to the owner.
>
> mBaba Metzia 3:2

According to the law, a lessee is not responsible for force majeure: if the cow expired for any reason beyond the lessee's control, he is exempt. The case is different with regard to a borrower. By law, he assumes full liability, since he does not pay for using the borrowed item. Even if the cow met a natural death, the borrower is responsible and liable. The focus of this Mishnah is the recipient of compensation for the dead cow. Is it forthcoming to the owner, who leased out his cow, or to the lessee, who rented out the cow to the borrower?

The Sages rule that the lessee must take an oath that the cow died a natural death and thereby exempt himself from liability, and the borrower must compensate the lessee. The lessee thus incurs a second, indirect, benefit in addition to the benefit of usage, for which he paid.

R. Jose disputes the lessee's right to enjoy such an indirect benefit. He rules that the borrower must compensate the **owner** of the cow, because "how can one do business with someone else's cow?!" On his view, the lessee is entitled only to the benefits he paid for, but not to any indirect benefits arising from his having lent out the cow, even if this bailment to a third party is not forbidden. R. Jose's view prevailed.

The distinction between the two kinds of benefits can now be applied to the question of the robber's use of robbed property. As we saw, a robber is exempt from paying for the use of the property he robs. But what is the rule regarding a robber who rents out such robbed property? Who is entitled to the profit thereby generated? If we regard any rental money earned by the robber as benefit **accruing directly** from the robbed object, rather than as accruing as a result of utilization of some legal arrangement, then he is exempt from handing over the rental fee to the owner. This position is endorsed by R. Joseph Caro:

> Since the rule is that "all robbers pay [restitution] according to the [value at the] time of the robbery," what difference does it make if he used it himself or rented it out to someone else?
>
> *Beit Yosef*, *Tur*, HM 362:5

But R. Moses Isserles rules that if the robber rented out the property to someone else, any profit thereby gained is not a benefit that is incurred directly, but rather an indirect benefit arising from utilization of a legal arrangement. Hence, he must hand the profits over to the owner. He arrives at this ruling by invoking R. Jose's opinion in the Mishnah about the borrowed cow: "if the lessee worked with the cow and it died, he is exempt [from compensating the owner], but if [the lessee] lent it to someone else and it died, compensation must be paid to the original owner."[48]

5 Unexpected profit received by an agent

5.1 Introduction

Sometimes a benefit accrues to an agent in the course of his agency, giving rise to the question of who this unexpected benefit belongs to. Although as we noted above, unexpected profit does not fall under the rubric of unjust enrichment, we will address this issue here because halakhic sources that have analyzed the issue have sometimes employed terminology ordinarily associated with unjust enrichment.

48 *Darkhei Moshe*, *Tur*, HM 363:5.

5.2 Talmudic source

> A widow's marriage settlement (*ketuba*) was [for the amount of] 200 [*zuz*, a unit of currency]; she sold assets [from her husband's estate] worth a *mane* [a unit of currency equivalent to 100 zuz] for 200 … her marriage settlement has been paid in full.
>
> mKetubot 11:4

The case at hand involves a widow who is entitled, by law, to a settlement of 200 *zuz* from her husband's estate, as well as to the customary additional payments. In order to partially realize this entitlement, the orphans, her husband's heirs, gave her land worth 100 *zuz* to put up for sale. She found a buyer who gave her 200 *zuz*, a sum that exceeded the estimated value. She claimed that she was entitled to keep the 100 'extra' *zuz* as her personal profit, and not as part of the settlement owed her. The orphans claimed that the windfall profit was theirs, and hence, that it served as payment of the remainder of the marriage settlement, which was thus fully discharged. The Mishnah states that their claim was upheld.

The Gemara maintains that she acted as an agent for the orphans, and states: "Here [i.e., regarding this Mishnah] Rabbi [Judah the Prince] has taught: It all belongs to the owner."[49] That is, the entire profit belongs to the principal, who sent the agent to buy or sell something, regardless of whether the latter bought or sold at a more-profitable-than-expected price. The agent cannot say that the profit is his.

The Gemara goes on to report a Tannaitic dispute over this matter:

> It was taught: If they added an extra item [to goods purchased by an agent], all [the profit] goes to the agent—so says R. Judah. R. Jose says, They share it. But is it not taught in a baraita, R. Jose says, 'It all belongs to the principal [lit., owner of the money]'? Rami b. Hama says, There is no contradiction, for in the one case we are speaking of something that has an established value, in the other we are speaking of something that does not have an established value.
>
> bKetubot 98b

The Gemara decides the matter, and its ruling is reiterated by the *Shulhan Arukh*. This ruling will be presented below.

First, however, let us flesh out the talmudic scenario. Reuben sends Shimon to the market to buy merchandise worth $100. Shimon gets a discount and hence buys additional merchandise with the sum at his disposal. If this is merchandise that does not have "an established value," that is, a fixed price, such as an article of clothing or fresh vegetables, and is sold according to an estimate of its value, it all belongs to the owner, since the seller agreed to lower his price, and is not adding anything to the

49 bKetubot 98b.

transaction. But if the price is fixed (Rashi cites dried legumes as an example of such a commodity), the owner and the agent split the additional merchandise. And indeed, the *Shulhan Arukh* rules accordingly:

> If the price is fixed and known, and to [the goods purchased by] the agent they added some extra in terms of number or weight or size—all that was added by the vendors belongs to both, and the agent shares the excess goods with the principal [lit., the owner of the money].
>
> *Shulhan Arukh*, HM 183:6

Sharing is mandated in cases involving commodities with fixed prices. As we are about to see, the Early Authorities were divided as to the rationale for this law.

5.3 Doubt as to the giver's intentions

> It was a gift: it might be said to have been intended as a gift to the agent, and it might be said to have been intended as a gift to the principal.
>
> *Rashi*, bKetubot 98b

Rashi's statement requires some explanation. First, we assume that the third party in question, the vendor, intended to give a gift; no other possibility is countenanced. In the case of a transaction involving a fixed price, it cannot be argued that the additional amount is included in the price paid, or that the vendor erred. He undoubtedly knew that he gave the buyer an additional amount, intending it as a gift, but we are uncertain as to whether this gift was intended for the agent or his principal. In contemporary terms, the question is what a reasonable individual would have intended. Did the vendor intend to give a gift to the agent, with whom he had come into contact, and with whose pleasant manner he may well have been impressed; did he perhaps hope to induce the agent to become a regular customer, as suggested by the Ritba ad loc., or was it his intention to give a gift to the principal?

Rashi's approach invites the following question: on the assumption that we have doubts as to the vendor's intention, should these doubts not be resolved by applying the standard decision-making rules that are in place for cases where there is a doubt (*safek*) as to who something belongs to? The rule that applies in cases like the one before us is that the burden of proof falls on the plaintiff. That is, the individual in possession of the contested item has the advantage, and no monies can be taken from him without adequate proof that his adversary is entitled to it. Hence the agent, who is in possession of the additional amount, need only make a declaration to the principal along the following lines: 'It is in my possession, and because there is doubt as to who the vendor intended to bestow the gift on, you cannot take it away from me.'

However, since the two claims are equally strong, we have to assume that the vendor—our presumed 'reasonable individual' — was fully aware of both. Thus this is not really an instance of doubt, but rather, a case where we have to make an assumption as to the vendor's intent, namely, that he intended to give it to both the principal and the agent. Indeed, Rashi himself did not use the word 'doubt,' but rather, the more cautious locution "it might be said to have been intended as a gift to the agent, and it might be said to have been intended as a gift to the principal."

5.4 The principal's instrumental role in the gift

Alfasi is of the opinion that the third party either intends to give the gift to the agent, or is indifferent as to which of the two is the recipient, and hence the agent acquires it by default, since he is the one who physically receives it. But Alfasi goes on to explain:

> Why does the agent split it with the owner? Because the benefit accrued to the agent due to the owner, so he shares it with him.
>
> *Alfasi*, bKetubot 57b (Alfasi pagination)

Here, it would seem, we come back to the concept, discussed earlier in the chapter, of an obligation arising from a benefit conferred by someone else. Had the agent not been acting on behalf of the principal, he would not have received the extra benefit, and hence, must share it with him.

This, however, raises two problems. The first is that if this is indeed a case of obligation arising from benefit conferred by someone else, why does the principal, who confers the benefit, get only half rather than all of the added benefit? In no other example, of those discussed above, is it the case that one who confers a benefit receives only half the compensation rather than the entire amount. In cases of 'improving someone else's property without permission,' for instance, the improver—the one who bestows benefit—is entitled to compensation, and the problematic issue is whether his payment will be calculated according to the value of a field earmarked for planting, or of a field not earmarked for planting. The idea of estimating the compensation to be the value of half a field was never even considered. Or take the case of R. Jose's rule regarding the borrowed cow—"how can this person do business with someone else's cow?!"—we saw that in the case of death, due to natural causes, of a cow first leased by someone and then loaned by him to someone else, the Sages maintained that the borrower must compensate the lessee, whereas R. Jose maintains that the borrower has to compensate the cow's owner, and no payment is made to the person who leased the cow, to ensure that he does not benefit indirectly from the owner's property. But there was no suggestion that the owner and the lessee share the compensation paid by the borrower.

The second problem points in the opposite direction. Why should this case be thought of as one where compensation should be paid for a benefit incurred from someone else's property? After all, as we saw in section 4.3, the key principle governing these matters is that "one who benefited, but the other did not lose, is exempt." In the case at hand, the principal has not lost anything, since he received full value for the money he spent, and what has he to do with the unanticipated profit?

It would thus appear that Alfasi does not mean to classify the case before us as, strictly speaking, one of benefit conferred by someone else, but simply intends to point out that because the profit is generated by the agent and principal jointly, they should share it. And indeed, regarding a similar situation, the Jerusalem Talmud makes the following assertion: "Here, by this man's money and that man's legs—they both share [the benefit]."[50]

The same idea is found in a story in the Midrash:

> Someone from Athens came to Jerusalem, saw a lad, gave him a few coins, and said to him: Go and buy for me some figs and grapes. He said to him: Good idea—you [provide] your money, and I my legs. When he returned, he said: Let us divide it.
>
> Lamentations Rabbah, 1.1.6[51]

Using modern terminology, we would say that the profit was generated jointly by the contributions of capital and labor—specifically, by the principal's capital and the agent's labor. From this perspective, Alfasi's principle that they should share the benefit is eminently reasonable.

5.5 Comparison of the views of Rashi and Alfasi

Later commentators noted a number of differences between the views of Rashi and Alfasi.

i Where the giver intends the agent to keep the windfall

In the case where the giver explicitly states that he is bestowing a gift upon the agent, then, on Rashi's view, the agent keeps the windfall. But on Alfasi's view, what is the law?

Commenting on Alfasi's aforementioned remark, R. Nissim Gerondi states:

> Even if the vendor explicitly gave it to the agent, nevertheless, because the benefit accrued to the agent due to the owner, he shares it with him.
>
> *Ran, Alfasi* ad loc.

50 jDemai 6:13 (25d).

51 This story is mentioned in *Biur Hagra*—the Vilna Gaon's commentary on the *Shulhan Arukh*—*SA*, HM 183:25.

R. Moses Isserles, however, rules in accordance with Rashi's view:

> But if the vendor explicitly said he was giving it to the agent, the agent keeps it all.
>
> *Rema, SA*, HM 183:6

ii Where the giver intends the principal to keep the windfall

What is the law when the vendor explicitly states that the extra amount is being given to the principal? According to Rashi, it is clear that the principal keeps the windfall. But according to Alfasi, we must ask whether the agent deserves half, given that the windfall resulted from his contribution as well, since had he not carried out his agency, there would have been no windfall.

R. Arye Leib Heller, a late eighteenth-century commentator, argued that the agent does not get a share of the profit:

> Just because someone gives a gift to his fellow via an agent, does the agent deserve a share in the gift!?
>
> *Ketzot Hahoshen*, HM 183:7

According to Alfasi, in cases where the gift is explicitly given to the agent, the agent's labor is a relevant factor in generating the windfall. But *Ketzot Hahoshen* argues that where the windfall is explicitly stated to be intended for the principal, the agent's labor is of no particular relevance. He has, after all, done nothing out of the ordinary, and it can be assumed that it was not his action that impelled the giver to confer the gift.

It is probable that in some cases the agent will claim that it is only the excellence with which he carried out his responsibilities that impelled the giver to make the gift. Despite such claims, however well-founded, the law is determined by the typical case, and typically, the agent does not bring it about that a gift is given to the principal.

iii Profit due to a mistake

The Early Authorities give much thought to the question of profit accruing as a result of error rather than due to a gift bestowed intentionally. The Tosafists, for example, report:

> R. Jacob Israel asked Rabbenu Tam, who answered him thus: regarding your question about Reuben who sent Shimon to collect money owed him by a Gentile, and the Gentile made an error in calculation, and afterwards could not be located....
>
> *Tosafot*, bKetubot 98b s.v. *amar*

Three different solutions to this question are put forward.

a. Rabbenu Tam's first solution: sharing the excess

There is no difference between a windfall profit that comes as a gift and that which results from error. Rabbenu Tam applies Alfasi's view that the excess should be split to the error scenario. He argues that the principal received what was due him and the excess has, from the perspective of the giver, been written off; it thus should go to the agent, but in view of the fact that this benefit is conferred on him by the principal, they must share the profit that results from the error.

b. Rabbenu Tam's second solution: the entire sum is the principal's

From comments by Asheri ad loc., we learn that Rabbenu Tam retracted his first solution and ultimately decided to adopt Rashi's approach to the matter, namely, that the giver's intentions are to be taken into account. In the case at hand, the giver was unaware of the excess; the monies were given with the intention that they go to the owner.

c. R. Isaac the Elder's solution: the entire sum is the agent's

R. Isaac the Elder endorses Alfasi's approach, but distinguishes the case of an error from that of a gift. In the case of a gift, we can say that the excess is related to the rest of the transaction: the vendor intentionally added to the merchandise that changed hands. But in the case of an error, there is no real connection between the excess and the actual transaction; the excess is a windfall received by the agent by chance. What claim does the principal have to this windfall? It is analogous to the agent's finding money on the road to his destination. To explain his reasoning, the Ri suggests a thought experiment: Suppose, for argument's sake, that the agent stole from the Gentile a sum in excess of the amount owing. Would the idea ever be entertained that the owner deserves to receive this sum? It does not suffice to say that were it not for the owner's having sent the agent to execute this transaction, the agent would not have had the opportunity to steal, since only when the transaction itself directly brings about the additional payment is there a 'partnership of capital and labor' in the sense discussed above.

The *Shulhan Arukh* rules as follows:

> If someone sent his agent to collect money owed him by a Gentile, if the Gentile erred and paid him too much [but afterwards could not be located], the agent keeps all the excess.
>
> *Shulhan Arukh*, HM 183:7

Appendix 1 *Responsa Maharam* (Prague edition), #39

Whether one who ransomed a prisoner is entitled to reimbursement

Question: And you asked about Reuben and Shimon, who were captured. And Reuben was rich and Shimon poor. And Reuben spent large sums on messengers to his mother so that she might win their release from prison. And now Reuben is suing Shimon to pay his share of the expenses, saying that his actions were undertaken at Shimon's direction and behest. And Shimon denies this and says that he said nothing.

I also received a question about this from Maideburck [Magdeburg].

And I was also asked about a tutor who had a sum deposited with his employer, and was imprisoned on false charges. And he told his employer not to redeem him.

Answer: And I wrote that he was to be redeemed against his will. And the proof is in the talmudic dictum, "One who says: Do not bury me at the expense of my estate, is not heard."[1] Were it not so, everyone would enrich their sons and make themselves a burden on the public purse. Further proof can be adduced from the *sugya* in Kidushin: "[A father who sold his daughter as a slave-girl] is coerced to redeem her against his will."[2] And the Talmud explains "against his will" as follows: the father objects to redeeming her, and we force him to do so, since otherwise it defames the family. And since the father is compelled to redeem his daughter, a fortiori we compel one who was captured to ransom himself, even if he gets up and shouts 'do not redeem me,' and all the more so in the present case where he said nothing....

And this comparison cannot be rejected on the grounds that in that case, the father acted criminally in selling his daughter into slavery, and for this reason is compelled to redeem her, since according to the law, the family of one who sold himself into slavery would have been forced to redeem him, even though they did not act criminally, were it not for the apprehension that he might sell himself again. How much more so, if someone was captured by evil non-Jews and held in torment, do all agree that he is redeemed with his own funds, even against his will, since otherwise it defames the family.

Another proof can be furnished from the case of a man of means who will not support himself [and would starve unless he was supported by charity].[3] The ruling is that they give [support] to him as a 'gift,' and later they, they recoup it from his assets. The Talmud questions this ruling on

1 bKetubot 48a.
2 bKidushin 18a.
3 bKetubot 67b.

the grounds that such a 'gift' can only be given once; the second time the man would refuse it [knowing that it was no gift at all]. R. Papa explains that this is taken care of by deferring the recovery until the man's death. It is evident that were it not for the apprehension that he would refuse the 'gift' a second time, we would have recovered it from him while he was still alive.

In the case before us, this apprehension is irrelevant, because, unlike food and sustenance, capture is not a daily occurrence, therefore he could be compelled to repay the money raised for his ransom while still alive. Since [in the other case], we use compulsion to provide daily maintenance, even when there is no imminent threat to life, but rather, the person merely lives a life of abstinence and bodily discomfort, how much more so may compulsion be used to save the captive from the non-Jews to prevent him from losing himself among them, or to save him from being killed, or being tortured unendingly, which is worse than death, lest he, due to the torment, consent [to their demands].... And even one who sold his burial ground — the family comes and buries him even against the buyer's will, since otherwise it defames the family.[4]

[Our case] is not comparable to 'one who settled the debt of another,' which is considered like 'scaring away a lion,' because even if the creditor pressured him, the beneficiary was merely saved from annoyance,[5] not from loss.... And even according to R. Isaac's ... interpretation—which says that paying someone else's debt is like 'scaring away a lion,' because the debtor could argue that he had friends who would have taken pity on him and paid his debts to save him from annoyance—this applies only to a legally contracted debt, not to robbery. This can be supported by a ruling of Rabbenu Gershom [Light of the Exile] concerning a nobleman who stole a horse from the house of a Jew, and sold it to another Jew. Rabbenu Gershom ruled that the second Jew does not have to return the horse gratis [to its owner], and R. Isaac ruled similarly.

And [our case] is not comparable at all to settling a debt [that someone else] owes to a Jew, because even if he does not pay the debt there is no certainty of harm [being incurred by the defaulter]. But one who falls into the hands of non-Jewish bandits has no hope, and is like "an antelope in a net" (Isa. 51:20) and anyone who acts promptly to rescue him is praiseworthy, and is reimbursed for whatever benefit he provided the other [i.e., the captive].

There is an even stronger proof from the Talmud. It says that a partner who improved a common property is regarded as one who has received permission, and therefore he is awarded expenses, even if he improved a field "not earmarked for planting."[6] Similarly, in our case, since he is to be

4 bBaba Batra 100b.
5 jNedarim 4:2 (38c).
6 bBaba Metzia 42b.

ransomed even against his will, in spite of his protests to the contrary, all the more so if he does not protest: [it is assumed] the ransomer acts with his permission and is entitled to reimbursement, and [the released captive] has to give his share.

For the same reason, this case is not comparable to the case in which one was surrounded by his neighbor's [fence] on three sides, where he is exempt. He would also have been exempt even if the neighbor had surrounded him on four sides and had fenced him in completely—were it not for the fact that he [the surrounding property owner] could say, You caused me extra expense due to the longer length—since there, he could argue that the fence was superfluous, and he is not compelled to build a fence against his will. But in the case of the ransom, even if he said that he did not want to be redeemed, he has to be redeemed against his will at his own expense; and all the more so when he said nothing....

It is also stated by the Talmud that one who sees his fellow drowning in the river must save him, and spare no expense in hiring help.[7] It is obvious that even if the drowning man shouted 'don't save me,' he must be saved, and the rescuer can take from him what he spent on the rescue.

To conclude, it seems obvious to me[8] that the ransomed prisoner must give his share. The calculation is based on the amount paid for him, not on the number of captives, because they were captured only for the money. It should not be argued that the captors might set them free for nothing, for lives must not depend on such uncertainties, but they must be ransomed even against their will. Furthermore, it is well known and a simple matter for every honest person, that one who falls into the hands of robbers does not escape with his body unharmed and money untouched.

And peace be upon you ... Meir the son of R. Baruch.

7 bSanhedrin 73a.
8 Literally, "simple as an egg in a bread pudding," cf. bEruvin 62b.

Appendix 2 *Unjust Enrichment Law, 5739–1979*

UNJUST ENRICHMENT LAW 5739–1979*

Duty of restitution	1. (a) Where a person obtains any property, service or other benefit from another person without legal cause (the two persons hereinafter respectively referred to as "the beneficiary" and "the benefactor"), the beneficiary shall make restitution to the benefactor, and if restitution in kind is impossible or unreasonable, shall pay him the value of the benefit. (b) It shall be immaterial whether the benefit was obtained through an act of the beneficiary, an act of the benefactor or in any other way.
Exemption from restitution	2. The court may exempt the beneficiary from the whole or part of the duty of restitution under section 1 if it considers that the receipt of the benefit did not involve a loss to the benefactor or that other circumstances render restitution unjust.
Deduction of expenses	3. The beneficiary may, in making restitution, deduct what he has reasonably expended or undertaken to expend or invested in order to obtain the benefit.
Person who pays another person's debt	4. A person who pays another person's debt without being under duty towards him to do so is not entitled to restitution unless the other person had no reasonable cause to object to the payment of the whole or part of the debt and not beyond the amount paid.
Person who acts to protect another person's interest	5 (a) Where a person, in good faith and reasonably, does any act to protect the life, physical integrity, health, honour or property of another person without being under duty towards him to do so, and in that connection incurs or undertakes to incur any expenses, the beneficiary shall indemnify the benefactor for his reasonable expenses, including obligations incurred by him towards a third party, and if damage is caused to the property of the benefactor in consequence of the act, the Court may order the beneficiary to pay compensation to the benefactor if it considers it just to do so in the circumstances of the case.

	(b) For the purposes of the duty of compensation under subsection (a), a person whose property is used for the protection of any of the aforesaid values shall be treated as a person who does an act for the protection thereof. (c) The duty of indemnification or compensation under this section shall not fall on a beneficiary who has objected or has had reasonable cause to object to the act or the use of the property or the amount of the expenses, unless the act is done or the property used to protect his life, physical integrity or health.
Scope of application and saving remedies	6. (a) The provisions of this Law shall apply where no other Law contains special provisions on the matter in question and no agreement between the parties provides otherwise. (b) This Law shall apply also to the State. (c) This Law shall not derogate from any other remedies.
Repeal	7. Section 3 of the Law of Torts Amendment (Repair of Bodily Harm) Law, 5724–1964,[1] is hereby repealed.

YITZCHAK NAVON President of the State	MENAHEM BEGIN Prime Minister	SAMUEL TAMIR Minister of Justice

* Passed by the Knesset on the 23rd Tevet (22nd January, 1979) and published in *Sefer Ha-Chukkim* No. 924 of the 4th Shevat, 5739 (1st February, 1979) p. 42. The translation here and on p. 80 are [sic] *unofficial*, prepared by staff of the Ministry of Justice.

[1] *Sefer Ha-Chukkim* of 5724, p. 77; *L.S.I.* vol. xviii, p. 64.

14 Free market competition in Jewish law*

1 Introduction

1.1 The free competition principle

A free economy and open markets are often regarded as the best and most efficient means of facilitating economic growth and advancing the welfare of society. The open market is characterized by limited government intervention in the natural dynamic that emerges from the interactions of

* Some material in this chapter is based on Sinai Deutch, "Business competition and ethics: predatory pricing in Jewish law," 17 *Dine Israel* (1993/94), 7–33.

the various players.[1] Countries with a market economy tend to minimize government ownership of companies and corporations, desist from regulation of wages and compensation rates, and are not eager to channel individuals toward specific occupations or locales. The presumption is that the free market can do all this better and more efficiently. The opposing view advocates a planned economy, contending that it enables the state to achieve optimal efficiency, as well as a more just distribution of resources among its citizens.

Free competition is a central pillar of the market economy. Competition is created by the market players, who are rivals in seeking to achieve certain goals. Competition may arise between employers who seek to recruit excellent workers, workers who seek to find the best jobs, consumers who seek to acquire scarce products, and merchants who seek to win the allegiance of customers. The latter—competition between merchants—is the classic example of business competition, and will be the focal point of this chapter.

Free competition between merchants takes place at two levels: (a) between merchants already active in the market, who initiate various steps with a view to attracting new customers, such as introducing novel or improved products, advertising, offering discounts, holding sales, and so on; (b) between merchants already active in the market, and new traders not yet active in the market. Entry of new traders into the market increases the competition, and may even create competition where none previously existed. The assumption is that the market itself will regulate the number of active merchants, by natural elimination of those who cannot survive in the competitive arena. On the one hand, free competition encourages enterprise, improves products and services, and lowers prices, but on the other, it contributes to the elimination from the market of those too inefficient to be commercially viable, that is, to compete successfully. The natural workings of the market bring it about that these individuals then seek their livelihood elsewhere, in a locale or business sector that will be more conducive to their success.

This chapter will explore the institution of business competition in the sources of Jewish law. Does Jewish law encourage free competition, and if so, in what manner? Does it impose any limits on competition, or make it contingent on fulfillment of any preconditions? An additional question arises due to the fact that Jewish law has been, and remains, operative over two millennia in a wide range of geographic regions and under an equally wide range of political regimes and economic systems. Is it at all possible to identify within Jewish law a consistent attitude to free competition, or have different attitudes crystallized from time to time in response to changes in the prevailing political and socioeconomic circumstances?

1 Adam Smith, the eighteenth-century economist and author of *The Wealth of Nations*, is generally credited with formulation of the theoretical and philosophical foundations of free market theory.

1.2 Problematics of free competition

Arriving at a principled stance vis-à-vis free competition is not a simple matter, as it entails weighing conflicting values. On the one hand, the principle of liberty would seem to support free competition. When the legal system does not permit someone to engage in a certain type of marketing, or prevents him from opening a business at a new location, it encroaches on his personal autonomy and constrains his freedom. On the other hand, values associated with social responsibility, such as equality and solidarity, might seem to support limits on competition. The upshot of business competition is victory of the (economically) strong over weaker rivals, who will no longer be able to support themselves with dignity. Unbridled rivalry may create a situation where small players of limited means are unable to compete successfully against players with strong financial backing. For instance, it might enable chain stores to push small businesses out of the market. Proponents of equality and social solidarity might, it would seem, prefer to limit competition so as to enable the weaker players to participate in commerce and to enjoy its fruits. And another value that enters into the equation is economic efficiency. If we regard economic efficiency and social wellbeing as worthy values, we may find support for free competition from a different perspective. On the assumption that free competition indeed produces economic efficiency and maximizes the wellbeing of all members of society, it should, indeed, be sustained and encouraged.

But conflicting desiderata vis-à-vis free competition are not found only in the realm of **values**; they are also to be found in the realm of **interests**. Three distinct—and arguably, incompatible—interests come into play in the framework of free competition. The first is that of the market player who initiates competition with a view to increasing his profits. This initiative may come from an existing business, or a newcomer seeking to open a new business alongside those already in existence. The second interest is that of the existing businesses, which may be harmed by the introduction of competition into the market. A merchant may lose customers to the new competitor, or suffer reduced profitability due to the loss of his de facto monopoly. The third interest is that of the consumer. Assuming that competition increases efficiency and enhances communal wellbeing, it is in the public interest to allow competition. In formulating a policy on whether to allow free competition, and if so, under which conditions, we must balance these three interests, while determining whether, and when, a particular interest should take priority.

Ordinarily, competition is beneficial to consumers, but this is not always the case: it may have no impact at all, and in some cases may even be detrimental. An example of the latter situation is the case of a natural monopoly, where considerations of consumer benefit and economic efficiency mandate the **prevention** of competition and maintenance of an existing player's monopoly.

1.3 Jewish law's qualified endorsement of free competition

Overall, as we will see, the mainstream of theoretical and applied Jewish law manifests a positive attitude to free and competitive economic life, including price competition and almost completely open markets. Nevertheless, emphasis is also placed on two considerations that may militate against free competition: concern for the interests of consumers, and avoidance of unnecessary damage to merchants. When all these desiderata are equally balanced, there is no doubt that the open market principle is endorsed and given free rein. However, when the benefit to consumers is not clear-cut, whereas the likelihood of ruinous damage to existing sellers can be demonstrated, Jewish law tends to forestall such damage by limiting uncontrolled competition. Jewish law, though cognizant of the benefits of a free market, also takes into consideration the interests of less-viable sellers.[2] It thus must confront the problem of reconciling one merchant's desire to maximize profits with another merchant's desire for a fair trading regime, or even some degree of intervention. This tension between encouraging free competition and protecting those who will otherwise be driven out of the market generates a certain multidimensionality in Jewish law's treatment of commercial rivalry.

Indeed, it would be an oversimplification to imply that Jewish law arrived at a formula for balancing the interests of the established player, the newcomer to the market, and the consumer. There may well be no unequivocal way to take into account all the possible configurations of these three key factors, but by studying various cases that came up in different periods and locales, and how they were resolved, we may be able to extract the principles that guided the halakhic authorities in their attempts to balance the said interests.

Another caveat: in exploring Jewish law on commercial competition, it should be kept in mind that Jewish law is a legal system with a very long history. The issue was addressed in sources as early as the Mishnah, and is still being considered in rulings of rabbinical courts today. Hence we must consider whether the ever-changing economic systems and commercial practices impacted rabbinical legal thinking on competition, in theory and in practice.

In the next section, we will explore the halakhic sources' basically positive attitude to free commercial competition. In section 3, we will examine ethical constraints on competition imposed by Jewish law, and analyze their legal implications. Section 4 will discuss the laws governing newcomers to the market: enterprises that create competition where it did not previously exist, a classic issue raised by free competition. In section 5, we examine the laws of price competition. Section 6 explores other issues

2 See Aaron Levine, *Free Enterprise and Jewish Law* (New York: 1979); *Moral Issues of the Marketplace in Jewish Law* (New York: 2005); Meir Tamari, *With All Your Possessions* (New York: 1987).

related to commercial competition that have been addressed in responsa and in cases that have come before rabbinical courts in Israel.

2 Support for free competition in Jewish law

Although the talmudic sources express a range of views on free commercial competition, the majority view, which is accepted as the law, endorses it.

In the chapter of the Mishnah that addresses laws governing commercial transactions, including laws governing misrepresentation, unconscionable prices, and consumer protection, we find the following passage:

> MISHNAH R. Judah says: A shopkeeper may not distribute dried wheat or nuts to children, because he thereby accustoms them to come to him. And the Sages permit it. Nor may he lower the price. And the Sages say: he is to be remembered for good [i.e., he is blessed]. . . .
>
> GEMARA What is the Sages' rationale? It is because [this shopkeeper] can say to him [his competitor]: I distribute nuts, you distribute plums. "Nor may he lower the price. And the Sages say, he is to be remembered for good" and so on. What is the Sages' rationale? [60b] It is because he eases the market price.
>
> bBaba Metzia 60a–b

In this Mishnah, R. Judah calls for two restrictions on free competition: sales must not be promoted by giving children promotional gifts, or by cutting prices. The Sages oppose this stance, and permit both practices. The law was decided in accordance with the Sages' view, which encourages free competition and competitive price reduction. Before examining this stance in more detail, however, let us first consider the rejected opinion, that of R. Judah.

2.1 R. Judah's position: limitations on free competition

R. Judah forbids shopkeepers to give free gifts to children who come to his store. Who is R. Judah seeking to protect with this injunction? This element of R. Judah's position—which appears to be an extreme protectionist stance—can be construed as intended to protect consumers, specifically, to protect children (or their parents) from being induced by the free snacks to spend money at the shop. Marketing ploys such as distributing free gifts to children may constitute misrepresentation, as the children think they are getting free prizes, whereas in fact the items given away are part of a sales promotion campaign. Today, such potentially misleading gifts to children are regulated in various jurisdictions. However, this understanding of R. Judah's legislative intent is problematic, given that R. Judah proceeds to prohibit price reductions, which are beneficial to consumers. This second rule is clearly intended to protect the shopkeeper's competitors from losing customers, who would flock to the store that had lowered its prices. It thus stands to reason that the rule prohibiting giveaways is also intended to protect the other shopkeepers by limiting competition. The giveaways would entice customers to change their shopping habits and patronize the store giving out the snacks. The Sages do not agree. They maintain that although influence is indeed being exerted on the young customers, the other shopkeepers can institute similar sales campaigns, and since they have this recourse, the marketing ploy of free giveaways should not be forbidden.

The leading decisors upheld the view of the Sages, but their respective presentations of this view indicate disparate understandings of the mishnaic dispute.

Maimonides rules in accordance with the Sages' view, as follows:

> A storekeeper is permitted to distribute dried wheat or nuts to children or maidservants, so as to accustom them to come to him; and to [sell for] less than the market price, so as to increase the number of those buying from him on credit. And the people of the market cannot prevent him from doing so, for this does not involve deception.
>
> *Code*, Laws concerning Sales 18:4

The ruling in the *Shulhan Arukh* appears similar, but is actually quite different:

> The shopkeeper is permitted to hand out dried wheat and nuts to the children, so as to accustom them to buy from him. And so too he may sell more cheaply than the market price, so that they will buy from him. And the people of the market cannot prevent him from doing so.
>
> HM 228:18

The ruling in the *Shulhan Arukh* reiterates that of Maimonides, but omits the words "for this does not involve deception." This omission is significant, and points to different understandings of R. Judah's intention, and the legal problem he sought to address.

Maimonides takes the shopkeeper's motive for lowering prices to be the desire to attract customers who lack the wherewithal to pay for the goods they have been enticed, by the giveaways, into buying, and need to have credit extended to them by the shopkeeper. Maimonides thus understands R. Judah's stance as intended to preempt deception on the part of the shopkeeper. The *Shulhan Arukh* apparently disagrees with this interpretation, and takes the issue at hand to be simply that of the competition between the merchants, and thus omits the final clause ("for this does not involve deception").

Although Maimonides entertains the possibility that deceit is involved, he nonetheless rules in accordance with the Sages' view, and permits the marketing ploys. The assertion "the people of the market cannot prevent him," is used by Maimonides to refer to the consumers, whereas the *Shulhan Arukh* uses it to refer to the other merchants competing in the market.

The *Shulhan Arukh*, apparently, sees the gist of this law as the dispensation to engage in free competition. Most of the decisors understand it similarly. Maimonides, however, regards it as pertaining to consumer protection. In his opinion, the gist of the law is that giveaways and reduced prices are not, in fact, misleading practices. Maimonides' concerns about consumer protection reflect the concerns of R. Judah in the Mishnah. The Sages, whose opinion was accepted as law, had no such apprehensions.

Maimonides' apparent deviation from the plain meaning of the Mishnah and the Gemara was noted by eighteenth-century Turkish authority R. Masoud Hai Rokeiah:

> I do not know why the Master [Maimonides] mentioned "deception" as a reason in this context, and did not invoke 'deprivation of one's fellow's livelihood,' for [as to the latter], wholesalers would lower their prices.
>
> *Maase Rokeiah*, Laws concerning Sales 18:4

What is the explanation for Maimonides' unique take on the law? Why did he see the intent of the law as the protection of consumers from being enticed into buying on credit rather than protecting merchants from unfair competition, as is implied by the Talmud? R. Judah's statement in the Mishnah, which expressly mentions children, may have evoked in Maimonides a sense that the thrust of the law was protection of the weak and naive. R. Judah forbids handing out snacks to children. Had his concern been unfair competition, Maimonides may have reasoned, then presumably he would have forbidden giveaways to adults as well. It seems that this impelled him to explain the Mishnah as addressing the issue of deception, even though this interpretation deviates markedly from that offered by the Talmud.

2.2 The Sages' position: free competition with limitations

Having examined the minority view, that of R. Judah, let us now turn to the majority view, that upheld by the Sages. As we will see, later generations gave this stance a range of interpretations, some broadening the scope of permissible competition, others limiting it.

The Talmud states that the Sages permitted shopkeepers to hand out giveaways to children because competing shops could do likewise. It also asserts that the merchant who lowers prices is 'to be remembered for good' because his action will lead to a general reduction of prices, thereby benefitting all consumers.

> What is the Sages' rationale? It is because [this shopkeeper] can say to him [his competitor]: 'I distribute nuts, you distribute plums.' "Nor may he lower the price. And the Sages say, he is to be remembered for good" and so on. What is the Sages' rationale? [60b] It is because he eases the market price.
>
> bBaba Metzia 60a–b

> *Rashi* ad loc.: "It is because he eases the market price"—those who have stocks of produce [lit. fruit], seeing that prices are being cut, will sell it more cheaply.

2.3 The decisors on free competition

The law was decided, as we noted, in accordance with the Sages' view, which became the primary textual anchor for the principle of free competition in Jewish law.

Though the legitimacy of free competition and related marketing practices was accepted in principle, the Sages' view, and even more so, Rashi's explanation of it, elicited extensive discussion as to the desirable limits of this policy. This discussion took place many centuries later, and came to be a classic controversy among the decisors. It generally involved analysis of a concrete case along the following lines. A merchant wants to lower his prices so as to attract more customers to his shop, but for various reasons, his competitors are unable to act similarly. The impediment to their so acting is either legal (e.g., if the temporal authorities forbid these competitors to lower their prices), or commercial, namely, the shopkeepers' inability to make a profit at the lower prices. We will explore three of these cases in detail. Clearly, however, a price-cut of the sort discussed in these cases could not in itself bring about a widespread reduction in the prevailing market price of the product in question. This being so, the halakhic authorities found it difficult to decide whether they could permit a price-cut intended to stimulate a merchant's business.

The answer to this question hinges on how we interpret the Sages' view, which can be understood in two different ways. It can be taken as **stating a necessary condition** that must be fulfilled if permission to engage in marketing ploys is to be granted: the condition that the said ploys be acts that can be performed by both the initiator of the marketing campaign, and his competitor. Actions that can only be taken by one side are impermissible. But it can also be interpreted as simply **illustrating** the general notion of business competition: in general, competition is such that if one side takes one tack, the other side takes another tack. Business competition in general routinely involves various marketing strategies, and giving away free samples falls squarely within the parameters of ongoing engagement in business. On this interpretation, the Sages permitted the distribution of the snacks because in principle, all the competitors could take similar steps, even if, for some reason, in practice one side was unable to employ the said tactic.

We must keep this interpretive question in mind as we examine three rulings about competition involving price reductions in the liquor trade, handed down by eighteenth and nineteenth century decisors. The merchants in question had businesses in neighboring locales. For reasons to be explained, in each case one of the merchants was able to lower the price of beer, while the others could not. The competitors argued that the cheaper price would lure away their customers, and they would have no recourse, since they were unable to lower the price they charged for beer. The question to be answered was, therefore, whether lowering the price of beer was a legitimate business practice under those circumstances.[3]

i *Responsa Panim Meirot*, 1, #78

The first ruling appears in a responsum written by R. Meir Eisenstadt, an early eighteenth-century authority. His main argument is that, as an mechanism for business competition, lowering prices—which can be injurious to the interests of competitors—is permissible only due to the benefit that will accrue to consumers from the price-cut's contribution to lowering the market price of the product in question. But if there is no expectation that it will bring about a general drop in the market price, he argues, there is no dispensation to employ this tactic.

> I was asked about licensees who held two village liquor franchises in the same district, each belonging to a different nobleman. One of [the licensees] wanted to sell liquor and beer more cheaply than the established market price in that province, and the other protested, saying that it would cause him damage, since by doing so, [his competitor] would get the residents of his village accustomed to going to his place to drink, and in this way, [the complainant] would incur a loss.
>
> Answer: ... Even in a town or in a Jewish neighborhood where the customers benefit [in principle, when prices are cut], nevertheless, even so, the other vendors of beer and liquor may restrain him. And this can be proven from the Talmud, where it says "Nor may he lower the price. And the Sages say, he is to be remembered for good." And it says "What is the Sages' rationale? It is because he eases the market price." Rashi comments: "those who have stocks of produce [lit. fruit],

3 An additional issue addressed in the rulings involved entry of a new trader into the territory of an established merchant. This aspect will be discussed below; here we focus on the tactic of lowering prices to increase sales.

seeing that prices are being cut, will sell it more cheaply." The talmudic query, "What is the Sages' rationale?" is not clear. Is it not obvious that he [is remembered for good because he] benefited his fellow Jews, his customers, and for that reason they put it in terms of 'he is to be blessed' and 'he is remembered for good'? So we have no choice but to conclude that where the vendors sustain a loss, we do not take customer benefit into consideration. And the prices have already been set, and stipulating prices is the law of the land, and falls under the rubric of 'the law of the kingdom is law.'

So the Talmud had to give the reason why [the merchant's price-cut] would bring about a change in the market price. And this is only germane to the sale of produce and grains, because those with stocks of produce, seeing that prices were being cut, would put all their stocks of produce on the market, and hence the market price would change. But with regard to the sale of beer, this in any event would not cause them to sell produce more cheaply, since everyone knows that the law of the land is that beer is expensive. And we can also argue that only in the specific case of produce is it true to say that the market price fluctuates in accordance with the quantities available, and when those with stocks of fruit see that the price is being cut, they take out all their stocks [and put them on the market], and it goes without saying that the market price changes. But with regard to beer and liquor, it is the law of the land, and their practice is to announce the going rate, and if they observe that it is appropriate to sell it more cheaply, they announce that it should be sold more cheaply. So it falls under the rubric of 'the law of the kingdom is law.' And we do not take customer benefit into consideration at all.... And to sell merchandise at less than the official market price if Jews do not benefit from it is forbidden ... particularly with regard to beer and liquor, [the prices of which] are subject to the law of the kingdom. And produce would not become cheaper as a result of selling beer more cheaply. It thus seems clear to me that the other vendors can protest. This is quite clear to me.... However, if he makes better beer than his colleagues—for usually one part grain is used to brew three parts beer, and he makes only two and a half [thereby brewing stronger beer]—and thereby gets customers used to [buying from] him, this is fine, as it is analogous to the case discussed in the Mishnah, where one party says 'I distribute nuts, you distribute plums.'

Responsa Panim Meirot, 1, #78

Careful examination of this responsum reveals two different arguments against permitting the price of beer to be reduced in the case in question. The first is that the government sets the prices of commodities, and in doing so takes consumer interests into account. On this argument, competition is needed as a means of lowering prices where there is no other mechanism for monitoring prices, but is redundant where there are authoritative bodies that fulfill this function.[4]

The second argument is that even if the good of the consumer does call for a lowering of the market price, individual merchants should not be permitted to sell at less than the market price when it is clear that such price-cuts cannot result in the desired **general** lowering of the market price. This was the situation in the case discussed in the responsum, since prices were under government control. The price-cut that the vendor sought to introduce was not expected to have any impact on the broader market price. Let us focus on this argument.

Note that R. Eisenstadt does **not** base his decision on the principle of fairness—he does not argue that one merchant may not reduce prices if others, being bound by the market price set by the governmental authorities, cannot do the same. Rather, he bases his decision on the principle of utility: the price-cut is not expected to have any real impact on the market price.

But if utility is his focus, his stance might seem to be inconsistent. While the price-cut in question is not expected to influence the market, that is, to improve the lot of **all** consumers, it can certainly be expected to benefit those customers who decide to switch their beverage-buying allegiance from a vendor who sells at the market price to the vendor in question. Why don't the interests of these consumers take precedence over the interests of the merchants who oppose the price-cut? Apparently, R. Eisenstadt is of the opinion that harming the interests of a merchant by way of unfair competition is so serious a matter that it can be justified only when it benefits all consumers. Competition that benefits only a smaller group would not justify the loss sustained by the merchants who, being bound by the market price set by the authorities, cannot compete, and lose business. The interest of a limited group of consumers, R. Eisenstadt is in essence arguing, does not take precedence over that of the undercut merchants. Only price-cuts that advance the interests of the whole body of consumers can justify one merchant's harming his fellow merchants.

ii *Hokhmat Shlomo, SA*, HM 228:18

Many decades later, R. Eisenstadt's responsum was criticized by R. Solomon Kluger of Brody.

R. Kluger was asked about a situation similar to that which had been addressed by R. Eisenstadt. R. Kluger rejected R. Eisenstadt's analysis of the matter, arguing that the fact that a price-cut brought about a general reduction of the market price for an item was not the

4 See J. Lieberman, *Business Competition in Jewish Law* (Hebrew), (Ramat-Gan, Israel: 1989), 41.

reason it was **permissible** for a merchant to cut his prices, but only the reason such a merchant was "remembered for good." The permissibility of a price-cut, he argued, is not dependent on its direct impact on the market price.

> I was asked by someone who lives in a village whether it is permitted to sell liquor more cheaply to people from another town or not. I answered him simply that there is, in Jewish law, no prohibition against reducing prices, for one is allowed to do as he wishes with regard to his own affairs. And it stands to reason that since dealers are allowed to sell for a lower price than other merchants in their own town, how much more so is it the case that a vendor can sell more cheaply than vendors in a different town. I was told that in a similar case, the author of *Panim Meirot* [R. Eisenstadt] prohibited selling at a lower price.... That view is questionable and unjustified, since the *Shulhan Arukh* and the *Tur* decided that a vendor is permitted to sell [his wares] more cheaply, and they did not distinguish between selling wheat and selling other products.... in any event, cutting prices is permissible whether it impacts the entire market or not.

R. Kluger's decision can be explained in terms of economics. A seller who lives in a village most likely has lower costs than one who lives in a town. The lower price he charges reflects the lower cost of operating his business, and is not an instance of selling below cost for the purpose of undercutting the competition to gain new customers. The decision clearly takes the principle of open business competition to be more important than the principle that existing businesses are to be protected.

iii *Responsa Shoel Umeshiv*, 1st edition, #20

The third ruling, by nineteenth-century Polish decisor R. Joseph Saul Nathanson, deals with a case where only one merchant could lower his prices.

A shopkeeper was delinquent in paying his local taxes, and therefore able to sell at lower prices than his competitors. In this case, the competitors were not prevented from cutting their prices by government price regulations, but could not cut their prices without selling at a loss, since they had to figure the local taxes into their costs, and price their wares accordingly. R. Nathanson concluded that under the circumstances, the conduct of the tax delinquent constituted unfair competition:

> And as to what we wrote above, namely, that the item may not be sold more cheaply, even though the *Shulhan Arukh* explains that if the item is sold more cheaply, [competing merchants] cannot impede this

> price-cut, because it is to the customers' benefit. But this only applies when a merchant reduces his prices because the others could sell more cheaply, but choose to sell at a high price. But in the case at hand, he is selling more cheaply because he does not pay his taxes. This being so, the others are charging [a price reflecting] the item's real value, and there is no merit in selling more cheaply. So it seems, in my humble opinion.

R. Nathanson permits a merchant to lower prices only where his competitors' price is exorbitant. Where the competitors are selling at a reasonable price—a price that cannot be reduced without rendering the said competitors unable to cover their expenses—undercutting them is not permitted. R. Nathanson's argument is based on the value of fair play, not that of benefit to the consumer. He contends that competing by lowering prices is permissible only where there is a level playing field; where one of the competitors has an inherent advantage, it is forbidden

Let us recapitulate our discussion thus far. We have seen that, basing itself on the mishnaic prooftext, the halakha generally recognized free competition as legitimate and even desirable. Nevertheless, with respect to the law intended for implementation, the decisors wrestled with the scope and limits of free competition. They sought to identify and exclude unfair competition, which they forbade. On R. Meir Eisenstadt's view, the primary consideration was the good of the consumer, and competitive actions that would impinge on the interests of other merchants were only permitted if expected to generate a market-wide reduction in the price to the consumer. This was disputed by R. Solomon Kluger, who endorsed merchants' taking the initiative vis-à-vis increasing their turnover. Citing the major decisors, he decried what he saw as uncalled-for attempts to prohibit that which was permitted. R. Saul Nathanson ruled that only fair competition was permissible, namely, when all competitors were able to take similar actions vis-à-vis marketing their wares. Competition was not permitted if only one party could lower prices, but his competitors, even for reasons having to do with their profitability, could not. These rulings demonstrate the importance of attending to the translation of theoretical law into practice, and drive home the dynamic character of the halakhic literature. The law codes set down the law in abstract terms, and responsists translate these abstract terms into concrete instructions.

3 Moral reservations about competing with an existing business

Let us now turn to another manifestation of business competition, namely, that which occurs when a new market player seeks to enter into competition with an existing enterprise. Notwithstanding the Talmud's support for the principle of free competition, its view on the specific question of new competition with an existing business is somewhat obscure. The Talmud censures one who enters into such competition, but it remains to be seen whether there is a legal norm prohibiting competition with an existing enterprise, or merely an ethical appeal to the competitor's conscience.

A talmudic *sugya*, bMakot 24a, discusses the feasibility of reducing the Torah's 613 precepts to a smaller number of more comprehensive precepts. In contemplating ways to carry out this reduction, the Talmud is, in essence, seeking to extract the fundamental values of Jewish law by defining the characteristic attributes of one who lives fully in accordance with the law. The *sugya* suggests that King David reduced the number of the precepts to eleven, invoking Psalm 15 as the basis for this idea:

> A Psalm of David: Lord, who shall sojourn in Thy Tabernacle? Who shall dwell in Thy holy mountain? [i] He that walketh uprightly, and [ii] worketh righteousness, and [iii] speaketh truth in his heart; that [iv] hath no slander upon his tongue, [v] nor doeth evil to his fellow … [vii] in whose eyes a vile person is despised, but [viii] he honoureth them that fear the Lord.… [xi] nor taketh a bribe against the innocent. He that doeth these things shall never be toppled.
>
> Psalm 15

After enumerating the eleven comprehensive precepts, the *suyga* proceeds to articulate the fundamental values embodied therein:

> "He that walketh uprightly"—that was Abraham, as it is written, "Walk before Me and be thou whole-hearted" (Gen. 17:1)…."Hath no slander upon his tongue"—that was our Father Jacob, as it is written, "My father peradventure will feel me and I shall seem to him as a deceiver" (Gen. 27:12). **"Nor doeth evil to his fellow"—that is he who does not encroach on his fellow's craft** (*yored leomanut haveiro*).[5]
>
> bMakot 24a

Evidently, the Talmud considers it wrong to deliberately enter into competition with a craftsman by setting up the same kind of business alongside him, though such conduct is not expressly prohibited. It is clear that 'speaking truth in one's heart' is a lofty moral norm to aspire to, but can hardly be regarded as a legal obligation enforceable in court.[6] The same applies to walking uprightly and honoring the God-fearing. It seems, therefore, that the Talmud regarded the admonition against entering into competition with an existing enterprise as a moral rather than a legal prohibition.

5 A slightly different version is found in bSanhedrin 81a.

6 On the distinction between lofty moral aspirations and legal obligations, see Chapter Eight, "Equity."

Furthermore, it is not clear whether this is the conduct expected of the average person, or that expected of the very righteous. Given that Psalm 15 speaks of the pious who sojourn in God's Tabernacle, and dwell on His holy mountain, it stands to reason that the Talmud is not setting down legal obligations binding on all, but rather sketching the moral high ground for those who aspire to particular righteousness and piety.

Elsewhere, the Talmud states that if someone hurled a terrible insult at his fellow, calling him a wicked man (*'rasha'*), the affronted individual may "encroach on his livelihood [lit., his life]."[7] There is some disagreement as to the interpretation of this dictum, and not all the commentators take it to deal with business competition.[8] But some do, such as R. Nathan b. Yehiel of Rome, who explains the dictum as meaning that when someone has insulted his fellow, the latter may open the same type of business as his affronter, right alongside, so as to reduce the affronter's livelihood. This implies, of course, that such competition is otherwise forbidden.

But how is this to be squared with the Talmud's overall positive attitude to business competition? To be sure, the preeminent decisors do not mention a formal prohibition against 'encroaching on his fellow's craft,' but this is merely an *argumentum ex silentio*, and suggests a need to clarify the matter further.

It seems that in speaking of one who "encroaches on his fellow's craft," the Talmud is not referring to the type of competition discussed above, but a different kind of competition. One who "encroaches on his fellow's craft" sets out to compete with his fellow's craft, that is, intentionally sets out to **start** a competing enterprise, as opposed to promoting competition with an existing business. This understanding is inferred from the literal meaning of the Hebrew verb, namely, 'to **descend** into one's fellow's craft.' R. Solomon Luria, the Maharshal, explains this as follows: "One has a certain craft, and his fellow plunges into it."[9]

There is, then, a fundamental difference between the two types of competition. Jewish law permits and even encourages competition between existing businesses, which advances the interests of the overall community. Some merchants may be adversely impacted by such competition, but such impacts are part of the ongoing workings of the market. Entering the market with the intention of ruining another trader, however, is something else entirely. Such conduct is reprehensible, or as the biblical verse puts it, "evil." The Talmud countenances recourse to such an act only in a hostile environment, that is, in response to a serious affront.

Let us analyze the distinction between the two types of competition. From the perspective of expected impact on market efficiency and

7 bKidushin 28a; see also *Rashi* ad loc.

8 See *Rashi*, bBaba Metzia 71a and *Tosafot* ad loc.

9 *Responsa Maharshal*, #36.

consumer benefit, it is doubtful whether a distinction need be made between increased competition with an existing business, and starting a new business, thereby creating competition. Both generate a net increase in competition and an increased supply of available goods, and thus improve the efficiency of the market and benefit consumers. It may well be that from the perspective of market efficiency, opening a new business in a location where no competition existed before is more important than merely adding to the competition between existing businesses by, say, introducing new sales ploys such as price-cuts and giveaways.

The difference clearly emerges, however, when we consider the situation from the perspective of the merchant seeking to increase competition. In the case of two already-existing businesses, there is benefit both to the consumers, who will enjoy lower prices, and the merchant, whose turnover will be increased. This dynamic supports the granting a dispensation to increase competition by lowering prices. Moreover, this is virtually the only way the merchant can increase his turnover.

But the situation is different with regard to a merchant who seeks to start a new business that will compete with an existing business. For such an individual had other options that would have caused no injury to the existing business. He could have started his new business in a different locale, where he would not be competing with an existing business, or started a different kind of enterprise, selling a different product or service. But because he did not exercise these options, but chose to compete with an existing business, the balance of interests between the previous players (the existing business and consumers) is upset by their having to accommodate a new player. The trade share of the existing merchant declines as business shifts to the new player. This negative dynamic explains why the new player is characterized as 'one who encroaches on his fellow's craft.'

Does 'encroaching on one's fellow's craft' generate any concrete legal consequences? Is there an actual legal norm enjoining us from starting a competing business, or is one who does so only subjected to moral disapprobation? Now whereas a legal norm is enforceable, the discharge of a moral obligation is voluntary. Generally, legal norms are addressed to all members of a community, whereas supererogatory ethical injunctions are addressed to the virtuous. And whereas legal norms are (ideally) clear-cut, moral obligations are often open-ended.

From the context, it would appear that the directive in question has the status of a moral norm, not a binding legal prohibition. One who refrains from 'encroaching on his fellow's craft' is conducting himself in an exemplary and meritorious manner. A person of exceptional moral scrupulousness, he likely also conducts himself in accordance with the other non-binding norms mentioned, such as keeping unspoken promises ("speaketh truth in his heart"). Also supporting this conclusion is the fact that the talmudic passages on not entering into competition—bMakot 24a and bKidushin 28a—are not cited by the leading codifiers.[10]

That the nature of the teaching that encroaching upon someone else's business turf is to be eschewed is that of an ethical admonition rather a binding legal prohibition comes to the fore in a responsum by the Rashba, R. Solomon b. Adret. R. Adret was asked to rule on a case involving a tailor who sought to set up shop within the business turf of a fellow tailor.

> Question: Reuben, a tailor, has worked for a burgher for a number of years. The burgher likes him, Reuben does all his work for him, and there is no other craftsman who does any work for him. The burgher used to give Reuben two dinars for every garment Reuben made for him. Then another tailor, Shimon, appeared on the scene, and sought to endear himself to the burgher. And he said he would do the work for less, one dinar for each garment. Reuben came and lodged a complaint against Shimon, who is causing him a loss, and robbing him in a number of ways: by undercutting his wages, and by entering his territory, since for the said [lower] price he could work in a number of other places in the town.
>
> *Responsa Rashba*, 3, #83

The Rashba is of the opinion that the new tailor cannot be prevented from tendering his offer, because "the Gentile [the burgher] gave him the work of his own free will." But he maintains that the matter cannot be ignored, and says that "it stands to reason" that Shimon should be reprimanded.[11] Now a reprimand is not a legal sanction, because in the end it is up to Shimon to decide whether to move his trade elsewhere, or not.

Nevertheless, a reprimand is a significant social sanction. In a society whose members hold the judicial system and its representatives—that is, the rabbinical court and the community rabbis—in high esteem, being chastised by the court exerts pressure that can be very powerful. Indeed, a social sanction imposed by the communal leadership may be more painful than a legal sanction—and a more powerful deterrent. As we said, a reprimand calls upon the offender to arrive at a decision (in our case, a decision not to proceed with the business enterprise in question) on his own, and not due to any coercion by the court. The function of the reprimand is to ensure that the offender is aware of the proper path, and encourage him to take it. Jewish law blurs, to a certain degree (perhaps intentionally), the boundary between law and morality, between voluntary actions and those subject to legal sanctions.

10 See Lieberman, n. 4 above, 55 n. 155.

11 R. Menahem Hameiri apparently concurs: "One who encroaches on his fellow's craft is called wicked" (*Beit Habehira*, bMakot 24a).

As we said, the silence of the main law codes (Maimonides' *Mishne Torah*, the *Tur*, and the *Shulhan Arukh*[12]) suggests that they did not regard 'encroaching' as prohibited in the legal sense, but later decisors were not in agreement on the matter. Some did uphold the view that the injunction was only a recommendation as to pious conduct, a position that appears to be in line with the spirit of the relevant talmudic sources. R. Yair Bachrach, a seventeenth-century decisor, for instance, asserts:

> Encroaching on the craft of one's fellow is clearly permitted even *ab initio*, except in the case of a resident of a different town.[13] And although this issue has been the subject of considerable discussion, it is certainly as I have stated it, and this is the custom in every Jewish community. In addition, we have forceful proof of this from the talmudic passage, "David came and subsumed them under eleven [principles], as it is written, 'Lord, who shall sojourn in Thy Tabernacle? … He that walketh uprightly, and worketh righteousness,'" and so on. And it is all explained there in the sense of pious conduct that is free of even the slightest taint of sin, and consult the text. And among these is the dictum: "Nor doeth evil to his fellow"—that is he who does not encroach on his fellow's craft." It follows that it is permitted, and it is only the humble and the devout who refrain from it.
>
> *Responsa Havat Yair*, #42

R. Moses Sofer upheld a diametrically opposed view:

> "Encroach on [one's fellow's] craft"–It would seem that this entire matter is scripturally prohibited, and [encroaching] is outright robbery according to the Torah …. And even though R. Joseph Caro explained that it is simply a Rabbinic rule … in my humble opinion, it is covered by the biblical verse "[and judge righteously between every man] and his brother, and the stranger who is with him" (Deut. 1:16). The Sifre interprets the expression "stranger who is with him" as including all who reside within his locale.… The Sages of the Talmud were thus authorized to adjudicate between every man and those residing near him, and accordingly, declared and enacted the prohibition [against encroaching]. And it was deemed scriptural law, and prohibited on the strength of the laws against robbery.
>
> *Responsa Hatam Sofer*, HM #79

R. Haim Hezekiah Medini, a nineteenth-century halakhic authority in the land of Israel, presents an analysis according to which the opposed positions can be reconciled:

12 Alfasi (bSanhedrin 18b) and Asheri (*Piskei Harosh*, Sanhedrin, ch. 9, sec. 3) do mention this prohibition, but expressly state that it is a moral and not a legal norm.

13 The term 'resident of a different town' is explained below.

"Encroaching on one's fellow's craft"... I saw a responsum by the learned author of *Responsa Havat Yair*, #42, quoted by the author of *Mayim Rabim, SA*, HM 16, in which the former asserts that 'encroaching on one's fellow's craft' is not prohibited at all, and it says that even a resident of an alleyway cannot prevent another resident of the same alleyway [from competing]. And it is permissible *ab initio* except in the case of a resident of a different town, as is explained in *SA*, HM 156.... It follows that it is permitted, and it is only the very scrupulous and the humble who refrain from it. And on the basis of this argument, he refuted what R. Solomon Luria wrote in a responsum, namely, that 'encroaching on one's fellow's craft' was the gravest transgression; and he suggested that what R. Solomon Luria had written was probably a scribal error. This is the essence of his holy words.

And the author of *Mayim Rabim* wondered how it could be considered permissible *ab initio*, for at the end of bSanhedrin 81a, the Talmud says "'nor did he defile his neighbor's wife' (Ezek. 18:6), for he did not encroach on his fellow's craft"—so we see that the Sages compared [one who encroaches] to one who defiles his friend's wife. And it states in bKidushin 28a that if someone calls his fellow 'wicked'—the latter may encroach on his livelihood [lit., his life], and Rashi interpreted this as meaning that he is allowed to reduce his livelihood by encroaching on his craft. It follows that otherwise [i.e., if not in response to a serious affront], it is forbidden....

And to resolve the apparent disagreement, he [the author of *Mayim Rabim*] wrote ... that encroaching on one's fellow's craft in the case where the encroacher says to him, 'You do [what you wish] on your property, and I will do [what I wish] on mine'—regarding such cases, the author of *Responsa Havat Yair* said that the law permits it, but the humble refrain from conducting themselves in that fashion. But as to the case of one who encroaches on his fellow's craft by driving out the existing business, that is, by doing the same work that his fellow is already doing—that is forbidden by law, and it was with regard to such conduct that they said [an encroacher] is like one who defiles his friend's wife. And this applies not only to an encroacher who completely drives out the existing business, but even to a case where the existing business is not driven out completely, but the [new craftsmen] work alongside him—it is still forbidden, for it reduces the existing business's share [of the market], which he has already earned.... With regard to that share, the encroacher has completely deprived him of the benefit [due him]. This is the thrust of his holy words.

Sdei Hemed, vol. 3, rule 45, letter 'yud'

Although R. Medini purports to set out a middle ground between the opposed views, it appears that he is inclined to forbid encroaching on one's fellow's craft. He seeks to distinguish between cases where the new business will not cause any loss to the exiting one, where the new business is permitted, though the scrupulous avoid such situations, and cases where the new business will cause the existing one to incur a loss, where starting the new enterprise is prohibited. But the former scenario is surely atypical, as the entry into the market of a new business does ordinarily impact existing businesses. If R. Medini accepts that encroaching is prohibited in the second kind of case, this is tantamount to regarding it as prohibited by law and not merely morally reprehensible. In effect, then, he concurs with the view of R. Moses Sofer.

A different interpretation of R. Medini's stance, however, is also plausible. In cases where each of the competitors pursues new contracts, or additional work, but the new competitor does not interfere with the existing enterprise's current contracts, the competition is, in principle, permitted, even though it may ultimately cause a loss to the existing enterprise. But should the new competitor interfere with jobs already contracted by his colleague, or contracts already entered into, with a view to terminating these contracts, the competition is not permitted. On this interpretation, R. Medini in principle supports competition, even if it will lead to losses for the existing business, and only prohibits competition involving the breach of existing contracts.

Both positions continue to find advocates and detractors. To illustrate the contemporary debate, let us consider the position of R. Yigal Ariel, a contemporary halakhic authority, who supports the dispensation to open a new business alongside an existing one.[14] R. Yigal Ariel distinguishes competition in urban centers from competition in small rural communities, and distinguishes between different types of business, such as shops, hotels, educational institutions, and so on. He argues that in large urban communities, there is no prohibition against opening a new shop next to an existing one, as long as the businesses in question are both open to the general public, and do not serve only members of a specific limited community. However, in cases where the opening of a competing business threatens to generate fierce competition, it is unethical, and the community can enact regulations to forestall such an outcome. In small rural communities, on the other hand, there is reason—in the case of businesses serving a limited clientele of local residents—to forbid certain modes of competition. Such a prohibition will be irrelevant vis-à-vis businesses serving a clientele of non-residents and tourists.

In conclusion, it seems that most of the controversies and debates over the nature of the injunction against 'encroaching on one's fellow's craft' can be attributed to a tension within the halakhic literature. This tension is rooted in competing desiderata: the encouragement of business competition, on the one hand, and on the other, the protection of vulnerable

14 R. Yigal Ariel. "Business competition in rural and urban environments" (Hebrew), *Tehumin* 10 (1989), 194–203.

market players—generally, small merchants—from potential injury from such competition.

4 Restrictions on freedom of entry

We have seen that the sources of Jewish law evince an essentially positive attitude to business competition, at least in theory. But thus far we have discussed only **local** competition, that is, competition between merchants conducting their business affairs in a single area. With respect to outside competition, however, there is less no consensus as to the permissibility of competition. Many of the halakhic rulings handed down on this issue call to mind traditional protectionist defenses against foreign merchants. Although this unwelcoming response to outside competition was not sufficiently strong to overcome the generally favorable attitude to free competition, it was strong enough to engender imposition of additional restrictions.

Interestingly, these restrictions are formulated in the context of the laws governing relationships between neighbors rather than that of the laws of business competition. Indeed, Maimonides does not list them in the *Code*'s Laws concerning Sales, but in the Laws concerning Neighbors. Similarly, in the *Shulhan Arukh,* they are classed under the rules governing damages inflicted by neighbors, rather than the rules of equitable trading. However, there is a straightforward explanation for the fact that these laws are categorized under the rubric of laws governing relationships between neighbors: it can be traced back to the Talmud, where the relevant laws are discussed in the context of laws governing damages perpetrated by neighbors (Baba Batra, ch. 2). Today, we would probably classify them under the rubric of 'immigration law' or 'international trade' rather than that of 'business competition.' To fully understand the law on freedom of entry that was ultimately endorsed by the decisors, we must examine how the issue unfolds in the talmudic sources.

4.1 Tannaitic and Amoraic sources

The question of whether to permit the opening of a new shop next to an existing one is discussed in the Mishnah, and it seems that there may have been some controversy as to the law in this regard. The Talmud quotes the following two Tannaitic dicta:

i One may open a shop next to his fellow's shop, or a bathhouse next to his fellow's bathhouse, and the latter cannot protest, because he can say to him, You do [what you like] on your property, and I do [what I like] on mine.

ii It was taught in a baraita: Residents of alleyways (*mevoot*) can prevent each other from settling a tailor, a tanner, a teacher of children, or any

> other craftsman, among them; but one cannot prevent his neighbor [from himself setting up a business]. Rabban Shimon b. Gamaliel says: even his neighbor can be prevented [from setting up a business].
>
> bBaba Batra 21b

The first dictum certainly has to do with the creation of a new business that will be competing with an existing one, and maintains that a craftsman or merchant already in business cannot prevent someone else from opening another business alongside his own.

But the subject of the second dictum is ambiguous. It states that the residents of an alleyway, call it alleyway A, have the right to keep those who live in a different alleyway (alleyway B) from opening a business in alleyway A. The Sages disagree as to whether this authority endows the residents of alleyway A with the authority to similarly prevent one of their own number from opening a business. This dictum can be construed as addressing the issue of starting a competing business, but can also be interpreted as addressing a completely different issue, namely, the quality of life of the alleyway's residents.

On the latter explanation, the residents of the alley seek to preserve the ambience of their surroundings, and do not want to change the neighborhood's character. They thus oppose the opening of new shops in their neighborhood. On the other hand, if the passage is interpreted as being about business competition, what the residents seek to protect are the business interests of those among them who earn their livelihood in the alleyway. They seek to keep outsiders from settling in their neighborhood and competing with the existing businesses and craftspeople.

Rashi does not accept the quality-of-life interpretation, on which the issue being addressed is the opening of a shop in a residential area without shops, and takes the view that the discussion is about opening a new shop to compete with an existing one: "'prevent each other from settling a tailor or a tanner ... among them'—this means not settling among them a tailor or a tanner from another place, and renting him a house in the alley when others there [already] engage in that craft."

If we interpret the second dictum as speaking of business competition, it implies that the Sages permit local businesses to protect themselves from outsiders seeking to compete with them by opening a business next to an existing one, but not from locals who seek to do the same. R. Shimon b. Gamaliel maintains that local tradesmen ought also be protected from such 'internal' competition.

Despite the ambiguity of the second dictum, the Talmud takes it to refer to business competition, continuing in the same vein as the first dictum.

The passage thus reveals conflicting dispositions, on the part of the Sages, vis-à-vis the opening of competing businesses. On the one hand, they permit—in principle—the opening of a competing business, at least when the two contenders are from the same locale. A proprietor cannot prevent his neighbor from opening a competing business. The first opinion cited in the second dictum, however, qualifies this dispensation, specifying that it does not apply to outsiders. An outsider seeking to open a business that will compete with the locals can be prevented from doing so, so as to protect the interests of the latter. R. Shimon b. Gamaliel disagrees, barring entry of any new competing business, even when initiated by a local resident.

Earlier in the *sugya*, R. Shimon b. Gamaliel's view was endorsed by the Amora R. Huna:

> R. Huna said: If a resident of an alleyway sets up a hand-mill and a fellow resident of the alleyway comes to set up [a mill] next to him, he can prevent him [from doing so], for he can say to him, 'You are putting an end to my livelihood.'
>
> bBaba Batra 21b

The debate about the permissibility of opening a competing business invites comparison with the debate between R. Judah and the Sages over marketing practices intended to draw in new customers. Might not R. Huna, who does not allow competing businesses to open, be taking the position upheld by R. Judah, who does not permit marketing ploys such as price reductions and giveaways? But the Talmud rejects this suggestion, concluding that the two debates are unconnected:

> Said Rabina to Rava: Could we not say that R. Huna is expressing the same view as R. Judah? For we have learned: "R. Judah says: a shopkeeper may not distribute dried corn or nuts to children, because he thereby accustoms them to come to him. And the Sages permit it."
>
> You may even say that he is in agreement with the Rabbis as well. For the Sages only took issue with the view of R. Judah there because [this shopkeeper] can say to him [his competitor]: 'I distribute nuts, you distribute plums.' But in the present case even the Rabbis would agree that [the proprietor of the established business] can say to the other: 'You are putting an end to my livelihood.'
>
> bBaba Batra 21b

Thus, the *sugya* distinguishes between business practices that can be introduced by both sides, and steps that only one side can take, and have an adverse impact on the competitor's business. The criterion for acceptability is the possibility of reciprocity. The Sages permit competition between existing businesses because if one enterprise starts a marketing campaign, the other can follow suit. But starting a new business that will compete with an existing business is a unilateral action that cannot be copied by the existing business.

This distinction between new and existing businesses ought not be understood literally: though opening a new business can indeed be seen as a unilateral action that cannot be copied, an existing business's lowering its prices can also be described as an action that is un-copyable by a new business, since by definition, it has no 'old' prices to lower. What is at issue is not whether the act taken can be matched by the competitor so much as the question of whether the *status quo ante* has been changed. A merchant who decides to hand out gifts to customers does not substantially change the overall business environment, because this marketing tactic is commonly used by merchants operating similar businesses. Hence, should the latter claim that they will incur a loss as a result of the gifts, their plea is not heeded. On the other hand, a merchant who opens a new shop has changed the status quo significantly, thrusting the existing shop into a competitive business environment.

To sum up the argument thus far, while there is disagreement as to the permissibility of a local resident's starting a new business in competition with an existing business, there is a consensus that an outsider may be prevented from starting a competing business.

The Talmud proceeds to define the meaning of 'local resident' and 'outsider':

> R. Huna the son of R. Joshua said: It is clear to me that a resident of one town can prevent a resident of another town [from competing with him], but if he pays the local taxes, he cannot be prevented; and [it is also clear] that a resident of an alleyway cannot prevent another resident of the same alleyway [from competing]. R. Huna the son of R. Joshua asked: Can a resident of one alleyway prevent a resident of another [from competing with him]? This remains unresolved.
>
> bBaba Batra 21b

In the opinion of R. Huna b. R. Joshua, an inhabitant of the same alley is certainly a local, and someone from another town is certainly an outsider. He is, however, in doubt whether someone from a different street in the same town is considered a local, and the Talmud leaves this question unresolved. It should be noted that R. Huna b. R. Joshua maintains that one who pays municipal taxes is considered a local resident even if he lives elsewhere.

4.2 Views of the decisors

The law was decided in accordance with the view of the Tanna Kama in the second Tannaitic source, the "residents of alleyways" dictum from bBaba Batra 21b, namely, the view that a local resident is permitted to open a business in competition with an existing business, but an outsider is not. For example, Maimonides rules as follows:

> Residents of alleyways (*mevoot*) can prevent each other from settling a tailor, a tanner, or any other craftsman, among them. If one of the residents of the alleyway was a craftsman, and [the other residents] made no protest, or there was a bathhouse, a shop or a mill in the alley, and other residents came and opened another bathhouse or another mill, in competition with it, the [established proprietor] cannot prevent him from doing so, and say to him, 'You are putting an end to my livelihood.' And even if he [who started a new business] was a resident of another street, they cannot prevent him [from doing so], since they have that very craft among them [there in the alley]. However, if a stranger from another town comes [intending] to open a shop adjacent to someone's shop, or a bathhouse adjacent to someone's bathhouse, they can prevent him [from doing so]. But if he contributed, along with the other residents, to paying the king's tax, they cannot prevent him.[15]
>
> *Code*, Laws concerning Neighbors 6:8

Although someone from another town cannot open a business that will compete with existing businesses, Maimonides rules, on the basis of the aforementioned talmudic passage, that if the outsider paid his due share of the local taxes, the market could not be closed to him, that is, he could not be prevented from opening a competing business. The prohibition against allowing outsiders to start businesses can therefore be explained as protecting local merchants against **unfair** competition: the outsiders, not paying the local taxes, have lower expenses, which constitutes an unfair advantage. Maimonides' rule was not accepted by all the subsequent halakhic authorities.

At this juncture, it should be noted that two enactments governing the right to settle in a new community were issued in medieval Ashkenaz due to extremely harsh local economic circumstances: a ban on accepting additional Jewish residents into a given community (*herem hayishuv*), and a boycott of outsiders competing with local merchants (*maarufia*). These enactments were local and temporary ordinances, and not part of the classic body of halakha on business competition.

Whether the distinction between external and internal competition is still relevant in the urban reality of contemporary life is open to question. This comes to the fore in an edifying responsum by R. Zvi Judah

15 Above, we saw that it was possible to interpret the Tannaitic dictum "Residents of alleyways can prevent each other from settling a tailor, a tanner, a teacher of children, or any other craftsman, among them" in two very different ways. Maimonides' rendering of the law encompasses elements of both interpretations. On the one hand, if a neighborhood is a residential area with no shops, he empowers residents to prevent craftspeople and shops from moving in. He then addresses the case of an alley with existing shops; here, the issue is business competition. Maimonides upholds the Talmud's ruling that a local resident, but not an outsider, may enter into competition with a local business.

Ben-Yaacov.[16] The responsum deals with the case of a store employee, A, who resigned his position and proceeded to open a similar store just fifty meters from his former place of employment. The owner of the first store argued that the new store constituted unfair competition, because his customers knew A, and would probably prefer to have him serve them in the new store, than to be served by the new employee hired to replace A. In his defense, A argued that there were several similar stores in the area, and, that everyone has the right to engage in business as he sees fit.

R. Ben-Yaakov's decision was that the employee was permitted to compete with his former employer. In his deliberations, he noted that there are specific laws governing business competition created by merchants from another town who do not pay their share of the local taxes. Where that is not the case, however, one merchant cannot prevent another from competing as long as the competition is fair and serves the customers' interests. But the merchants' interests do not take precedence over the interests of the customers. In a large urban center, where there are many stores, not only is there no legal obligation to refrain from competing with existing businesses, there is also no moral obligation to do so.

4.3 Market day

An incident described in tractate Baba Batra involved out-of-town merchants who sought to sell their wares at a certain market. The local dealers sought to prevent them from doing so. The court ruled that since the incident took place on a market day, the outside dealers were permitted—even though they did not pay the local taxes—to sell their wares, seeing as there were also many out-of-town purchasers at the market.

> Certain basket-makers brought baskets to Babylon [to sell]. The townspeople came and stopped them [from doing so]. They came before Rabina. He said to them: They have come from outside [lit., the world at large] and they can sell to outsiders. And this ruling applies only to the market day, but if it is not a market day, it does not apply. And even on the market day, it is only applicable to those who sell at the market, but not to those who go back and forth [Rashi: who go around in the streets and from house to house].
>
> bBaba Batra 22a

Maimonides decides the law in accordance with Rabina's ruling:

> Traders who take their merchandise to sell in towns can be prevented from doing so by the townspeople. And if they sell only on the market

16 *Mishpatekha Leyaakov* (Israel: 1999), vol. 3, article 23, 301–309.

> day, they are not prevented from doing so, provided they sell in the market [only], but do not go door to door, even on the market day.
>
> *Code*, Laws concerning Neighbors 6:10

Although various limitations were imposed on the dispensation to 'compete' on the market-day,[17] there is no doubt that it made a significant contribution to broadening the possibilities open to outsiders—even those not paying local taxes—vis-à-vis entering into commercial competition with locals.

Some contemporary halakhic authorities have, in recent years, imparted new meaning to the 'market-day' proviso, the effect of which has been to further reduce the restrictions on entering the market. The classic rules that protected local merchants were based on the commercial reality of local businesses in the pre-modern period. At the time, most people purchased goods and services in the locale where they lived. Today, when the manufacture and sale of household goods, foodstuffs, and other consumer products take place at the national, international, and even global levels, these barriers are no longer relevant. This consideration was emphasized in an Israeli rabbinical court decision (see Appendix). The court explained that the notion of a 'market day' is not to be understood literally, but in terms of the institution's rationale. Businesses that are not local in nature, such as insurance brokers, or Bar-Mitzvah teachers, can therefore enter the market not only in the town in which their owner resides or their shop/office is located, but in other towns as well.

4.4 When existing businesses face bankruptcy

A more protectionist stance has also been voiced by several eminent halakhic authorities. The originator of this line of thinking was the medieval decisor R. Eliezer b. Joel Halevi of Bonn (Rabia). The Rabia ruled that if there is a shop in the inner part of a closed alley, and someone else intends to open a shop at the entrance to the alley, so that every customer first has to pass by the upstart competitor's shop, the owner of the existing shop can prevent the upstart shop from opening.[18]

Many commentators took the Rabia's rule to be in line with the Talmud's protectionist minority view in the *sugya* in bBaba Batra 21b—that is, R. Huna's view—which was not accepted as the law. Hence the Rabia's rule did not gain acceptance either.[19] But this is not the only way to understand the Rabia's stance. It may be the case that he is not endorsing protectionism, but merely adding a qualification to the majority view.

17 E.g., the decisor R. Joshua Falk Katz writes that "On the market day, merchants from elsewhere are permitted to sell at the market even to local residents.... The only proviso is that they may not go door to door" (*Sefer Meirat Einayim, SA*, HM 156:20).

18 Quoted in *Mordekhai*, Baba Batra, ch. 2, sec. 516.

19 *Hagahot Maimoniot*, Maimonides, *Code*, Laws concerning Neighbors 6:10.

The Rabia is speaking of a closed alley and not a central market-square that is accessible from various directions. His view may simply be that the rules of an open market apply to an accessible commercial area, but not a local store in the inner part of a closed alley. So understood, he does not reject free competition in an open market.

Some commentators who tend to restrict free competition nonetheless contend that restrictions on free competition are in fact in harmony with the majority rule of the Talmud and the codifiers. Business competition is permitted when the existing business is not excluded from the market, and prohibited only when it leads to the complete ruination of the existing business.[20]

This law is not set down in the works of the major codifiers,[21] but cannot be ignored, since it is sometimes invoked in the responsa literature. It might appear to reflect the moral principle that protecting merchants from complete ruination—in other words, from bankruptcy—takes precedence over protecting the interests of the consumer. But in view of the fact that the leading talmudic and post-talmudic sources clearly support both free competition and protection of consumers, this explanation is overly simplistic. Other justifications for the halakhic authorities' tendency to uphold limitations on free competition have been suggested. One such explanation was offered by a contemporary scholar, Aaron Levine.[22] He begins by citing our *sugya*, bBaba Batra 21b:

> May we say that [R. Huna's] view is supported by the following: Fishing nets must be kept away from [the hiding place of] a fish [which has been spotted by another fisherman] the full length of the fish's swim. And how much is this? Rabbah son of R. Huna says: A *parasang* –fish are different because they look about [for food].
>
> bBaba Batra 21b

Levine then adduces the interpretation of this passage offered by R. Joseph ibn Migash, who he characterizes as taking a "protectionist" stance. Ibn Migash asks why a territorial preserve is conferred on fishermen, but not tradesmen, and explains this disparity as follows. The capture of a large fish that has been sighted, he argues,

> is effectively frustrated when another fisherman places his net between this fish's hiding place and the bait. The second fisherman's action has the effect of intercepting the swarm of little fish that surround the large fish. Insofar as the large fish will change direction as

20 *Reponsa Hatam Sofer*, HM #79.

21 Alfasi, Maimonides, *Tur*, *Shulhan Arukh* and the Rema's gloss thereon.

22 A. Levine, "The deprivation-generating criterion," *Free Enterprise and Jewish Law* (New York: 1980), 24–26, reproduced in *Torah U-Madda Journal* 10 (2001), 114–115.

> soon as he notices that the small fish have been caught, the action of the intruder effectively deprives the first fisherman of his catch. In contrast, the arrival of a new firm on the competitive scene in no way forces customers to discontinue their patronage of the entrenched firm. With the new entry generating no deprivation effects on the established firm, the latter is denied a territorial monopoly.

Levine then proceeds to invoke the views of two more recent decisors, R. Moses Sofer, the Hatam Sofer, and R. Moses Feinstein:

> The foregoing leads R. Moshe Sofer to reconcile the dispute between R. Huna and R. Huna b. Joshua: R. Huna's protectionist philosophy is restricted to instances where the effect of the new entry would be to ruin, not merely reduce, the livelihood of the established firm. The free-entry advocacy of R. Huna b. Joshua, on the other hand, is confined to instances where the effect of the new entry would be merely to reduce the profit margin of the entrenched competitor and not deprive him of his livelihood entirely.
>
> The complainant's wealth and the number of his sources of livelihood are, according to R. Moshe Sofer, irrelevant in considering the merits of a ruinous-competition case. To qualify for judicial intervention, a complainant need only demonstrate that a particular source of his livelihood is cut off as a result of his competitor's action.
>
> Concurring with R. Sofer's deprivation-generating criterion, R. Moshe Feinstein would enjoin a new entrant whenever the latter's expected impact is to reduce the established firm's earnings below the mean earnings of his socioeconomic peer group. Deprivation, in R. Feinstein's formulation, is not associated with below-subsistence earnings. A complainant, depending upon his socioeconomic status, may aspire for protection of an earnings floor above the margin of subsistence.[23]

On the basis of these halakhic opinions, Levine presents what he takes to be legal restrictions on the general rule of free competition, restrictions that apply even in a fair competitive environment. In light of these restrictions, he argues, rabbinical court judges adjudicating cases involving competition must decide, not just on the basis of moral principles, but on the basis of the law itself, how best to balance the values of free enterprise, on the one hand, and not depriving someone of her livelihood, on the other. This position would seem to conflict with the majority view in the talmudic sources, which is upheld by most of the decisors.

There is also another conceivable rationale for the views adduced by Levine. Opening a second business may ruin the existing business. Such a

23 Levine, n. 22 above, 115.

development is not beneficial to consumers, since in the end only one shop will remain; and there is no guarantee that the new business will be any more advantageous to consumers than its predecessor. It could be argued that when competition may destroy an existing business, yet the benefit to consumers is far from certain, the existing merchant's interest takes precedence over unbridled business competition. Several halakhic authorities have rejected this rationale, as it is not certain that the existing business will be ruined by the competition. They maintain that the free competition principle remains valid, and takes precedence over other considerations.

Before concluding our discussion of the tendency of certain halakhic authorities to restrict the dispensation to compete against an existing business, another point should be mentioned. As we saw, in limiting the scope of the dispensation, both R. Moses Sofer and R. Moses Feinstein relied on the view of the Rabia, regarding it as law intended for implementation (*halakha lemaase*). Yet, at least on the face of it, the Rabia's ruling does not appear to have been upheld by the major decisors, who do not adduce it in their codifications of the law. How is this divergence to be explained?

One possible explanation is that the views of R. Moses Sofer and R. Moses Feinstein reflect the harsh economic conditions faced by Jewish merchants in certain communities. But while this explanation might be plausible with regard to R. Moses Sofer, it cannot explain the rulings of R. Moses Feinstein, who lived in the United States in the twentieth century. Let me suggest another explanation, though it is only conjecture and in need of empirical substantiation. It is possible that R. Feinstein's ruling constitutes a reaction to the secularization of large segments of the Jewish people. The role and function of the decisor is not to regulate the market, but rather to guide a religious community that seeks to live in accordance with its legal rules and moral principles, and accepts his authority to interpret those directives. Contemporary responsa are not directives for the wider Jewish community, whose members do not all accept the authority of the halakha, but are issued to a self-selected group whose members are highly committed and devout. This being so, R. Feinstein's rulings may tend to emphasize moral obligations and constraints beyond the strict letter of the law. This could—though as we said, this hypothesis has yet to be substantiated—explain why R. Feinstein upholds the Rabia's restrictions on competition.

Moreover, R. Feinstein's responsum does not address a classic case of business competition, but an exceptional situation, as attested by the details of the case, which Levine does not go into. The case dealt with the complaint of a rabbi who owned a synagogue building, and presided over the congregation housed therein. Several members of the congregation quarreled with him, withdrew from the congregation in a huff, and built a synagogue of their own nearby. They also incited other members of the congregation to leave and join their new synagogue. This led to a decrease in the rabbi's income, and also lowered the value of the synagogue building. These dissident members were the addressees of the responsum. Attending to two unique features of the case will allow us to understand R. Feinstein's apparent hostility to free competition.

First of all, Jewish tradition ascribes great importance to preserving harmony within a congregation and upholding the honor of its leader. The dissidents were not merely encroaching on an existing 'business,' but also brought about dissension among its membership and disrespect for its leader. Secondly, the competition here has no potential to benefit the 'customers,' seeing as there are no products that are being improved or provided at a lower price. Indeed, there are no 'consumers' here, as there are only two conflicting interests—that of the established congregation and that of the new congregation. It is a conflict between two competing sides, and there is no third 'side' whose interests can help decide between the competitors. Taking these two elements into account can help explain R. Feinstein's disapproval of the breakaway faction.

5 Price competition and predatory pricing

As we have seen, outside competition with local businesses was generally taken to be prohibited, unless the outsiders paid the local taxes. R. Joseph ibn Migash qualifies this limitation, stipulating that it holds only if the out-of-town merchants will be selling at the same price as the local dealers. But if the merchandise is of better quality, or its price is lower, the limitation does not apply. Ibn Migash explains that when competition generates direct benefit to consumers, the existing merchant's interest does not take precedence.

> Thus we can conclude from this that residents of a town can prevent merchants from another town from coming to their town to sell their wares if it is not a market day....
>
> However, apparently all this applies only where the consumers do not lose thereby – for example, if the prices are the same and the merchandise is also the same – since consumers do not stand to benefit from it. Hence the Rabbis made an enactment for the benefit of the local traders so that their businesses will not be ruined and their livelihood will not be threatened. But where their merchandise is the same yet their prices are not the same, or their prices are the same but their merchandise is not the same, we check if the customers in the town are Gentiles. If so, the locals may still prevent the outsiders [from conducting business in their town]. But if the customers in that town are Jews, it stands to reason that the Rabbis would not have made an enactment for the benefit of the merchants, for where the customers stand to lose thereby, there is no dispensation [to prevent entry of new merchants]. Hence where the customers stand to benefit, the merchants

have no power to make enactments that protect their livelihood at the expense of others.

R. Joseph ibn Migash, cited in *Shita Mekubetzet*, bBaba Batra 21b s.v. *naktinan*

R. Joseph ibn Migash presents his remarks as a minor qualification of an accepted limitation on the entry of outside traders into a local market. Yet it appears that this 'qualification' will apply to virtually every case of outsiders seeking entry into the market, because it can definitely be expected that these traders will utilize marketing measures such as giveaways and offering better quality goods and lower prices. Hence the practical import of the Ri Migash's qualification is a dramatic curtailment of the restrictions on the entry of outsiders. This bears out a thesis put forward by Haym Soloveitchik, a noted historian of Jewish law, who contends that as a rule, the rabbinical authorities prefer issuing dispensations of limited scope to announcing dramatic changes in and reversals of the law. The halakha, he argues, "addresses problems one by one, and does not tend to issue comprehensive dispensations. It prefers to come up with a series of limited dispensations, the cumulative effect of which is the de facto annulment of the prohibition as opposed to its abrogation or restriction in principle."[24]

Although Maimonides does not mention ibn Migash's opinion—which is noteworthy, given that Maimonides' father was ibn Migash's student, and Maimonides himself had great respect for ibn Migash—it was accepted by many halakhic authorities.[25] In essence, ibn Migash, recognizing that the interests of the consumer are ordinarily best served by allowing free market competition, asserts that this factor takes precedence over the merchant's interest, even when the competition is not on equal terms. That is, he maintains that competition is permissible even when one competitor has an advantage such as greater size or lower expenses, for instance, if the business does not pay local taxes.

This approach appears to conflict with the position upheld by the Talmud, which does not permit the participation of outside traders in a local market if they do not pay the local taxes. It does, however, reflect the basically positive attitude of Jewish law to free competition. Ibn Migash concurs with the traditional stance that when the issue of benefit to the consumer is moot–that is, when a competing outside merchant seeks to sell at the same price—the interests of the local merchants take precedence over implementing the free competition principle. But if the outside dealers offer deals that clearly benefit consumers, the free competition principle prevails.

24 Haym Soloveitchik, *Principles and Pressures: Jewish Trade in Gentile Wine in the Middle Ages* (Hebrew), (Tel Aviv: 2003), 136.

25 See, e.g., *Tur*, HM 156:11.

This approach was criticized by Nahmanides, who argues that the Mishnah endorsing price competition is limited to cases where competition from outsiders will lead to a general price reduction; where that is not the case, outside competition is not allowed. He further argues that if we accept the notion that price-cuts justify permitting outside competition, then outside competition should always be permitted, since it is "impossible" that some price reduction will not result from the entry of new competitors into the market. As to protection of the consumer's interests, Nahmanides maintains that this should be achieved by price controls on the part of communal leaders. Only in cases where the merchandise is of significantly better quality and can thus be considered a different product does Nahmanides concede that outside competition is permissible.

> R. Joseph Halevi [ibn Migash], of blessed memory, says that the rule that craftsmen can prevent other craftsmen from a different town [from opening a shop in their market] applies only if their merchandise is the same and their prices are the same, but where they are not the same, and the customers of the town are Jews, they cannot be prevented [from doing so].
>
> And this [statement] is not clear to me, because the Mishnah states: "[R. Judah says,] Nor may he lower the price." And even though the Sages proceed to say, "He is to be remembered for good ... because he eases the market price," this applies only to residents of the place in question, because they can say to [the would-be competitors], 'Lower your prices and you can sell [in our market].' But craftsmen from a different town can be prevented [from entering the market] ... and if the locals wish to lower their prices, they can stipulate a fixed price, or appoint someone from their town [to enter the market]. But they can certainly prevent someone from elsewhere [from opening a business in their market]. Were it not so, [outsiders] could never be prevented [from entering], for it is impossible that the price will not go down [at least somewhat] when there are many who engage in the same craft, and it certainly benefits the customers.
>
> It follows that if [local businesses] stand to lose thereby, [merchants from another town] do not have [the right to enter a market], for merchants from another town cannot benefit the customers if they are depriving local traders of their livelihood. But local residents may stipulate that [merchants] are to sell for such-and-such a price ... as long as they set a moderate price that is fair to both [buyers and sellers] alike. However, if the wares [of the locals and outsiders] are not the same, all would certainly agree that they can say to them: 'Your wares are inferior and ours are superior,' and it is considered a different business, because one product is not like the other.
>
> *Nahmanides*, bBaba Batra 22a s.v. *zilu*

Although ibn Migash's position was widely accepted,[26] some halakhic authorities endorse Nahmanides' stance.[27] Others attempt to harmonize the views of ibn Migash and Nahmanides. One example of an attempted harmonization is that of the fifteenth-century Spanish decisor R. Joseph Habiba.

> It seems that the opinion of the Master [ibn Migash], of blessed memory, applies only when [the outsiders] sell at a very low price. But if they sell it only slightly more cheaply than the town's own vendors do, it is certainly possible to prevent them [from entering], for were it not so, [outsiders] could never be prevented [from entering], for it is impossible that, when there are many who engage in the same craft, the price will not go down. And for such a trifling improvement, merchants from another town do not have the right to [do something that would] cause a loss [to the local merchants] and benefit [the local customers]. For if the locals wanted to reduce prices, they could either stipulate a fixed price or appoint someone from their own town to enter the market. This seems to me to be the opinion of Nahmanides, of blessed memory.
>
> *Nimukei Yosef*, bBaba Batra 11a (Alfasi pagination)

R. Joseph Habiba, the Nimukei Yosef, claims that there was no disagreement between ibn Migash and Nahmanides. He argues that ibn Migash agrees that a token price reduction by new merchants does not justify their entry into the market, which will harm the existing businesses, and takes Nahmanides to agree to their entry if they offer significant price-cuts. The Nimukei Yosef thus accepts the principle implicit in ibn Migash's stance, namely, that price reductions justify admitting non-local merchants to the market, qualifying this with the caveat that the price-cuts must be significant.

R. Joseph Caro rejects R. Joseph Habiba's attempt at harmonizing the views, and insists that there is indeed a substantive disagreement between ibn Migash and Nahmanides:

> Whether the price-cut was paltry or substantial, according to R. Joseph Halevi [ibn Migash] they cannot be prevented [from entering the local market], and according to Nahmanides, they can be prevented [from doing so].
>
> *Beit Yosef, Tur*, HM 156

R. Joseph Caro maintains that ibn Migash and Nahmanides disagree both over the case where the outsiders sell at a significantly reduced price, and

26 *Rema, SA*, HM 156:7, citing Asheri and the Tur. See also *Pithei Teshuva*, HM 156:11; *Responsa Beit Efraim*, HM #26–27.

27 E.g., R. Yehiel Mikhel Epstein, *Arukh Hashulhan*, HM 228:14, R. Naftali Zvi Berlin, *Responsa Haamek Sheeila*, HM #1, and see Lieberman, n. 4 above, 31–36.

over the case where the outsiders offer a token reduction. And indeed, contra R. Joseph Habiba, Nahmanides' remarks manifest an explicit and unambiguous disagreement with ibn Migash. Nahmanides considered the whole issue of price-cuts to be moot, as he maintained that the community could take care of price levels by itself, and there was no need for outside merchants to come and force down prices by competitive marketing tactics. And since ibn Migash took price-cuts, regardless of their size, to be indicative of improved products, for him too, the degree of the price-cut makes no difference.

Nahmanides contended that price regulation by communal leaders was preferable to price adjustments resulting from free competition between merchants. In practice, however, the former was not a feasible means of protecting the consumer, given the realities of Jewish life in Europe in the Middle Ages, and competition was the main mechanism for maintaining fair prices and reasonable product quality. This claim has been disputed by some scholars, who argue that price regulation on the part of community leaders was indeed the prevailing price control mechanism.[28] However, there seems to be little, if any, evidence in the responsa literature attesting to the **actual** enforcement of price controls in Jewish law. While there are, indeed, numerous rules referring to price controls in the various codifications of Jewish law, there is a pronounced absence of such references in the responsa literature. There is, in other words, a sizeable gap between the law on the books, which calls for the imposition of price controls by community leaders, and the almost total disregard of these rules in actual case law.

This conclusion is endorsed by a contemporary scholar of halakhic business law, Meir Tamari:

> It would seem that Jewish law and thought tends to accept as its basis the mechanism of the market place, adjusted, however, to meet the demands of morality, benevolence and justice. Furthermore, at various periods of their history, the Jews were forced to live a marginal economic life, making the application of economic liberalization an act of physical suicide. In those periods, Jewish law and communal action operated to create a more restricted and regulated economy.[29]

6 Business competition in responsa and rabbinical court rulings

As we have seen, various issues pertaining to business competition and predatory pricing are addressed in the responsa literature, which records

28 I. Warhaftig, "The economic system according to the Torah" (Hebrew), in S. Ishon and Y. Bazak (eds.), *Studies in Economics and Law according to the Halakha* (2004), 19–39.

29 See M. Tamari, "Competition, prices and profits in Jewish law," *Bar Ilan Annual 10 (H.M. Shapira Memorial Volume)* (1972), 73–147. The quote is from the English summary, p. 159.

halakhic case law. As noted, there is sometimes a gap between the theoretical law, and the law applied in concrete cases. Study of the responsa literature enables us to see how the laws of business competition have been applied in practice. These responsa attest to a sizeable disparity between the law on the books, and the law implemented in practice. This can be explained in large part by the fact that in adjudicating actual cases, the judges must take into consideration more than the laws of business competition. Both the context of the case, and its socioeconomic sub-text, so to speak, must also be taken into account.

6.1 R. Moses Isserles on competition between printers

The first responsum we will consider was written by R. Moses Isserles (Rema). The position he upholds in this responsum appears to conflict with the rule he presents in his glosses on the *Shulhan Arukh*, a discrepancy that calls for explanation. In the latter work, *Hagahot Harema*, he adduces ibn Migash's rule that outside competitors are permitted to compete in a market if they offer their wares at a price lower than that charged by the local merchants. It is thus surprising that in the responsum, R. Moses Isserles forbids purchase of a new edition of Maimonides' *Code* being offered for sale at a price lower than that of the existing edition, printed by another printer. The apparent inconsistency between these stances has been noted by many commentators.[30]

Let us first look at R. Moses Isserles' ruling in *Hagahot Harema*:

> There are some who say that townspeople can protest outsiders' [entry into the market] only when consumers do not stand to lose thereby, for the outsiders sell at the same price as the local townspeople, and their merchandise is not superior to that of the locals. However, if they sell more cheaply or their merchandise is superior, consumers benefit thereby, so the local merchants cannot protest.
>
> *Hagahot Harema, SA*, HM 156:7

Keeping the foregoing ruling in mind, let us now examine the seemingly contradictory ruling in the responsum:

> This concerns a man from abroad whose name is known far and wide … our teacher and rabbi R. Meir of Padua. And he collected his interpretive leanings, ideas, and thoughts, in collaboration with an important man in his country, a printer of books.[31] Together they entered into an agreement to print the great opus *Mishne Torah*.… And

30 See Lieberman, n. 4 above, 37–8.

31 The renowned Alvise Bragadini of Venice; see Neil Weinstock Netanel, "Maharam of Padua v. Giustiniani: the sixteenth-century origins of the Jewish law of copyright," *Houston Law Review* (2007), 822–70.

having decided to undertake this [project], they commenced the work, with God's help, and have only recently completed it. And R. Meir has edited it with his acute intelligence, removing even the slightest chaff that may have become mixed with the wheat, and smoothing the path until there remained on it not a single stone. Subsequently, another gentleman, one of the wealthiest in the land,[32] came and declared, I too will do this for my own financial gain, and I too will print it, and so he did. And his principal reason for doing this was that the aforementioned eminent scholar did not collaborate with him, and he did it in order to anger the said scholar and cause him a financial loss, God forbid. For it was known that were the scholar unable to sell his books, the ensuing burden would be too great to bear.

And now, in ruling on this matter in accordance with Jewish law, I will rule 'as if' the aforementioned two individuals were Jews according to our holy Torah, and prove that the aforementioned scholar wins the case. And we will address four main issues, which will be the four foundations of our discussion of this matter. And I assert that the law is that this scholar is right, and he should sell his books first. And insofar as, due to our many iniquities, we are unable to enforce the law as set down in our Torah, in any event we will not forego our duty, but we will declare that no Jew may buy any volume of the new edition of Maimonides' work, but may only buy volumes published by the aforementioned scholar or those acting on his behalf. And there are four reasons for our decision.[33]

The first fundamental reason appears in the Talmud in bBaba Batra 21b: "R. Huna said: If a resident of an alleyway sets up a mill and a fellow resident of the alleyway comes to set up [a mill] next to him, he can prevent him [from doing so]." And the import of the words "set up next to him" is that he did so with his [the first miller's] knowledge, but even so, he may prevent him [from setting up the mill]. Accordingly, in the present case, by our law, the second gentleman may not print the books. That is the rule, and the aforementioned scholar could have prevented him [from printing the books], as we demonstrated above. And rabbinical court judges are also obliged to do so. But due to our iniquities, only Gentile law is enforceable and we cannot enforce our judgments. In any event, though, we shall do that which it is our mandate to do, and decide the law as set forth above.

And even though R. Alfasi and the Rosh ruled against R. Huna, whose view is the minority opinion, I nevertheless find that his opinion must be taken into account, because the *Mordekhai*[34] cites the *Aviasaf*[35]

32 The Venetian printer Marco Antonio Giustiniani.
33 We will cite only the first, which suffices to illustrate the point in question.
34 Baba Batra, ch. 2, sec. 516.
35 A mostly non-extant work by R. Eliezer b. Joel Halevi of Bonn (the Rabia).

as follows: "In the case of an alleyway that is enclosed on three sides and has an entrance on one side only, where Reuben lives at the closed end and Shimon came to live near the open end, so that Gentiles [i.e., customers] cannot enter the alleyway without passing Shimon's door, then the law is that Shimon can be prevented [from plying the same trade as Reuben there], as R. Huna ruled."

This being so, it follows that the *Aviasaf* adopted R. Huna's ruling. So we must distinguish the case where damage will be caused, such as the case of the alleyway. [In such a case,] where it is certain that damage will be caused [to the craftsman who already resided there], all agree that the law is in accordance with the view of R. Huna. Accordingly, in the case at hand, it is also certain that damage will be caused, because the second gentleman has declared that he will sell every book for one ducat less than the scholar. And who would see this and not go to him to purchase [the books] from him!? And he is able to reduce the price because he is one of the richest men in the land. Hence in this case too, the law is in accordance with the view of R. Huna.

Responsa Rema, #10

It appears, then, that there is a manifest contradiction between the Rema's ruling in his gloss on the ruling in the *Shulhan Arukh*, and the decision he hands down in the responsum. How might this contradiction be reconciled? I would argue that the Rema takes the position that, while in principle business competition is to be encouraged, the responsum deals with an exceptional case, where there is real danger that the first merchant will be harmed. The second printer's declaration that he intends to sell for a ducat less than the first indicates that he is willing to sell his books at a loss. As his motivation is the desire to exclude other printers from the market, he is prepared to sell below cost and lose money on printing the volumes in question. Being extremely wealthy, the interloping printer can afford to engage in such behavior. Entering a market with the sole intention of ruining the business of a competitor by undercutting his prices and selling at a loss is predatory behavior, and thus prohibited.

This position can be justified by invoking considerations of fairness and efficiency. From the perspective of fairness, the case involves a competition where *ab initio*, only one side can participate, and the other side, lacking the wherewithal to weather selling at a loss, is doomed from the outset to lose the competition and forfeit its entire investment. More specifically, the existing printer has no marketing ploys to which he can have recourse in response to the second printer's price-cut, since any price reduction he might introduce would be more than matched by his wealthy adversary, to the point where he cannot continue selling at a loss and is bankrupt. In essence, this is the thrust of the Rema's ruling—in line with that of the Rabia—forbidding the entry into the market of a new merchant who will not only adversely affect the interests of the existing merchant, but ruin him altogether, removing him from the market. This is not a price competition but a calculated attempt to overthrow and supplant an existing merchant.

The Rema's ruling can also be justified in terms of considerations of market efficiency. To be sure, reduced prices benefit customers in the short term, but it is clear that the second printer will not be able to go on selling at a loss indefinitely. After getting rid of the existing business, he will either raise the price—reverting to the price at which the now-defunct printer sold the books, or even price the books higher than the original price, to recoup some of his losses. Hence, in the long-term, the interests of the customers are not better served by the second printer.

To enhance our understanding of the Rema's ruling, it should be understood against the background of the late medieval printing industry. At the time, to be viable, the publication of works of Jewish scholarship apparently mandated a natural monopoly. The latter occurs when production costs are so high that, if the venture is to be feasible, exclusive production rights must be given to a single company. If two companies are allowed to compete, it will not be worthwhile to either one to produce the product, as neither company would recover the initial outlay.[36] The high costs of printing and the limited number of potential buyers of scholarly books resulted in "the creation of natural monopolies in the printing industry, where the activity of competing firms could not be justified."[37] In other words, only one printer could survive the competition. The market conditions were such that two printing businesses could not both be sustained at the same time. Against this background, we can see that the Rema had good reason to protect the existing publisher.

6.2 R. Samuel di Modena on the impact of socio-political change on the rules of market competition

In *Responsa Maharashdam*, HM #407, R. Samuel di Modena (Maharashdam), a sixteenth-century authority in Saloniki, was asked about a case involving competition law. Outside merchants had entered the market and reduced the prices of goods. The local merchants had difficulty competing with the newcomers, and asked the Maharashdam if it was possible to proscribe market competition by out-of-town merchants.

In his answer, the Maharashdam explained that the distinction between local and outside market players had been relevant in the past when each town was a jurisdiction unto itself, but was no longer relevant in the sixteenth-century Ottoman Empire, when the market was open to everyone

36 This is frequently the case with respect to utilities (e.g., hydro and nuclear power plants), since the high cost of setting up and running such plants can only be recovered if the company is granted a monopoly and consumers have no choice but to use its services.

37 Lieberman, n. 4 above, 38–39.

subject to the Sultan's law. In what was essentially a free-market economy, there was no room for restrictions on new business ventures. The Maharashdam further asserted that since all could come and sell their wares, there was no justification for requiring only Jewish merchants to refrain from competing with existing businesses:

> These and similar laws, which are set out in the Talmud in tractate bBaba Batra, and quoted by the decisors, of blessed memory, and also in compendia of responsa, were relevant to those times when the Jews lived under the jurisdictions of many different local lords, some under lord A and some under lord B. But in this vast kingdom, long may it thrive, which opens its gates to all comers, from anywhere in the world, and we Jews all dwell within its territory, and are under its aegis and protection, it seems that these laws do not apply as they did in those other times and places.

Now what is the difference between the case addressed by the Rema and that addressed by the Maharashdam? The latter involves an environment where the entry of new merchants into the market is expected to harm the existing merchants, but not to cause them to lose their livelihood altogether. But in the case addressed by the Rema, the livelihood of the existing merchant is at stake. Granting the second printer a dispensation to compete with the first will effectively ensure that the existing printer is forced out of business, as he will either be deprived of his income, given that customers can buy for less elsewhere, or will lose his assets by selling at a loss in order to compete. This explains why the Rema rules that competition is to be curtailed, whereas the Maharashdam endorses competition.

The Maharashdam recommends asking the out-of-town merchants to pay the local community expenses and taxes, though they are not legally bound to do so. He argues that they should be encouraged to do so, that is, to act in a supererogatory manner (*lifnim mishurat hadin*), so as to avoid generating conflict between the local Jewish community and the Ottoman authorities. Although the facts of the case are not clear, it seems likely that the outsiders' entry into the local marketplace was responsible for a decrease in tax payments to the authorities. Accordingly, although there was no legal basis for requiring outsiders to pay their share of the local taxes, the Maharashdam recommends calling upon them to pay these taxes voluntarily, as under the circumstances, they have a moral obligation to do so.

Both ibn Migash and the Maharashdam extend the dispensation for outside merchants to enter the market. But whereas the former based his decision on the benefit that would accrue to consumers, namely, lower prices and better quality products, the latter based it on the reality of free market competition under the Sultan's reign. Both rulings had a similar outcome, rendering permissible the virtually unrestricted entry of new merchants into the market. But the halakhic methodologies these decisors used to attain this outcome differ dramatically. As we saw, ibn Migash, while presenting himself as upholding the law as written, introduced a seemingly minor qualification to it. Yet he thereby rendered permissible many—if not most—instances of outside competitors entering into competition with local merchants. In other words, under the cover of conservative rhetoric, ibn Migash significantly broadened the scope of the law. This approach has the advantage of preserving the law's stability, and thus protecting the stability of the legal order more generally, while at the same time introducing changes, sometimes profound, to the law as practiced, thereby enabling it to accommodate changing times and circumstances.

The Maharashdam, on the other hand, declares from the outset that changed circumstances have rendered the old laws irrelevant, and henceforth the entry of outside merchants into the market will no longer be subject to restrictions. His rhetoric is much more radical than that of ibn Migash. To be sure, this method undermines the stability of the law, but does so in order to reflect the full extent of the changes that have transpired in the world, changes the law is now in harmony with.

The disparate methodologies are rooted in another difference. Ibn Migash bases his dispensation on halakhic argumentation, that is, engagement with the halakhic rules of business competition. He argues that in considering the entry of outside merchants into the market, the interests of existing businesses should not take precedence over the interests of consumers. Hence, when new merchants are expected to benefit consumers, their entry should be permitted. The Maharashdam, on the other hand, bases his dispensation, not on halakhic arguments, but on the changed socio-political circumstances of the Jews of his day, and in particular, the rules imposed on them by the non-Jewish political regime. He assumes without question that the halakha seeks to accommodate the changed circumstances. It could be argued that whereas ibn Migash's dispensation introduces flexibility into the laws governing the admission of outsiders into the market, the Maharashdam's dispensation almost voids them altogether.

6.3 R. Haim Halberstam of Sanz on competition in the sale of spirits

In this section, we will examine two responsa by R. Haim Halberstam of Sanz (Poland, 1793-1876) that address the question of competition in the sale of spirits. The first responsum clarifies the limits of permissible business competition.[38] R. Haim was asked whether a tavern-keeper was allowed to sell liquor at prices lower than those of his competitors. The competitors complained of unfair competition: this particular tavern-keeper, they said, could afford to sell at a lower price because,

38 *Responsa Divrei Haim*, HM 1, #18.

for some reason, he paid lower taxes than the rest of the tavern-keepers. They argued that if the prices were not raised, their livelihood might be endangered. In his answer, R. Halberstam distinguished between two scenarios: where the price was fixed by the authorities, and where there was no fixed price. In a fixed price situation, selling for less than the official price is illegal and constitutes unfair competition, because sellers who abide by the law cannot compete with the prices offered by the lawbreaker. But where the price is not fixed, competitive price-cuts are legal and therefore halakhically permissible. Provided that vendors do not engage in unfair competition—as they were alleged to have done in the case he was asked about—there is no moral prohibition, he contends, against competing by lowering prices.

Following the Maharashdam, R. Haim Halberstam suggests a further argument that well illustrates the practical concerns that arise in the context of business competition, concerns the decisor must be sensitive to. R. Haim argues that since the purpose of the restrictions sometimes placed on free competition is to protect existing businesses, they should only be imposed when and where they will be effective. For instance, there is no point in restricting some merchants when others can do as they please. In the market in question, some of the merchants are not Jewish, and thus, of course, not bound by the halakhic laws of competition. As these merchants can cut their prices at will, imposing a prohibition against price-cuts achieves nothing, and indeed handicaps the Jewish merchants. Moreover, the Jewish tavern-keepers generally acted as agents of Gentile landowners:

> In the matter at hand … since he [the tavern-keeper who lowered his prices] is acting on behalf of a Gentile, and this Gentile can sell at whatever price he wishes, why should this [tavern-keeper] be at a disadvantage just because he is Jewish, heaven forbid!? Therefore the prevailing custom is that one cannot protest when [a competitor] introduces a price-cut.

This is a significant determination. It implies that the halakhic rules of free competition were, from the outset, intended only for markets whose players are Jews who accept Jewish law as binding. But if there are players in the market who are not bound by Jewish law, the halakha intentionally desists from limiting the market activities of observant merchants where such limitations could put them at a disadvantage vis-à-vis conduct acceptable to their Gentile market colleagues.[39]

39 Similar questions were presented to other halakhic authorities during the same period, but the circumstances of those cases were very different, and the decisors ruled that price reductions were prohibited; see, e.g., *Responsa Panim Meirot*, 1, #71; *Responsa Maamar Mordekhai*, #11.

Another responsum by R. Haim Halberstam indicates the broader considerations that can influence concrete halakhic rulings concerning entry of new merchants into the market.[40] These considerations do not pertain to harm or benefit to either merchants or consumers, that is, to the questions treated within the context of competition law in itself, but arise out of other legal concerns and general policy questions.

> A lord granted licenses to sell liquor. He granted this right to Jewish dealers if they paid a certain tax, on condition that the liquor be sold at a fixed price. Other Jews, however, sold liquor illegally at a very low price. Upon hearing this, the official threatened to expel all the Jews from the district. The question is whether such illicit sales are halakhically permissible.

R. Halberstam approaches the issue from three different directions. He first discusses it in terms of the laws of business competition, comparing the case to that of the competing printers addressed by R. Moses Isserles. He concludes that price-cuts of the type in question are forbidden, though it is evident that he is not entirely comfortable with this conclusion; it seems unlikely he would have reached it were the laws of competition the only consideration he took into account.

He then considers the situation from the perspective of the laws of sales. Specifically, he addresses the question of rights accruing to the merchants who bought the concession allowing them to sell liquor. R. Halberstam takes the concession to create a twofold right: the right to sell liquor, and the right to assume—that is, the assurance—that other concession-holders will not undercut the concession-holder's prices. Hence, a merchant selling at a lower price would not merely be harming the said dealer's business interests, but also infringing the rights he acquired from the lord. Consequently, even were the said price-cuts permissible from the perspective of the laws of business competition, they would still be forbidden in the case at hand, since they infringe the concession-holder's rights. R. Halberstam argues that violating this right is tantamount to theft, hence the case should be governed not only by laws of business competition, but by the laws of theft as well.

> Those who bought the *arenda*s [concessions] in the villages, also bought from the lord the assurance that [liquor] would not be sold in the town for less than what it sells for in the villages. If so, one who sells it for less is robbing his fellow Jews. And it is full-fledged robbery, and prohibited.

40 *Responsa Divrei Haim*, HM 1, #19.

Thus the same conclusion is reached from the first two perspectives considered by R. Haim Halberstam.

The third consideration R. Halberstam takes into account is that of maintaining communal peace. The lower prices offered by the said merchants endanger communal peace and harmony, since they entail violation of the concession's rules, and could cause the lord to impose sanctions—notably, expulsion—on the entire Jewish community. Consequently, even were the said price-cuts permissible from the perspective of the laws of business competition, the local halakhic decisor has the authority to forbid them on the basis of wider considerations as to the public good. For the decisor does not reach his decision solely on the basis of the specific rules governing business competition in Jewish law, but must also take into account any legal and social issues that have bearing on the question being decided.

> In the case at hand, the lord is seeking to expel hundreds of people, and if things deteriorate, heaven forbid, perhaps the town's entire population. Hence these individuals—the tavern-keepers who conduct themselves sneakily—are obligated to stop [what they are doing], and turn away from this path, for if they do not heed this [admonition], they will be burned by robbery and misappropriation [i.e., they are likely to commit graver misdeeds, such as violating the prohibition against robbery].

6.4 A rabbinical court ruling on competition between private tutors

We will conclude our discussion with some comments on a contemporary rabbinical court ruling.[41] In their decision, the judges point out that halakhic thinking vis-à-vis competition has undergone considerable change in recent years in the wake of the transition from commerce based on small local markets to commerce based on national or even global markets. As we saw, the main restrictions on market entry apply to merchants from elsewhere who seek to trade in a local market. The local merchants, that is, the existing businesses, are viewed by the halakha as deserving of protection from outside competition, but not from the competition of other local merchants. But this way of framing the issue of competition presupposes that the market is small, and local players can be readily identified and distinguished from outsiders. With the growing complexity of the market, and the ongoing expansion of commercial activity, both geographically and in terms of the sophistication of the products involved and the ways in which they are marketed, the distinction between local and outside merchants has become less and less relevant. The rabbinical court ruling applies this insight to a claim of encroachment

41 See Appendix.

on someone else's commercial turf brought by a tutor against a competitor.

7 Conclusion

Jewish law is basically supportive of free market competition: many commentators take the legal rules governing business competition to unambiguously endorse free competition over restrictions on entry into the market. Moreover, the good of the consumer generally takes precedence over the good of the merchant. Even these pro-competition halakhic authorities, however, maintain that competition may be restricted if there are moral considerations warranting such restriction, though they are not always in agreement as to what these considerations are. There are also a number of halakhic authorities who contend that restrictions on competition are to be imposed. It is likely that some of these opinions were influenced by the harsh economic conditions of the places and times in which they were formulated, or by other social constraints; they should be viewed as inapplicable to the present day, with its free and open economic climate.

Appendix File No. 9635/65 Rabbinical Court (TA) A v. B, 6 PDR 90 (Isr.) [1965]

TEL AVIV-JAFFA DISTRICT RABBINICAL COURT

Before the Honorable Judges Rabbis S.B. Werner, Y. Goldschmidt, E. Azoulay

…

Facts and Arguments

The plaintiff's plea: He has resided in the G neighborhood for some twenty-three years, and during all that time has earned his living as a teacher who prepares boys for their Bar Mitzvah, teaching them the laws of phylacteries and other laws, preparing them to give a talk on the Bar-Mitzvah day and to read the Haftara for that week, and so on. For the past eight years, the defendant, who does not reside in G, has been encroaching on his territory and accepting boys from G and the surrounding area for Bar-Mitzvah lessons. He further claims that the defendant visits the homes of parents of children and solicits them to send their children to him to prepare them for their Bar-Mitzvah.

The plaintiff maintains that the defendant is adversely impacting his livelihood and encroaching on his territory, given the plaintiff's status as the local teacher in the G neighborhood.

The defendant's reply: He is a resident of Tel Aviv and teaches all boys from the city who come to him for lessons; he does not inquire as to their addresses. He denies that he visits the homes of parents of boys to solicit them to send their children to him for Bar Mitzvah lessons.

…

When asked by the Court if he would accept pupils from Ramat-Gan and Bnei Brak [nearby suburbs] if they came to him for Bar Mitzvah lessons, the plaintiff answered that he would readily do so, and that he would conduct the lessons in the synagogue in neighborhood G.

Following the signing of an arbitration agreement by the parties, and after hearing the parties' pleas, the Court finds that the following questions must be addressed:

- **(a)** Can a craftsman who resides in a certain neighborhood prevent a craftsman from a different neighborhood from competing with him, just as he can prevent a craftsman from a different town from doing so?
- **(b)** Is teaching an occupation to which the prohibition against competition is applicable?

[If so,] is every kind of instruction, at every level, covered by the prohibition?

(c) Does the prohibition against competition also apply to contexts where residents of a town go elsewhere, viz., to a different town, to make purchases?

(d) What is the law with respect to occupations whose practitioners do not work in one particular place, and what is the law with respect to the concept of the 'market day'?

Let us proceed to resolve these problems one by one.

...

(c) Competition in a context where customers come from elsewhere

There is another reason why we believe that the plaintiff's claim should be rejected. The rule that a resident of an alleyway (A) may prevent someone who lives in a different alleyway (B) from plying his trade in A's alleyway only addresses A's right to prevent B from entering A's alleyway. But if the residents of A's alleyway go to a craftsman outside the alleyway, it is incontrovertible that A cannot prevent them from making purchases in a different alleyway or even in a different town.

Since the defendant claims that he does not visit the homes of parents of prospective pupils, but rather, they contact him at their own initiative, or at the recommendation of friends, others parents and teachers, there are no grounds for preventing the defendant from accepting pupils who contact him.

(d) Competition in a business that is by nature not local

Furthermore, it can be argued that the right to prevent a resident of a different alley from plying his trade in one's own alley is not applicable to all occupations. For certain occupations are by their very nature not limited to any particular street or neighborhood, and there is an intrinsic element of interchange, as one person goes to a business on his fellow's street while his fellow comes to his street. One example is insurance agents, who are not limited to the neighborhood in which they reside. Each agent has, among his clients, friends and relatives who reside throughout the city, and even in other cities. In the halakhic sources, there is an example of this in bBaba Batra 22a:

> Certain basket-makers brought baskets to Babylon [to sell]. The townspeople came and stopped them [from doing so]. They came before Rabina. He said to them: They have come from outside [lit., the world at large] and they can sell to outsiders. And this ruling applies

> only to the market day, but if it is not a market day, it does not apply. And even on the market day, it is only applicable to those who sell at the market, but not to those who go back and forth [Rashi: who go around in the streets and from house to house].

. . .

We can conclude from this that the right of townspeople to prevent a resident of a different town from selling his wares in their town applies only if the buyers are from that town alone. And hence someone from another town has no right to encroach on [the local merchant's] territory, impact his business adversely, and sell to the local townspeople. But on a market day, when sales are not limited to the local townspeople alone, since large-scale inter-urban trading takes place, with customers coming from other towns to buy there, [someone from another town who comes to trade at the local market] is not encroaching on the local merchant's territory, but selling to "the world at large."

. . .

Moreover, with regard to occupations where the customer base [is not local but] covers a broad area, it can be assumed that an implied stipulation has been agreed to, as in the case of market days, as explained in [R. Samuel Kalai's] *Responsa Mishpetei Shmuel*, #49:

> The wording of the Talmud should not be taken literally to mean that the 'market day' must be a special fixed day; it means any time when buyers and sellers come together to meet and trade. What is important is not the precise wording [of the talmudic rule], but its underlying rationale.

. . .

Accordingly, in the matter at hand, since it is customary to accept pupils from every locale, and teachers and instructors are not limited to teaching [pupils from] their own neighborhoods—indeed the plaintiff himself declared that if approached by pupils from Ramat Gan or Bnei Brak he would readily accept them—it is clearly the custom of these teachers to accept pupils without inquiring into their place of residence, and they teach anyone who comes to them for lessons. Therefore, we must rule that the prohibition against encroaching on someone else's business territory does not apply, because no teacher or instructor has any particular territory to call his own.

In view of all the aforesaid, the Court rules to reject the plaintiff's claim. No order is made as to costs.

Rendered this day, 29 Kislev 5725 (December 1964).

List of halakhic authorities and scholars

R. Aaron b. Joseph Halevi (Spain c. 1235–c. 1303), Talmud commentator, decisor

R. Abdallah Abraham Joseph Somekh (Baghdad, 1813–1889), responsist

R. Abraham b. David (Rabad; Raavad), (France, c. 1120–c.1198), Talmud commentator, responsist, critic of Maimonides

R. Abraham b. Solomon Akra (Italy, late 16th c.), author of *Meharerei Nemeirim*

R. Abraham ibn Ezra (Spain, 1089–1165), Bible commentator, poet, philosopher, grammarian, astronomer.

R. Abraham Isaac Kook (Greiva [Courland] 1865–Jerusalem 1935), influential religious thinker and responsist, first Ashkenazic chief rabbi in the land of Israel

R. Abraham Isaiah Karelitz (Hazon Ish), (Kosova 1878–Bnei Brak 1953), leading haredi decisor

R. Aha of Shabha (Babylonia, 8th c.), one of the greatest scholars of the Geonic period, author of the *Sheiltot*, the first post-talmudic halakhic work

Arukh Hashulhan see R. Yehiel Mikhel Epstein

R. Aryeh Grossnass (1912–1996)

R. Arye Leib Heller (Galicia, 1745–1813), author of *Ketzot Hahoshen*, a seminal commentary on *Shulhan Arukh*, HM

R. Asher b. Yehiel (Asheri, Rosh), (Germany 1250–Toledo 1327), eminent decisor, responsist, and Talmud commentator, authored *Piskei Harosh*, a widely-used summary of talmudic rulings

Asher Gulak (Dankira, Latvia 1881–land of Israel 1940), one of the founders of modern academic study of Jewish law, professor of Jewish law at the Hebrew University

Bah see R. Joel Sirkes

Beit Yosef see R. Joseph Caro

R. Bezalel Ashkenazi (Egypt c. 1520–Jerusalem c. 1592), author of *Shita Mekubetzet*, an anthology of commentaries on the Talmud

R. Chaim Ozer Grodzinski (Ivye [Belorussia] 1863–Vilna 1940), preeminent decisor, responsist, leader of the ultra-Orthodox community, one of the founders of Agudath Yisrael

R. David b. Samuel Halevi (Taz), (Ludmir 1586–Lemberg 1667), author of *Turei Zahav* commentary on the *Shulhan Arukh*

R. David ibn Avi Zimra (Radbaz), (Spain 1479–Safed 1573), Talmud commentator, chief rabbi in Egypt for decades, prolific responsist

R. David Pardo (Venice 1719–Jerusalem 1792), author of *Hasdei David* commentary on the Tosefta

R. David Tzvi Hoffman (Verbo [Slovakia] 1843–Berlin 1921), scholar, commentator, leader of German Orthodoxy

Rabbenu Efraim of El-Kala [North Africa], a student of Alfasi

R. Efraim b. Aaron Navon (Constantinople 1677–1735), decisor and responsist, author of *Mahane Efraim*

R. Eliezer b. Joel Halevi of Bonn (Rabia, Raavya), (Germany, c. 1140–c. 1220), Tosafist, liturgical poet

R. Eliezer b. Nathan (Raban; Raavan), (Germany, 1090–1170), Tosafist, liturgical poet

R. Eliezer Waldenburg (Jerusalem, 1915–2006), influential responsist and decisor, authority on bio-medical halakhic issues

R. Elijah b. Haim (Raanah), (Turkey, 1530–1610), responsist

R. Elijah b. Solomon of Vilna (Gra, Vilna Gaon), (Vilna, 1720–1797), acclaimed halakhic leader, one of the greatest eighteenth century halakhic minds, commentator of encyclopedic breadth, opponent of Hasidism

Ephraim Elimelech Urbach (Poland 1912–Israel 1991), scholar of rabbinical literature and history of the talmudic and medieval periods

R. Ezekiel Landau (Opatow 1713–Prague 1793), author of *Responsa Noda Biyehuda*, leading decisor, chief rabbi of Prague

Rabbenu Gershom b. Judah (Light of the Exile), (Metz 960–c. Mayence 1028), one of the founding halakhic authorities in Ashkenaz, enacted important communal ordinances, authored responsa, commentaries, and liturgical poetry

R. Hai b. Sherira Gaon (Babylonia, 939–1038), Talmud commentator, last head of the Pumbedita academy, decisor, responsist, and influential shaper of halakhic thinking

R. Haim b. Isaac Alfandari (the Younger), (Constantinople, mid 17th c.–Jerusalem 18th c.), kabbalist

R. Haim b. Menahem Algazi (Turkey, c. 1640–c. 1710), author of *Bnei Hayai*, novellae on the *Shulhan Arukh*

R. Haim Benveniste (Turkey, 1603–1673), author of *Shiurei Kneset Hagedola*, an anthology of halakhic rulings

R. Haim David Halevi (Jerusalem 1924–Israel 1998), Sefardic chief rabbi of Tel Aviv-Jaffa from the 1970s to the 1990s

Haim H. Cohn (Lubeck 1911–Jerusalem 2002), Israel Supreme Court justice, scholar of Jewish law

R. Haim Halberstamm of Sanz (Tarnogrod 1793–Sanz 1876), decisor, responsist, hasidic rebbe

R. Haim Hezekiah Medini (Jerusalem 1832–Hebron 1904), author of *Sdei Hemed*, a comprehensive halakhic encyclopedia, served as rabbi in the Crimea for decades, and later, as rabbi of Hebron

R. Haim Joseph David Azoulay (Hida), (Jerusalem 1724–Livorno 1806), decisor, kabbalist, historian, bibliographer

R. Haim Or Zarua (Germany, 13th c.), son of R. Isaac of Vienna (Riaz); student of the Maharam of Rothenburg, responsist

R. Haim Palagi of Smyrna (Smyrna, 1788–1869), prominent decisor

Rabbenu Hananel b. Hushiel (Kairouan [North Africa], died c. 1056), Talmud commentator

Hatam Sofer — see R. Moses Sofer

Hazon Ish — see R. Abraham Isaiah Karelitz

Hida — see R. Haim Joseph David Azoulay

ibn Migash — see R. Joseph ibn Migash

R. Immanuel Jakobovits (Koenigsberg 1921–England 1999), a pioneer in the field of Jewish biomedical ethics and chief rabbi of the United Kingdom from 1967–1991

Don Isaac Abarbanel (variant: Abrabanel), (Lisbon 1437–Italy 1508), Bible commentator, philosopher, royal financier

R. Isaac Alfasi (Rif), (El-Kala [North Africa] 1013–Lucena 1103), one of the first codifiers, and author of *Sefer Hahalakhot*, a classic compendium of the Babylonian Talmud's rulings

R. Isaac Arama (Spain c. 1420–Italy 1494), Bible commentator, philosopher, homilist

R. Isaac b. Abraham (the Younger) (Ritzba) (France, d. 1209), brother of the famed Rash of Sens (R. Samson b. Abraham), Tosafist, headed the yeshiva at Dampierre after R. Isaac the Elder's death

R. Isaac b. Asher (Riva), (Germany c.1055–c. 1130), one of Rashi's preeminent students, first Tosafist in Germany

R. Isaac b. Moses of Vienna (Riaz, Or Zarua), (Germany, c. 1180–c. 1260), author of the *Or Zarua*

R. Isaac b. Samuel of Dampierre (France, 12th c.), known as Ri (the Elder), great-grandson of Rashi, and one of the most prolific Tosafists

R. Isaac b. Sheshet Perfet (Ribash), (Spain 1326–Algiers 1408), prolific and influential responsist

R. Isaac of Corbeil (France 1210–1280), eminent Tosafist and codifier, author of *Sefer Mitzvot Katan*

R. Isaac the Elder see R. Isaac b. Samuel of Dampierre

R. Isaac Jacob Weiss (Hungary 1902–Jerusalem 1989), responsist, head of Eda Haredit rabbinical court in Jerusalem

R. Isaac Judah Schmelkes (Galicia, 1828–1905), headed rabbinate in Brzezany, Przemysl, and Lemberg, author of *Responsa Beit Yitzhak.*

R. Isaac Liebes (d. New York 2000)

R. Isaiah Horowitz (Shela), (Prague c. 1565–Tiberias 1630), mystic, homilist

R. Israel Isserlein (Trumat Hadeshen), (Regensburg 1390–Wiener-Neustadt 1460), leading decisor of 15th c. Ashkenaz, responsist

R. Israel Meir Kagan of Radin (Chofetz Chaim), (Zhetel [Dvorets] 1838–Radin 1933), known by the name of his seminal work on the laws of defamation, author of the *Mishna Brura*, a commentary on the Orah Haim section of the *Shulhan Arukh*

R. Issachar Ber Eilenburg (Poznan 1550–Austerlitz 1623), Talmud commentator

R. Jacob b. Asher (Tur, Baal Haturim), (Germany 1269–Spain 1343). Fled Germany with his father, the Rosh, settling in Spain; author of the seminal four-part code *Arbaa Turim*

R. Jacob b. Moses Lorberbaum of Lissa (Poland, c. 1762–1832), author of numerous works, including *Netivot Hamishpat* commentary on the Hoshen Mishpat section of the *Shulhan Arukh*

R. Jacob Emden (Yaavetz), (Altona, 1697–1796), commentator and responsist, critic of claims regarding the Zohar's provenance, anti-Sabbatean polemicist

R. Jacob Ettlinger (Karlsruhe 1798–Altona 1871), commentator, responsist, leader of German Orthodoxy

R. Jacob Joshua Falk (Pnei Yehoshua), (Cracow 1680–Offenbach 1756), Talmud commentator, opponent of Sabbateanism

R. Jacob of Marvège (France, late 12th–13th c.)

R. Jacob of Orleans (d. England 1189), Tosafist and student of Rabbenu Tam; killed at the coronation of Richard I (the Lionhearted)

R. Jacob Reischer (Bachofen), (Prague c. 1670–Metz c. 1736), responsist

R. Jacob Tam (Rabbenu Tam), (France, 1100–1171), grandson of Rashi and brother of the Rashbam, leading Tosafist, decisor, and poet

R. Joel Sirkes (Bah), (Lublin 1561–Cracow 1640), author of the *Bayit Hadash* commentary on the *Tur*, responsist
R. Joel Teitelbaum (Sighet 1887–New York 1979), Satmarer Rebbe, responsist
R. Joseph b. Solomon Colon (Maharik), (France 1420–Padua 1480), responsist
R. Joseph B. Soloveitchik (Pruzhany 1905–Boston 1993), talmudic scholar and philosopher, leader of American modern Orthodoxy
R. Joseph Babad (Tarnopol c. 1800–Safed 1874), author of *Minhat Hinukh*
R. Joseph Caro (Spain 1488–Safed 1575), preeminent codifier, author of the *Shulhan Arukh* and *Beit Yosef*, responsist
R. Joseph di Trani (Maharit), (Safed 1568–Constantinople 1639), responsist and leader of communities in Egypt and Turkey
R. Joseph Habiba (Nimukei Yosef), (Spain, early 15th c.), Talmud commentator
R. Joseph ibn Migash (Spain 1077–1141), Alfasi's student and successor as head of the Lucena yeshiva, Talmud commentator, responsist
R. Joseph Saul Nathanson (Brzezany 1810–Lemberg 1875), prominent decisor and communal leader, chief rabbi of Lemberg, prolific responsist
R. Joshua Boaz (b. Spain, d. Italy, 1557), author of *Shiltei Hagiborim* commentary on Alfasi's *Sefer Hahalakhot*
R. Joshua Falk Katz (Lublin 1550–Lemberg 1614), author of the *Sefer Meirat Einayim* (*Sema*) commentary on the *Shulhan Arukh*, and the *Derisha* and the *Perisha*, twin commentaries on the *Tur*
R. Judah Ayash (b. Morocco–d. Jerusalem 1760), head of Algiers rabbinical court, decisor and responsist
R. Judah Gershuni (Poland 1908–Israel 2000)
R. Judah Loew b. Bezalel (Maharal) of Prague (Poznan c. 1525–Prague 1609), talmudist, philosopher, communal leader, homilist
R. Judah the Pious of Regensburg (Speyer 1150–Regensburg 1217), mystic, author of the ethical treatise *Sefer Hasidim*

Maharal	see R. Judah Loew b. Bezalel
Maharam	see R. Meir of Rothenburg
Maharashdam	see R. Samuel di Modena
Maharit	see R. Joseph di Trani
Maharsha	see R. Samuel Halevi Edels
Maharshal	see R. Solomon Luria
Maharsham	see R. Shalom Mordekhai Schwadron
Maimonides	see R. Moses b. Maimon

R. Masud Hai Rokeiah (Smyrna 1689–land of Israel 1749), halakhic leader of various Mediterranean communities, including Leghorn and Tripoli
R. Meir b. Todros Halevi Abulafia (Rama), (Burgos c. 1170–Toledo 1244), Talmud commentator, authority on the masoretic text of the Scriptures
R. Meir Eisenstadt, (1670 Poland–1744 Austria), author of *Responsa Panim Meirot*, Talmud commentator, rabbi of Eisenstadt and the famed "Seven Communities"
R. Meir Hakohen of Rothenburg (late 13th–early 14th c.) author of *Hagahot Maimoniot*, student of the Maharam of Rothenburg
R. Meir of Lublin (Lublin, 1558–c. 1618), responsist
R. Meir Posner (Poland c. 1728–Danzig 1807), decisor, author of *Beit Meir*
R. Meir of Rothenburg (Maharam), (Worms 1215–Ensisheim 1293), Tosafist, decisor, leader of 13th c. Ashkenaz; teacher of R. Asher b. Yehiel

R. Meir Simha Hakohen of Dvinsk (Lithuania 1843–1926), author of the *Meshekh Hokhma* commentary on the Pentateuch and the *Or Sameiah* commentary on Maimonides' *Mishne Torah*, Talmud commentator, philosopher

Meiri see R. Menahem b. Solomon Hameiri

Menachem Elon (b. Dusseldorf 1923), scholar, prominent advocate of the 'Mishpat Ivri' approach to the halakha, Israel Supreme Court justice

R. Menahem b. Solomon Hameiri (Meiri), (Provence, 1249–1316), Talmud commentator

R. Menahem Kasher (Poland 1895–US 1983)

R. Menahem Mendel Haim Landau of Strykow (Poland 1862–Otwock 1936)

R. Menahem Mendel Krochmal (Cracow 1600–Nikolsburg 1671), author of *Responsa Tzemah Tzedek*

R. Meshulam Rata (Roth), (Horodenka [Galicia] 1875–Israel 1962), rabbi of Czernowitz during the Holocaust years, responsist

R. Mordekhai b. Hillel of Nuremburg (Germany, 1250–1298), author of the *Mordekhai*, which supplemented Alfasi's *Sefer Hahalakhot* with rulings of Ashkenazic authorities, was martyred with his family in the Rindfleish massacres

R. Moses b. Jacob of Coucy (France, 13th c.), Tosafist, author of *Sefer Mitzvot Gadol* (*Semag*)

R. Moses b. Maimon (Rambam, Maimonides), (Cordoba, Spain 1138–Fostat, Egypt 1204), preeminent commentator, codifier, responsist, philosopher, communal leader and physician. His codification of the law, the *Mishne Torah*, also known as the *Yad Hahazaka*, is herein cited as the *Code*

R. Moses b. Nahman (Nahmanides) (Gerona 1194–land of Israel 1270), commentator on the Pentateuch and Talmud, responsist, kabbalist, communal leader

R. Moses Feinstein (Uzda [Belorussia] 1895–New York 1986), responsist, decisor, halakhic authority for North American Orthodoxy

R. Moses Halevi Mintz (Maharam Mintz),(Germany c. 1415–c. 1480), decisor and responsist

R. Moses Isserles (Rema), (Cracow, 1530–1572), authoritative glossator of the *Shulhan Arukh* for Ashkenazic Jewry, decisor and responsist

R. Moses Khalfon Hakohen (Djerba, 1874–1950), author of *Responsa Shoel Venishal*, chief rabbi of Djerba

R. Moses Margalit (Keidan [Lithuania] 1710–Brody [Galicia] 1781), author of *Pnei Moshe* commentary on the Jerusalem Talmud

R. Moses Sofer (Hatam Sofer), (Frankfurt 1762–Pressburg (Bratislava) 1839), leading decisor and responsist, led struggle against the Haskala and the incipient Reform movement

Moshe Silberg (Skaudvile [Lithuania] 1900–Jerusalem 1975), jurisprudential scholar, Israel Supreme Court justice

R. Naftali Z. Berlin (Netziv), (Mir 1817–Warsaw 1893), Bible commentator, responsist, headed the renowned Volozhin Yeshiva for decades

Nahmanides see R. Moses b. Nahman

R. Nathan b. Yehiel of Rome (Italy 1035–1110), authored the *Arukh*, a dictionary of talmudic terms

R. Nathan of Igra (Italy, died first half of the 16th c.), one of the leading Italian decisors, rabbinical court judge in Venice in 1531

Netziv see R. Naftali Z. Berlin

Nimukei Yosef see R. Joseph Habiba

R. Nissim b. Reuben Gerondi (=of Gerona) (Ran), (Spain 1310–c.1375), decisor, Talmud commentator, responsist, and philosopher

R. Nissim Solomon Algazi (Turkey c. 1610–Jerusalem c. 1683), leading opponent of Shabbetai Zvi

R. Ovadiah of Bartenura [Bertinoro], (Italy c. 1445–Jerusalem c. 1516), author of highly popular commentary on the Mishnah

R. Ovadiah Yosef (b. Baghdad 1920), decisor, prolific responsist, served as Rishon Lezion (chief rabbi of Israel's Sefardic/Mizrahi community) from 1973–1983, and remains its foremost spiritual and intellectual leader

Rabad see R. Abraham b. David

Raban see R. Eliezer b. Nathan

Rabbenu Tam see R. Jacob Tam

Rabia see R. Eliezer b. Joel Halevi

Radbaz see R. David ibn Avi Zimra

Rama see R. Meir b. Todros Halevi Abulafia

Rambam see R. Moses b. Maimon

Ramban see R. Moses b. Nahman

Ran see R. Nissim b. Reuben Gerondi

Rashba see R. Solomon b. Adret

Rashbam see R. Samuel b. Meir

Rashbash see R. Solomon b. Shimon Duran

Rashbatz see R. Shimon b. Tzemah Duran

Rashi see R. Solomon b. Isaac

Rema see R. Moses Isserles

Rif see R. Isaac Alfasi

Ritba see R. Yomtov of Seville

Rosh see R. Asher b. Yehiel

R. Saadia Gaon (Egypt 882–Sura, Babylonia 942), communal leader, biblical commentator, grammarian, and philosopher

R. Samuel b. Meir (Rashbam) of Ramerupt (France, 1085–c. 1174), Bible and Talmud commentator, Tosafist, grandson of Rashi, brother of Rabbenu Tam

R. Samuel b. Moses Kalai (Turkey, 16th c.), author of *Mishpetei Shmuel*

R. Samuel di Modena (Maharashdam), (Salonika, 1506–1589), halakhic authority throughout the Balkans and beyond, communal leader, prolific responsist

R. Samuel Halevi Edels (Maharsha), (Poznan 1555–Ostrog 1631), Talmud commentator, also wrote a commentary on the Talmud's Aggadic material

R. Saul Lieberman (Motol [Belorussia] 1898–Israel 1983), commentator on the Jerusalem Talmud and the Tosefta

R. Saul Yisraeli (Slutzk 1909–Israel 1995), decisor, author of *Amud Hayemini* on the issues arising from Israel's statehood

R. Shabtai Hakohen (Shakh), (Vilna 1621–Holleschau [Moravia] c. 1662), decisor, author of the *Siftei Kohen* commentary on the *Shulhan Arukh*

Shakh see R. Shabtai Hakohen

R. Shalom Mordekhai Schwadron of Brzezany (Maharsham), (Galicia, 1835–1911), eminent decisor and responsist

Shela see R. Isaiah Horowitz

R. Shimon b. Tzemah Duran (Rashbatz), (Majorca 1361–Algiers 1444), decisor, responsist, and communal leader

R. Shimon Efrati (Bessarabia 1908–Israel 1988), rabbi of Bendery, rabbi of Holocaust survivors in post-war Warsaw

R. Shimon Kaiara of Basra (Babylonia, 8th c.), author of *Halakhot Gedolot*

Shita Mekubetzet see R. Bezalel Ashkenazi

R. Shlomo Goren (Zambrow [Poland] 1917–Israel 1994), Ashkenazic chief rabbi of Israel from 1972 to 1983

R. Shneur Zalman of Liadi (Baal Hatanya), (Liozna [Belorussia] 1735–Piena [Belorussia] 1813), founder of Chabad hasidism

Shulhan Arukh see R. Joseph Caro

Simha Assaf (Osofsky), (Lyuban [Belorussia] 1888–Jerusalem 1953), scholar of rabbinical literature, esp. the Geonic period, Supreme Court justice

R. Solomon b. Adret (Rashba), (Barcelona, 1235–1310), Talmud commentator, responsist, leader of Spanish Jewry

R. Solomon b. Isaac (Rashi), (Troyes, 1040–1105), greatest of the Bible and Talmud commentators, communal leader, responsist

R. Solomon b. Shimon Duran (Rashbash), (Algiers, 1400–1467), responsist and philosopher

R. Solomon Efraim of Lunschitz (Leczyca [Poland] 1550–Prague 1619), Bible commentator and homilist, author of the *Kli Yakar* commentary on the Pentateuch

R. Solomon Kluger of Brody (Galicia, 1785–1869), prolific responsist and commentator, defended traditionalism against the Haskala

R. Solomon Luria (Maharshal), (Poland, 1510–1573), author of *Yam Shel Shlomo* commentary on the Talmud, decisor

R. Solomon Zalman Auerbach (Jerusalem, 1910–1995), decisor, wrote extensively on halakhic issues pertaining to agriculture, technology, and medicine; responsist

Trumat Hadeshen see R. Israel Isserlein

Tur see R. Jacob b. Asher

R. Tzvi Hirsh Kalischer (Lissa [Leszno] 1795–Thorn 1874), proto-Zionist thinker and activist, opponent of the Reform movement

R. Vidal of Tolosa (Spain, 1283–1369), author of *Magid Mishne* commentary on Maimonides' *Mishne Torah*

Vilna Gaon see R. Elijah b. Solomon of Vilna

R. Yair Haim Bacharach (Moravia 1638–Worms 1702), important decisor, author of *Responsa Havat Yair*, prolific writer

R. Yehiel Mikhel Epstein (Bobruisk 1829–Navarodok 1908), author of *Arukh Hashulhan*, codifier and decisor

R. Yekutiel Asher Enzil Zusmir (Mahariz Enzil) of Stryj and Przemysl (Poland, 19th c.)

R. Yekutiel Judah Teitelbaum of Sighet (1808–1883) (Yetev Lev), hasidic rebbe, great-grandfather of R. Joel Teitelbaum

R. Yomtov Lipmann Heller (Wallerstein 1579–Cracow 1654), commentator on the Mishnah, communal leader and rabbinical activist

R. Yomtov Lipmann Muhlhausen (Prague, 14–15th c.), scholar and polemicist

R. Yomtov of Seville (Ritba), (Spain, c. 1250–1330), one of the foremost Talmud commentators, responsist

Index of names

Index of rabbinical authorities

Subject index

Index of sources quoted*

* Only direct quotations at least several words in length are indexed

Responsa

Contributor affiliations

Hanina Ben-Menahem is Professor of Law at the Faculty of Law, Hebrew University of Jerusalem

Sinai Deutch is Professor of Law at the Law School, Netanya Academic College

Arye Edrei is Professor of Law at the Faculty of Law, Tel Aviv University

Arnold Enker is Professor of Law (Emeritus) at the Faculty of Law, Bar Ilan University

Simshon Ettinger is Professor of Law at the Faculty of Law, Bar Ilan University

Neil S. Hecht is Professor of Law (Emeritus) at Boston University's School of Law and Founding Director of its Institute of Jewish Law

Berachyahu Lifshitz is Professor of Law at the Faculty of Law, Hebrew University of Jerusalem

Benjamin Porat is a Lecturer at the Faculty of Law, Hebrew University of Jerusalem and head of its Institute for Research in Jewish Law

Eliav Shochetman is Professor of Law (Emeritus) at the Faculty of Law, Hebrew University of Jerusalem and Shaarei Mishpat College

Daniel Sinclair is Professor of Law at the School of Law, College of Management Academic Studies (Rishon Lezion) and Fordham University

Itamar Warhaftig is Professor of Law (Emeritus) at the Faculty of Law, Bar Ilan University

